Spain's New Wave Novelists

1950-1974

Studies in Spanish Realism

by

RONALD SCHWARTZ

The Scarecrow Press, Inc.

Metuchen, N.J.   1976

Library of Congress Cataloging in Publication Data

Schwartz, Ronald, 1937-
    Spain's new wave novelists, 1950-1974.

    Bibliography: p.
    Includes index.
    1. Spanish fiction--20th century--History and
criticism. 2. Realism in literature. I. Title.
PQ6144.S38 1976   863'.03   75-44366
ISBN 0-8108-0854-4

For my wife
AMELIA,
beautiful, courageous, indefatigable.

And in memory of my beloved parents,
MINNA and IRVING

ACKNOWLEDGMENTS

I wish to extend my thanks to the Kingsborough Community College Library Faculty, especially Professors Gordon Rowell, Florence Houser, Adele Schneider, Coleridge Orr, Frances Eagon, Anna Brady and Angelo Tripicchio, without whose help and good cheer I could not have completed this book as well as my first, Gironella. Grateful appreciation to these librarians as well as to my wife, also a librarian, is long overdue. Secondly, I would like to thank several colleagues in the Department of Foreign Languages, notably its chairperson, Dr. Julio Hernández-Miyares, for his patience and continued encouragement in completing this project over the past two years, and professors Elio Alba, Evelio Pentón, Margaret Rockwitz, and Irving Gersh for their continual intellectual dialogues with me as this book was being written. Finally, I wish to thank my friends in the Department of Foreign Languages and our secretary, Mrs. Rhona Silverman, and my typist, Mrs. Lourdes M. Tariche, for their continual confidence in me and my work.

I also wish to thank the following for permission to reprint material appearing in this volume:

Sra. Josefina Aldecoa and Editorial Noguer for Parte de una historia.
Ediciones Anaya, Las Americas and Rafael Bosch for his La novela española del siglo XX, vol. II.
Juan Benet Goitia and Ediciones Destino for Volverás a Región.
Camilo José Cela and Editorial Noguer for La colmena.
Editorial Cuadernos para el Diálogo for José Corrales Egea's La novela española actual.
Editorial Destino for J. L. Castillo-Puche's Paralelo 40, Miguel Delibes' Parábola de un náufrago and Ana María Matute's Primera memoria.

Editorial Gredos for Eugenio de Nora's La novela española
 contemporánea (1927-1960), vol. III, and Gemma
 Robert's Temas existenciales en la novela española
 de postguerra.
Grove Press for Juan Goytisolo's Marks of Identity as trans-
 lated by Gregory Rabassa.
Editorial Guadarrama for M. García-Viñó's Novela española
 actual and G. Gómez de la Serna's Ensayos sobre la
 literatura social, both in the Colección Universal de
 Bolsillo--Punto Omega Series, Madrid.
Editorial Labor for José Domingo's La novela española del
 siglo XX, vol. II.
Pantheon Books, a division of Random House, Inc., for Ana
 María Matute's School of the Sun, translated by Elaine
 Kerrigan.
Editorial Península for Ramón Buckley's Problemas normales
 en la novela española contemporánea.
Editorial Planeta for José María Gironella's Los cipreses
 creen en Dios and with the author's personal permis-
 sion.
Ediciones Prensa Española for Gonzalo Sobejano's Novela
 española de nuestro tiempo.
Editorial Seix Barral for Pablo Gil Casado's La novela so-
 cial española, Alfonso Grosso's Guarnición de silla,
 and Juan Marsé's Ultimas tardes con Teresa.
Editorial Taurus for Juan Alborg's Hora actual de la novela
 española, vol. I and II.
Eliseo Torres and Sons for E. Guillermo and J. A. Hernández' La novelística española de los 60.
Twayne Press for Janet W. Diaz's Miguel Delibes, Diaz's
 Ana María Matute, and Kessel Schwartz's Juan Goyti-
 solo.
University of Missouri for David W. Foster's Forms of the
 Novel in the Work of Camilo José Cela, copyright
 1967 by the Curators of the University of Missouri,
 Columbia.

One last note of appreciation to Dr. Alfred Borrello at
Kingsborough Community College whose own scholarship and
encouragement helped me to finish this book.

                                        Ronald Schwartz

TABLE OF CONTENTS

Preface   ix

PREFACE

The twenty-two chapters that follow will define, criticize and place in chronological perspective the latest developments in novel writing in modern Spain over the past twenty-
five years. After a short definition of nouvelle vague in
Spanish terms and setting the literary scene between 1950 and
1974, I will discuss the life and leading novel of Spain's eighteen outstanding writers with a view towards defining the current state of evolution of the novel genre in Spain. This book
is not intended as a refutation of the opinion of Spain's leading literary critics, such as Ramón Buckley, Eugenio de Nora,
Antonio Iglesias Laguna, M. García Viñó, Gonzalo Sobejano
or Rafael Bosch among others, but rather intends to systema-
tize and develop a theory of criticism and trace the evolution
of one of Spain's leading literary currents most commonly
misunderstood by today's readers, writers and critics alike.

Through a detailed analysis of each of the New Wave
writer's leading works and a dissection of a choice passage
in the manner of explication de texte (see the Appendix), I
will demonstrate the reasons each writer belongs to the New
Wave and how each has individually contributed to the development of the genre and the regeneration of the modern Spanish novel despite the rigors of present-day censorship.

A fairly extensive bibliography concerning each author,
his or her major works and leading critical articles about
him or her, will provide the reader with a guide for future
reference as well as an accounting of each author's major
impact on Spain and the international literary world.

A note on English translations: unless they are cited
as by another, they are my own and are used where they
were thought beneficial to the reader. Texts in Spanish were
sometimes left in the original so the reader might be able to
savor the original thoughts of the author and his or her use
of the Spanish language.

I must express a debt of gratitude to the Research Foundation of the State University of New York for a recent grant which provided the travel funds to interview Ana María Matute, Juan García Hortelano, Ignacio Aldecoa and José María Gironella on a return trip to Spain and for the opportunity to present much heretofore unpublished material about the lives and works of these writers in the chapters that follow.

Ronald Schwartz
Professor of Romance Languages
Kingsborough Community College
    of the
City University of New York

New York City
January 1975

Chapter 1

THE LITERARY AND HISTORICAL BACKGROUND

The Spanish Civil War of 1936-1939 is Spain's most tragic and unsettling event in the country's history; its resonances are still felt over the past thirty-five years by Spain's creative artists. With the outbreak of civil war in 1936, the majority of Spanish novelists who were mainly Surrealist stylists abandoned their dedication to their current work which had vitiated an approach to the social and historic realities of the late 1920's and early 1930's. Many Spanish novelists became politically active. They embraced Communism, Fascism or some other current political ideology. The Civil War not only interrupted the normal development of all literary creations, especially in the novel genre, but placed authors in opposing political camps. Some lived harmoniously under the Nationalist policies of General Franco. Others who defended Republican Spain were forced into exile after the war.

Regardless, all Spanish literature, irrespective of genre, suffered a division of creative effort as a consequence of the war. Many emigrant writers who resided chiefly in Latin America tried to reestablish their literary reputations. Through the bitterness of their defeat and in exile, they attempted to elucidate the reasons for the war. However, in Spain itself, a new generation of young writers in the early 1940's, concerned with the traumatic effects of the war and living under Franco's Nationalist regime, engendered the true resurgence of the Spanish novel. Many of these younger writers remember the war and some participated in it. Reviving the Realist tradition of nineteenth-century novelists, their novels dealt with social themes of contemporary Spanish society and the Civil War. They utilized documentary and photographic evidence and some cultivated new forms of the novel as a stylistic outgrowth of the mechanical and dehumanized Surrealist techniques of the writers of the mid-1920's and the early 1930's. Other writers proved their manifold skills by writing sociological treatises, literary criticism or

1

highly stylized works in which they created an entirely new
esthetic. Camilo José Cela's tremendismo is an example of
a new esthetic evolved as the result of an attempt to reproduce contemporary reality from a personal, profound, graphic
and highly stylized basis as demonstrated in his novel La
familia de Pascual Duarte (1942). Some novelists combined
fantastic motifs with reality, exoticism with mundane themes.
Others seriously portrayed their war experiences autobiographically or semiautobiographically. Still others attempted
to reproduce reality photographically, describing their experiences in the new realm of realistic perception tempered by
a Surrealist's sensibility.

        Certain writers in the early and mid 1950's revived
the Spanish tradition of nineteenth-century Realism. Some of
their novels represented a break from the introspective, esthetic and intellectualized pre-Civil War novel. The trauma
of Civil War experiences caused a return to Realism and to
the exterior world with its imperative political and social
problems. Many of these writers are serious ones, living in
Spain, who reflect both their personal traumatic experiences
of the war and the realities of postwar Spain in their work.

        Apart from the authors of the 1930's and 1940's, a
new generation of writers arose--the Generation of 1950 or
nueva oleada (New Wave). Never having known the fears and
dangers of the Civil War, they continue the Realist trend in
fiction and in their social novels. Whereas the 1940 generation of novelists like Cela described the social significance of
their era, some New Wave writers preferred to act as critics, denouncing the effect of the present regime. Camilo
José Cela and Juan Goytisolo among others, utilizing the contributions of their predecessors, have reduced the descriptive
element in their works. Their creations are sober, direct
works which, deceptive in their simplicity, suggest a number
of undeveloped themes. Some writers such as Cela have been
equally formative and susceptible to these newer intellectual
currents. Cela's consistent flexibility demonstrates the author's formation and assimilation of the new watchwords of
the New Wave novelists. Federico Saínz de Robles sums up
succinctly some of the new characteristics of the 1950 New
Wave writers:

                ... realism, objectivity, description, a documentary
                style in their colloquial and exacting use of language.
                They share an abhorrence for metaphor, for para-
                dox, for the subtle poetic image and for feelings of

eroticism without their complexities or delights.
In portraying these qualities, the writers of the
1950's [and 1960's] use a coldly written style, almost scientific.   Their comprehension of beings
and of things depend[s] only upon their attraction to a
particular temperament, on their laborious studies
of submissive or inverted mentalities and on their
pretensions to portray excited psychological states
in sensitive, exasperated personalities. [1]*

It is only fitting then, that this critical work begin
with an analysis of Cela's La colmena (The Hive) because of
his own virtuosity in the novel genre, indicating his refusal
to submit to Spain's literary paralysis.   In fact, the brilliance
of Cela's literary career which already spans two "literary"
generations and may possibly help to engender a third in the
1970's may be revealed either as a commentary upon modern
man or upon Cela and the New Wave novelists, writers who
are constantly in search of themselves and their society.

To fully comprehend the writing of the New Wave novelists
and their emergence, a brief summary of the leading historical and political events during their lifetimes is imperative
at this point.   Any and all Spanish political action which af-
fects or affected these novelists is rooted in the fact of General Francisco Franco's emergence as chief of state or cau-
dillo after the Spanish Civil War ended in 1939.

During the years 1931-1936, Alfonso XIII was deposed
as King of Spain and a Republic was established.   Economic
and political unrest culminated in an army revolt under the
leadership of General Franco in Spanish Morocco.   Franco,
in semi-exile on the Canary Islands, took command of the
forces in Morocco, the most powerful segment of the Spanish
Army; he led them in the invasion of Spain and three years
of civil war began (1936-1939).

Internal support for Franco came from the country's
conservative elements, including the Fascist Falange Party
(founded in 1933 by Primo de Rivera); the defending Loyalists
were backed by the Popular Front and the Basques and the
Catalans.   Franco received substantial aid from Nazi Germany and Fascist Italy; the Loyalists, handicapped by the

---

*Notes to Chapters 1 through 22 begin on page 329.

non-intervention policies of many great powers, received
help from an idealistic band of mercenaries from the Soviet
Union.   Factionalism ate into both sides; it was a situation
the Communists used to gain the upper hand in the Loyalist
camp; Franco, on his side, managed to hold ascendancy over
the army-Fascist rivalries in his ranks.   Finally, by early
1939, the insurgents for Franco won the revolution.   Franco
became comander-in-chief, prime minister and head of the
Falange Party.   He made Spain a corporate state under authoritarian rule and all opposition was rigorously suppressed.

In July of 1942, Franco reestablished the Cortes
(Parliament) with elected, ex-Officio members without genuine popular representation.   Spain stayed neutral during
World War II but morally supported the Axis powers.   Its
relations with these Fascist powers and support for repressive measures caused its exclusion from the United Nations
in 1946.   In 1947, Franco declared Spain a monarchy by
promulgating the Law of Succession, and governed Spain under a regency council, but with himself as chief of state for
life.   Leading prospects for the crown, not available until
Franco's death, were then Don Juan de Borbón and his son,
Prince Juan Carlos.

It was more than a decade after World War II that
Spain was readmitted to the United Nations.   But closer to
home, in Europe, membership in the Common Market was
vetoed by the anti-Franco traditions of such countries as
Great Britain, Belgium and the Netherlands.   In December
of 1966, a new Constitution, called the "Organic Law," was
approved by the people in a plebiscite.   The new law implied
a liberalization of government policy in the areas of religion,
the press, trade unions and other social aspects of Spanish
life.   It also curbed the political power of the Falange Party.
In July of 1969, General Franco and the Cortes designated
Prince Juan Carlos, then 31 years old, as the future king
and chief of state, to assume office in the event of the death
or incapacitation of General Franco who was then 76 years
old. (Juan Carlos is the son of the pretender to the throne,
Don Juan de Borbón.)   However, dissatisfaction with the
Constitution made itself felt in strikes and university unrest
which led to severe police repression.   The deep wedge
driven between the people by the Civil War continued to
cause serious internal unrest and even the Church faced a
widening rift between its young liberals and the conservative
hierarchy.

In spite of these events, Spain has strengthened its
ties with the United States and in an agreement first signed
in 1953 and renewed in 1963 and again in 1970, the United
States, in return for the use of Spain's air bases, promised
to support the Spanish defense system and underwrite it with
loans and equipment, stressing Spain's importance for Mediterranean security.   President Nixon appeared to place
American approval behind the regime of Franco and his
chosen successor, Prince Juan Carlos, by making successive
visits to Madrid and inviting Juan Carlos to Washington.

Nevertheless, the Spanish government waved both the
carrot and the stick before foreign opinion.   A new labor law
introduced some democracy in the conduct of Spanish unions.
But on the other hand, in 1970, six Basque separatists were
sentenced to death on terrorism charges.   Franco commuted
these sentences following world outcry that included a plea
from Pope Paul.   In a 1972 article in the New York Times,
correspondent Henry Giniger no longer foresees any hope of
Spain's joining the European Common Market.   In fact, the
title reads: "Spain Appears to Resist Liberalization Required for Full Role in Europe. "2   Most European nations
believe Spain cannot enter the Common Market unless it
demonstrates substantial changes in the authoritarian nature
of the present regime.   The Spanish government, in effect
in its thirty-eighth year, shows increasing resistance to political change.   Several publications and prominent public
figures who favor the democratization of Spanish life have become open targets for their criticism and have been fined and
jailed accordingly.   Surveillance of the press is accompanied
by a close watch over the universities and worker groups,
two sources of discontent where radical influence is particularly strong.

On the international level, diplomats from other nations view the Spanish problem somewhat differently.   "It is
in the interest of Europe that Spain evolve a democratic system.   If we can help, we must do it.   Otherwise we will
have a regime like that of the Greek colonels or anarchy. "3
Neither diplomats who share this view nor any Western Euro-
peans expect any change while Franco continues in power.
But they believe Franco's heir, Prince Juan Carlos, will
bear the full weight of this problem some day although Juan
Carlos himself has recently reaffirmed his loyalty and adhesion to his Generalísimo--ironically and coincidentally on
the anniversary of Spain's "Thirty-six Years of Peace. "

Thus, Spain's New Wave novelists lived and continue to live in a climate of repression unrelieved by various supposed liberalizations of policies. Though the repression in Spain is a far cry from the bloody reprisals and prison terms meted out by the Civil War victors in 1939, a Spaniard still gets in trouble if he or she openly defies the regime. In 1971, Ana María Matute, one of the leading New Wave novelists, was jailed and fined in Barcelona for speaking out against the censorship policies of the Franco regime. Yet there is a new outspoken mood in Spain, with criticism of the government widespread. It is in this mood many of the leading novelists in Spain find themselves today as they seek to create in their respective fictional worlds an image somewhat daring and multifaceted that, indeed, mirrors Spanish society with an astonishing realism never attempted before 1950.

Chapter 2

WHAT IS THE SPANISH NEW WAVE?

One leading Spanish critic, Federico Saínz de Robles, has suggested a definition for this literary phenomenon known as "New Wave"--quoted in the preceding chapter. Since the early 1950's, many Spanish literary critics have written and commented upon this current in Spain's literary world which erupted at that time and has sustained a large group of talented writers over the past twenty-five years.

One of our major considerations will be to judge if the Spanish New Wave is really Spanish at all or if it originated with the beginning of a New Wave, for example, in French cinema which began at approximately the same time. Another consideration is if indeed, there exists an authentic Spanish New Wave. One literary critic, José María Castellet, writing in 1963 views in the Spanish novel, a "nueva ola"[1] of writers and goes on to say that two currents of writing persisted over the past fifteen years--"realismo histórico y realismo crítico."[2]

Before considering in depth the points of view of any particular Spanish literary critic, a closer examination of the term, "New Wave," is relevant at this juncture. Afterwards, I will attempt to treat Castellet, Laguerre, Sobejano, in short, mostly all of Spain's major literary critics, in alphabetical order to discover whether or not they have brought any new ideas to bear on the concept of what a "New Wave" writer or style really is and if these authors have genuinely contributed to the progressive development of the novel genre in Spain.

Curiously, a French novelist and critic, Alain Robbe-Grillet, was chiefly responsible for the term nouvelle vague and its wider application to French arts and belles lettres.

"If in many of the pages that follow, I readily employ the term New Novel, it is not to designate a school, nor even a specific and constituted group of writers working in the same direction; the expression is merely a convenient label applicable to all those seeking new forms for the novel, forms capable of expressing (or of creating) new relations between man and the world, to all those who have determined to invent the novel, in other words, to invent man. ...

"Flaubert wrote the new novel of 1860, Proust the new novel of 1910. The writer must proudly consent to bear his own date, knowing that there are no masterpieces in eternity, but only works in history; and that they survive only to the degree that they have left the past behind them and heralded the future. ...

"The novelist, more than a creator in the strict sense, is thus a simple mediator between ordinary mortals and an obscure power, a force beyond humanity, an eternal spirit, a god.... ...

"That passion to describe ... is certainly the same passion we discern in the new novel today. Beyond the naturalism of Flaubert and the metaphysical oneirocriticism of Kafka appear the first elements of a realistic style of an unknown genre, which is now coming to light. It is this new realism whose outlines the present collection [of essays] attempts to describe. "[3]

Robbe-Grillet also used the following characterizations:

"The New Novel is not a theory, it is an exploration ... merely pursuing a constant evolution of the genre ... interested only in man and in his situation in the world ... aiming only at a total subjectivity ... addressed to all men of good faith ... and does not propose a ready-made signification. "[4]

Clearly, the nouveau roman in France is responsible for the use of the words nueva novela or nueva ola in Spain. However, Robbe-Grillet's attempts to define the New French Novel, no matter how interesting they are in themselves, have really very little to do with the conception of novel writing or Spanish New Wave as we know it today. Jacques Siclier, a French film critic, attributes the term New Wave correctly to "Operation New-Look, " a term used in the

Parisian salons in 1948 to renovate post-World War II fashion. "Le rapport est pourtant direct entre la haute couture
et le cinéma français d'aujourd'hui quant à l'étiquette."[5]
French Cinema took on a "new look" which one called "nouvelle vague" or "new wave" and the term, according to Siclier, became the basis for the literary movement "jeune
roman" or "nouveau roman" developed by Robbe-Grillet,
Michel Butor, Nathalie Sarraute and others. Above all, the
term, nouvelle vague, says Siclier, "... est infiniment plus
séduisant a l'oreille et plus poétique que celui d'avant
garde...."[6]

Simply then, New Wave writers in Spain deal with one
particular aspect of novel writing--Realism or the reproduction of reality. "Realism is, in the broadest sense, simply
fidelity to actuality in its representation in literature.
...The Realist centers his attention to a remarkable degree
on the immediate, the here and now, the specific action,
and the verifiable consequence."[7] Many leading Spanish literary critics, in their attempts to define the Spanish New
Wave and identify its writers, have used Realism as a point
of departure to examine the modern Spanish novel and its
present state of fertility and regeneration.

In his 1958 essay, "Lo que falta a nuestra novela,"[8]
Juan Luis Alborg states his preference for the nineteenth-
century novels of Flaubert, de Maupassant and Balzac, believing the French used their realism to perfection. The
French novel reached its apogee intellectually as well as its
greatest degree of profundity by explicating its thematic and
stylistic values through Realism. For Alborg, a great novel
carries a bit of "authentic human philosophy," and the great
writers certainly knew how to create an entire world, "describing their society, its characters, with a particular atmosphere, rhythm and pulse of life." Although Alborg makes
no direct statement regarding the New Wave authors in his
examination of several of them, he prefers the style of
Realism, citing Dickens, Balzac, Pérez Galdós, and Erskine
Caldwell as his favorites. He feels that Cela, Matute, Castillo Puche, Aldecoa, Delibes, Quiroga and Sánchez Ferlosio
"maintain a certain tonality"[9] in their novels and each one
contributes the perceptible and undeniable stamp of their personality to each of their works.

In another essay, "Subjectivity and Objectivity in Today's Novel,"[10] Alborg restates his preference for Realism,
citing Stendhal's famous definition of the novel as "a mirror

passed along the road." Alborg is not interested in the
"novel-novel," the one which feigns Realism. Rather, he
prefers the kind of novel based upon the author's subjectivity
rooted in a genuine realism which the author portrays. After remonstrating with the definitions of the novel genre proposed by Fernán Caballero, Zola, Stendhal, Flaubert, Goethe
and Gide among others, Alborg affirms today's Spanish novel-
lists have renounced "objectivity" and have centered their total interest on "the expressions of their own egos." "Un
artista no es el que copia bien, sino el que saca de sí mismo, como un gusano de seda, la madeja de su propio mundo." Until 1950, Alborg believed the Spanish novel, precisely because of its impersonality, represented an "island without contact with the great continental literatures." The trend
has turned toward greater subjectivity and his idea of the reality contained in the novels published between 1950 and the
present is based solely upon a greater exposition of the
novelist's ego (personal reality) and the development of his
own intellectual preoccupations for which the action of the
novel (or plot) is generally a pretext. The subjective or intimate novel is the logical result of an evolution which, for
the novelist, represents the unavoidable true reality of the
events it narrates. Alborg feels in the 1950's that a crisis
exists among Spanish novelists because of the proliferation
of media--films, television, radio, magazines, xerox copying, etc.--and that the novel-novel, the one that is for mere
entertainment and without realistic or transcendental or
spiritual values, will gain popularity from the Spanish masses
and eclipse the subjective novel, its truly prestigious predecessor. To save the reading public from this crisis, Alborg
declares a professional novelist must renounce the idea of
writing to please the public. Taking this stand, he must
delve into the profundities of Spanish life in order to capture
the paradoxical "intimidad universal" or universal intimacy
through his own profound conception of reality.

In his Introduction to his two-volume work, La novela
española del siglo XX, Rafael Bosch declares literary realism is "a creation of the modern spirit,"[11] a thoroughly
Spanish creation tied to the Spanish invention of the novel,
although the novel is not the only genre which accommodates
the expression of Realism. He traces the development of
the Spanish novel, describing three distinct periods of time
and three different forms Realism has taken over the past
few centuries before he arrives at his lucid discussion of the
novel of the 1960's and his ideas of Realism and how they
affect the New Wave novelists.[12] Bosch views Realism as

used in the novels of the fifties and sixties based solely upon objectivism. "El concepto de objectivismo es algo mucho
más complejo--no pertenece a la dimensión exagerada o
desproporcionada del naturalismo, sino a su miopía, que
trata de sustituir la realidad por su epidermis--se funda el
objetivismo en toda una serie de tendencias, prejuicios,
paradojas y errores de la literatura contemporánea." Nevertheless, Bosch sees objectivism as a relatively new tendency
in the Spanish novel, as a technique for writers creating
their own idea of Realism. For Bosch, this writing style is
nothing new but is a rather hard and cold look at those
events which mattered little and have minor significance as
they are related by the novelist from a totally intellectual
(objectivist) point of view. Bosch feels the kind of reality
that objectivist authors portray is really a pretense. True
reality is a collection of intuitive impressions based upon
subjective values. Bosch sees the Spanish novel of the
1960's as a portrayal of reality which is divided in tone--
some novels are simply informative, others, vibrant but repressed. It is through the "objectivist style" which portrays
its realism that a chill and lack of interest in reality arises
in the novel. This pretension or belief that "things exist by
themselves without the necessity of poetic construction" often
reduces the novels of the 1960's to commonplace works.

     The best novels today are those that remain furthest
from this "objectivist" style of writing and have a natural
(subjective) tone. Nevertheless, to explicate reality as
graphically as possible, many Spanish novelists have chosen
objectivism as their modus operandi, especially Juan Goytisolo and Daniel Sueiro among others. Today's Spanish novel
distinguishes itself by its use of dialectics and many aspects
demonstrate social class differences. Greater attention to
dialogue, interior monologue, a new collective sense of time,
existential overtones, inventions of new uses of the present
tense to convey the past are some of the innovations or,
rather, re-inventions of the 1930's that are currently being
used to describe the realities of the 1950's and 1960's.
Bosch predicts there is no single stylistic or thematic means
of expression that captures reality which will be successful
in Spain. He foresees a type of baroque subjectivism initiated by Carlos Fuentes in 1958 in his novel La región más
transparente (Where the Air Is Clear) which will dominate
Spanish letters for many years to come--a subjectivist style
based upon the "isolation of modern man"[13] which may have
its merits and defects. This style tends to give the socialist or realist novel a new kind of "duty" to describe reality

with a highly developed type of social consciousness. For
Bosch, style or the means to capture reality is not the important factor. It is the novelist's goal to achieve a kind of
reality that is, above all else, valid, if it answers the social
motivations and the profound cultural imperatives which border on true greatness and ennoble the Spanish spirit.

        Another leading Spanish critic, Ramón Buckley, views
the problem of defining Realism somewhat differently. In
his book, Problemas formales en la novela española contemporánea, he discusses Realism from three points of view:
objectivism, selectivism and subjectivism, intending to give
a new, perhaps experimental, critical focus since he believes
the Spanish novel to be in the throes of intense experimentation and stylistic renovation especially during the early
1960's. Buckley presents the problem of the definition of
the "new" Spanish novel formally in an eclectic manner, de-
riving many of his critical arguments from Alain Robbe-
Grillet, Lucien Goldmann, Nathalie Sarraute, Michel Butor,
Baquero Goyanes, Guillermo de Torre, J. María Castellet,
Juan Goytisolo, Eugenio de Nora, John McCormack, Miriam
Allott, Sir Percy Lubbock and David W. Foster. He believes
essentially, "the novel [genre] is a solution to a formal
problem posed by the author."[14] Whether this problem is
conscious or subconscious, primary or secondary, an end in
itself or a vehicle to develop other themes is immaterial
since each contemporary modern novel has become experimental in nature, its technique and form somewhat imprecise
and vague. Buckley associates these developments in the
novel with the internal structure of the novel and the author's
own relationship to his work. A writer may be absent, omniscient or omnipresent. The author can see and interpret
reality as it is or imagine reality (that is, be omniscient)
or continue to be invisible to the reader while the latter
reads his work (typical of the selectivist style of writing for
which Buckley cites Miguel Delibes as his best example).
A subjectivist author is one who tries to create an unreal
world, or one that appears "unreal" or "mythical" in his attempt to interpret reality. An objectivist author who presents his concept of reality from a "behavioristic" view belongs to another school of novelists who view reality from
this vantage point.

        Buckley reaffirms J. M. Castellet's critical emphasis,
stating whatever point of view the author chooses, be it objectivist, selectivist or subjectivist, the only way to understand the meaning of the novel is to investigate and define

the distinct "point of view" the novelist offers to his readers.
The novelist's "point of view" is the key to discover his concept of reality or whether he is present, absent or invisible
(subjectivist, objectivist or selectivist) from his work. At
this juncture, Buckley relies upon Robbe-Grillet's and Juan
Goytisolo's definitions of the novel, re-emphasizing that each
novel, in essence, "creates itself according to its own rules"
and each novelist "invents his own form or composition of
his novel."[15] The rest of Buckley's critical work is divided
into three sections where he defines and illustrates his meaning of his categories, selecting and analyzing representative
novels of Spain's New Wave novelists: (1) objectivism and
the novels of Juan García Hortelano and Rafael Sánchez Ferlosio, (2) selectivism and the novels of Miguel Delibes including a lengthy critical analysis of Cinco horas con Mario
(Five Hours with Mario), and (3) subjectivism and the novels
of Juan Goytisolo and Luis Martín-Santos. Buckley offers
no conclusions concerning the success or failure of these
novelists to portray realism. He gives us only definitions
of the "categories of experimentation" of several of Spain's
New Wave novelists in his rather lengthy, eclectic, verbose,
jargon-laden but penetrating critical work.

Juan Carlos Curutchet's short work, Introducción a la
novela española de postguerra, attempts to abandon the myth
that Spanish realism is an unchangeable, singular entity.
Rather, Curutchet supports the conviction that an ideal style
of "Realism" does not really exist but is an attitude which
is created through the methodology of novelists such as Cela,
Fernández Santos and Juan Goytisolo among others. After
presenting a panoramic view of the Spanish novel which
flourished through the period 1939-1964 and giving special
emphasis to the novels of Juan Goytisolo and Jesús Fernández Santos, Curutchet presents his idea of Spanish Realism
apropos several New Wave writers in his last chapter, entitled "Entre el realismo crítico y el realismo histórico."
His ideas of critical realism and historical realism are
really borrowed from an original article by José María
Castellet who first created these literary categories in 1963
in his "Veinte años de novela española (1942-1962)." Before turning to Castellet however, Curutchet reminds us of
Albert Camus' words concerning reality, emphasizing that
reality cannot do without a minimum of interpretation and
arbitrariness. "To reproduce the elements of reality without choosing would be, if it were imaginable, to repeat its
creation in a sterile manner."[16] Critical and historical realism are another matter taken up more deftly by Castellet.

José María Castellet created the categories of critical
and historical Realism merely to describe the two distinct
groups of writers who deal with Realism as a consequence
of their generation. "Critical realists" were born between
1910 and 1922, those writers who were old enough to have
witnessed and participated in the Spanish Civil War or at
least have some direct, personal contact or precise memory
of it. The "historical realists" represent a group of writers
born after 1924, who may have lived through the war but
were not aware or did not have the capacity to act and were
mere witnesses or victims as children. Castellet cites Cela
and Delibes, among others, as belonging to the "critical
realist" school, and Goytisolo, García Hortelano, Matute and
Fernández Santos, among others--essentially the New Wave
novelists--as belonging to the group of "historical realist"
writers.

> Casi obsesivamente los jóvenes novelistas, entre
> el recuerdo de una guerra civil an la que no parti-
> ciparon y un incierto futuro político, intentan es-
> tudiar, analizar, describir y explicarse a ellos
> mismos la situación actual de su país, su estruc-
> tura social, las consecuencias de la guerra civil,
> etc.... Es decir, se adhieren consciente o in-
> conscientemente a una literatura testimonial, com-
> prometida, realista. [17]

Castellet hits the mark and defines the kind of "realism" of the New Wave writers and their thematic outlook.
He is surprised by the lack of novels emanating from "pure
imagination" or those with an essentially aesthetic or artistic point of view as late as 1963, types of fiction which
other members of the New Wave will take up in succeeding
years. He believes the "historical realist" writes novels
that deal essentially with the social situation, Spain's rural
life, industrial problems, urban living, interior provincial
immobility, etc. Some novels describing this kind of reality
may be social documentaries although other novelists may
have chosen to discuss the same themes differently, viewing
their reality through their creative imagination, demonstrating
a social and political conscience not necessarily from a documentary point of view. Castellet cites Goytisolo, Sánchez
Ferlosio and Matute among others as sharing this point of
view. The novelistic efforts of New Wave writers have not
fallen into the category of social novels, novels of the proletariat or agrarian novels so common in Europe, American
and Soviet literatures. Castellet maintains there are two

important reasons for this: first, because of the Civil War
and World War II, Spanish writers had no tradition of writing
to fall back upon, since the novel as a genre lay dormant
until 1942 and most novelists were fighting or reading the
fictional output of other nations rather than actually writing
themselves and second, political censorship extended into all
phases of Spanish life including literature--so much so that,
consciously or unconsciously, Spanish novelists exercised a
kind of auto-censorship, treating "social themes" in a rather
prudent and subtle fashion, adopting new stylistic techniques
in order to comply with governmental restrictions. This
being the case, the New Wave writers have contributed to
world literature a "novel of repression" or a novel reflecting "historical realism"--realities encompassing their memories of the Civil War, disagreement with the present regime
and censorship. Their novels also contain a spirit of hope-
fulness, hopeful of a constructive future presided over by
faith in a democratic "realism" which is now being perpetu-
ated in several Spanish novels of the late 1960's and 1970's.
Castellet's view of the New Wave is the most perceptive
and intelligent article we have encountered thus far which
accurately describes the kind of realism, thematic concerns
and intent of this group of novelists.

Guillermo Díaz-Plaja's latest book of criticism, Cien
libros españoles: poesía y novela (1968-1970), is a compendium of reviews of the fifty best poets and fifty best
young novelists and their work in Spain today. Limiting
himself to four categories, invention, reality, experience
(implying psychological experience, conscious or unconscious)
and history, Díaz-Plaja presents a critique of each new
novel but offers no unified series of conclusions regarding
Spanish fiction in general or its present direction (nor was
it his intention to do so). For as many multi-faceted novels
he examines critically, there are as many glimmers into the
nature of Realism or lack of it for each writer discussed
but there are also few substantial conclusions about their
novels. Perhaps the best inference we may draw from
Díaz-Plaja's reviews is that Spanish novelists today are ex-
perimenting with Realism, rejecting it, submerging it,
creating a supra-kind of Realism as well as relying upon
their indefatigable notion of Spanish Realism conceived in
their own particular style and from their own unique points
of view. Most important, the Spanish novel during the period 1968-1970 continued to be a fertile, even prolific genre.

Taking a slightly different view, Juan Ignacio Ferreras, in his excellent and thorough critical work, Tendencias
de la novela española actual (1931-1969), describes the
Spanish novel after World War II as basically a continuation
of the traditional Realist novel. He proposes to place these
novels written after 1945 into three "realist" categories:
(1) realismo restaurador or traditional realism restored,
(2) realismo renovador or traditional realism "transformed"
(or renovated), and (3) realismo novador or "innovative"
realism.

The first category, "traditional realism restored," is
the kind that corresponds to the "moral" or "idealist" type
exemplified by writers in the decadent portion of the nineteenth-century (or after 1885) and is currently utilized in
Spain by such writers as Gironella, Delibes and several
others. "Transformed realism," his second category, however, is really the basis of the writing style for most New
Wave novelists. Those novelists who use this style employ
"traditional" realism as their inspiration, however through
greater narrative skill and new experimental writing techniques, they explore the problems of modern Spain, bringing
their readers up to the absolute present moment, no matter
what theme they care to dissect. Ferreras cites Matute,
Quiroga, Castillo Puche, Sánchez Ferlosio, Goytisolo, Aldecoa, Fernández Santos and García Hortelano as the principal
practitioners of this style of realism. He further subdivides
"transformed" realism into three categories: first, realismo
intelectual or "intellectual" realism in which novelists such
as Sánchez Ferlosio and Luis Martín-Santos create an entire
fictional universe in order to explore a thoroughly intellectual
problem; second, realismo moral or "moral" realism in
which novelists such as Miguel Delibes create a fictional
world to deal with a moral, religious or philosophical problem; and third, realismo de crítica-social or "social-critical"
realism in which certain novelists like Matute, Quiroga,
Castillo-Puche, Fernández Santos, Lera, Goytisolo and García Hortelano among others take a critical position against
the Spanish middle class, defending their own "bourgeois"
position at the same time. Ferreras believes "social criticism is the common denominator of all types of realism,"[18]
whatever system or categories he chooses to define. Finally,
"innovative" realism, Ferreras' third category as used by
Lera, Antonio Ferrés or Alfonso Grosso is a new classification which manifests itself in authentic "social" problems,
especially the class struggles within Spanish society.

In a series of conclusions, Ferreras discusses the multiple missions of the New Wave novelists and their diverse uses of Realism to graphically explicate themselves and their society. He believes the contemporary postwar Spanish novel is systematically linked to the historical past and Spain's novelists either "oppose, exalt, ignore the postwar period, sometimes creating an unreal world or a real world without coming to grips with its problems in their search for the 'real' Spanish reality." He feels the contemporary Spanish novelist searches for the "real" Spanish reality but his use of Realism, however pervasive, is frustrated by certain inhibitions. This was the case until 1957 when Spanish novelists began to recapture the true kind of Realism necessary to deal with their themes. Ferreras describes the truthful "new Spanish novel" as "an accurate reflection of the society as it is, not as a creation in itself or conceived pointlessly" or in a void. For Ferreras, Realism and the Realist novel exist when "there is a correlation of relationships in a homologous universe and a parallel exists between the society created in the novel and the actual one from which the novel itself emerges."[19]

Turning from Spain to Latin-America for a brief moment, it is often valuable to peruse the literary criticism of Latin American writers and gain their perspective of Spain and the novel genre. The Latin American novel itself has experienced an exciting resurgence over the past ten years. Writers such as Julio Cortázar, Gabriel García Márquez, Alejo Carpentier, Mario Vargas Llosa and Carlos Fuentes have contributed greatly to this growth and spectacular interest in the Spanish language novel. Without delving into these writer's thematic approach, a view of their perspective of Realism is valuable because of the Latin American novel's tradition, linguistic ties to Spain and its persuasive influence which has had its effects on one or more of Spain's New Wave writers.

A well-known Mexican novelist and literary critic, Carlos Fuentes, in his book La nueva novela hispanoamericana, begins his work with a fine definition of the novel: "the novel is myth, language and structure."[20] Fuentes contends the novel died as a genre in Latin America as well as its chief frame of reference--Realism--which presupposes a descriptive and psychological style of observing individuals in personal and social relationships. With the resurgence of the Latin-American novel, Fuentes notes reality is better expressed by the "language of myths and the prophecies of an

epoch whose true stamp is not a capitalist-socialist dichoto-
my (as in the bourgeois novels of Realism of the nineteenth-
century) but a summation of events that in reality have
transformed life in industrial societies: automation, elec-
tronics, peaceful use of atomic energy."21

Social Realism and neocapitalistic Realism are the
two currents which have prolonged the nineteenth-century
Realist novel into the twentieth.   Fuentes believes these
views of realism no longer serve the genre or the society.
He prefers the "new novel" based upon the poetic roots of
a culture in which the novelist may first create a conventional type of Realism that appears "total," when in actuality,
he creates a second, parallel reality by means of a myth in
which his readers may recognize the true, significant side
of life as conceived in a unity of time and space.   In the
creation of this "new" reality, the Latin-American novelist
finds himself in conflict since first, he aspires to capture
the universal elements of reality (derived from a European
cultural tradition) and second, he is at odds with his own
"national" perspective, directing his novels to readers of his
own cultural and linguistic community.   Fuentes believes
this conflict of interests is more apparent in South American
writings, but all novelists share in this problematic dichoto-
my.   Of all writers treated in this excellent short critical
work, he singles out the Spaniard, Juan Goytisolo, as the
only New Wave novelist presently writing the kind of novel
in Spain with its particular brand of Realism that is nearly
identical to the best novelistic efforts of the Latin-American
"new wave" writers of today--novelists who demonstrate
through myths, new language and new structure a new truth
and "real" reality.

Juan Goytisolo himself has set down his own ideas on
novel writing in two short works, Problemas de la novela
(Problems of the Novel) and El furgón de cola (The Caboose).

In Problemas, Goytisolo discusses the novel's limitations, the French, Italian and American novels, the "new"
psychology, Robbe-Grillet and the nouveau roman, Ortega y
Gasset's views of the novel, the picaresque novel and its
heritage and cites in an appendix appropriate selections from
the criticism of Malraux, Lukacs, Pingaud, Brecht and Vit-
torini with which to justify his own views of reality.   Discussing essentially the novels of Sánchez Ferlosio, Fernández Santos and Cela (El Jarama, Los bravos and La colmena
respectively), and citing Albert Camus, Goytisolo believes

"realism cannot preclude a minimum of interpretation and arbitrariness.... Even the best photographs betray reality because they are born from selection and present limitations as to what they do not contain. ...To reproduce the elements of reality without choosing would be, if it were imaginable, to repeat creation in a sterile manner."22 Using Camus as his point of departure, Goytisolo feels the contemporary Spanish novel must show us the Spaniard in society as he really is, not just as he thinks he is. Writers must mirror reality, not manipulate it. The truly good novelist combines the lyrical (poetic) elements with this notion of reality and relates it to social motivation, which is, for Goytisolo, the purpose of all literary creativity. To become truly universal, the Spanish novel must become both national and popular. It is the duty of every author to fight against tyranny and try to reveal the truth about subjects of vital importance, no matter how difficult the task. In order to achieve truth in fiction, a dialogue between author and public is necessary, but an author may objectively record exterior actions of characters without entering directly as narrator. Goytisolo feels the novelist must be judged primarily by his ability to interweave technique and life and not his ability to create fictional characters. To create a thoroughly realistic novel, Goytisolo adopts many of the forms of the "new realism": dialogue, stream of consciousness techniques, flashback, time travel, translations of sounds as if by phonographs or tape recorders, interior monologue and cinematic techniques. Touching off a literary debate in Insula with highly esteemed Spanish critic Guillermo de Torre, the latter felt it was precisely these "techniques" that disfigure or falsify the very reality the New Wave writers purportedly seek. Although Torres' opinions have been since discredited because of the publication of Goytisolo's Señas de identidad (1967) and his Count Julian (1970), proving decisively that Goytisolo has written "national novels" capably outside of Spain and has done much to disseminate the Spanish New Wave novels and their influence abroad, Problemas is somewhat dated now, since Goytisolo himself has revised his earlier beliefs that only through "objectivism" and the objectivist novel (based upon a synthetic and real appreciation of man's ordeals, a style in which he no longer writes exclusively) can true reality be achieved in writing fiction.

El furgón de cola (The Caboose) is Goytisolo's only major collection of essays dealing with a wide variety of subjects such as the influence of Larra on Spanish censorship,

anarchic poet Luis Cernuda and his works, the opinions of
critic Menéndez Pidal, the "ideal" and "reflective" realities
of language, the literary heritage of the Generation of 1898,
literature and euthanasia and an author's conscience (probably Goytisolo's). Borrowing the title for these essays from
a famous quote of poet Antonio Machado, "We keep maintaining faithful to our traditions, our position at the tail end of
the caboose,"23 Goytisolo becomes a social critic, judging
Spain's epoch of modernization and industrialization out of
keeping with the anachronistic traditions held in vogue by its
reigning, impermeable intellegentsia. Destroying the myths
of nobility and history, Spain must uncover the cowardice,
hypocrisy and egotism beneath its masks of pride and nobility
to re-create itself as a modern nation. Considering intellectual censorship the single most devastating blight on the nation, Goytisolo considers his own literary generation as the
most rebellious, leftist, agnostic and vital. "The new writers of the New Spain must strive for the passion of personal
experience, emotions and ideas to achieve the necessary tension which will illuminate a new reality--this new world needs
a new, anarchistic and virulent language, for only by destroying antiquities can one create anew...."24 The essays of
El furgón de cola are written much in the same tone as his
novel Señas de identidad, one of denunciation (of the Spanish
language and myths of Spanish history). In Spain, literary
critics do not know what to make of Furgón, believing the
collection of essays to be a bitter, ironic outcry, but posing
the dilemma as to whether it is really criticism or just plain
palaver. Without taking sides, most critics in Spain concur
"lo demás es silencio" ("the rest is silence"),25 but as we
know outside of Spain, we must read between the silences to
comprehend Goytisolo's full and vitriolic meaning. As American critic Kessel Schwartz puts it, "Goytisolo has been one
of the most outspoken critics of the Spanish government and
the shrillest voice stressing the social purpose of contemporary literature and the responsibility of intellectuals; he has
also espoused the vogue for technical and artistic reform.
... It is his refusal to accept authority in conflict with his
moral code which makes him the leading Spanish novelist of
his day."26 Furgón's essays are an "intellectual scream,"
another aspect of Goytisolo's literary ability and genius. In
a recent interview about his critical and fictional writing,
Goytisolo declared: "My own praxis [of writing] has shown
me the exactitude in that celebrated observation of Roland
Barthes in The Zero Degree of Writing: all born writers
contribute to the process of literature. My true birth as a
writer coincides in fact, with the destruction of my literature,

the molds of the novel, that, routinely, were taken from
borrowed traditions. "27 As critic and novelist, Goytisolo is
the arch iconoclast, the single writer whose artistic works
make us tremble because of the brilliance and excitement of
his critical and literary perceptions. Goytisolo incarnates
the hue and cry of the New Wave. It is his spirit of "critical realism," "cultural revisionism" and "demythification"
that has been partially responsible for the resurrection of
the Spanish novel during the late 1960's and early 1970's.

Two critics that add minor insights into our views of
the New Wave novelists, attempting classification of the
latter's works, and presenting definitions of "social realism"
and "intellectualism realism" as the basis for their points of
view while providing interesting chapter analyses of many
New Wave writers are M. García-Viñó and Pablo Gil Casado.

In García-Viñó's work, Novela española actual, 28 he
examines the careers of Delibes, Castillo-Puche, Laforet,
Sánchez Ferlosio, Cunqueiro, Torrente Ballester, Matute,
Bosch and Rojas. Believing social realism to be detrimental
to the progress of the novel genre, García-Viñó favors an
intellectualized concept of the novel. "La verdad ... es
que la llamada literatura social no ha dado un sólo novelista
que sobrepase la mediocridad. " In his Epilogue, he states
the novel should not be based upon economic circumstances
as in the intrigues of most novels of social realism, but the
fundamental realities, "analyses in profundity, in search of
true feeling, taking into account originations such as religion,
love, ideas, the human being, the world and death. " García-
Viñó feels the proponents and continuers of social realism
will never raise the level of the Spanish novel artistically
until they fully intellectualize the need for profundities, not
escape from them and finally reject their tradition of "social
realism. " With "social realism" so engrained in Spanish
society, one wonders how a novelist living in contemporary
Spain can fully "intellectualize" his problems and not deal
with the "social realities" of his daily world and how García-
Viñó's dream of "intellectual realism" on the highest artistic level be fulfilled.

After summing up in five cardinal points the main
characteristics of Spain's new novelists under scrutiny in
his book, García-Viñó concludes:

En definitiva, dos características, que resumen
todas las demás, pueden quedar incuestionablemente

anotadas en el haber de esta nueva novela española:
Primero: concepción de la novela como forma de
conocimiento del hombre antes que de la historia;
es decir, como contemplación de la realidad universal, invisible, más que como reflejo fotográfico
de lo inmediato y visible. Segundo: preocupación
estética, culta, universitaria, por el género, que
se toma como medio de expresión intelectual, como
un arte, independiente, por tanto de todo tipo de
servidumbre política.

One year later, in an essay entitled "La nueva novela
española," García-Viñó adds very little to his own view (or
ours) of Spanish Realism but provides a presentation containing many excellent bibliographical references and a listing
of characteristics of the new Spanish novel into which he inserts several works under discussion in this book. Re-
emphasizing his idea of total or universal realism, he divides the new novels into the following groups of those pos-
sessing these qualities: exoticism, utopistic, poetic, infra-
realistic, symbolic, metaphysical and theological, qualities
in harmony with his view that contemporary Spanish novelists
have a "university talent and mentality" (used positively),
treat the "invisible reality" rather than the "visible," concern themselves with non-conformist attitudes, stand their
ground on "social issues rather than the spiritual." Earlier
in this essay he declared, "Los novelistas españoles, se
dice, no abordan temas de interés universal. La crisis de
la novela española es una crisis de temática."[29]

Contrastingly, Pablo Gil Casado's excellent critical
work, La novela social española, assumes that the Spanish
novel between 1950 and 1966 fundamentally deals with social
realism and classifies all novels and novelists under discussion into six main thematic categories: (1) abulia or
lack of will, (2) the countryside, (3) the worker and the em-
ployee, (4) daily living, (5) travel and (6) alienation.[30] Gil
Casado believes social realism is the only kind described in
Spanish novels and it truly reflects the society with all its
multifaceted problems. In his final chapter, he sees the
novel of social realism and intention as a "new" phenomenon
in modern Spain and believes that the present social novel

represents the continuation of the Castillian literary tradition. This evolution, clearly, adjusts
itself to the artistic conception of different epochs,
but in the analysis of the society, it finds itself

> not only in the period that follows the (civil) war
> but also in the one that precedes it, in the 1898
> writers, in the works of naturalist-realist writers,
> in nineteenth-century Naturalism and Realism in
> full flower and in Realism in transition. One
> could establish a realist line linking Goytisolo-
> Cela-Zunzunegui-Sender-Baroja-Blasco Ibáñez-
> Clarín-Galdós. 31

Gil Casado feels the novel of social realism is a continuing
genre, with its characteristics and tendencies already firmly
established among Spain's new novelists.

Antonio Iglesias Laguna's extremely detailed first
volume of his two projected tomes, entitled Treinta años de
la novela española (1938-1968), is another example of literary criticism that creates a set of fixed categories (not too
clearly defined themselves) and assigns names of authors con-
forming to a preconceived point of view with the end result
that what appears to be a historical view of literary criticism turns out to be nothing more than a colossal encyclopedia with little profundity. Iglesias Laguna takes the Spanish literary phenomenon of Realism for granted, and without
defining it, divides it thematically, placing his predilect authors according to these categories: (1) "objective" realism
in the novels or Lera, Salvador, et al., (2) "historical"
realism in the novels of Gironella, Agustí, et al., (3) "ironic" realism in the novels of Cela, García Pavón, et al.,
(4) "intimate" realism in the novels of Quiroga, Castillo
Puche, Delibes, et al., and (5) "lyrical" realism in the
novels of Cunqueiro, Torrente Ballester, et al. He situates
authors into these categories by virtue of the "generation"
to which they belong as well as his own personal criteria
and proceeds to give a fair sketch of each writer and an
overview of his or her novels in succeeding chapters without much penetration. Unfortunately, Iglesias Laguna adds
little to our knowledge of the multi-faceted definition of
Spanish Realism linked with the New Wave novelists. The
single eclectic critical remark he makes about the "new
Spanish realism" is borrowed from a French critic, Roger
Garaudy: "Ser realista no significa imitar la imagen de lo
real, sino su actividad; no quiere decir preparar un dupli-
cado de las cosas, los hechos y los hombres, sino partici-
par en el acto creador de un mundo en devenir, descubrir
su ritmo interno."32 Iglesias Laguna feels the lyrical realism of Spain's New Wave novelists comes closest in capturing the "real" reality Roger Garaudy described so aptly.

Marra-López' Narrativa española fuera de España
(1939-1961) also sheds very little light on what is currently
happening in Spain concerning the Spanish novel's regeneration. Most of the writers he treats of, for example Max
Aub, Francisco Ayala, Arturo Barea, and Ramón Sender,
are exiles who continue the pre-Civil War tendencies of most
Spanish writers in the Galdosian tradition of the nineteenth-
century tempered with an "intellectualism" and "dehumanization" characteristic of the early 1930's. Their exile from
Spain causes the "realist" novel they write to degenerate into idealizations of their one central theme--the Civil War as
well as a tendency to intellectualize their experiences. Because they live elsewhere, their "lyrical" realism produced
by nostalgia gives way to rationalizations which depart even
further from their idea of Spanish Realism. The "pure objectivity" that New Wave authors are capable of is not possible for these exiles to achieve in their portrayal of the
war. Their novels either exalt, condemn or are raised to
a new level of abstraction which is construed as "anti-
realism. " The exiles have become apolitical before the "in-
vading reality" of the Civil War and consequently, in Spain,
certain New Wave novelists have taken up this anti-realist
trend of the exiles--such as Castillo Puche and Luis Goytisolo in Las afueras. Anti-realism, however, as a writing
style has had negligible impact on Spain's New Wave novelists. Perhaps the saddest plight of the Spanish novelists in
exile is expressed in the words of Francisco Ayala: "For
whom are we writing? I, a Spaniard in America? For
whom does a Spanish academician, on this side of the ocean,
continue cultivating his specialty? Well, if we answer the
questions ourselves--we write for everyone and no one,
would be the answer. Our words go with the wind--we are
confident that some of them may not be lost. "[33] Clearly,
these novelists live in a vanishing reality, expatriated and
with little persuasive influence on modern peninsular Spanish
novelists and intellectuals.

In the third volume of Eugenio G. de Nora's expansive and heavily detailed three-volume work, La novela española contemporánea, which treats the Spanish novel of the
period 1927-1960, he acknowledges "la nueva oleada" in his
fourteenth chapter and places this group of writers stylistically between "el relato lírico and el testimonio objetivo. "[34]
Nora agrees with the majority of critics discussed previously that Realism is the dominating tradition in their novels
but regards the North American novel, Italian neo-realism

(both literary and cinematic), the French nouveau roman and social realism of the Russian novel as the most stimulating and pervasive influences on the new Spanish novel. Because of their "generational situation," their realistic orientation predominates as well as a critical intention which each writer uses proportionately, according to his or her own personality. Nora examines in depth the careers of Matute, Sánchez Ferlosio, Mario Lacruz, Fernández Santos, Goytisolo, Aldecoa, Carmen Martín Gaite, López Pacheco, Luis Goytisolo-Gay and García Hortelano as the novelists most representative of the New Wave. Nora's greatest strength is his liberal examination of the major novels of each writer treated as well as a large section of bibliographical entries regarding each novelist. However, he too merely accepts Spanish Realism as a continuing current tempered by international influences with little penetration into the utilization of these influences by his own selection of New Wave authors.

Domingo Pérez Minik devotes only the last four pages of his 348-page volume, entitled Novelistas españoles del siglo XIX y XX, to Spain's New Wave. He states the novelist has "separated himself more and more from the fiction he writes," taking a new point of view concerning reality. His discovery of objectivity and the new social novel of the masses as exemplified by Sánchez Ferlosio are his only statements about the direction of the New Wave. For Pérez Minik, the Spanish novel in 1957 was in its formative stages based on the premise that a "subjective system of knowledge was being converted in principle into an objective order of things."[35] Pérez Minik felt the success or failure of the New Spanish novel rested entirely on this premise.

Writing about the same time as Pérez Minik, Federico Carlos Saínz de Robles, in his critical work entitled La novela española en el siglo XX, traces the novel and its main authors from the nineteenth century through 1957, giving over his last few pages to a few new and young novelists such as Delibes, Aldecoa, Sánchez Ferlosio, Castillo-Puche, Goytisolo, Matute and Quiroga. Rather than discuss the "realism" of the New Wave novelists, he simply describes their qualities and sums them up succinctly as we have already noted in Chapter 1. Saínz de Robles adds that these writers return to Realism, however, in a distinctly new social setting with different political factors operating, and with new states of consciousness and new stylistic experiments. Documentary and cinematic points of view, not exclusive to the Spanish New Wave, are also new inroads towards

expressing this new Realism.   Regarding the introduction of
new themes, Saínz de Robles is rather pessimistic.   "The
themes are eternal ... " and concerning the new writers,
"they have neither invented nor renovated [the genre]. "36

One of the best books of literary criticism to come
out of Spain by a Spanish professor living and teaching in
New York City is Gonzalo Sobejano's Novela española de
nuestro tiempo (en busca del pueblo perdido), in which the
author deals exclusively with two mainstreams--existential-
ism and socialism.   He subdivides the existential novel accordingly: Cela and the novel of alienation, Laforet and the
novel of disenchantment, Delibes and the novel in search of
authenticity and under a heading labeled "other novelists,"
he groups the "conventional" realists, the "conflictive" realists such as Castillo-Puche and Lera, and the "every-day"
novelists.

Within his category of the social novel, he devotes
single chapters to Sánchez Ferlosio's style of "invariability,"
Fernández Santos' "apartness" from society and Juan Goytisolo's search for "pertinence" while using the novel genre.
He further subdivides his social novel category into those
novelists who orient their novels (1) about the Spanish
masses, as do Aldecoa, Luis Goytisolo, Antonio Ferrés and
Alfonso Grosso; (2) against the Spanish bourgeoisie, like
those of García Hortelano, Sueiro, Martín-Santos, and (3)
about their own personalities, as exemplified in the novels
of Matute, Trulock and Bosch.   Sobejano's thesis is the
following:

> Ser realista significa tomar esa realidad (de la
> guerra civil) como fin de la obra de arte, y no
> como medio para llegar a ésta: sentirla, com-
> prenderla, interpretarla con exactitud, elevarla a
> la imaginación sin desintegrar ni paralizar su ver-
> dad, y expresarla verídicamente a sabiendas de lo
> que ha sido, de lo que está siendo y de lo que
> puede ser.   La consecuencia más general de la
> guerra, en lo que concierne a la novela, ha sido
> la adopción de este nuevo realismo: nuevo porque
> sobrepasa la observación costumbrista y el análisis
> descriptivo del siglo XIX mediante una voluntad de
> testimonio objetivo artísticamente concentrado.   En
> este nuevo realismo pueden señalarse dos direc-
> ciones extremas que ponen a prueba la condición
> humana (novela existencial) y hacia el vivir de la

> colectividad en estados y conflictos que revelan la
> presencia de una crisis y la urgencia de su solu-
> ción (novela social). [37]

At this point, Sobejano analyzes the writers of his choice,
placing them in his categories. The best two chapters are
the summations of the qualities shared by these authors regarding their choice of theme, characters, society, technique and inter-relationships. Sobejano assigns to the realism of Spain's existential novel the following qualities:

> insolaridad, incertidumbre, incomunicación, vio-
> lencia, rutina, ensimismamiento, angustia cuida-
> dosa, exploración de la tierra incógnita: tales
> son, creo algunos rasgos esenciales del contenido
> de muchas novelas que podemos estimar expresi-
> vas de un realismo existencial. ... Tendencia
> a la objetividad a partir de un subjetivismo todavía
> difícil de sobrepasar, pero en ningún caso gratuito,
> sino representativo; alejamiento del análisis
> psicológico, viva atención al contexto social, ini-
> ciación en nuevos ensayos estructurales, son ras-
> gos que distinguen a la generación de la guerra de
> su predecesora y la vinculan con la siguiente. Su
> insolidaridad, su incertidumbre, su desgarradura y
> su angustia son las cualidades que en sí misma
> podrían definirla.

In a later chapter, Sobejano cites from Juan Goytisolo's critical work, Problemas de la novela, the following
three points: the novelists of this generation (a) lack ideological content in their novels, (b) display an absence of
psychological analysis of their characters and (c) lack any
"message" or intention in writing their novel. Their novels
are "realist," but their Realism is saturated with intentions.
In his last chapter, Sobejano contends the "social novelists"
continue the trends of the "existential novelists," stressing
the following themes:

> infructuosidad, la soledad social y la guerra como
> recuerdo y en sus consecuencias. ... Predominan
> ... los ambientes de intemperie: campo, mar,
> aldeas, riberas, carreteras, trigales, viñedos,
> olivares, arrabales.... El tiempo de acción ...
> suele ser la actualidad, como corresponde al
> común intento de iluminar el presente. ... Soli-
> daridad, infructuosidad, soledad social, paciencia,

esfuerzo, tentativas de compromiso, exploración
de una España maltrecha por absentismo o central-
ismo: tales serían algunos rasgos típicos del con-
tenido de muchas novelas que pueden estimarse
representativas del realismo social.

Concerning realism, Sobejano finds there are three
basic components of the social narrative: (1) Realism,
(2) society or sociability and (3) formal experimentation
within the realist tradition preferred by the new novelists
emanating from Spanish, American and Italian sources.
Citing Michel Butor, another renowned French critic and
nouveau roman advocate, Sobejano shares his view that
"realism is a sine qua non of the new novel and to this new
situation, a new consciousness of relationships on a more
advanced level of Realism is born and on several different
planes through new language, style, composition and structure. "

Summing up his position, Sobejano optimistically concludes that the post-Civil War novel is in a state of "splendid renaissance. " He insists the major purpose of the New
Wave novelists has been to "open the novel genre to life. "
Using Max Aub's term, "transcendent realism" from his
well-known critical but dated work, Discurso de la novela
española contemporánea, published in 1945, Sobejano concludes it is this kind of Realism which represents the "actual" reality and all novelists should approach this kind of
Realism--to better humanize both socially and historically
the "actual" reality. "Art should not be enclosed within the
pride of its own autonomy but should be a centrally focused
art, concentric and integrated into actual reality. "38

Torrente Ballester's 700-page critical work, Panorama
de la literatura española contemporánea, offers little more
than a repetition of the critic's works previously discussed.
It is only in his last twenty-five pages that he treats the New
Wave. He views the Realism sought by these novelists between 1950 and 1964 as part of a "novela-testigo" (novel as
witness) or "novela-reportaje" (novel as documentary). Taking José María Castellet's view of Realism with its historical
and critical polarities but not his optimism, Torrente Ballester, however, pessimistically views the novel of the 1960's
as a genre in decadence, blaming the Spanish public for this
development since it prefers novels of "poor quality and ...
without aesthetic values. "39

Another fairly well-known Spanish author-critic, Carlos Rojas, also has very little new to add to our understanding of New Wave novelists and concepts contained in his article, "Problemas de la nueva novela española. " Echoing the
thoughts of Juan Goytisolo, Rojas believes the mission of the
new artist is to show that "man's destiny is man and to
transform his destiny by his own conscience. " Rojas' final
statement shows the direction the New Wave is taking in
1968:

> De Los desastres de la guerra (Goya) al tremendis-
> mo (Cela) pasando por Picasso y los esperpentos
> (Valle-Inclán), la humanización del monstruo fué
> constante obligada del arte español. El realismo
> objetivo ha venido a desdecir la obra de aquellos
> moralistas: los hombres transformados en mon-
> struos, sin advertirlo y sin proponérselo. [40]

Perhaps the best written essay tracing the Spanish
novel from Pérez Galdós to the present and describing the
New Wave appears in Edenia Guillermo and Juana Amelia
Hernández' 1971 publication, La Novelística española de los
60, [41] in which the authors also provide excellent discussions
of six leading writers--Martín-Santos, Marsé, Delibes, Goytisolo, Benet and Matute. Somewhat eclectic, they review
past criticism as I have done in this chapter but do provide
some new thoughts. These critics are mainly concerned
with Realism of the 1960's and view 1960 itself as the crucial year when Spain's frontiers were finally opened because
of increased tourism, possibility of admission into the European Common Market, growing industrialization and better
working conditions. Spain's novelists had their first opportunity to open their eyes and paint into their works a kind
of "photographic realism" that never existed before. Spanish
novelists were free at last to experiment and write works of
transcendental value approaching a kind of "universal novel. "

Guillermo and Hernández stress the Spanish novelists'
great insistence upon new language and a total linguistic
realization which has been the greatest accomplishment of
Spain's modern novel. Those critics believe most Spanish
authors to be susceptible to Marshall McLuhan's "the medium is the message" philosophy that maximum communication
is the basis of all possible relationships and the essential
necessity of man. Towards achieving this end, the treatment of reality by the New Wave is of utmost significance.
Generally, all New Wave writers depart from the realities of

contemporary Spain as their starting point, or events that
are vital and concrete, but try to penetrate them intimately,
distrusting surface appearances.   Some writers try to transcend these realities, believing there is always something
beyond the visible, the tangible.   These critics believe the
true confrontation with reality occurs when there is a symbi-
osis of the "external" reality and the internal "ideal" reality
which, when united, act as a single "vital" reality.   Guillermo and Hernández define other forms of describing reality
such as the humoristic, the ironic, sarcastic, psychological,
the caricature, black humor and the cruel joke.   The new
Spanish novel also opens a new path towards fulfilling a new
perspective of "totality" with a kind of realism that com-
prises, they say, "the natural and supernatural, the living
and dreamed, the conscious and subconscious, the imminent
and transcendental. "   The two authors give, in the penulti-
mate paragraph of their Introduction, extraordinary insights
into the novel of the 1960's which are worth repeating here:

> Búsqueda, inquietud, cambio, movimiento, indaga-
> ción, disconformidad, destrucción de mitos, trans-
> formación social, ansia de renovación, desesper-
> anza, frustración voluntad de vivir, sueños y re-
> alidades, tradición y ruptura.   Es evidente que la
> narrativa española de nuestros días ha superado
> la etapa de experimentación, anda por nuevos
> caminos en busca de nuevas metas y refleja una
> perspectiva distinta ante una realidad nacional
> cambiante, sustentada en sus viejas raíces eternas,
> pero de espaldas a un pasado que ha dejado atrás
> definitivamente para ir al encuentro de nuevas posi-
> bilidades más a tono con la hora de un mundo en
> marcha.

Clearly, the most perceptive analyses of the New
Wave and their realism came from the critiques of Castellet,
Ferraras, Sobejano, and Guillermo and Hernández.   There
is little I can add at this point that would be an origianl perception of these writers--perhaps the value of the present
work is my personal cosmos offering the reader, through the
next twenty chapters, a knowledge of each of eighteen novelists, his or her best work and an "in-depth" portrait of his
or her style and use of Realism.   In essence, then, there
is nothing new under the Spanish sun.   The Spanish New
Wave is merely a refurbishing of a nineteenth-century style
made popular by Dickens, Balzac, Pérez Galdós and the like.
The Spanish temperament is rooted in this Realism that has

known its expression from the days of the stoics to the present.   It was my intention in this chapter to gather the major, relevant critical materials with a view to understanding the historical development of Realism since the nineteenth century as well as to explain the New Wave, its followers and their interpretations of Realism.   New Wave, then, is a literary category for a group of writers who use Realism to demonstrate their particular major thematic concerns.   In short, Realism, from our view, is simply a writing style. The intention of the following chapters is to reveal how this Realism (style) has been tempered artistically according to the modern sensibilities of eighteen outstanding writers. [42]

Chapter 3

CELA and LA COLMENA
(The Hive) (1951)

    Camilo José Cela was born in Padrón, a small Gali-
cian town in the northwestern corner of Spain in 1916. As
a young child he lived in England and later returned to Spain,
spending several years in Andalusia and Barcelona before
making Madrid his permanent residence. The son of a Spanish father and English mother, Cela went to the university
and studied law, philosophy and medicine. Before he was
twenty, however, he was writing poetry, short stories and
newspaper articles. His first novel, La familia de Pascual
Duarte (The Family of Pascual Duarte), published at age
twenty-six, brought him fame all over Europe. It was an
extraordinary international success as well. Since then,
Cela has continued to produce novels, essays, short stories
--in short, diverse material in all genres, incorporating his
youthful spirit and knowledge of popular dialects in his works.
He currently lives and writes in Madrid, occasionally lecturing in the United States on the contemporary Spanish novel
and his own works. His sixth novel, La colmena (The Hive)
was such a sensation when it appeared in 1951 that it became an international best seller and the fourth of his novels
to be translated into English in the United States. It established Cela as a prominent novelist of insight and compassion
capable of wider horizons than the tremendista tradition he
initiated in his first novel, Pascual Duarte.

    Before we enter into a discussion of La colmena, a
paragraph devoted to tremendismo is necessary in order to
establish Cela's stylistic point of view and some ideas of
his thematic concerns previous to La colmena, since that
novel, revolutionary in itself for its time, is however not
unusual as a development in Cela's own literary progress.
Tremendismo is a supra-realistic writing style, perhaps

close to the nineteenth-century French Naturalism of Emile
Zola and the Goncourt brothers in which Cela deliberately
accentuates the horrific, "tremendous" events of life--over-
powering events larger than the reality that contains them,
violent events conceived in an exaggerated, naturalistic esthetic, fortified linguistically by the crude, lewd, low-life
terminology which spices nearly all of Cela's major novels.
Perhaps the best view of tremendismo and its pessimistic
philosophy in English is given by Chandler and Schwartz:

> Tremendismo, a new kind of Naturalism starting
> after the Spanish Civil War partly because of the
> disillusion stemming from it in the early 1940's,
> exhibits many ... Existential traits. (Man wants
> to know what he is and where he stands. He is
> concerned with his own existence, since as a ra-
> tional animal he must question the meaning of that
> existence. Man is a stranger in the world and
> comes here by accident. Danger besets him on
> all sides, but he must meet the challenges of his
> environment courageously. Face to face with
> nothingness, he reaches a state of despair from
> which he may, perhaps, be rescued by his resolve
> or faith. ... Man must decide at each moment
> what he is going to do and what he is going to be.)
> Tremendismo derives its name, however, from
> another aspect of its themes. It deals with situa-
> tions and events which are truly terrible or tre-
> mendous. It differs from Naturalism in accenting
> environment rather than heredity as the major de-
> terministic factor. In its feeling of abandonment
> and hopelessness before the various boundary situa-
> tions faced by its characters, it is completely Ex-
> istential as already mentioned. Even when the
> bloodthirsty elements are missing, the constant
> conflicts and clashes of personalities, the incessant
> frustrations and anguish of the major characters,
> contribute to the tremendista aspects. The very
> youngest writers, born after 1925, mix their new
> themes with a continuing tremendismo, as they find
> it impossible to expunge their grim memories and
> continue to write about them. [1]

Needless to say, Pascual Duarte, as character and
representative of a new style of Realism revived the post-
Civil War novel, if any at all really existed. La colmena,
however, comes at another point of crisis, when the Spanish

novel as a genre is experiencing difficulty, burdened with
its own problems, a restless conscience and no meaningful
way of expressing itself. As in 1942, Cela revivifies the
Spanish novel with his trenchant prose, his expresivness of
the crude, harsh reality we remember in Pascual Duarte,
his intellectualism so demanding of the Spanish reader. Of
course tremendismo has given way to Realism as a writing
style for which Cela, intimately preoccupied by the anxieties
and problems and delusions of modern man, has made the
theme of his prolific, apocalyptic novel, La colmena.

 In the 1971 edition of La colmena, Cela recapitulates
in his own words his varied points of view about the novel,
its original conception and style as adapted from the first
four introductory notes written over the past twenty years
which are, in essence, the highlights of his thinking. However, within these same twenty years that the novel has been
in print, Cela reaffirms his position on Realism and his expectations of La colmena, which, parenthetically, took him
some five years to write while living in Madrid. "La
colmena no es otra cosa que un pálido reflejo, que una hu-
milde sombra de la cotidiana, áspera, entrañable y dolorosa
realidad. "[2] Cela presents his definition of Realism: "Esta
novela no aspira a ser más--ni menos, ciertamente--que un
trozo de vida narrado paso a paso, sin reticencias, sin ex-
trañas tragedias, sin caridad, como la vida discurre, ex-
actamente como la vida discurre" (p. 9). Cela calls his
novel "un grito en el desierto" (p. 14) and emphasizes its
feelings of sadness which permeate his readers. He views
all ideas, whether they be religious, moral, social or political ones, as manifestations of the unbalanced nervous system, atavisms that are illnesses and sadness as a product
of this reversion to the primitive. For him, ideas and
scruples are nothing but hindrances. In his most pessimistic commentary, Cela believes we follow the same useless
negative patterns in life and there is little hope. Cela believes La colmena is not a novel but history and like life
itself, history continues, muted by its own sordidness and its
sadness, both of which are highly atavistic qualities. In
Cela's attempt to portray reality, he feels this work of fiction, this particular story or historia was conceived as the
world turns on its axis in its "valley of tears. " His role
is to write and to hope that his words express, at the very
least, some measure of faithfulness to himself and to his
image of the world. Cela believes "nothing is really important outside of the truth or the 'mask of truth' that each
person discovers for himself" (p. 16). Finally, literature,

for him, is not a charade. It is an attitude which demands
discipline for writers and readers alike.

                              *   *   *

          Before we turn to a detailed analysis of La colmena,
a definition of the novel as genre is vitally important at this
point.   Thrall, Hibbard and Holman in their revised A Handbook to Literature devote six pages to a description of the
"novel," its several types and general characteristics.
Their most important words for the purposes of this book
and its evaluation of the eighteen Spanish novels follow:

> The novel is used in its broadest sense to desig-
> nate any extended fictional prose narrative. In
> practice, however, its use is customarily restricted
> to narratives in which the representation of charac-
> ter occurs either in a static condition or in the
> process of development as the result of events or
> actions.   Often the term implies that some organiz-
> ing principle--plot or theme or idea--should be
> present in a narrative that is called a novel.
> ... All novels are representations in fictional nar-
> rative of life or experience but the form is itself
> as protean as life and experience themselves have
> proven to be. ... Basically what we are saying
> here is that the subject matter of the novel defies
> cataloging or analysis. ... In shaping the various
> material to the formal demands of fiction, the
> novelists have displayed an equal variety. ... But
> however diffuse and various the novel is as a form
> it has always submitted itself to the dual test of
> artistic success and imitative accuracy of truth.
> Its best definition is ultimately the history of what
> it has been. 3

At this point the authors trace the roots of the European and
American novel, from birth through maturity, summing up
their thoughts by broadly classifying the novel with a unique
series of adjectives such as "detective," "psychological,"
"sentimental," "regional," etc.   For us, however, "the
principal modes in which novelists write are the general
modes of their ages; such modes are the products of style,
literary convention and the author's attitude toward life. "4

*   *   *

La colmena is composed of six basic chapters of
varying length including a final note and an alphabetical listing of its 346 personages (real or imagined) complete with
short descriptions.   Each chapter is episodic in nature and
contains either a dialogue or description or a combination of
these.   La colmena is a presentation of life in Madrid in a
series of loosely connected vignettes.   Its action is concen-
trated into three days in December 1943 and covers a period
from the afternoon of the first day to the night of the second
with an epilogue or Final taking place one morning four or
five days later.   D. W. McPheeters explains it thus: "The
first and second chapters are in chronological order--the
afternoon and early evening of the first day.   The third
chapter interrupts the sequence to jump to the afternoon of
the second day, to be interrupted in turn by the fourth which
returns to the night of the first day.   The fifth chapter jumps
forward to the night of the second, while the sixth returns
to the morning of the same day."[5]   David W. Foster in his
excellent book on Cela gives the best and most succinct outline of Cela's plot of the novel.

"The locale for all but one of the narrative units is
doña Rosa's café in Madrid.   Here a wide range of individuals are presented, all inter-related on the basis
of their varying degrees of attachment to the café.
... The main character of the novel is presented mid-
way in the chapter.   Martín Marco, unable to pay for
his order and expelled from the café has all eyes
turned upon him, thus bringing together briefly the interests of the tertulianos.   Although doña Rosa dominates the chapter as the overwhelming proprietress of
the café, she serves in this first chapter as a spring-
board for Marco's introduction through her hardhearted-
ness in having thrown him out.

"The first narrative unit [of Chapter II] re-enacts
the expulsion from the café from Martín's point of view
and in his way establishes him as the dominant figure
of Chapter II.   He appears several times throughout
the first two-thirds of the chapter.   The last third is
devoted to the events surrounding the discovery of the
murder victim doña Margot.   Marco is not mentioned
in connection with the murder.   But the fact that he is
the central figure of the novel, that the murder is the
only real event of the novel, and that in the Final

Marco is wanted by the police for questioning tend to point a strong link here.

"Chapter III ... portrays scenes in the café and elsewhere. Martín appears briefly only three times.

"Chapter IV ... consists chiefly of night scenes. Martín dominates this chapter, and it closes with him in the arms of a prostitute [Pura], where he has sought refuge from the winter cold.

"Chapter V tells of the evening of the second day and follows Chapter III in time. Don Roque and his family are highlighted. ... Events of several days previous are seen in flashbacks. Martín appears only twice.

"Chapter VI ... is a short chapter and surprises several by now familiar characters in the process of facing the new day. Martín is prominent among them.

"The Final concentrates on Martín a few days later as he takes a morning stroll. The newspaper under his arm contains the yet unread notice of the warrant out for his detention. Cela alternates accounts of Marco's stroll with sketches portraying the reaction of his friends and relatives to the notice that they read and commented upon. "[6]

By tracing Martín's somewhat "picaresque" wanderings throughout the novel, we are able to meet a wide variety of characters and discover their happy or sordid histories-- Doña Rosa and Celestino, the principal café proprietors, Pablo and Paco, Martín's respectively rich and poor boy-hood friends, Pablo's affair with Laurita, another friend, Ventura Aguado and his amours with a prostitute ironically named Purita, and Julita, the daughter of Don Roque and Doña Visi (Doña Visi being sister to Doña Rosa, proprietress of the café where most of the action of the novel takes place). The novel follows the affairs of Don Roque with Lola, Celestino with Petrita (the maid of Martín's sister, Filo), Martín's date with an old, prosperous girl friend, Nati Robles, Martín's conversations in a bar with La Uruguyana, a prostitute, Martín's visit to Doña Jesusa's brother where he sleeps with Pura. The narrative is particularly good in describing Petrita's affair with the policeman Julio García Morrazo, Martín's conversations with Seoane, the poor musician who plays

at Doña Rosa's café. Besides presenting extended canvasses
of Suárez, the aging homosexual, and Elvira, the aging prostitute, both habitueés of Doña Rosa's café, as well as other
minor characters, it presents a whole panorama of lesser
persons generally unnoticed such as the serenos (night watch-
men), the camareros (waiters), the cerilleros (match-sellers)
and the limpiadores (bathroom attendants), people who function in the twilight world of the café, whose lives and problems go generally unnoticed but without whom the society of
Madrid would be sorely lacking.

        For all its 241 pages, La colmena in a dense novel
consisting of an interplay between dialogue, description and
character development. Its constant tension between dialogue and description has been noted by most leading critics
of Cela as well as its one continuous interplay of people and
fragmented chronology. It has been often thought that John
Dos Passos' Manhattan Transfer served as Cela's model for
La colmena because of the novel's portrayal of a single,
whole society with its mosaic of interrelationships whose
single protagonist is, in reality, the city of Madrid. Its
plot (as outlined beforehand) is of minor importance, since
this work is one of actions, daily living by ordinary and vulgar people portrayed on a universal level, not a personal
one. Cela presents through his vignettes not only a micro-
scopic but simultaneously a panoramic view of a particular
section of Madrid, a Madrid of low life and unproductive
people. His choice of symbol for the city, the "beehive,"
works quite well for throughout the novel, one feels the continuous hum of action, incidents, life scurrying by. For
Cela, this particular "hive" serves as an inverse metaphor
since bees are generally productive insects, laboring vigorously to produce honey. Cela's "hive" is exactly the re-
verse--one murder is committed and mostly all the personages are engaged in a struggle for survival. They are
tragic creatures, discontented and singularly unproductive.

        Thematically, it has been said La colmena deals es-
sentially with money and sex. It is true that nearly all the
characters are concerned with money and sex in one way or
another, but their concerns proceed from Cela's initial pessimism about mankind. Essentially, man does not differen-
tiate himself from the beasts. The human being, for him,
is not a rational creature but a primitive animal interested
only in food, reproduction and destruction. Food and survival serve as the leitmotif for the early chapters of the
novel; sex (both perverse and commercial) is also high-

lighted; destruction and death are the themes seen in the
latter part of the novel--the unexplained murder of Doña
Margot suffocated to death with a towel and the cruel, sadistic killing of a dog on the street.

One wonders why such a pessimistic novel, dealing
with the lives of several people in Madrid during the winter
of 1943, a period of hardship suffered by most Spaniards
after their own Civil War and in the midst of World War II,
would indeed receive such international acclaim.   McPheeters called the novel "completely lacking in any depiction of
physical beauty; the settings are conceived in ugliness, and
there is a remarkable dearth of references to physical at-
tractiveness or to its lack in a story where sex is so important. "[7] In fact, La colmena at times gives the impression of not being a novel at all.   Apart from lacking the
"Jamesian" sense[8] of the novel form that Foster speaks of,
the narrative of La colmena gives the impression the author
originally wrote it sequentially and then taking shears, arbi-
trarily cut up the logical narrative and placed sections at
random into different chapters, deliberately upsetting the time
sequence.   Foster however sees Cela's fragmentation of
chronology as his "means to create an illusion of simultaneity. "[9] Granted, the work is a novel since it is a reflection
of human experience and although the author prefers not to
create the illusion of characters unfolding their personalities
before us with an awareness of themselves in society or revealing themselves in situations as is the Jamesian ideal,
La colmena, if somewhat unsatisfying to me, is still worthy
as an experiment seeking to revive the Spanish novel genre
through its new use of Realism.   Although banning its publication in Spain did help to publicize its notoriety, the novel
really comes as an outgrowth of Cela's own tremendista
style and fits comfortably into the prevailing literary experiments of Robbe-Grillet and Michel Butor (objectivism), the
Existential philosophy of Jean-Paul Sartre, the American
"behaviorist" trend as in Dos Passos' Manhattan Transfer,
and the Neo-realism of the Italian cinema as seen in De
Sica's films and as written in Moravia's novels.

The core of La colmena's success is based upon
Cela's use of Realism.   Departing from the epical narrative
Realist traditions of the late nineteenth and early twentieth
centuries, Cela creates the illusion of a closed world, the
actions of a variety of men and women in their day-to-day
routines.   He portrays the relative similarity and simultaneity of events in the lives of the three hundred or so

characters he creates. He presents his characters as they
are, through dialogue or internal monologue or biographical
descriptions in tense, colloquial language without any logical
connection to a principal narrative thread. The absence of
a narrator also destroys the logical presentation of events
and characters since Cela prefers to use dialogue and description to reveal the multiplicity of situations and circumstances. For Cela, his brand of Realism may be best defined this way: "it is essentially only that life be observed
and recorded while it is in motion."[10] For Madrid is a
teeming metropolis, a city in motion and Foster attributes
Cela's success to his personal use of Realism: "In La
colmena, by doing away with a center of intelligence within
the narrative, Cela has achieved a distance that renders his
novel less charming but all the more clinical and penetrating."[11] McPheeters goes a bit further: "Cela is not attempting to write the erotic novel; his is the clinical view."[12]

        Throughout the novel, this critic always felt detached
because of the extreme coldness of the events, the lack of
emotion of the personages, the complete detachment of Cela
himself. This may be attributed to Cela's use of an almost
cinematic style.   John J. Flasher's excellent article on
Cela's style in La colmena gives credence to this thought:

> The novel is a multiplicity of snapshots or sketches
> that follow in quick succession. To obtain them
> Cela uses a camera with three lenses: close-up,
> wide-range and telescopic. Within the field of the
> finder he perceives a small teeming universe with
> unusual intensity and accuracy of observation. His
> snapshots are a device that enables such a degree
> of concentration on each individual character and
> incident that there is barely any feeling of sus-
> pense. [13]

Foster calls La colmena essentially a novel of seeing and
one "based upon the rewards of voyeurism."[14] Cela, as author, stays completely out of the novel, as does the reader,
which accounts for the complete coldness and objectivity of
the author. Foster makes it quite clear that once the reader masters Cela's clinical objectivity in taking "the pulse of
life to chart its vital functions,"[15] he will be able to accept
Cela's neutrality of position. The key to Cela's novel is his
complete striving for objectivity or objective Realism, destroying the lines between what is observed and the observer
(the author in this case).

La colmena comes off also as a literary contrivance
over which Cela has complete control of characters, events,
actions. Without warning, Cela changes his vantage point--
from one locale to another, from biographical sketch to action. Just as in the filmed freezes of action in François
Truffaut's marvellous Jules et Jim, so does Cela literally
"freeze" the action of the novel by taking the reader back in
time and discussing a past event or a biographical detail.
Cela also uses another film artifice, the flashback, to great
and fine effect. Cela's flashbacks are the kind that often
repeat past events in present time. For example, an incident such as Marco's ejection from Doña Rosa's bar is first
presented while happening and then discussed by two characters in a later chapter who literally see the incident occur
once again. Foster notes that Cela always allows himself
"the liberty ... to report the same incident twice or, better,
to record the same dialogue twice, both times differently,"[16]
to create for his readers the illusion of reality by viewing
from two different perspectives the same incident. Foster
also sees Cela in Unamunian terms, "arranging reality in
order that the reader may most conveniently understand
whatever it is that the novelist would have him understand."[17]

Foster best sums up Cela's technique in the following
words: "Cela has come to believe that the function of the
novel is to give the illusion of reflecting life as it is being
lived, although, of course, the final result is but one novelist's personal vision."[18] Foster warns most perceptively
that Cela's opponents are the critics and readers who see
Cela's departure from the Romantic-Realist novelistic tradition. It is evident that Cela deals on the level of universals
(and on the basest levels thematically) and not with individuals as the Realist novels tend to create.

For all of Cela's efforts to create a good novel, there
are several aspects of his new Realistic style that hamper
his work. We are almost stopped from continuing with the
novel because of a "sameness" of tone in so many of the incidents and lives of the people of the story. Also there is
an insistence upon the rude, crude realities so objectively
seen that it tends to depress and discourage the reader from
penetrating into the novel any further. Because of the lack
of any unity of character or theme, the novel appears aimless, going nowhere. Some critics have found this aspect
part of Cela's "free form" or experimental use of the novel,
part of his protean quest for reinvigorating the genre. If
Cela has done anything new, he has successfully used the

Spanish language to create a type of photographic Realism
that startles, excites and sometimes depresses. In the following passages, note Cela's extraordinary use of language,

(1) descriptively in the manner of Dos Passos:

> Los portales llevan ya algún tiempo cerrados, pero
> el mundo de los noctámbulos sigue todavía goteando,
> cada vez más lentamente, camino del autobús.
>
> La calle, al cerrar de la noche, va tomando un
> aire entre hambriento y misterioso, mientras un
> vientecillo que corre como un lobo, silba por entre
> las casas.
>
> Los hombres y las mujeres que van, a aquellas
> horas, hacia Madrid, son los noctámbulos puros,
> los que salen por salir, los que tienen ya la iner-
> cia de trasnochar: los clientes con dinero de los
> cabarets, de los cafés de la Gran Vía, llenos de
> perfumadas, de provocativas mujeres que llevan el
> pelo teñido y unos impresionantes abrigos de pieles,
> de color negro, con alguna canita blanca de cuando
> en cuando; o los noctívagos de bolsillo más ruin,
> que se meten a charlar en una tertulia, o se ve de
> copeo por los tupis. Todo, menos quedarse en
> casa [p. 144].

(2) naturalistically in his portrayal of the death of a dog:

> En la calle de Torrijos, un perro agoniza en el
> alcorque de un árbol. Lo atropelló un taxi por
> mitad de la barriga. Tiene los ojos suplicantes y
> la lengua fuera. Unos niños le hostigan con el
> pie. Asisten al espectáculo dos o tres docenas de
> personas. ... Unos basureros se acercan al gru-
> po del can moribundo, cogen al perro de las patas
> de atrás y lo tiran dentro del carrito. El animal
> da un profundo, un desalentado aullido de dolor,
> cuando va por el aire. El grupo mira un momen-
> to para los basureros y se disuelve después.
> Cada uno tira para su lado. Entre las gentes hay,
> quizás, algún pálido que goza--mientras sonríe
> siniestramente, casi imperceptiblemente--en ver
> cómo el perro no acaba de morir... [p. 234].

(3) realistically in the following interior monologue of Martín:

--¿De qué tengo yo miedo? ¡Je, je! ¿De qué
tengo miedo? ¿De qué? ¿De qué? Tenía un
diente de oro. ¡Je, je! ... A mí me haría un
diente de oro. ¡Qué lucido! ¡Yo no me meto en
nada! ¡En nada! ¿Qué me pueden hacer a mí si
yo no me meto en nada?... ¡Este es un mundo
de locos!... Si tuviera dinero, mañana le regala-
ba un diente de oro a mi hermana. ¡Je, je! Ni
Isabel la Católica, ni la Vicesecretaría, ni la
permanencia espiritual de nadie. ¿Está claro?
¡Lo que quiero es comer! ¡Comer!... [p. 174].

and (4) once again in the tradition of Dos Passos and the
Realist novel, a passage which sums up the novel symbolically:

La mañana sube, poco a poco, trepando como
un gusano por los corazones de los hombres y de
las mujeres de la ciudad; golpeando casi con mimo,
sobre los mirares recién despiertos, esos mirares
que jamás descubren horizontes nuevos, paisajes
nuevas decoraciones.

La mañana, esa mañana eternamente repetida,
juega un poco, sin embargo, a cambiar la faz de
la ciudad, ese sepulcro, esa cucaña, esa colmena...
[p. 229].

These four passages stylistically represent Cela's
technique of Realism. Foster also makes a very good case
for the biographical sketch and juxtaposition to show contrast
and delineation of personality in achieving the kind of technical realism that displays character portrayal. In fact, he
stresses this technique as Cela's chief modus operandi, believing "once the reader has accepted [this] and the constant
interplay between the characters' dialogues and the author's
commentaries upon them, he may achieve a rather complete
understanding of the motives of the personalities in La
colmena."[19]

Throughout the novel, various personages proffer certain philosophical adages, which although tend to etch them
as characters realistically in one's mind, offer little else
except to show their banal existences. Doña Rosa says at
the very beginning of the novel, "--No perdamos la perspec-
tiva, yo ya estoy harta de decirlo, es lo único importante"
(p. 19). Padilla, the match-seller at one point, while

conversing with Elvira, a prostitute says to her: "Lo mejor
es que cada cual viva su vida, ¿no le parece a Vd. ?" (p.
42).   Another personage, Don Leoncio Maestre says to himself while thinking of Elvira, "Cada vida es una novela" (p.
47).   Later Doña Rosa says to one of her customers, "Aquí
estamos para ayudarnos unos a otros; lo que pasa es que no
se puede porque no queremos.   Esa es la vida" (p. 51).
And so on.   Despite the heavy pessimism and the determinis-
tic philosophy inherent in these remarks, it is these bits of
conversation and character, mixed with various refrains such
as "a veces la mala uva pone buena cara" (p. 53) etc., that
endear the characters such as they are to me.

        Cela has an excellent ear for dialogue, great empathy
with his characters (despite his clinical approach to their
portrayal) and a profound understanding of human hearts.   He
has caught the very heartbeats of his world of the life in
Madrid's cafés through his descriptions and dialogues.   Just
as Cela listens intently, he sees acutely.   In fact, one of
his personages says somewhat philosophically that "cada vida
es un misterio, pero la cara sigue siendo el espejo del
alma" (p. 89).   La colmena is replete with faces, visuals,
as well as sound portraits of people in a city in flux.   This
kind of Realism has the sweep of Honoré de Balzac's comedie
humaine and lacks the psychological depth of a Galsworthy or
a Proust or Romain's roman à fleuves but, in its own way,
La colmena may be considered a multifaceted gem because
of the kind of reality it spews forth.   In many instances,
Cela recalls Pérez Galdós' world as seen in Fortunata y
Jacinta and Torquemada en la hoguera from a thematic view.

        What makes Cela's work so alive is his new use of
Realism and in this particular novel, a kind of experiment in
style, which, to my own view, works fairly well on some
levels and fails on some others.   When we follow the aimless
wanderings of Martín Marco, we feel a proximity to the
character; we are anxious to know his opinions on whatever
touches him and sometimes, we would like to know more
about a certain person or groups of persons with whom he
associates.   But Cela's idea of chronology or lack of it so
interrupts and confuses the reader that Martín's literal bondage to his state of affairs, his failure as a poet, his unproductive nature as a part of a city of masses trapped by their
circumstances, his plight viewed always clinically, cooly,
pessimistically and above all, fragmented by Cela, leaves
me in a state of stress.

The novel has no sense of fulfillment or completion.
In fact, one of its amazing features, that it offers a Censo
de personajes or "Listing of Principal Characters," which
some critics say must be used as a guide to follow the actions of one particular character, is equally mystifying, confusing and unnecessary for a novel of this particularly short
duration.   Somewhat in the vein of the fairly successful
Rayuela (Hopscotch) of Julio Cortázar, Cela is an intellectual
who indeed presents us with an elaborate puzzle and a key
to his mosaic, but unless the novel is of gargantuan proportions (e.g., Proust's fourteen-volume classic, A la recherche
du temps perdu), such a listing of personages and page numbers inflates the novel and gives its characters and their
chronology a technical importance originally underemphasized
by Cela throughout the course of the novel itself.   A key to
this work should certainly be disregarded as a means of com-
prehending it.

Nevertheless, La colmena stands out as the very first
novel in Spain that heralds the coming of a New Wave of
writers and novels.   With the publication of La colmena,
Cela was at the peak of his creativity.   He gave the Spanish
novel new life and international significance by reviving a
current of social literature through his own brand of social
Realism, perceived through a new kind of photographic technique or clinical objectivity that was heretofore unseen in
the Spanish novel.   He also invested the genre with a new
sense of experimentalism through his insistence upon fragmentation, lack of chronology, pictorial and aural presenta-
tions of character, colorful and colloquial language.   His
main importance however is his insistence upon two-dimensional photographic Realism, objectivism and at times a
voyeurism that makes his novels visual rather than simple
word pictures that inhabit the imagination.   Cela is a continuer of the school of the Realist novel, although his techniques in writing were invented by him principally to contradict and possibly renounce his own association with the very
same Realist school of writers.   One of his shortcomings is
his tendency to alienate his readers with his clinical techniques as well as his choice of themes and his own personal
pessimism or even sadistic view of human nature.   Cela's
La colmena is a cold work, without any real conclusions.
In fact, some critics enjoy his "slice-of-life"-without-conclu-
sion technique; others feel a lack of completion when coming
to the last page.   Few threads of plot or character are
gathered up in the final chapter, perhaps because Cela had
intended this volume to be the first in a trilogy of novels

with the general title Caminos inciertos (Uncertain Roads).
As yet, successors to La colmena have not appeared and it
is doubtful if Cela will continue down the road of La colmena.

Cela has been most fortunate since La colmena's appearance in 1951. He was elected a member of the Royal
Spanish Academy in 1968 and has written many works of differing genres since the early 1950's. But La colmena stands
out as the very first attempt to depart from his tremendista
and Existential philosophies to cope with or create an illusion
of reality, a kind of Realism which he structures and ar-
ranges very much like his predecessor Miguel de Unamuno
so that the reader will be guided into Cela's own views,
thoughts, and pictures of contemporary life in Madrid.   La
colmena is a "human document ... an unretouched picture of
life. "20

Looking at Cela's entire literary output, Foster judges
that "Cela's novels stand back to record the scurrying and
the scuffle, both tragic and comic, of everyday life.   In doing so he has expressed his belief that man is essentially unaware of the role he plays in the vast complex of human
existence. "21 It is generally agreed by most critics that
Cela is a very good story teller and that his chief interest
is the modern Spaniard and his way of life.   While dramatically departing from his Regional novelist forbears who were
concerned primarily with Spain in its national setting, of
paramount importance to Cela is the international reading
audience.   Cela is part of a New Wave of writers, a serious and talented group of novelists who are dedicated to
their craft and who would like to elevate the level of Spanish
literature to international prominence.   "For not only has
Cela been responsible for re-vitalizing the Spanish novel by
giving it impetus with a series of artistically excellent works,
but he has chosen as well to make his career one of a complete re-examination and re-consideration of the novel as an
art form. "22 For further evidence of this revitalization and
proof of Cela's role as one of the foremost initiators of the
Spanish novel's resurgence, consult the Appendix of this
volume for a fairly complete explication de texte of an exemplary passage of Cela's La colmena.   La colmena is the
key novel of this group of New Wave writers that is making
Spanish narrative prose fiction the most dynamic genre in
Spain today.

THE WORKS OF CAMILO JOSE CELA

La familia de Pascual Duarte.   Madrid: Editorial Aldecoa,
     1942.
Pabellón de reposo.   Madrid: Afrodisio Aguado, 1944.
Nuevas andanzas y desventuras de Lazarillo de Tormes.
     Madrid: La Nave, 1944.
El bonito crimen del carabinero y otras invenciones [stories].
     Barcelona: Lauro, 1947.
Viaje a la Alcarria.   Madrid: Revista de Occidente, 1948.
La colmena.   Buenos Aires: Emecé, 1951.
Timoteo, el incomprendido.   Madrid: Editorial Rollán,
     1952.
Mrs. Caldwell habla con su jijo.   Barcelona: Ediciones
     Destino, 1953.
Baraja de invenciones [stories].   Valencia: Editorial Cas-
     talia, 1953.
Historias de Venezuela: La catira.   Barcelona: Noguer,
     1955.
El molino de viento, y otras novelas [stories].   Barcelona:
     Noguer, 1956.
Del Miño al Bidasoa, notas de un vagabundaje [travel].   Bar-
     celona: Noguer, 1956.
Judíos, moros y cristianos.   Barcelona: Destino, 1956.
Cajón de sastre.   Madrid: Ediciones Cid, 1957.
Cuaderno del Guadarrama.   Madrid: Arión, 1959.
Primer viaje andaluz [travel].   Barcelona: Noguer, 1959.
Tobogán de hambrientos.   Barcelona: Noguer, 1962.
Las compañías convenientes y otros fingimientos y cegueras.
     Barcelona: Destino, 1963.
Garito de hospicianos.   Barcelona: Noguer, 1963.
Viaje al Pirineo de Lérida [travel].   Madrid: 1965.
El ciudadano Iscariote Reclús.   Madrid: Alfaguara, 1965.
Páginas de geografía errabunda [essays].   Madrid: Alfaguara,
     1965.
Vísperas, festividad y octava de San Camilo del año 1936 en
     Madrid.   Madrid: Alfaguara, 1969.
El Tacata oxidada.   Barcelona: Ed. Noguer, 1973.
Oficio de tinieblas 5 [essays].   Barcelona: Ed. Noguer,
     1973.
Obras completas [complete works].   6 vols.   Barcelona:
     Destino, 1962-1965.

SELECTED STUDIES ON CELA

BOOKS

Foster, David William.   Form of the novel in the work of
    Camilo José Cela.   Columbia: University of Missouri
    Press, 1967.
Ilie, Paul.   La novelística de Camilo José Cela.   Madrid:
    Editorial Gredos, 1963.
Kirsner, Robert.   The novels and travels of Camilo José
    Cela.   Chapel Hill: University of North Carolina
    Press, 1964.
McPheeters, Dean William.   Camilo José Cela.   New York:
    Twayne, 1969.
Prjevalinsky Ferrer, Olga.   El sistema estético de Camilo
    José Cela; expresividad y estructura.   Valencia: Edi-
    torial Castalia, 1960.
Suárez Solís, Sara.   El léxico de Camilo José Cela.   Ma-
    drid: Alfaguara, 1969.
Trives, Eduardo.   Una semana con Camilo José Cela.   Ali-
    cante: Gráficas Vidal, 1960.
Zamora Vicente, Alonso.   Camilo José Cela.   Madrid:
    Editorial Gredos, 1962.

ARTICLES

Alvarez, Federico.   "La familia de Pascual Duarte a los
    veinticinco años," Revista de la Universidad de
    México, Suplemento, vol. 23, no. 5-6 (enero-feb.
    1969), 4-6.
Bueno Martínez, Gustavo.   " 'La colmena,' novela behavi-
    orista," Clavileño, no. 17 (sept.-oct. 1952), 53-8.
Cano, José Luis.   "La colmena," Insula, no. 67 (15 julio
    1951), 4-5.
Carenas, Francisco.   " 'La colmena': novela de lo con-
    creto," Papeles de Son Armadans, vol. 183 (julio
    1971), 229-55.
Durán, M.   "La estructura de 'La colmena,' " Hispania,
    vol. 43 (1960), 19-24.
Foster, David William.   "Cela's Changing Concept of the
    Novel," Hispania, vol. 49 (1966), 244-49.
G[onzález] C[orugedo], F[ernando].   "El léxico de C. J. C.,"
    Papeles de Son Armadans, vol. 166 (enero 1970),
    79-82.
González López, E.   "Camilo José Cela, 'La colmena',"
    Revista Hispánica Moderna, vol. 20 (1954), 231-2.

Ilie, Paul. "Primitivismo y vagabundaje en la obra de C.
    J. C.," Insula, no. 170 (enero 1961), 170.
Kirsner, Robert. "Spain in the Novels of Cela and Baroja,"
    Hispania, vol. 41 (1958), 39-41.
Kronik, John W. "Cela, Buero y la generación de 1936:
    Raigambre de una visión histórica," Symposium, vol.
    22, no. 2 (verano 1968), 164-71.
M. C. "C. J. C.: 'La colmena," Clavileño, no. 9 (mayo-
    junio 1951), 67.
Ortega, José. "Importancia del personaje Martín Marco en
    'La colmena' de Cela," Romance Notes, vol. 6, no.
    2 (1965), 92-5.
_____. "Símiles de animalidad en 'La colmena,'" Ro-
    mance Notes, 8, no. 1 (1966), 6-10.
_____. "El humor de Cela en 'La colmena,'" Cuadernos
    Hispanoamericanos, no. 208 (abril 1967), 159-64.
Predmore, R. L. "La imagen del hombre en las obras de
    Camilo José Cela," La Torre, no. 33 (1961), 81-102.
Solero, F. J. "Camilo José Cela: 'La colmena,'" Sur,
    no. 201 (julio 1951), 112-3.
Torrente Ballester, Gonzalo. "'La colmena,' cuarta novela
    de Camilo José Cela," Cuadernos Hispanoamericanos,
    no. 22 (1951), 96-102.
Torres Rioseco, Arturo. "Camilo José Cela, primer
    novelista español contempráneo," Revista Hispánica
    Moderna, vol. 28 (1962), 166-71.
Uriarte, Fernando. "Apuntes sobre San Camilo, 1936,"
    Papeles de Son Armadans, vol. 177 (dic. 1970), 323-
    35.

Chapter 4

GIRONELLA and LOS CIPRESES CREEN EN DIOS
(The Cypresses Believe in God) (1953)

José María Gironella is one of the most successful authors living in Spain today, essentially because he has achieved in his own country as well as internationally the fame accorded to a popular novelist. His best and most widely translated work is The Cypresses Believe in God which appeared in 1953. It is a long, huge novel (some nine hundred pages) written in the roman à fleuve tradition. Gironella is a master story-teller and his forte lies in explicating graphically the panorama and problems of the Spanish Civil War, a heretofore verboten theme for Spanish novelists in the early 1940's and 1950's.

Gironella was born in the town of Darnius in the Catalan-speaking province of Gerona in northeastern Spain on December 31, 1917. He spent his childhood and adolescence there, not receiving any formal education. As a youth he was obliged to work at a series of jobs that ran the gamut from factory apprentice to day laborer to bank clerk. Throughout his life Gironella had ambitions to become a priest but he never achieved this goal. When the Civil War broke out, Gironella was nineteen years old. He enlisted with the Nationalist Army and served three years with the Ski Patrol at Huesca until the end of the war. During this period, he began to write first letters, then love poetry. Immediately after the war, he returned home and became a newspaper reporter and later worked as a correspondent for an Italian newspaper in Rome. Gironella read voraciously at this time. Essentially self-taught, he began to try his luck writing a novel. In 1946, his first one, Un hombre (Where the Soil Was Shallow) won the highly touted Nadal Prize. It is an average first novel that displays all the romantic zeal of a young writer trying to discover himself and his métier through literature. The critics were very

kind indeed to promote Gironella's first effort. 1   After marrying his long-time sweetheart, Gironella published La marea
(The Tide) in 1949.   It was another experimental novel for
him in which he successfully integrated history with a highly
fictional and improbable love story set in Germany during
the Second World War. 2   The novel, however, went virtually
unnoticed nationally and internationally.

       It was after a nervous breakdown in 1951 and exten-
sive travel and electroshock therapy in various clinics
throughout Europe that Gironella began his famous Cypresses.
Completing it in 1953, it became an immediate international
best seller in Spain and in my opinion, his best novel to
date.   Following Cypresses, Gironella published two sequels
--One Million Dead and Peace After War--both of which are
of lesser importance as successors, although as sequels they
have achieved a degree of prominence based upon the fame
of Cypresses.   Except for several travel books, one highly
praised collection of short stories entitled We Are All Fugi-
tives and a new best-selling novel in two volumes entitled
Condemned to Live, Gironella has not achieved again the
great success of his highly praised award-winning The Cypresses Believe in God.   This is partly because his career
as a novelist has been somewhat erratic, his ventures into
other genres have not brought him the success for which he
had hoped and Gironella himself is indecisive about his vocation as a serious novelist, historian, world traveler, political theorist or essayist.

       Despite Gironella's own personal vacillations about
his career, as a novelist he firmly believed that he was always free to write about virtually any theme he chose to.
Of the group of New Wave writers under discussion in this
book, Gironella indirectly led the battle against government
censorship, inspiring other novelists to take up the theme of
the Spanish Civil War, since in 1953 the Spanish government
had left his manuscript of Cypresses virtually untouched.
The fact that Cypresses received such popular acclaim gave
inspiration to the "nueva oleada" to approach heretofore controversial subjects.   This is perhaps Gironella's greatest
contribution to his fellow authors of the New Wave generation.   Cypresses was also the first novel of Gironella's that
gave him literary prominence in Spain simply because he insisted upon writing about "things Spanish. "   Combined with
the prolonged and voluminous character of this work and its
inventory of human types and the Spanish spirit, Gironella
attained the goals he set for himself with the publication of

this novel. He also believed that Cypresses and its sequels
escaped condemnation and censorship because in 1953 and
later, Spain anticipated entering the European Common Market and at that time, General Franco had suspended restrictions on most cultural activities, preferring to project a
liberal image. Gironella took advantage of this prevailing
but short-lived period of liberalism and in doing so, achieved
the success he had longed for throughout his life at the young
age of 36.

It is indeed strange that a novel such as Cypresses
would achieve such a resounding success in Spain and elsewhere especially since the New Wave writers were seeking
new ways of invigorating a genre that was practically mori-
bund in Spain. In fact, Cypresses, if anything, is furthest
from the new kind of prose we found in Cela or the experimentalism within the genre that has been practiced by many
of Gironella's contemporaries. Gironella himself acknowledges the great nineteenth-century Spanish novelist Benito
Pérez Galdós as his first teacher and like him, Gironella
integrated history and fiction, fusing them for greater truth
within the historical frame of the Civil War he chose for
this most successful novel. With this literary aesthetic in
mind, Gironella wrote Cypresses, where his Alvear family
of Gerona typically represents all Spanish families between
1931-36. Ignacio Alvear, the novel's hero is a fictional pro-
jection of Gironella himself and consequently, Cypresses is
an excellent example of Gironella's attempt to fuse history
with biography and fiction, combining his own sense of freedom to express his personal thoughts on the subject of Spain's
Civil War.

When The Cypresses Believe in God was published in
1953, it won Spain's National Prize for Literature. It was
certainly Gironella's most ambitious work at that point in his
career and his largest in scope, breadth and depth up to that
time. The novel itself is organized into five sections that
cover the pre-Civil War period from April 1931 to July 1936.
All of the action takes place in Gerona (Catalonia). Its leading protagonists are the Alvear family who live in a large
apartment on the Ramblas overlooking the Ter River. The
father, Matías, is a clerk at the local telegraph office. He
is married to Carmen, a devout Catholic. They have three
children, César, Pilar and Ignacio. César is an intellectual,
physically weak and desirous of entering the priesthood. Pilar is presented as a rather sequestered girl, obedient to
family and church. Ignacio, the novel's hero, is restless, in-

secure, the prototype of Gironella himself. It is through
Ignacio's eyes that Cypresses comes alive for the novel is
essentially his story, the tale of his growth from adolescence to maturity.

        Structurally and stylistically, Cypresses is conceived
on three levels: the immediate fictional problems of the Alvears and their daily life; the Alvear family as microcosm
of the families who lived through the Civil War; and the universal level, when Gironella transcends his historical and
fictional perspectives and elevates the Alvears' struggle as
symbolic of every family's plight for survival during a war.
The prose is clear, lucid, pierced with historical truths and
descriptions of human foibles. The characters are presented descriptively, gradually revealed in the style of Realism of Gironella's nineteenth-century models. And, in the
Dickensian tradition of serialized fiction, a whole range of
personages other than the Alvears emerge, too numerous to
mention here. Like Cela's novels, Cypresses also has a
listing of characters which helps to clarify the relationships
between the Alvears and their acquaintances. But essentially,
Cypresses is Ignacio's story and we may follow his actions
alone throughout this chronologically conceived novel, since
his story is of prime importance.

        The novel begins in April 1933 with a generally broad
description of the city of Gerona and also a portrait of the
entire Alvear family. The action quickly narrows to highlight Ignacio's decision to enter the priesthood and then after
a brief period of time, his renunciation of this ideal. His
brother César, a solitary wanderer of cemeteries impassioned
by thoughts of the afterlife and martyrdom, is Ignacio's an-
tagonist and the only member of the family to enter the Roman Catholic Seminary at Collell. Ignacio secures a job as
a clerk at the Arús Bank and at the same time decides to
work for his bachelor's degree (bachillerato). Gironella frequently interrupts the fictional narrative with historical passages that describe the political entanglements and intellectual arguments occurring before the outbreak of civil war.
He also describes Gerona and its institutions such as the
Café el Neutral, the Telegraph Office, the Arús Bank, the
Orpheum Theatre, the Cycling Club and others. In doing
this, Gironella notes the changing values of the city, increasing modernization and its effects upon the people of Gerona.

        Gironella also develops within the fictional narrative
a description of real events and people during this epoch,

providing a "semblance" of history and reality. Ignacio
takes no particular political position despite his exposure to
discussions of all political parties and platforms. Only when
his cousin, José, arrives from Madrid does Ignacio begin to
become politically active. Gironella describes Ignacio's newly found anarchic spirit and his discovery of romantic ideals
and sexuality. Against the background of strikes, the failure
of Spain's Second Republic and general anarchy in Gerona,
Ignacio becomes estranged from his family, fails his examinations for the bachillerato and instead, turns to politics and
becomes caught up in a sexual and political whirlwind. Ignacio also intellectualizes his faith and after a stimulating
argument with Mosén Alberto, the family's chief spiritual
adviser, Ignacio's alienation is complete. However Gironella
deemphasizes Ignacio's problems and subordinates it at times
to the larger context--the Alvears' personal drama as a
family while confronting the Civil War. Ignacio finally com-
pletes his bachillerato at a time when the Falange Party
emerges the strongest nationally.

     After the academic year ends, the family vacations at
San Feliû de Guíxols where Ignacio enjoys his first real romance with Ana María, young daughter of an aristocrat he
met accidentally on the beach. He returns to Gerona and
they continue their relationship through letters. Strikes
break out once again and Ignacio fears for César's life.
His parents surprise him with a gift of law texts and Ignacio's thoughts turn from Ana María to his law studies. The
description of their romance wanes as Ignacio's concern with
politics takes up the narrative. War breaks out in Gerona
when the Republican Army marches into the city. Political
prisoners are taken and tribunals mete out justice to the opposition. The Falange (Nationalist) Party emerges from ob-
scurity and in retaliation they decide to set fire to the forests,
the very cypresses that for Ignacio's brother César are conducive to belief in God. Gironella suggests here that a godless Spain is in the offing.

     Ignacio's political ideas remain unclear as he does
not take part in any political party. Gironella is quick to
point out Ignacio is an individual, somewhat immature and
adolescent. To show Ignacio's immaturity, Gironella describes his first "love affair" with Canela, a prostitute, and
his subsequent gonorrhea. As the novel proceeds, Ignacio
finally obtains his bachillerato, and then later passes the
first half of his law examinations at the University of Barcelona to the delight of the entire family. At about this

time, he meets Marta de Soria, a Falangist leader with
whom he falls desperately in love.   Gironella ties in their
romance with the successes of the Falange Party in Gerona.
Another outbreak of hostilities brings the revolution to Gerona in full force.   Meanwhile, Ignacio tries to complete
his law degree and continues his "middle-of-the-road policy"
politically as a desire for General Franco to establish law
and order in chaos appeals to Communists and Falangists
alike.   However, unable to be insensitive to events, he is
forced to take a stand on political issues.   The murder of
Calvo Sotelo, a leading political figure, ends the Republican
government and with it, full-fledged civil war finally breaks
out and Cypresses moves to its swift conclusion.

       Barcelona falls to Falangist control as Communists
burn churches and kill priests.   César is separated from
his family and is detained by a Revolutionary Committee because of his attempts to preserve consecrated hosts by
swallowing them.   Ignacio tries to save him after the Alvear
family learns of his arrest.   César, however, is executed,
achieving the martyrdom he himself desired, but his death
serves no other purpose than to accentuate the confusion of
the political situation.   César is shot down with one hundred
other prisoners before Ignacio can intercede.   His death
ends the novel and gives it a feeling of completion.   We are
not surprised that One Million Dead, the sequel to Cypresses,
begins in the cemetery outside Gerona where Ignacio discovers César's body among the others executed.   However,
at the end of Cypresses, our hero is seen unsuccessfully
searching for his brother while the war continues around
him.   We see Ignacio rushing towards César at the climax.
César is given the supreme dramatic moment of the novel in
its last lines: "And then César heard a shot and he felt
something sweet penetrate his skin.... Later his eyes
closed.   He felt a kiss on his brow.   Then his heart stopped
forever. "3

                    *   *   *

       The Cypresses Believe in God is one of the best no-
vels to come out of Spain in the past twenty-five years despite its melodrama, stereotyped characters and extensive
historical descriptions.   The reason for its great success is
that Gironella revived the narrative of epic proportions in
the tradition of Balzac and Pérez Galdós and returned to the
Realist novel of the nineteenth-century for his inspiration.

Gironella's use of Realism to explicate the Spanish Civil War
and the Alvear's fictional story caught up in the historical
events have an almost photographic quality that is both typically Spanish and authentic.   Gironella's Realism manifests
itself in his complete blend of fact and fiction so that it is
very difficult for any reader to distinguish between history,
autobiography and Gironella's imagination.   Because he
traces the trajectory of the Alvear family while integrating
the important historical and political events of the pre-Civil
War years so well, the novel takes on an epic quality, a
pace and movement that is continually shaped by the whirlwind of experience.   Like Cela, Gironella does not delve
deeply (psychologically) into the actions of his characters.
They merely serve as springboards to discuss Gironella's
real problem--the war, its causes and effects.   Through his
style of Realism, Gironella describes the intellectual convictions, the psychologies of those his protagonists encounter
while moving through the novel, creating an organic view of
Spain through his own relationship to the war.

     Despite Gironella's use of Realism, certain critics
have elucidated several obvious points where the narrative
seems to fail.   Some believe Ignacio's lack of emotion--or
Gironella's failure to provide believable emotions for his
characters--is one of the great defects of the novel.   On the
other side, Gironella has been complimented for his character creations, portrayed as both truthful and realistic when
they do not surrender to purely fictional events.   Gironella's
prose presents the realities of the Spanish character.   His
personages act and talk like real Spaniards, naturally, sym-
pathetically, realistically.   Gironella's Realist style is terse,
direct, stripped of all aesthetic pretensions.   It is an ambitious Realist novel and some critics believe it represents a
reaction to Romanticism, stemming from Gironella's own
pessimism.   Others believe it is a careful blend of truth and
fiction that appraises the problems of the war fairly accurately.   Still others feel the novel to be the great Catholic novel
to come out of Spain over the past twenty years. [4]

     Stylistically, Cypresses is artfully written and at
times, even poetic.   It is Gironella's best novel of the entire trilogy (and intended pentology) because its happy balance between history and fiction synthesizes an organic and
full-scale portrait of prewar Spain in the best tradition of
Realism.   It achieves a harmony of character and incident,
both real and fictional in a clear Realist prose style that
also shows a talent for dialogue and occasional sharp insights

into character.   Gironella's descriptions of his leading characters are written in the frame of nineteenth-century Realism:

> Matías Alvear was forty-six years old, a civil
> servant working for the Telegraph Office and part
> of a group of outsiders in Gerona.   He originally
> came from Madrid and spent five years in Gerona
> and appeared acclimated to the city [p. 18].

> Carmen Elgazu bore the stamp of a new arrival to
> Gerona.   Of average height, her jet-black hair was
> gathered into a bun and her head was well-placed
> between her shoulders.   A look at her waist indi-
> cated she had given birth to several children.   Her
> legs were the columns that supported her family's
> existence [p. 19].

Although he intends to individualize his characters, they become types.   Gironella also shows a talent for romantic description in the following passage:

> The most important thing was to be a man, to ad-
> vance, to get ahead in his career.   Now he would
> spend the next two weeks, dreaming.   ...   About
> love, the truth is that he understood very little.
> Suddenly he didn't know what had happened.   A
> blue balloon drew near him from the sea and, boom!
> It seemed like his heart swelled.

> Ana María could hardly breathe.   Her legs re-
> mained immobile.   Besides she had just realized
> that the pedal boat was also named Ana María, the
> one that Ignacio had just selected without realizing
> it [p. 298].

His prose is also imbued with a sense of lyricism as exemplified in the following passage recounting the death of César:

> Minutos después oyó una voz que decía:

> --Yo te absuelvo en nombre del Padre, del Hijo y
> del Espíritu Santo.   --Una voz que se iba acercando
> y repetía --:   Yo te absuelvo en nombre del Padre,
> del Hijo y del Espíritu Santo.   --También oía gemi-
> dos.   Abrió un momento los ojos.   Vió un milici-
> ano de rodillas, que iba sacando de su reloj de

pulsera pequeñas Hostias y que las introducía en
la baco de sus vecinos caídos. Reconoció, en el
miliciano, a Mosén Francisco. Luego, sus ojos
se cerraron. Sintió un beso en la frente. Luego
se cerró su corazón [pp. 870-1].

Gironella also has a very good ear leading to a natural
quality in his dialogues. In this passage, Ignacio reveals
to Mateo an "intimate" detail:

--Tú crees que tengo la gripe, ¿verdad?

--Claro...

--Pues... No es cierto. Tengo una enfemedad
venérea. Mateo quedó estupefacto. Sacó el
pañuelo azul.

--Pero...¿cómo ha sido? No comprendo. ¿Algo
grave?

--No. Hace unos años lo hubiera sido. Ahora se
cura.

--Pero... ¿quedarás bien...?

--Completamente.

Mateo no sabía qué decir.

--No me sermonees--cortó Ignacio. --Sé que es
culpa mía. Soy un imbécil [p. 454].

Finally, Gironella's Realist prose is at its strongest when
he appeals to our documentary sense, whether he is recon-
structing historical events or re-creating the political atmosphere during those turbulent prewar years. Note how Gironella presents the ideals of the Falange Party as Mateo Santos, son of an aristocrat, talks to his father about their plat-
form:

The Falange was a revolutionary organization!
Much more revolutionary than any of the Syndi-
cates, which limited themselves to promising better
economic conditions. The Falange claimed first,
to convince the producers that they were not the
proletariat but men, persons. Second, they tried
to explain to them that economic factors are not
everything, that apart from satisfying the bare
necessities, there are a thousand spiritual roads
by which to progress. Third, they tried to make

men love their families and their work.   Fourth,
they gave them a similar 'collective illusion' of
life.   Fifth, they made them understand the meaning of their native land [pp. 405-6].

Also Gironella's general descriptions of historical events
have a great sense of timeliness and flow as in this description of Franco's triumph in Africa:

Hasta el día siguiente, 18, las radios no empeza-
ron a dar noticias algo precisas.   Lo de Africa
era un hecho, y no se trataba solamente de la
Legión.   Todas las fuerzas marroquíes y todas las
guarniciones: Melilla, Ceuta, Tetuán, Larache....
En el Banco hacían semana inglesa y el subdirector
se pasaba las horas oyendo emisoras de onda corta.
El Hermano de la Doctrina Cristiana estaba a su
lado.   El aparato lanzaba gritos de '¡Viva España!'
En los llanos de Axdir, el Caid había convocado a
los guerreros de Beni Urriaguel y les había dicho:
'¡Por la gloria de Dios, por la fuerza y el
poderío que residen en El.   Al glorioso héroe, tan
afortunado de mano, alma y corazón: al general
Franco. ' ¡Que las bendiciones divinas sean sobre
ti y los que contigo combaten en la buena senda!
Nosotros no regresaremos de España hasta que los
mayores y los menores gocen de vuestra paz.
Porque Dios ayuda al siervo tanto como dure la
ayuda del siervo a su hermano.   ¡Y veréis como
a nuestros heróicos hombres no les importa la
muerte [p. 792].

Gironella's best novel, then, The Cypresses Believe
in God, demonstrates his sympathy with the average man as
his Realist prose displays his characters as typical of their
society and era.   But it is of prime importance because with
his fellow Spanish authors, he shares his interest in explain-
ing the complexity of the Civil War.

                    *   *   *

Gironella's career as a novelist began in 1945 and
continues to change under the dynamic impulses of his talent.
He has published works in a variety of genres and displays
vital energy and a capacity for experimentation.   He is popular in Spain because of his utilization of personal and univer-

sal experiences to establish, in a slowly developing but a
real talent, the validity of the singular complex event which
dominated his entire life--the Civil War. His talent is still
in its formative stages and his career is always in a state
of flux. Despite the "transitional" nature of Gironella's career, he is included in the group of New Wave writers because of his revival of Realism (in his case, as a literary
anachronism) and his war novels are worthy of comparison
with the romans fleuves of Galsworthy, Martín du Gard,
Rolland, Romains and Dos Passos. Like them and his fellow New Wave writers, Gironella attempts to create a panoramic view of society and a common humanity in characterization. In fact, one literary critic elevated Cypresses to
the level of Cervantes' immortal classic Don Quixote: "If
the Quixote offers us the most ample and capable vision of
Spain in its time associated with the figure of that incredible
lunatic, Gironella's vision also affords us a very diverse
panorama of contemporary Spain in a manner that informs
us through uncommon daring. "5

      In the traditions of the Realist novel, Gironella
evokes in Cypresses his greatest success--a focus for the
problems of the Spain of his own Civil War generation.
Like the New Wave novelists, he is skillfull at handling controversial and sometimes intractable material. In Cypresses
as well as other works, Gironella suggests several social
and political problems of contemporary Spanish life such as
alienation, psychological illness, etc. , that other New Wave
novelists (for instance, Goytisolo, Delibes, García Hortelano
and Matute) have taken up but without their conscious cultivation of poetic lyricism. 6 Gironella's career then, may be
considered transitional since, on one hand he does revive
the Realism of the nineteenth-century tradition and on the
other, he attempts experiments with the novel form, the
creation of the fictionalized essay and other forms typical
of the New Wave.

      When Cypresses was published in 1953, William J.
Grupp had this to say about Gironella and his novel: "It
would seem that in the person of José María Gironella,
Spain has a novelist of international stature, a man who
combines an excellent command and understanding of the
novelist's techniques with a clear perception of the spiritual
tensions of the world he portrays and the courage to face
these tensions realistically and truthfully. "7 Gironella's diverse, complex and stylized work in other genres demanding
artistic concentration also places him in this class of writers
who are "always seeking some new thing. "

What makes Cypresses unique, however, is that within this new period of experimentalism, Gironella has returned
to describe events and people with a semblance of history and
reality. Stylistically, his use of Realism dazzles us because
of his revelations of universal, yet simple, intimate truths
(like Cela) but with a minimum of emphasis on language. He
portrays a man's world best and his best novels deal with
the Civil War and Gerona, his birthplace. Like the New
Wave writers, he is interested in revealing his own feelings,
Catalan attitudes about war, sex, religion, philosophy, politics, love, life. And unlike the historical novels of Pérez
Galdós and Balzac, Gironella deemphasizes individualized
qualities and subordinates their roles to the larger context
of one family caught in the years of pre-Civil War.

Perhaps the real story of Cypresses is the history of
Spain, but basically, Cypresses is still a novel that vividly
dramatizes the coming of war through the eyes of the Alvears. Unlike Cela, Gironella constantly shifts the narrative towards a new problem or personage and ties nearly all
loose ends of the plot by the conclusion of the novel, assur-
ing a basic continuity. (Curiously, the second and third
volumes of the trilogy contain lists of personages so the
reader will not lose the narrative thread, although Cypresses
is so dominated by the tale of the Alvears that the minor
personages, well-delineated as they appear, are relatively
unimportant within the context of the events of the pre-Civil
War years.)

Like his New Wave counterparts, Gironella uses symbolism, but in a very limited sense. The single symbolic
act, the burning of Gerona's forests, of the very cypress
trees that for César are conducive to a belief in God, provides the title of the volume and the symbol for a godless
Spain as well as a refutation of nature. Cypresses had en-
joyed such popular success in Spain because Gironella insists upon qualities such as happiness, optimism, faith in
nature, God and himself that he is an "inspirational" novelist
and Cypresses, an inspiring novel. Even the epic proportions of Cypresses do not eclipse the fundamental integrity
of its simple people and their problems. The novel's popularity is also abetted by another primary thematic concern--
the life-death struggle, a basic theme of most New Wave
writers.

Like the New Wave experimentalist authors, Gironella introduces journalism into the novel form which some

critics have thought weakened the artistic elements of Cypresses, [8] but in my view, it is a valid inclusion since Gironella's ulterior purpose is to stress the complexity of
Spanish politics and the inevitability of Civil War.   His use
of Realism encompasses three qualities: visual, documentary
and fictional.   Cypresses does not neglect any essential dimension because everything Gironella writes about functions
dynamically within the narrative.   If Gironella had excised
much of the historical detail from Cypresses, he might have
had a more cohesive, but less successful fictional work.
As the New Wave is essentially interested in high artistic
standards to revive the novel genre, it also applauds the
success and popularity of their fellow writers.

        Cypresses may not be the "artistic" sensation of 1953
Gironella had hoped for, but its breadth of characterization
(not depth) and re-creation of the Spanish social climate with
relevance to contemporary problems insured Gironella the
chance to write two sequels with two volumes yet to be published in his "proposed" pentology.   Most important, Cypresses originated as a natural outgrowth of Gironella's personal necessity to come to terms with himself and his generation.   That Cypresses appeared in 1953 simultaneous to the
eruption of the nueva oleada is an accident of chronology,
nothing more, since Gironella shared a basic ethic with his
fellow writers--sincerity in reproducing life as it really is
despite government censorship of the arts.   From this point
of view, Gironella maintained his sincerity in telling the
truth realistically, as he saw it about both sides of the conflict.   It is for that reason he indirectly side-stepped the
issue of censorship and Cypresses is not just a mere phenomenon continuing the Galdosian tradition of the realist novel.
Cypresses represents a real intellectual breakthrough for the
New Wave to treat the formerly untouchable subject of the
Civil War and with it, a myriad of other contemporary problems heretofore untreated in Spanish fiction.

THE WORKS OF JOSE MARIA GIRONELLA

Un hombre.   Barcelona: Ed. Destino, 1946.
La marea.   Barcelona: Ed. Planeta, 1949.
Los cipreses creen en Dios.   Barcelona: Ed. Planeta, 1953.
El novelista ante el mundo [criticism].   Madrid: Ed. Rialp,
        1954.   Out of print.
Los fantasmas de mi cerebro [non-fiction].   Barcelona: Ed.
        Planeta, 1958.

Muerte y juicio de Giovanni Papini [story].   Barcelona: Ed.
    Planeta, 1959; out of print; usually included in Los
    fantasmas de mi cerebro.
Un millón de muertos.   Barcelona: Ed.   Planeta, 1961.
Todos somos fugitivos [stories].   Barcelona: Ed.   Planeta,
    1961.
Mujer, levántate y anda.   Barcelona: Ed.   Planeta, 1962.
Personas, ideas y mares [essays].   Barcelona: Ed.   Planeta,
    1963.
El Japón y su duende [travel].   Barcelona: Ed.   Planeta,
    1964.
China, lágrima innumerable [non-fiction].   Barcelona: Ed.
    Planeta, 1965.
Ha estallado la paz.   Barcelona: Ed.   Planeta, 1966.
Gritos del mar [non-fiction].   Barcelona: Ed.   Planeta, 1967.
En Asia se muere bajo las estrellas [travel].   Barcelona:
    Plaza & Janes, 1968.
Conversaciones con Don Juan de Borbón [non-fiction].   Ma-
    drid: Ed. Afrodisio Aguado, 1968.
Cien españoles y Dios [non-fiction].   Barcelona: Ed. Nauta,
    1970.
Gritos de la tierra [non-fiction].   Barcelona: Ed.   Planeta,
    1970.
Condenados a vivir.   Barcelona: Ed.   Planeta, 1971.

TRANSLATIONS

The Cypresses Believe in God.   Trans. by Harriet de Onís
    (New York: Knopf, 1955).
Where the Soil Was Shallow.   Trans. by Anthony Kerrigan
    (Chicago: Henry Regnery, 1957).
One Million Dead.   Trans. by Joan MacLean (New York:
    Doubleday, 1963).
On China and Cuba.   Trans. with Prologue by John F.
    Byrne (Notre Dame, Ind.:   Fides Publishers, 1963).
Peace After War.   Trans. by Joan MacLean (New York:
    Knopf, 1969).

SELECTED STUDIES ON GIRONELLA

BOOKS

Alborg, Juan L.   Hora actual de la novela española.   Ma-
    drid: Ed. Taurus, 1958.
Hoyos, Antonio De.   Ocho escritores actuales.   Murcia:
    Aula de cultura, 1954.

Schwartz, Ronald. José María Gironella. New York:
Twayne, 1972.
Zamarriego, Tomás. Tipología sacerdotal en la novela es-
pañola contemporánea: Bernanos, Mauriac, Gironella.
Madrid: Ed. Razón y Fe, 1959.

ARTICLES

Alborg, Juan L. "Los novelistas: José María Gironella,"
Indice de artes y letras, no. 94 (Oct. 1956), 9.
Angeles, José. "Review of Gironella's 'Ha estallado la paz',"
Books Abroad (Norman: Univ. of Oklahoma Press),
vol. 41, no. 4 (Autumn 1967), 451.
Bergin, Thomas G. "Spain in Chaos," Saturday Review,
vol. 38 (April 16, 1955), 14-5.
Boyle, Kay. "Spain Divided," Nation, vol. 180 (June 11,
1955).
Calvo Sotelo, Luis Emilio. "Crítica y glosa de 'Un millón
de muertos'," Ya (Apr. 16, 1961-June 30, 1961);
articles unnumbered.
Cano, José Luis. "Los libros del mes: 'Un hombre' de
Gironella," Insula, no. 18 (June 15, 1947), 5.
_____ . "Los libros del mes: 'La marea' por Gironella,"
Insula, no. 49 (Jan. 15, 1950), 4.
_____ . "Los libros del mes: 'Los cipreses creen en
Dios' por Gironella," Insula, no. 89 (May 1953), 6-7.
_____ . "Los libros del mes: 'Los fantasmas de mi
cerebro' por Gironella," Insula, no. 151 (June 15,
1959); supplement.
_____ . "Carta de España: dos libros sobre la
guerra civil española," Asomante, vol. 17 (1962), 59-
61. Cano reviews the leading novels on the Spanish
Civil War.
Clancy, William J. "Review of 'The Cypresses Believe in
God'," Commonweal, vol. 62 (Apr. 15, 1955), 53.
García-Luengo, Eusebio. "Gironella tardíamente; 'Los ci-
preses creen en Dios'," Indice de artes y letras, no.
64 (June 30, 1953); supplement.
Gich, J. "Los libros de quincena: 'Los cipreses creen en
Dios'," Correo Literario, no. 70 (April 15, 1953), 4.
Gómez de la Serna, Gaspar. "Reseña de 'Los cipreses
creen en Dios'," Clavileño, no. 22 (July-Aug. 1953),
70-1.
_____ . "El nuevo episodio de J. M. Gironella," in Es-
paña en sus episodios nacionales (Madrid: Ed. del
Movimiento), 1954, 199-236.
Gramberg, Edward J. "J. M. Gironella ¿novelista?"

Cuadernos del Congreso por la Libertad de la Cultura,
      no. 79 (Dec. 1963), 62-8.
Grupp, William J.   "J. M. Gironella, Spanish Novelist,"
      Kentucky Foreign Language Quarterly, vol. 4, no. 3
      (1957), 129-35.
Kerrigan, Anthony.   "J. M. Gironella and the Black Legend
      of Spain," Books on Trial, vol. 14 (April-May 1956),
      343-5.
Klibbe, Lawrence H.   "Gironella's 'Where the Soil Was
      Shallow'," Catholic World, vol. 188 (Feb. 1959), 399-
      402.
Marías, Julián.   "Gironella y los planos de su mundo," La
      nación (Buenos Aires), Sept. 13, 1959, 27.
Schuster, Sister Scholastica.   "Song of a Catholic World,"
      Catholic World, vol. 183 (Spring 1956), 433-6.
Urbanski, Edmund Stephen.   "Revolutionary Novels of Gi-
      ronella and Pasternak," Hispania, vol. 43 (May 1960),
      191-7.
_____.   "El revisionismo en la valoración de las letras
      y cultura contemporánea de España, Hispania, vol.
      48 (Dec. 1965), 816-25.
Van Doren, Mark.   "Thousand Faces of Spain," Reporter,
      vol. 12 (June 16, 1955), 35-7.
Vasquez Dodero, J. L.   "Sentido de una novela," Nuestro
      Tiempo (Feb. 8, 1955), 35-7.
West, Anthony.   "Review of 'The Cypresses Believe in God',"
      New Yorker, vol. 31 (May 28, 1955), 120-2.

Chapter 5

QUIROGA and ALGO PASA EN LA CALLE
(Something Happens on the Street) (1954)

Before dealing with Elena Quiroga and her contribution to the Spanish New Wave, it is of interest to know how this author figures in Spain's literary world which consists mainly of male novelists. Spain is notorious for its male domination of the arts, particularly its writers. Except for Fernán Caballero and Emilia Pardo Bazán in the nineteenth century, very few women writers contributed any leading works to the development of the Spanish novel. Sadly, this situation persists into the twentieth century with this minor exception--there are numerically many more noteworthy female writers now than in the previous century who have made considerable strides intellectually in their practice of the novel as an art form. Among the best are Carmen Laforet, Ana María Matute and, of course, Elena Quiroga, whose fourth novel, Algo pasa en la calle places her firmly among all Spanish novelists as one of the leading exponents of the genre.

Elena Quiroga was born in Santander in 1919 of Galician parentage. She spent her early years in the fishing village of Valdeorras and later, moved to La Coruña where she married and finally took up permanent residence in Madrid. She published her very first novel in 1949, La soledad sonora (Clear Solitude). Her second novel, Viento del norte (North Wind) however received high critical praise and won her the Nadal Prize. Her third novel, La sangre (Blood), although highly regarded by many Spanish critics, was the turning point for Quiroga to cultivate her art as a novelist and she begins to approach her craft with maturity and taste.

Algo pasa en la calle (Something Happens on the Street), her fourth novel, was published in 1954 and is par-

ticularly interesting to us because of its author's attempts
to provide her readers with a different notion of reality.
Algo essentially is the story of Agatha and her investigation
into the "accidental" death of her father Ventura. As Agatha
pursues the mysterious circumstances behind the accident,
Ventura's liaison with his mistress Presencia is revealed.
Other family members and their thoughts about Ventura's
life and death are also presented such as Froilán, Agatha's
husband, Remedios, her mother, tío Fermín and tía Luisa,
Ventura's brother and Agatha's uncle and aunt, Esperanza,
her sister and Asís, Ventura's and Presencia's illegitimate
son. The novel unfolds essentially from Agatha's point of
view and utilizes many stylistic devices such as flashback,
interior monologue and straight dialogues that strip bare the
artifice of "straight descriptive realist prose" in order to
probe more deeply into the "psychological realities" of each
of the protagonists. To attempt to set down a plot description of Algo pasa en la calle would be an onerous task since
there is little physical action. Algo concerns itself mainly
with the revelation of the thoughts of Agatha in Madrid, her
disillusion with life, her marriage, her family, her entire
world. Ventura's death acts as the emotional trigger for
everyone concerned with him to reveal his innermost feelings.

Structurally, the novel's 220 pages are organized into
about twenty chapters. Its title is derived from an incident
from Antonio Machado's Juan de Mairena. A student is asked
by his teacher to render in poetic language the following
thought: "Los eventos consuetudinarios que acontecen en la
rúa." He writes simply, "algo pasa en la calle," the title
of our novel. This quotation from Machado's 1936 critical
essay sets the tone for the entire novel. Quiroga is trying
to write a poetic work about daily events in the lives of her
characters. Structurally speaking, the novel is also somewhat cyclical since its first and last chapters describe the
death of Ventura. Quiroga avoids inserting any sense of
mystery although we are never quite sure if Ventura died
"accidentally" or committed suicide. For Agatha and her
sister Esperanza, the turbulence of life has been momentarily suspended with their father's death and both sisters spend
time remembering incidents in their respective childhoods
and adult lives, experiences that moved them profoundly in
their relationship with their father.

We feel and hear Esperanza's resentment of Ventura
when his affair with Presencia is first discovered and we are

aware of its effect on his daughters through their thoughts.
We hear Ventura speak throughout the novel (his words appear italicized) as the sisters reproduce in their minds past
exchanges of dialogues with him or while they are presently
speaking, words and thoughts that are sometimes complimentary, and at other times contrary to what they are saying or thinking.   This is Quiroga's attempt at using most
naturally the stylistic device of interior monologue in poetic
fashion, which, incidentally works very well throughout the
novel since thoughts, spoken words and actions of all the
characters function in close harmony.   There is not one dis-
cordant note through any of the character's revelations about
their family situation and death of Ventura.   Ventura's actual
death is presented many times and from several points of
view--Agatha's imagination, a priest's eyewitness account,
Presencia's narration of it after discovering him on the
street surrounded by the police and a crowd of passers-by.
Mention of his death and portrayal of the actual scene is
fragmented throughout the novel like shafts of light that when
seen in the aggregate by the time we reach the end of the
novel, these figures or fragments of light form a continuous,
uninterrupted picture of the man, the scene and resolve how
Ventura "accidentally" fell from the balcony of his apartment
in downtown Madrid.

There are some tightly controlled emotional scenes
between Ventura's mistress and his legitimate daughters.
But most touching to me are the chapters which concern
themselves with the onset of the romance between Ventura
and Presencia.   They give the novel an elevated romantic
tone, an exuberance and delight in youth which in contrast to
other parts of the novel (and other protagonists) is sorely
lacking.   Quiroga also displays certain feminist attitudes and
the sheer delight in being a woman especially when it concerns love:

> Being in love for her was simply to breathe near
> him, to have him for a companion, to be able to
> say 'Ventura' and for him to turn his head towards
> her.   To walk anywhere, no longer alone from one
> street to another but together, without saying a
> word and knowing their steps would join each other
> as they traversed the streets.   And when stopping,
> that slight squeeze on the arm; they were as if
> alone, absolutely and purely alone in the wide and
> magnificent world of God. [1]

This passage accurately reflects Presencia's feelings of intense love for him when she simply walks with Ventura.

On reality, Elena Quiroga curiously only mentions the
word once when Presencia notices her son's eyes catching
the sun's rays, filtering "reality." Reality for Asís on this
level is only visual. Quiroga's reality manifests itself mostly in the revelation of her protagonists' thought patterns or
in the mixtures of Ventura's words and each protagonist's
thought processes. Algo is a novel of thoughts, not images.
Quiroga also describes a character's feelings when they fan-
tasize. For example, because of Ventura's affair with
Presencia, Esperanza imagines her father in a garden, first
with her mother, then with his mistress until she becomes
so angered that she tears up his photo and says all men are
despicable. "¡Qué asco los hombres! ¡Qué asco!" (p. 171).

Sometimes Quiroga sidesteps direct commentaries by
having her female characters make generalizations about the
world of men. For example, at one point near the novel's
conclusion, she says: "Men live in stagnant compartments:
work [their vocation] and life--life and love [love as human
passion not being necessarily sexual] or life and family.
Life and family is the most homogeneous and the central
axis [for most men, especially Ventura]" (p. 181). With regard to the category of life and family, Agatha remembers
Ventura's words about her home, her friends, her position
in society:

> It's so absolutely superficial.... You don't do
> anything, nor do you think about anything profound-
> ly human. It's not a question of class, but a per-
> sonal one, of your determined ambience--to have
> the best house, good friends, not to leave any
> space for anything transcendent. It's all very bor-
> ing and besides you wouldn't do it as a penitence.
> Spending the whole day with a composed, smiling
> face. It makes one feel exhausted, mortally tired
> of so much constraint of the soul. Because it isn't
> elegant to let light enter the soul. It may carry
> it away and that would be indiscreet to say the
> least [p. 108].

As Ventura's words attack the hypocrisy of feminine attitudes,
Quiroga also tries to impart a feeling of the moral decay that
is choking her female characters in Algo. Her males become her most ardent and courageous speakers. Only in

matters of emotion and love do Quiroga's women speak most
convincingly (see the explication de texte in the Appendix).

I believe the most poignant revelation in the novel
comes to us through Agatha, when at the conclusion, just
before Ventura's burial, she realizes her father was thinking
only of her just a few minutes before he died when she was
told he had carried some notes intended for her in his pocket, messages that expressed his love for her and his mistress Presencia.   At another point in the novel, Agatha also
realizes after her father's death, life must go on and she
wants to embrace life herself by becoming a mother.   "Life
is what she wanted to give, not death" (p. 178).   And so the
novel ends with a recapitulation of the accident, the tale of
the faulty iron grille, Ventura's burial and everyone picking
up their lives as Ventura's illegitimate son Asís, in sil-
houette looks on at the mourners.

                              *   *   *

Algo pasa en la calle is a good, well-modulated
novel, poetic, simple in its structure and plot but complex
in its psychological implications.   It describes fairly well
the society of Madrid of the 1950's.   Although it is decidedly not a mystery novel, we still have no clear answer as to
whether Ventura fell accidentally or committed suicide.   Of
major concern to us is Ventura's revelations through the
thoughts of his family about the society in which he lives
and the people he dealt with on a daily basis.   Eugenio de
Nora believes that "if this man had not been killed, he still
had no great reason to go on living because his life had
been one of complete frustration."[2]   Nora also comments
upon the revelations of character, the cold egoism, cheap
vanity, the clash of an "idealized" love relationship with the
institution of modern marriage.   The novel also demonstrates
the "incompatibility between the aspiration to be men and
women totally integrated in society or being merely capsulized in the mould of the married bourgeois."[3]

One also notes Quiroga's tendency towards poetic
lyricism, which diffuses the action of the novel, as well as
the lack of psychological analysis of the motivations, conduct
and beliefs despite the heavy reliance upon interior monologue to reveal the realities of her protagonists.   We never
have a clear idea of how the characters look or what they
do.   Nevertheless, Algo is definitely a New Wave novel and

Quiroga is firmly entrenched in this group precisely because
of her efforts to renew the novel genre, inject it with poetic
lyricism, deal with contemporary problems and probe her
protagonist's psyches through the use of interior monologue.
In this way, Quiroga definitely departs from nineteenth century Realism.

Other Spanish critics besides Nora have justly accorded Quiroga and her novel Algo pasa en la calle their
proper accolades. According to Iglesias Laguna, the outstanding feature of this novel is Quiroga's manipulation of
"time on objective and subjective planes, giving the reader
a sensation of timelessness and a feeling of the predetermi-
nation of events."[4] José Corrales Egea classifies this novel
as "reconstructiva"[5] or one of those that reconstructs the
life and deeds of a dead or missing character by the people
who knew him and the events that shaped his life. Gonzalo
Sobejano views Algo as "a study of consciences, accomplishing its aims in Faulknerian fashion by reducing time and
space, mixing past and present by means of monologues
sparked by memories and presenting a variety of views by
the personages."[6] He feels Quiroga's main theme was to
present in a frank, adult manner the problem of an "illicit"
affair imbued with authentic love versus a legitimate relationship (marriage) without love in a society without the recourse of divorce laws.

Juan Ignacio Ferreras feels Quiroga has written an
extraordinarily "coherent and realist novel"[7] in which a collective investigation by her characters becomes the universe
created to determine the truth with regard to the circum-
stantial death of Ventura. Finally, Juan Luis Alborg believes the novel literally 'breathes with a deep and unrivalled sincerity"[8] not heretofore felt in the Spanish
novels of this period and that her stylistic "sobriety," and
thematic interest make Algo one of the best novels published
in 1954.

Quiroga's character creations do speak frankly and
thrill us realistically. She is concerned with Spanish society as it is, implicit with its moral and social implications. Although some of her characters do not reach a
level of reality for me because they seem more imaginary
than real and because at times she refuses to concretize
their feelings, heavily insisting upon poetic lyricism, Quiroga is still one of the few novelists, in keeping with the
New Wave, who has tried to give new directions to the

Spanish novel. Although we may consider her use of interi-
or monologue, flashback, dichotomies between what is thought
and said rather stylistically archaic now, we must have
thought Eugene O'Neill mad in the 1920's when Strange Interlude was first presented on Broadway and his characters
stepped out of their roles to talk to the audience and directly
reveal their thoughts to us. In similar fashion, Quiroga does
this in her novels of the early 1950's, but her insistence on
writing about contemporary themes combined with an easy
facility with words and a marvelous creative sense make her
one of the leading novelists of modern Spain today.

THE NOVELS OF ELENA QUIROGA

La soledad sonora. Madrid: Ed. de la Excma. Diputación
        Provincial de la Coruña, 1949.
Viento del norte. Barcelona: Ed. Destino, 1951.
La sangre. Barcelona: Ed. Destino, 1953.
Algo pasa en la calle. Barcelona: Ed. Destino, 1954.
La enferma. Barcelona: Ed. Noguer, 1955.
La careta. Barcelona: Ed. Noguer, 1956.
Plácida la joven. Barcelona: Ed. Noguer, 1957.
La última corrida. Barcelona: Ed. Noguer, 1958.
Tristura. Barcelona: Ed. Noguer, 1960.
Escribo tu nombre. Barcelona: Ed. Noguer, 1965.
Presente profundo. Barcelona: Ed. Noguer, 1973.

SELECTED STUDIES ON QUIROGA

ARTICLES

Alborg, J. L. "Los novelistas. Elena Quiroga," Indice de
        Artes y Letras (Madrid), no. 92 (sept. 1956), 8-9.
        This article appeared in an expanded form in Alborg's
        Hora actual de la novela española (Madrid: Taurus,
        1958), 191-9.
Anonymous [A. Albalá?]. "La libertad, tema clave en las
        novelas de E. Quiroga," Ya (11 mayo 1958), 19.
Baeza, F. "Diario de un lector. E. Q.: 'Algo pasa en la
        calle y La enferma'," Indice de Artes y Letras (Ma-
        drid), no. 84 (oct. 1955), 23-4.
Brent, A. "The Novels of E. Quiroga," Hispania, vol. 42
        (1959), 210-13.
Cano, J. L. "E. Q.: 'Viento del Norte'," Insula, no. 66
        (15 junio 1951); "La sangre," ibid., no. 89 (15 mayo

1953); and "La última corrida," ibid., no. 144 (15 nov. 1958).

Castillo-Puche, J. L. "Séptima edición del Premio E. Nadal" [E. Quiroga]," CHA, vol. 11 (1952), 32, 277-80.

Corrales Egea, J. "Carta de París" ['Viento del Norte'], Insula, no. 79 (15 julio 1952), 12-13.

Domingo, José, "Dos novelistas españoles: Elena Quiroga y Daniel Sueiro," Insula, no. 232 (marzo 1966), 3.

Entrambasaguas, J. de. " 'La soledad sonora', de E. Q.," Cuadernos de Literatura (Madrid), vol. 7 (1949), 16-18, 205-6; "La sangre," Revista de Literatura (Madrid), vol. 3 (1952), 195-200; "Algo pasa en la calle," Ibid., vol. 6 (1954), 384-7.

Fernández Almagro, M. "Algo pasa en la calle," ABC (9 enero 1955); "La careta," Ibid. (15 enero 1956), 26.

G[ómez] de la S[erna], G., " 'La sangre,' de E. Q.," Clavileño, no. 19 (1953), 76-7.

Laforet, C. "Viento del Norte," Destino (Barcelona), no. 718 (12 mayo 1951), 1.

Plans, Juan J. "E. Quiroga: 'Escribo tu nombre'," El, no. 330 (6 nov. 1965), 17-8.

Torres Rioseco, A. "Tres novelistas españolas de hoy" [C. Laforet, A. M. Matute and E. Quiroga], Revista Hispánica Moderna (New York), no. 31 (1965), 418-24.

Vázquez Dodero, J. L. "Algo pasa en la calle," Nuestro Tiempo (Madrid), no. 9 (1955), 118-21.

Chapter 6

JESUS FERNANDEZ SANTOS and LOS BRAVOS
(The Savage Ones) (1954)

The year 1954 was crucial to the development of the Spanish novel because of the emergence of New Wave novelists in full force and the so-called "new" qualities contained within their novels. It was the year in which three major works were published: Elena Quiroga's Algo pasa en la calle (Something Happens in the Street), Juan Goytisolo's Juego de manos (Sleight of Hand), and now Jesús Fernández Santos' Los bravos (The Savage Ones). What was stylistically evident in Quiroga's Algo, the use of interior monologue and a preponderance of mental over physical action, is carried to further extremes in Santos' novel within his own framework of Realism. Apparently the kind of journalistic and colloquial Realist prose that depicted exterior states had given way to the cultivation of poetic prose, novels of greater sensibility, feeling, imagination and interiority. Exterior Realism evolved into the new "intimate" novel, the novel of thought as action, the novel of greater psychological penetration in contrast to ones of greater exterior description. For Fernández Santos the new Realist novel portrays anonymous beings, abstract thoughts in contrast to novels containing descriptive portraits of actual people, real identities and palpable realities as painted in words by the nineteenth-century Realist writers and their followers.

Los bravos, written in 1952, is Jesús Fernández Santos' first published novel but according to Rafael Bosch it is really his second fictional work--written after En la hoguera (On the Hearth), which was published late in 1956. 1 J. F. Santos was born in Madrid in 1926 of parents whose origins were in the mountains of León in northwestern Spain. A student of arts and letters at the University of Madrid, he first began his artistic career in the university's theater,

74

first as director and later as an actor in the Teatro Nacional
de Cámara and for several theatrical radio programs produced by Radio Madrid. F. Santos also wrote several screenplays for the Spanish cinema and was a student at Madrid's
Institute for Investigation and Experimentation of Cinema,
eventually directing several films, particularly one on the
life and work of Francisco de Goya y Lucientes. Los bravos,
his "first" (published) novel was a natural outgrowth of his
creative energy. A true member of the New Wave, he seeks
his own unique direction in writing novels and to establish
his own particular view of Spanish society as well as his
own concept of reality. In an interview about his work with
French critic Claude Couffon, he declares that "Cela is the
writer of the Spanish middle class. The [Spanish] people
read The Cypresses Believe in God by Gironella to convince
themselves of their own reason for existence. They read
for compensation the books of Cela, who makes them tremble. Cela, a master of language, entertains them. He has
had and still exerts great influence on the young writers.
Influence on me? I don't think so. I cannot judge. Perhaps yes, although his kind of perspective is not so great
that it may please me" (or that it may have affected Santos'
work). 2 Rather than risk comparison with his contemporaries, F. Santos declared in another interview as cited by Eugenio de Nora in 1959: "When I began to write, I admired
the American writers a lot. Now they bore me with equal
intensity. On the other hand, I consider Baroja just as before, ahead of everyone including Galdós. "3 To understand
the numerous influences on F. Santos' writing style, a detailed examination of Los bravos is necessary to discover the
extent of his own contribution to the New Wave and his individual view of Spanish Realism.

Fernández Santos' first published novel has been
categorized by leading Spanish critics as belonging to the
school of "social realism" or "objective realism" or simply
as "New Wave. " To definitively categorize the novel is
somewhat futile at this point since other "-isms" may be
applied to its qualities such as regionalism, paisajismo
(novels about the land), as well as other generic qualities
such as comedia bárbara (a play about local rustics), or a
tragedy of picks and hoes. Los bravos is simply a story of
a small town near Asturias, its people and its daily routines
and problems, its monotonous, abulic existence in one particularly hot summer. Its protagonist is a young country
doctor, embarking on his career in this town and the novel
deals with approximately two weeks in his life during a

particular sultry Asturian summer. The so-called plot re-
volves around the doctor, his care for his patients, his falling in love with a beautiful servant girl, Socorro (her name
is symbolic of the help the doctor needs), and his decision
to remain the town's doctor after a series of daily but un-
surprisingly routine events dealing with life, death, deception or simply the "stuff" of human nature. His affair with
Socorro is precipitated because of boredom, sensuality,
desolation and his idealism to liberate her from the almost
feudal life she lives in the employ of Don Prudencio. Socorro indeed reflects within her the desolation of all the
farmers in the town. Our young doctor wants to free her
from this bondage, to live with her but without the ties of
matrimony.

        A sub-plot, the arrival of a "traveler" who asks the
farmers to invest their life savings in a bank--which offers
them 4 per cent interest on their money and in reality turns
into an enormous swindle--peppers the novel with some intrigue and action but on a relatively minor scale. The
swindler is discovered, badly beaten and almost lynched by
the townspeople. He is finally rescued by the doctor who
promises to deliver him over to the local police official.
The townspeople demand vengeance but the doctor resists
them and delivers the estafador over to the authorities.
"--After I heal him, I'll turn him over to Amador. But
they knew he was lying to them and dragging the victim by
the arms, they tried to get him off the horse. "[4]

        The narrative continues with descriptions of scenes
of country life, demonstrating the beauties of our anonymous
small town near León. It reveals in detail the work of a
country doctor who cares for the ignorant, indigent, savage
and uncivilized and introduces many, many minor characters.
Among these, the most interesting are Alfredo, wounded by
the Civil Guard for illegal trout fishing in the river; Pepe,
owner of the town's only taxi service who dreams of living
in the big city; Manolo, his brother, who owns the local
country store and tavern; Amador, the President of the town
whose child has been ill and bedridden for many years;
Antón Gómez, secretary of the township, who is always pursued by his fat and ugly wife; Pilar, the old maid; Amparo,
the innocent young girl seduced by the swindler; and many
other characters of minor importance (other pastors, farm
hands and cowboys), all incidental to the development of the
plot but important in demonstrating the doctor's profession-
alism and skill.

Central to the development of the plot is the doctor's
own growth and maturity, molded by his career and shaped
by transitions in thought that lead him to remain with the
town as their doctor despite much stubborness, frustration,
ignorance, scorn and the abulic attitudes of the townspeople.
Don Prudencio's heart attack and eventual death at the
novel's end is the major incident that liberates his mistress
Socorro. Our "country" doctor buys Prudencio's house and
continues to live with Socorro, probably remaining in the
town until the end of his life.

F. Santos began Los bravos with a quotation attributed to J. Wasserman: "The destiny of a town is like the
destiny of a man. Its character is its destiny." Pablo Gil
Casado believes the entire novel is shaped by Wasserman's
words, assuming that the destiny of this unnamed town in
Los bravos is always subject to a leader's will (Don Prudencio) and as a consequence, the town's character is abulic and
indigent of spiritual values because of its leader. [5] Gil Casado also believes when Don Prudencio dies, the town will
fall into the hands of the country doctor (who has already
bought Prudencio's home and taken his servant-mistress as
his own) and consequently suggests the doctor will now shape
the town's character by exercising his own tyranny over the
people. Gonzalo Sobejano believes Gil Casado's interpretation of the novel's conclusion is erroneous simply because
the characters of each man (Don Prudencio was old, a feudal
landlord, egocentric, lewd, and the doctor is young, enam-
ored of life, just, charitable and basically decent) are so
completely opposite that it would be virtually impossible for
the young "enlightened" doctor to exercise the same kind of
tyranny over the townspeople as did Prudencio. [6] My own
view supports Sobejano's comments on this controversy with
one reservation--the novel's conclusion is ambiguous and
life goes on for everyone. The doctor will continue to serve
the townspeople. Gil Casado is more interested in viewing
Los bravos as a social-realist work and Sobejano refutes
this conception although in his own book, he places Los bravos into the "social novel" category. My own view departs
from these critical opinions: in fact, Los bravos is more
of a Realist novel with minor social pretensions cast in the
mold of the nineteenth-century Realist writers such as Pérez
Galdós or Pardo Bazán. It is however more up-to-date because of Santos' new techniques of writing which he superimposed on a basically traditional fictitious work common to
the aforementioned novelists. What makes Los bravos essentially New Wave is Fernández Santos' concept of style.

Los bravos begins or fades-in "after the titles" with
a horse stopping in front of the local cantina. It is about
1:30 p. m. A local farmer enters and inquires of Manolo,
the proprietor, the whereabouts of the doctor. The farmer
looks back to his horse, worriedly glancing at his son whose
bleeding right hand is wrapped in blood-soaked rags. Manolo and the farmer run outside to the prostrate child clinging
to the horse. Manolo tells the farmer to take his son off
the horse and rest in the cantina until the doctor comes and
offers him help while the latter lifts the boy off the horse.
It is 2:00 p. m. when the doctor finally arrives and in a
brief dialogue, he tells the farmer that his son's finger must
be amputated. Fade-out. Fade-into the cantina's kitchen
two hours later. It is 4:00 p. m. Manolo asks the doctor if
he can look at the child's amputated finger lying in the cantina's kitchen wrapped in some paper. His wife then tells
him to bury it, but he leaves it on the kitchen counter.
Manolo asks "what does one feel when one's finger is cut
off?" The doctor or Manolo's wife answers, "One doesn't
feel anything, but it only hurts a little. " Long shot of the
town, deserted, empty, silent, hot. Fade-in. The doctor
is seen walking down the street towards the garage where
Manolo's brother Pepe parked his car. Pepe is dismantling
the motor. The doctor asks him what happened. Pepe tells
him he probably flooded the carburetor. We watch the doctor help Pepe clean the motor's cylinders. Fade-out.

I have deliberately reproduced the first six pages of
this novel in cinematic terms, stripping the excess Realist
narration or description of exterior and added the cinematic
terms of fade-in, fade-out, and long shot because Los bravos
is (or was) essentially planned as a film scenario. There is
a preponderance of dialogue, and attention is given to visuals,
interpreted through extremely Realist descriptive prose. The
dialogue is expository, alive, fluent, rapid, concise. The
reader is able to "see" the reality of the personages. F.
Santos also handles the narration in his 236-page novel extremely carefully. There are no formal chapters, only
short scenes in which he presents one character, one problem, one view of the town, one spectacle of nature and then
continues to build upon each of these scenes successively so
that in the aggregate we are given the entire view of the
leading character developed slowly and carefully in short
sketches.

For example, according to Gil Casado, Fernández
Santos inserts details of Don Prudencio's illness at the very

beginning of the novel and delves into them nearly two hundred pages later, when Prudencio must visit a heart specialist in the neighboring big city. [7] Gil Casado also comments upon the "anticipatory" character of Santos' writing style. [8] F. Santos is also careful not to point out interrelationships between characters and events but lets the reader envisage for himself the nature of these relationships. For example, the arrival of the swindler is seen by everyone. No one knows his identity but his arrival triggers a series of conversations about money, Don Prudencio, Socorro, the country doctor, Amador and his sick child, and then in almost circular fashion, the dialogue returns to the swindler who, still unknown to everyone first begins to talk about investments. "You give us your money, we keep it for you" (p. 55). Gil Casado feels the method of presenting the swindler and avoiding presentation of his total identity is another unique stylistic concept of the author which encourages his reader's interest by his refusal to reveal everything about a situation or a character, preferring instead to let the character reveal himself by means of his actions and his words. [9]

It is evident Fernández Santos prefers to begin slowly, building an event or a character from an ambiguous state to a concrete one. (See the explication de texte section in the Appendix where I demonstrate, through a very well-known passage, Santos' Realist, cinematic style employing this ambiguous-to-concrete stylistic device.) When you read Los bravos, you are impressed by the "simultaneity of actions, words, events, the continuity of time, the successiveness of events by hours, days, changes of place, weather, mood, milieu. Asterisks mark transitions. Transitions between scenes are elided ... all the scenes have one common denominator determined by a spacial unity--the town itself. "[10] Sobejano best sums up Fernández Santos' writing style with the following words: "Relief of concrete details, peaceful aggregation of moments, descriptive process from the unknown ambiguity to clear representation, reticence, cinematic perspective--these constitute the peculiar notes of technique of Fernández Santos in his first novel and in the rest of his work. "[11]

Sobejano sees F. Santos as a practitioner of "objective realism" because the author never presents a personal view or idea about a character. We come to know his characters through an accumulation of the facts we learn about them and their own qualities as revealed in their

words or deeds. The major themes of this novel, then, are
revealed indirectly--poverty, isolation, brutish female domination, lack of help or guidance, sterility, the helpless nature of the farmers, the loneliness of the ill, the spiritual
vacuousness of the environment, the discouragement of
progress, the narrowness of opinions, injustice.

        Sobejano also sees the role of the doctor as an indi-
vidual who is trying to harmonize and administer the qualities of "love and justice." In terms of love, he helps everyone as a dedicated professional. In terms of justice, he
defends the swindler from being lynched in spite of public
opinion (which is always against him) because he is a man
who firmly believes in principles of law and order. In reality, this country doctor likes his work, the townspeople,
and is destined to remain there. Spanish critics have often
compared him to Andrés Hurtado in Pío Baroja's El árbol
de la ciencia (The Tree of Science), a dedicated doctor who
on the other hand, felt it would be better for him to escape
from the provinces rather than cope with rural problems.

        Despite my own preference for Sobejano's view of
Los bravos over Gil Casado's rather controversial one, I
feel the latter tries to make a very good case for viewing
Los bravos purely as a social-realist novel conceived in the
narrative spirit of Pérez Galdós--although he acknowledges
the influences of Unamuno (because of the unilateral nature
of his characters), Baroja (because of his concise dialogues),
and Cela (because of his cinematic style). Gil Casado notes
the lack of explicit social criticism in Los bravos but then
reverses himself, preferring to believe the novel is fused
with a critical intent and that because of this Los bravos
properly belongs to the category of social-realism since it
retains all of the following characteristics of social-realist
fiction: (1) a diffuse theme--despotism in a small town,
(2) kaleidoscopic vision--parallel and multiple development
of characters and events or struggles between the cacique
(leader) and the townspeople, (3) social criticism--the injustices committed by landlords, (4) exposition through dia-
logue--lively dialogue that has the strength and character of
a testimonial, (5) integration of narration and documentary
material--the novel is seen as a document presenting social
conditions to expose the realities, (6) personages with "class"
characteristics--the novel depicts types although in Los
bravos, everyone except the doctor and Prudencio is seen
as poor and lacking any will, (7) appropriate use of vocabu-
lary--colloquialisms of the region, (8) a concise prose style

--the type of short phrasing used in Los bravos gives its
readers a plastic and imaginative vision as described by
brilliant metaphors and daring images, and (9) complex
technique and construction--the use of dialogue that antici-
pates the action and the "cinematic" techniques of Fernández
Santos. 12

     Gil Casado has interestingly placed together nine
characteristics of the novel of social-realism.   To his way
of thinking, Los bravos shows all nine qualities although I
would refute the placing of it in G. Casado's category of
social-realist novel since the novel does not have a diffuse
theme, a kaleidoscopic vision, overt social criticism, or
documentary material and does not make extensive use of
colloquialisms.

     In an excellent chapter of criticism dedicated to Fer-
nández Santos, Juan Carlos Curutchet deals with Santos' essential investigation of man and reality in Los bravos.   Citing Carl Jung, Curutchet believes that "only through the
mystery of self-sacrifice can man arrive to feel himself renewed" and suggests this as the country doctor's motive for
remaining in the provinces, to renew himself through his
work, through his explorations into the human condition.   He
suggests Los bravos is Santos' exploration of the human condition and that he has written a perfectly conceived work of
art in the manner of Carlo Levi and William Faulkner, 13
demonstrating through his protagonist that each human being
discovers his own anguish before loneliness, his own destiny
before death.

     Man appears as physically insignificant with regard
to Santos' view of nature but Curutchet feels Los bravos contains a "fervent exhaltation for life, a calling to men of good
will to change the structures of life that are choking them."14
He believes Los bravos is a Realist novel in which Santos
does not idealize reality but rather accepts it and describes
his world without misrepresenting it.   Curutchet painfully
accepts the human condition as is and for him, Los bravos
portrays "the petrification of human and social relations in
a region of Spain. "15   Our eager critic also compares
Faulkner's Sound and Fury and Levi's Christ Stopped at Eboli
to Los bravos, asserting F. Santos' profound vision of humanity and humility as a novelist because the latter demonstrates the universal qualities and elements of life situations
on the "same level of greatness and miraculous revelation
as a Levi or a Faulkner. "16

Simply, Los bravos is a Realist novel, stylistically
well-conceived on a cinematic level, with excellent dialogues
and marvelous exterior descriptions of the land of Asturias.
It is not a complex work and neither is its protagonist, the
country doctor, especially deep or complex. There is little
we learn about him through his thoughts. There is little, if
any, use of interior monologue or any well-developed physical or mental portrait of his protagonist. The enormous
appeal of Los bravos lies in its descriptions of nature, its
author's ability to visualize scenes, to record conditions,
dialogues, in fact, to have lived this type of experience himself. Our country doctor may have some thoughts about his
"superiority" to the farmers, but we never get really close
to him or inside the man to hear what he is really thinking
or feel what he is really feeling.

Fernández Santos' strength as a novelist lies in his
manipulation of descriptions and dialogues. His portrait of
this anonymous small town on a Sunday morning, a town
wedding, the local cantina, the heat, swimming in the river,
a local dance, remind me of the best folk paintings of Juan
de Sorolla or Thomas Eakins. Santos has caught the narrowness, the brutality of the uneducated provincials but without
aluding to colloquialisms or provincialisms. No one speaks
in a rude or ugly fashion. In fact, everyone speaks in the
very same tone as the doctor, author, narrator. There is
nothing terribly sensual about the doctor's affair with Socorro, no highs or lows in depiction of feeling states--just
beautiful but sometimes monotonous description and dialogue
punctuated with the pessimistic philosophy of the narrator:

> The world mattered little. To work, to work al-
> ways in winter and in the autumn, to see the har-
> vest, from the kitchen, in this epoch, how quickly
> life went by. To hear the children chase each
> other, to run throwing the green fruits of summer
> at each other's faces. ... Year after year. At
> night he went to bed battered, tired, without know-
> ing against what or against whom to rebel, later
> to have moved himself hour after hour all day long
> like the donkey around the waterwheel, towards a
> profit which he had not seen clearly [p. 155].

Characters would say things to the doctor like: "What can
you expect here? Disgust, nothing more. ... From here
you will leave this village poor" (p. 216). One has to get
out from here; here we spend our lives without taking our

heads out of the hole.... What's the use! One has to
leave, friend. To see the world, to stretch your legs... "
(p. 218).

Occasional insights into the doctor are found scattered
through the text. One of the best passages in the novel occurs after the doctor has rescued the swindler from the
angry townspeople.

> He thinks to himself: 'I am a doctor, only a doc-
> tor. I'm nobody in this town. Let them do what
> they like.' But he knew well that more than a doc-
> tor, he was a man, and in that town or in any
> other, through his own heart or interest, by means
> of his own survival, life was not going to let him
> remain at the margin of things [p. 298].

Gil Casado feels the doctor's personality is well-developed,
complex, "magnificently seen, well presented, self-developing
through what he thinks, says and does."[17] What astounds is
Gil Casado's assertion that the doctor's conduct is the result
of an inferiority complex which leads him to escape reality
by locking himself into a miserable small town and also,
one of the key problems of the novel is supposedly the doctor's decision to stay or to leave there. The doctor does
feel and think about his superiority to the townspeople and
consciously meditates upon his own decision to stay there,
but his occasional thoughts are not "psychologically" revealing or terribly complex or absorbing. In fact, the novel
itself is not complex in any sense but rather a series of
fragmented incidents with occasional short lapses into interiority. F. Santos departs from Quiroga and his generation
of New Wave novelists by returning at times to the mold of
the traditional Realist novel, adjusted somewhat with twentieth-century stylistic perspectives to suit our "modern" sensibilities.

Some of Fernández Santos' descriptions are reminiscent of John Steinbeck's portrait of Southern California's
wine country in the latter's famous novel The Grapes of
Wrath and parallel the best Realist writing of José María
Gironella. For example, let us note F. Santos' portrait of
moonrise in our small town:

> There appeared a resplendent shadow on the moun-
> tain situated to the rear of the houses. The sky
> cleared rapidly, extinguishing its stars, crannied

by the growing arc of the moon that was outlined
on the peaks of the hairy Cytisus and the hazel-nut
trees. Black silhouettes, twisted, darkened for
an instant by a yellowish halo, like captives of a
distant fire. The globe continued rising, each
time smaller as it gained altitude until it remained
there, hanging immobile in the heavens [p. 25].

Whether F. Santos describes the joy of swimming, a sudden
rainfall, or sunrise on a Monday morning, his descriptive
powers capture the common denominator of all men and
their experience of participating with nature. In fact, these
descriptions are so well impregnated with "universal" qualities that they are timeless and free of geographic limitation.

One of the problems of the novel manifests itself in
the "anonymous" nature of the doctor as well as the town
itself, the swindler, and others. While reading Los bravos,
I was constantly seeking a detail such as a name, a physical
description of the man or the town, stripped of "universal
elements" that would help to fix in my own mind the identity
of the country doctor, his town, etc. Objective writers run
the risk of losing their readers if their descriptions of
places or people deal in universals and ambiguities rather
than concrete examples which clarify physical and personality
characteristics. In my mind, I cannot describe our country
doctor because he is faceless, devoid of personality, charac-
terless. On the other hand, Don Prudencio comes off much
better descriptively because he is revealed to us with much
exterior detail about his physical nature, his illness, his
home, and his relationship with his servants (especially Socorro, his servant-mistress). In particular, his interior
thoughts about his illness are presented in two to three
pages of intense, descriptive writing.[18] Such sustained passages are rare in F. Santos' novel and they reinforce my
own view that although the author is capable of experimentation with new writing styles like his fellow New Wave novelists, he is still very much tied to the nineteenth-century idea
of Realist fiction in the vein of Pérez Galdós and consequently does his best work when his novel includes similar passages. Perhaps what the novel cries out for is a more personal view of F. Santos' characters and a less objective one.

Santos once said, "a writer always uses several situations and characters to define himself, although he may not
always succeed to do it."[19] Juan Luis Alborg feels Santos
never picks up his pen until he is absorbed in the particular

reality of the situation in which he is working and that he
is an authentic writer of promise with an objective style, [20]
a true artist who has given modernity with this objective
style to the old costumbrist novel. [21] M. García-Viñó is
concerned with Santos' "functional" use of language which
takes on a certain scenic expressionism, [22] a poetic climate
and at times certain explorations into the surreal. [23] He
views F. Santos' main function as writer is to depict a reality objectively but not to give it profundity. [24] Corrales
Egea views F. Santos' role as author to be "distant" from
his work but not necessarily passive. [25] Eugenio de Nora
finds F. Santos' novel is "graphic, simple, dynamic; dialogues are fresh and lively but imperceptibly elaborated,
reduced to the essentials; [some] psychological introspection
with a minor preoccupation for originality; light and briefly
etched descriptions of great conciseness and plasticity. "[26]
Clearly, F. Santos has not written anything new thematically.
What he has done is simply transformed the traditional
Realist novel (with occasional lapses into its traditional
style) into a new work demonstrating truly "modern values"
of Realism but, as Ignacio Ferreras has stated, he has
kept some of the same values of the traditional realist novel
intact--"solid construction, ample description, compact personalities and above all, objectivity. "[27] A cinematic style,
together with objective writing are the new elements that
began to resuscitate the Spanish novel of the early 1950's
and Fernández Santos is its most able practitioner.   His
later novels, En la hoguera (On the Hearth) (1957) and
Laberintos (Labyrinths) (1964) demonstrate further use of
the same stylistic elements already discussed in this chapter.

THE NOVELS OF JESUS FERNANDEZ SANTOS

Los bravos.   Valencia: Editorial Castalia, 1954.
En la hoguera.   Madrid: Ediciones Arión, 1957.
Cabeza rapada.   Barcelona: Seix Barral, 1958.
Laberintos.   Barcelona: Seix Barral, 1964.
El hombre de los santos.   Barcelona: Ediciones Destino,
        1969.
Las catedrales.   Barcelona: Seix Barral, 1970.
El libro de las memorias de las casas.   Barcelona: Seix
        Barral, 1971.
Paraíso encerrado.   Barcelona: Seix Barral, 1973.

SELECTED STUDIES ON F. SANTOS

Couffon, Claude. "Recontre avec Jesús Fernández Santos," Les Lettres Nouvelles, no. 62 (julio-ag. 1958), 127-32.

Domingo, José. 'Narrativa española; Análisis de una sociedad conformista," Insula, no. 274 (oct. 1969), 7.

Gil Novales, Alberto. "Los bravos," Insula, no. 120 (dic. 1955), 6.

_____. "En la hoguera," Cuadernos Hispanoamericanos, no. 112 (1959), 74-5.

Martín Gaité, Carmen. "15 años después de 'Los bravos'," La Estafeta Literaria (1 ag. 1969).

Núñez, Antonio. "Encuentro con Jesús Fernández Santos," Insula, no. 275-6 (oct.-nov. 1969), 20.

Rodríguez Padrón, Jorge. "Jesús Fernández Santos y la novela española de hoy," Cuadernos Hispanoamericanos, no. 242 (feb. 1970), 437.

Sánchez Ferlosio, Rafael. "Una primera novela: 'Los bravos'," Correo Literario, no. 6 (oct. 1954).

Chapter 7

RAFAEL SANCHEZ FERLOSIO and <u>EL JARAMA</u> (1956)

Rafael Sánchez Ferlosio was born in Rome on December 4, 1927, to an Italian mother and a Spanish father, Sánchez Mazas, who was a foreign correspondent residing in Italy at that time. The entire family returned to Spain during the 1930's and Rafael spent his childhood mostly in Madrid. He studied for a liberal arts degree at a university in Madrid and is now married to the novelist and short story writer Carmen Martín Gaité (whose <u>Entre visillos</u> (Between the Blinds) (1958) is her best known novel). Little else is known about Sánchez Ferlosio and his personal life.

Sánchez Ferlosio has written only two novels himself. The first, entitled <u>Industrias y andanzas de Alfanhuí</u> (Traffic and Events in the Life of Alfanhuí) (1951), created a minor sensation in Spain according to several literary critics because it revealed him as a writer of profound sensibility, talented and with a precise poetic style, having the ability to create an entire "fairytale" world. When his second novel, <u>El Jarama</u> (The Jarama River), was published in 1956, Sánchez Ferlosio's "fantasy-world" created in <u>Alfanhuí</u> was quickly forgotten since <u>El Jarama</u> is considered now by most Spanish critics as one of the key novels of the Spanish New Wave and a literary milestone which has regenerated the entire novel genre in Spain. It is the first novel written by a young author of twenty-eight or twenty-nine years to exhibit a rigorous, truly "objective" technique of writing, lacking in rhetoric, description, and emotion and totally removed from the author and his personal point of view. It is completely opposite in style and content to his first fictional work and to date is Sánchez Ferlosio's last written and most critically controversial novel.

<u>El Jarama</u> won the Nadal prize in 1955. Structurally it consists of fifty-eight sections broken down in the following

manner: two describe geographically the Jarama River,
twenty-four deal with a group of young Madrileños who are
spending their Sunday outing on the banks of the river,
twenty-two are situated in Mauricio's tavern and describe
his actions and conversations with his customers, five sections deal generally with the groups themselves in the tavern
and their interaction with the young Madrileños, two are devoted to describing the countryside, two portray the actions
of a local judge and one deals with the actions of two Civil
Guards.[1] Before beginning his story, Sánchez Ferlosio has
provided a quotation from Leonardo da Vinci: "The water
which we touch in the rivers is the last of those which went
down to the sea and the first of those which will return--
just like the present day." The novel's first section opens
with a description of the Jarama River and its course and
tributaries, and closes in its fifty-eighth section with another narrative section about the Jarama running into the
Atlantic Ocean, indicating a circular pattern of structure and
artistic conception of the novelist as well. S. Ferlosio is
concerned with a single day in the lives of the Madrileños
who spend their time at the river or in the tavern or both
and consequently, is concerned with all the events, both
major and minor, conversations and actions of these groups
of people.

It is unfortunate that the novel's 365 pages (ironically
matching the number of days in a normal year) is not really
of major significance as fiction; this is so simply because it
contains truly minor episodes, actions or conversations that
defeat the definition of what we might call a good fiction.
Certainly El Jarama is narrative writing with a heavy insistence upon dialogue drawn from S. Ferlosio's imagination.
Rather than letting his imagination run free for his readers
to enjoy or be instructed, edified, persuaded, aroused or
just be generally interested in his fictional world, S. Ferlosio prefers to subordinate these estimable values of fiction
to the communication of his own particular vision of the nature of reality in "objective" terms. Consequently, El Jarama is an exercise in style, creating a new kind of "objective realism." It retains few "traditional" fictional elements.

Given the quotation from Leonardo da Vinci, it is
evident that S. Ferlosio proposes to deal with time by capturing that particular momentous Sunday "like a palpitating
wave, to recall the past and [open our eyes to] the future."[2]
The river, like time, is symbolic for S. Ferlosio of a reality that is "transmuted, in effect like the reflections of a

day and its hours"[3] which pass minute by minute next to the
Jarama.   The novel begins at 9:15 a.m. and ends at nearly
1:00 a.m. on that particular summer Sunday.

It is also possible to view the novel's structure on
three spatial planes: the description of the river and its
vicinity, the interior of the tavern, and the garden surrounding the tavern.   It can also be said that the novel follows
closely a structure parallel to the "classical unities" of time
(one day), space (one locale--the river and its local tavern
and garden), and action (revelations of all the people's conversations, actions, thoughts, gestures, silences).[4] The
fifty-eight moments in time which comprise the novel are
presented in an alternating rhythm, giving the reader a feeling of simultaneous action.   Structural elements in the novel
predominate over plot essentials.

El Jarama's plot can be summed up very briefly.
One hot August Sunday, a group of about twenty middle-class,
working boys and girls from Madrid, all in their early
twenties, all friends, come together in order to spend the
entire day swimming and picnicking on the Jarama River.
They come from all walks of life--garage mechanics, department store employees, factory workers, clerks, cafeteria workers.   After arriving by bicycle, they leave their
belongings at the tavern run by Mauricio and go down to the
banks of the river to swim, chat, eat, drink, stroll, play
ball, kiss, frolic in the water.   They left their homes in
the morning with the illusion that they were going to spend
a day of fiesta.

As the day progresses, we meet a variety of young-
sters--Lucita, Tito, Daniel, Mely, Miguel, Fernando, Sebas,
Santos, Alicia, Paulina.   We hear them chat and emote
about love, cigarettes, kissing, suntans, singing, drinking,
fighting, cavorting.   At the tavern, we meet a great number
of customers as well--besides Mauricio, there are Lucio,
Demetrio, Justina, Claudio, Carmelo, Chamaris, and others,
who chat about their daily troubles, and give their opinions
about life, love, politics, food--all conversations without any
transcendental value.   The eleven couples from Madrid left
their homes originally with the illusion that they were going
to spend a wonderful day, but as the day progresses, the
tedium of their working days overrides them, infiltrates
them and destroys their own illusions of fiesta because they
become bored, disillusioned and finally sickened by the tragedy of the drowning of one of their friends, Lucita.

The drowning scene, the only "real happening," occurs in Section 49 after two-thirds of the novel is spent in tedious, adolescent conversation by the youths who are seemingly resigned to a "vegetative" life, preferring not to transcend the monotony of their own existence.[5] After Lucita's tragic death, an investigation takes place by the Civil Guard, the secretary and the judge of the local township. Their handling of this serious incident is just as vulgar and banal as the young group's mentality, and thus the novel concludes on an extremely pessimistic note. It is ironic that Lucita, kissed by Tito (who was apparently mildly intoxicated and who cried because of Tito's kiss without knowing why), should be the author's victim of this chance drowning accident. With this event, all the "aspects of insignificance, the climate of boredom evaporate."[6] An interrogation of Lucita's friends takes place and all the youngsters from Madrid bicycle home after collecting their belongings at the tavern. The tavern-keeper Mauricio is thinking (at about 12:50 a.m.) of what he will do tomorrow as his clientele pedal homeward past the olive groves towards Madrid. And the Jarama slowly rolls on its way towards the Atlantic Ocean.

Thematically, El Jarama deals with the insipid and insensitive conversations of youths on an outing and those of the clientele of the local tavern. The novel does possess a unity of action, time and place and was written within a rigorous, disciplined framework. The characters reveal themselves. They are neither introduced by the author nor described by him. There is narrative description in El Jarama only of the physical settings. However the action of the novel is principally conceived in its dialogue. El Jarama has been described as having the kind of "prose that captures the minuscule detail, characteristic and expressive of a moment of popular talk [reflecting] the monotony, triviality, including the repetition of events already narrated."[7] Here are two short sample conversations demonstrating these points:

--You didn't bring the Bisontes, Mely?

--Yes. I have them in my pocket. Pass me the pack.

--Okay, said Fernando. Let Mely give us a light cigarette [un rubio].

--I'm sorry, guys, but these are not for you.

> You guys will have to smoke the dark kind [los negros]. 8
>
> . . .
>
> --How dark you are! What have you been doing to become so dark?
>
> Two of the girls held up Santos' cloak like a curtain, while the others took off their clothes.
>
> --You won't believe it, but I've hardly been in the sun.
>
> --Yeah, kid. Looking that dark, I wish I could beat you up. I on the other hand, if I ever wanted to be as dark as you--the summer would have already passed before I ever got as brown as that [p. 42].

Conversations such as these are the substance of the novel and none have transcendent value. They deal with suntans, bathing suits, wine, drunkenness, buying peanuts, soccer, infantile conflicts. All conversation is on the juvenile level with skirmishes that resolve themselves in the name of innocent camaraderie and puerile friendships. If one of the essential views of the writer is to expose the "triviality and total mental poverty of our society,"9 or portray the Realism of group interaction, or describe in detail the actions and reactions of a particular homogeneous class of Spanish society, then Sánchez Ferlosio has succeeded in writing a social novel analogous to Cela's La colmena. If Ferlosio wanted to demonstrate to his readers through monotonous, reiterated dialogue, completely lacking in ideas or ingenuity, the emptiness of many lives without enthusiasm or horizons, without ideals, and lives suffering from boredom (the real "protagonist" of the novel), 10 then he has succeeded. If the author intended "to see, hear and set down the things that happened without the slightest intervention, interpretation or judgment about the values or sentiments of the acts and words uttered by his characters,"11 then he has also been successful.

Why then, has this "novel," totally lacking in traditionally sound fictional elements and evoking only the most banal characteristics of plot and theme, been such a sensation in Spain? The answer rests solely upon S. Ferlosio's style and view of Realism. Following in the footsteps of Cela's La colmena, he proposed to create an entire world based upon "objective testimony." Reading El Jarama is

like listening to an unedited tape recording of groups of
people talking unabashedly about their daily lives. Obviously,
S. Ferlosio carried his idea of an "objectivist-realist style"
to its limit since the author himself functions almost like a
tape recorder, objectively recording what his characters say
and do. "Conversations are reproduced with minuscule fidelity and concentration; movements are drawn with the sugges-
tive sobriety of a motion picture camera."12

Reading El Jarama gives us the impression that, after
another workweek in Madrid, the same kinds of people will
return to bathe at El Jarama, full of illusions that will be
destroyed by the same tedium and monotony of their daily
preoccupations. El Jarama is a novel of loneliness, desolation, of the unconscious death of unrealized lives, of paralysis of the will, and tedium. It is a novel that also contains,
apart from the negative values of Spanish life, a treasure
trove of the popular language and slang of Madrid, alive and
brimming with the authentic flavor of daily city life.

El Jarama has provoked much controversy among
Spanish and French critics alike simply because of its appearance in 1956 as a "novel" (a supposed "social novel"),
its "realist-objective" style, and because its position among
the "New Wave" writings published at that time was extremely difficult to appraise. El Jarama is certainly a novel.
But because it deals with some negative aspects of Spanish
life and contains no transcendent values in itself, most critics
prefer to think of it as mere "reportage." Rafael Bosch has
noted the influence of El Jarama to have been enormous, although the novel was written on an extremely base level.
He feels its "illumination of the vulgar and its vulgar and
insipid language gives it significance to other writers who
are more interested in portraying reality than Sánchez Ferlosio."13 He considers the novel "nothing more than a mon-
ument to the vices of naturalism"14 and his characters totally lacking in human sympathy.

Like Torrente Ballester, Bosch does not consider El
Jarama an objective-realist novel. Torrente even feels "El
Jarama is an authentic tranche de vie [slice of life] ... like
life itself, flowing, amorphous, uniform, continuous. ...
[L]ike Ulysses, like A la recherche du temps perdu, El
Jarama is a great 'destructive' novel, through which one imposes the reconstruction of an art and of a genre."15 Torrente recognizes the novel's value, not in itself but as a
trend setter, a key to the regeneration of Spanish novelists

and the Spanish novel of the 1950's.   He views S. Ferlosio's
objective technique as better than the objective-realist experiments of Alain Robbe-Grillet or Michel Butor but concedes
their heavy influence upon his work.

    At this point, one must discover if S. Ferlosio is a
Realist, social realist, objective-realist or Naturalist writer.
Rafael Bosch feels that Ferlosio has written a "naturalist"
novel and has used Ortega y Gasset's objectivist concepts in-
appropriately. [16] In his masterwork, The Dehumanization of
Art, [17] Ortega speaks of portraying the events of a novel by
themselves, without interpretation.   He did not intend to found
a school of revitalized writers who would create a body of
novels that dealt only with superficialities and exclusively exterior matters.   Ortega felt that if writers dealt with events
themselves, they must still retain a sense of reality in which
these events are shaped, events that also primarily deal with
important matters.   Bosch feels S. Ferlosio has reversed
this trend and his objectivist style represents the vices of
reinterpreting Ortega's words.   S. Ferlosio deals only with
events from an exterior, superficial view and narrates objectively the "unimportant" conversations of life.   Bosch
feels S. Ferlosio's copying of an entire geographic description of the Jarama River and inserting it into the novel has
nothing to do with the novel itself. [18]

    Ignacio Ferreras comes out strongly against Corrales
Egea and Sobejano by firmly stating El Jarama is not even
a "realist novel, but has the temerity of stating falsely, the
problem of objective realism. "[19]   Ferreras provides four
important reasons: (1) all Realist novels have to be of significant value or have an expressed problem (El Jarama
demonstrates neither of these points); (2) there are incoherencies concerning the novel's content (El Jarama's personages
lack expressed problems); (3) there are incoherencies regarding the novel's form (there are changes of structure,
pace, rhythm, language that disobey the novel's own internal
structure); and (4) the novel seems to be more of a rigorous
exercise or experiment rather than a real novel (because of
its discipline, it lacks naturalness and becomes a literary
problem, an experiment, a dilettante's effort). [20]

    Nevertheless, Ferreras feels El Jarama tries to
evoke "pure Realism" and is one of the most important of
the postwar period because it presents the problems of using
a completely objectivist style.   He feels it is not successful
as a novel because of its "intellectualized realism, " which

is so exaggerated by its insistence on "photographic values"
that whatever Realism there is in the novel is "lessened,
falsified."[21] Juan Luis Alborg, on the other hand, feels
"El Jarama is not of minor interest because of its technique
and literary style--this novel represents possibly the extreme limit to which Realism has advanced [as portrayed] by
our novelists. ... [T]he penetration of this technique, of
absolute photographic values and presence, with the world
of personages that are its object, is perfect and total."[22]
Alborg also speaks of the "universal elements"[23] and "arche-
types of a particular type of humanity"[24] that make the
readers of El Jarama feel compassionate about S. Ferlosio's
novel.

        Reactions to El Jarama vary from reader to reader
and critic to critic. M. García-Viñó read the novel as "an
adventure" which not only at times "bored him," but contra-
dictorily interested him so thoroughly that it "inflamed, empassioned him."[25] Whatever gifts for literary criticism or
talent a critic may have, in short, whatever perception he
brings to a novel, helps to bring that novel's values, either
good or bad, into sharper focus. El Jarama's Spanish critics both for and against are always passionate about their
beliefs. Just as Ignacio Ferreras refused to assign El Jarama any stature as a Realist novel but considered it an intellectual experiment with objectivist stylistic intent, M.
García-Viñó's views El Jarama as a pure work of art, a
novel in dialogue, "the reflection of Stendhal substituted here
by the tape recorder."[26] Perhaps he reads more into the
novel's worth when he strikes a parallel between El Jarama
and Hermann Hesse's Demian, believing Ferlosio's intent,
like Hesse's, was to prove that "each human being is not
only the same but is also at one point, the most particular,
always important and singular."[27] El Jarama is an "impressionist portrait,"[28] a "total vision,"[29] not mere entertainment but an "aesthetic and intellectual pleasure and that
only on rereading can its true value and significance be attained."[30] He calls El Jarama a magnificent document
which "discovers within it the hidden poetry that there is
within the people"[31] and believes Ferlosio "succeeds to elevate [to the level of symbols] the situation and characters
[he deals with]."[32]

        Comparing the novel to those of Robbe-Grillet, Gar-
cía-Viñó feels El Jarama has social and sentimental (human)
content whereas the leading practitioner of the noveau roman
is often technical and formal. He disagrees with Alborg

about the "cinematic vision" of the novel but agrees a tape
recorder is more apropos to describe Ferlosio's objectivist
style.   "If Cela had used a tape recorder, he would have
caught totally different things--many more scatological and
arousing ones.   If Graham Greene would have used one, he
would have captured something more transcendental.... "33
García-Viñó by means of inflated critical attitudes certainly
elevates El Jarama to a position much higher than it really
deserves.   He calls the language of El Jarama "literary,
poetic,"34 "romantic and dramatic,"35 and feels that the author "loves his creations and makes his readers love them,
too. "36

     Although García-Viñó has seriously overestimated S.
Ferlosio's second novel, his opinions tend to show what the
novel is certainly not.   His words are strong but deceptive.
El Jarama is not a work of art, a magnificent document, an
Impressionist portrait or a total vision that affords its readers intellectual or aesthetic pleasures.   It deals neither symbolically, socially, humanistically, cinematically nor dramatically with its material.   It does however, present a virgin
look (mirada virgen, to use Sobejano's phrasing) at one of
the many stylistic possibilities available to Spanish writers
seeking to renovate the novel genre.   More particularly, it
demonstrates "the perpetual monotony of dealing with just
reality, viewed without any psychological penetration. "37

     El Jarama does present a singularly penetrating vision
of the lower middle class of Spanish workers from Madrid
and the boredom that encircles their lives.   But this essential theme could have been presented with fewer characters,
in a much shorter space of time and in fewer pages.   Sánchez Ferlosio's only use of a true fictional motif occurs
when he has Lucita drown.   Otherwise the entire "novel" reduces itself to eating, drinking, bathing, chatting, etc.   The
novel's greatest weakness lies in the large number of incidents of minor importance--Fernando's anger at Tito for
throwing him into the river, Daniel's refusal to eat, the
kissing scene between Tito and Lucita.   Like Pablo Gil Casado, I believe the novel's value lies in its style "to describe the insipid reality of its characters by means of their
words and reactions. "38   Gil Casado views El Jarama as a
"behaviorist" novel, with "its ultimate purpose being to give
an impression of veracity by means of testimony. "39

     One of Sánchez Ferlosio's great problems with ob-
jectivist techniques is that his readers rarely get close to

his characters.   While reading El Jarama, I was impressed
by the enormous number of slang words used by the group
throughout their conversations, and as a linguist, I tried to
recall their exact meanings when I lived in Madrid.   Approaching a novel linguistically is one point of view available
to literary critics.   However to be driven to this recourse
constantly because of a lack of character development, an
impoverishment of ideas, a constant repetition of thoughts,
conversations and minor themes leaves me little sympathy
with the novelist or his creation.   If we accept El Jarama
as an experiment in style, which is certainly what it appears
to be, rather than a well-conceived novel, then we cannot
feel too upset after reading through 365 pages of superficialities, prose that is poor in content, a lack of character
development, and scarcity of psychological revelations by
our author.   Perhaps S. Ferlosio refuses to experiment in
the novel genre, preferring to work in linguistics rather than
write a new novel. 40

        I share the view with several astute Spanish critics
that El Jarama is neither a novel, a social novel nor a copy
of the nouveau roman, but a prose work using an objective
technique that is not limited to dialogue but employed in descriptions as well which in themselves are a linguist's dis-
play--flashes of poetic prose that retain a lively feeling for
life and nature.   (See the explication de texte in the Appendix.)   El Jarama succeeds as an experiment because its
form and content are inextricably fused and represent a
cross-section of Spanish society as it actually was in 1955.
Controversy surrounding this experiment has developed because the work is considered by some as "artistic" despite
its apparent lack of transcendent values.   Since nothing really happens in the novel, or for that matter during the 1950's
in Spain, the question arises by critics and readers alike,
as to the work's real meaning.

        Most critics agree that S. Ferlosio rose to the oc-
casion and artistically transposed in the best style he could
master--always careful of the censorship prevalent in the
1950's--his ideas regarding the suffocation of Spanish society by immersion into its own trivialities, and its total
mental impoverishment.   Perhaps Lucita's death is symbolic
of the "drowning" or suffocation of the Spanish intellect
which no Spanish critic dare mention explicitly or even im-
ply in his writings.   Juan Carlos Curutchet, in a book published recently (1966) in South America mentions "the rigid
censorship which obliges Spanish writers to treat certain

themes with prudence and a wiliness that causes them to
adopt stylistically certain curious forms. "41 S. Ferlosio,
like many of the New Wave writers, had to resort to the
subterfuge of style, to mask his highly symbolic content,
which to the American reader becomes more apparent only
when the novel is viewed in its social and historical context.
If El Jarama represents a new kind of novel--Realist, social,
or an objectivist experiment testifying to the negative aspects of Spanish life without criticizing them explicitly but
letting its readers comprehend the basic problems of the so-
ciety--only from this perspective then can S. Ferlosio's
work be truly appreciated.

       S. Ferlosio's El Jarama most certainly represents
the new Spanish Wave precisely because of his cultivation of
a realist-objectivist style, one that "narrates the action of
the novel as a movie camera would, without either intervention or commentaries from the author, a style which has
permitted him to evade the heavy presence of censorship. "42
Most Spanish critics residing in Spain have avoided discussing the real significance of the novel's title. El Jarama
recalls the site of one of the most furious and bloodiest
battles fought during the Spanish Civil War.   Perhaps the incidents in the novel may be viewed "symbolically" as minor
skirmishes of the present, a pallid reflection of the past, a
constant but irksome reminder of a society currently experiencing moral decay as it did during the 1930's, a sick society, suffocating and without hope.

       It is indeed unfortunate that the novel's real signifi-
cance does not appear between its covers. El Jarama consequently comes off as a work without much art, profundity,
insight or guts, simply because the author's preoccupation
with an objectivist style and the problems of censorship in
Spain precluded his direct revelation of the social criticism
of the Spain he knows too well and in which he continues to
live. Other writers of his generation, like Matute and Goytisolo, have proven themselves more courageous and artistically ebullient. Thus, El Jarama, if anything represents for
me a work of great frustration. I see it as a paradox since
it pretends to reveal objectively the problems of a cross-
section of Spain's lower middle class yet in actuality it reveals little directly about its characters or the society in
which they move. We can consider El Jarama a successful
experiment in writing if we take the author's word that he
has completely realized his novel according to the limits he
himself set for it--the parameters of action, time and place.

El Jarama is quizzical, episodic, prolix, fascinating at
times, but totally frustrating. Its style results from the dimension of an aesthetic that is not purely eclectic if we
agree by conjecture on its huge French influence by the pur-
veyors of the nouveau roman.

     Sánchez Ferlosio himself is a question, a perpetual
promise; Spanish letters must still await his evaluation.
Although El Jarama as a novel would not augur well for
psychological insights, it does succeed in establishing a new
direction, a new style for other New Wave novelists to emu-
late. However, if we consider that "style is art" and that
all great art is founded on distance, on artificiality, on what
Ortega calls "dehumanization," then it is possible to stretch
our convictions and judge El Jarama to be a true art work
since the novel contains the elements of distance, artificiality and style. From my own view, El Jarama is more of a
document, a trend setter, an experiment, a startling new effort (in 1955) to renovate the decaying novel genre in Spain,
a transitional work exemplary of "something rendered as a
certain handling of the ineffable,"43 perhaps a work of "art"
more potent for its silences than for what it expresses.

THE WORKS OF RAFAEL SANCHEZ FERLOSIO

Industrias y andanzas de Alfanhuí.   Madrid: Talleres Cies,
     1951.
El Jarama.   Barcelona: Destino, 1956.
Alfanhuí y otros cuentos [stories].   Barcelona: Destino,
     1961.

SELECTED STUDIES ON S. FERLOSIO

ARTICLES

Cabot, J. T.   "La narración behaviorista," Indice de Artes
          y Letras, no. 147 (marzo 1961), 8-9.
Cano, José Luis.   "El Jarama," Arbor, no. 126 (1956),
          313-4.
Castellet, José María.   "Notas para una iniciación a la
          lectura de 'El Jarama'," Papeles de Son Armadans,
          no. 2 (1956), 205-17.
Coindreau, Maurice Edgar.   "Los jóvenes novelistas espa-
          ñoles: Rafael Sánchez Ferlosio," Cuadernos del Con-
          greso por la Libertad de la Cultura, no. 27 (nov. -

dic. 1957), 67-71.

Gil Novales, Alberto. "El Jarama," Clavileño, no. 39
(mayo-junio 1956), 71-3.

Izcaray, J. " 'El Jarama', o la hora de España," Nuestras
Ideas, no. 1 (1957), 94-6.

Jiménez Martos, L. "El tiempo y 'El Jarama'," Cuadernos
Hispanoamericanos, no. 80 (sept. 1956), 186-9.

Ortega, José. "Tiempo y estructura en 'El Jarama',"
Cuadernos Hispanoamericanos, no. 201 (sept. 1966),
801-8.

Quiñones, Fernando. " 'El Jarama' de Rafael Sánchez Ferlosio," Cuadernos Hispanoamericanos, no. 80 (ag.
1956), 138-42.

Villa Pastur, J. "El Jarama," Archivum, no. 2-3 (mayo-
dic. 1955), 11-3.

Chapter 8

LUIS GOYTISOLO-GAY and LAS AFUERAS
(The Outskirts) (1958)

      Luis Goytisolo was born in Barcelona on March 17,
1935. He lived there throughout his youth and received most
of his education there although he never completed his law
studies at the university. He turned to writing in 1955 and
published his first series of short stories, winning the Sesame Prize for them in 1956. He is the youngest son of
three boys of the renowned Goytisolo family. His brother
Juan is already established as one of Spain's leading novelists. With his brother he shares a passion for writing, and
in 1958 he won the coveted Biblioteca Breve prize for his
first novel Las afueras (The Outskirts). While at work on
his second novel, Las mismas palabras (The Same Words)
(published in 1963), he was thrown into jail in 1961 because
of "political reasons," although he was released after four
months. He is considered one of the youngest and best
writers of the New Wave, having published Las afueras at
age twenty-one. Like Sánchez Ferlosio, little else is known
about his personal life or subsequent work. The Spanish
public is awaiting his third novel.

*   *   *

      Las afueras received excellent reviews internationally.
It has been called "a book written with sensitivity, tenderness and with a fine murmuring humor, bittersweet at times
and bitter at others--a poetic book of impeccable style,
terse and agile, full of delicate nuances and of excellent
artistic qualities."[1] "The book is written with extraordinary
narrative power. It captures, at times prodigiously, the
characters and ambience. Everything is seen in the clean
simplicity of its essential elements.... The book leaves one

with a rounded feeling of complete creation, of a fulfilled
authenticity in all its elements. "2 "The pages of Las afueras
reveal to us a gifted writer with a fine sense of Realist and
psychological observation. "3 "There doesn't exist a novel
coming out of Spain that has made such a great impression
internationally in the last ten years. "4

"I am sure that Luis Goytisolo is already an authentic revelation in our letters. His sensitivity is extraordinary
and his prose has an evident descriptive power. Las afueras
abounds in pages of great beauty and in lively drawn characters. "5 "With Las afueras, Luis Goytisolo has succeeded in
writing a structurally perfect work. The characters, from
their introduction, in a Barcelona of 1953-55, are those
which form a society that is the true protagonist of the action and from which emanates a force that can be considered
either light or darkness. "6 "The most beautiful narrative
design of Las afueras not only constitutes one of the best
collections of stories and short novels that has been established in Spain, but is one that reveals the domination and
mastery of an authentic story teller, who possesses the secret of telling a story and the gift of converting it into a
true work of art. "7

Judging by these "glowing" reviews, Las afueras, for
all of its two hundred pages and seven chapters is most certainly considered an international blockbuster, having been
translated into six languages by the end of 1959. It is a
novel set in Barcelona in 1957, eighteen years after the end
of the Civil War. According to its blurb, it is a

> novel of a fragmentary and broken world, a story
> developed in seven chapters without any apparent
> initial connection but, page by page, the charac-
> ters interlock, superimpose themselves upon each
> other and complete themselves until they form a
> single collective drama where their chief charac-
> ters, like impulses of an internal dynamism, ap-
> pear destined to penetrate into the background of
> the tranquil and desolate outskirts of a large city.
> The names, places and situations repeat themselves
> because history is the same for everyone and what
> at the beginning may seem to be a series of short
> stories juxtaposed reveals itself to us as an entire-
> ly closed and coherently unified work. Here and
> today are the coordinates of drama and if among
> the actors, who are at the same time the victims,

> we want to find a leading character, it will have
> to be the small child Bernardo whom we will se-
> lect, since he is the silent and unrelenting witness
> to the greatness and misery of his elders. 8

Using this blurb as an introduction to the novel itself,
Las afueras may be seen as a "unique" work because it consists of a series of short stories related by the unity of
place, time and characters whose relationships between each
other at times prove confusing to the reader since the characters exercise different roles while using the same names
throughout the course of the novel.   One must approach Las
afueras then, by a discussion of each of its seven chapters
since each one demonstrates a different refinement of Realist
style, use of narrative technique and story themes.   Rafael
Bosch has already noted the influence on Goytisolo's work of
Cesare Pavese's En la playa (On the Beach); it too deals
with the description of poor types and those of other social
classes which, through a series of apparently unconnected
narratives or seemingly independent short stories, provide
the novel with its single unique vision, scope and depth. 9
Iglesias Ferreras does not consider Las afueras an "experimental" fictional work, but rather, it is "the author's intention to show us a universe sociologically incapable of per-
mitting a rational solution to the human beings that compose
it. "10   Nora calls it "una novela unanimista [a complete
novel] [where] each reader will retain not the impression of
a novel but of a series of totally independent short stories
... and in which the author ... has introduced ten or eleven
series of characters who are not related nor appear to be
related but who all have the same name. "11   Nora believes
it is the "interconnection, the historical and social condition
of each concrete human life, consciously or subconsciously
that has been and is the basic theme of the great novelists.... "12   He defends the elaborate form of Las afueras,
believing Goytisolo insisted upon a definite thematic nucleus
in order to show the

> plurality of circumstances, the differences within
> personal conditions, the same interconnecting fate
> [or fortune] that neither cancels nor twists funda-
> mentally the character and feeling of those lives
> in their particular framework, lives conditioned
> by their particular historical or sociological situa-
> tion. 13

                            *   *   *

          Chapter One is the longest section of the novel's
seven parts. Its fifty-three pages deal with Victor, an old,
tired ex-soldier, who returns to a farm on the outskirts of
Barcelona, where he lived with his wife many years ago, to
discover Claudina, an embittered old woman now living there
with her teenage daughter Dina in an old house gone to ruin.
Victor spends his time hunting rabbits for food, sometimes
never firing a shot, or going to the local Café Moderno,
conversing about the Civil War or gambling with his old
friends Adrián, Roig, Fredo and Mario. He takes up with
Claudina and Dina, giving them money for his room and
board and shares their lives and problems.

          Claudina's husband Ciriac was jailed by the Civil
Guard for stealing and as a consequence, she and Dina had
to fend for themselves to survive. Victor wants to take
charge of his "adopted" family and bring up Dina, but he is
opposed by Claudina. One evening, after receiving a letter
with simply one written word "No!," Victor gets drunk and
brutally beats Dina. Hugging her pink bathrobe afterwards,
he falls asleep, intoxicated and dreams erotically. On the
following day, he apologizes to Dina as he stands by the
hearth watching the firewood from the carob-tree blaze.

          Victor's story is similar to many old people in Spain
whose very existence lack any kind of social commitment,
people who spend their lives on the outskirts of society surviving, waiting to die. The emptiness in Victor's life (perhaps "existence" is a better word) is reflected in the town's
people, their petty concerns, their loneliness. Gonzalo Sobejano suggests the "repressed vitality" of Victor is counterpointed with the "succulent portrait of the landscape, as if
nature may compensate a little, with all its beauty for the
daily pain of that world of outcasts."[14] Goytisolo's Realist
writing suggests so many of the cinematic possibilities that
for example Vittorio de Sica, in his great film, Umberto D,
or Luis Buñuel, in his equally triumphant film, Tristana,
have seized as themes: the emptiness of the lives of old
people and their repressed sexuality.

          Chapter One comes alive only when Goytisolo de-
scribes the outskirts of the city, nature and Victor's hunting
expeditions, especially when the latter kills rabbits (a metaphor so beautifully used by Carlos Saura in his recent film
La caza (The Hunt)). Sometimes Goytisolo criticizes his

fellow Spaniards or the urbanites of Barcelona when Victor
says in a conversation with his old buddies in the cafe that
they are "bad people, bad people. They're close-mouthed,
routinized, they distrust everyone and everything. To speak
to them is a waste of time. They say 'yes, yes' and continue just as before. ... [They have] little initiative, love
and take few chances. ... What people! What a country!"15
Perhaps one of the most poignant scenes is the discussion
about Patalino, an ex-soldier friend of Victor's who lost his
feet during the war (they were machine-gunned) and then his
farm, and finally hanged himself from the carob tree, symbol of one of the beauties of nature and fuel for survival for
these old people on the outskirts of Barcelona. Another interesting passage deals with Victor's memories of his father
and mother, Don Augusto and Doña Magdalena, as he thinks
about them while looking through some old mildewed books
he read as a child in the now dismal, decaying attic.

        Goytisolo develops Victor's character fully but does
not provide any psychological motivations to explain his im-
promptu beating of Dina. The most outstanding feeling I had
while reading Chapter One was Goytisolo's revulsion towards
city life or, rather, his indictment of the city as an anti-
life force, stultifying its inhabitants, perverting their characters, killing their motivations.

        Chapter Two continues the novel's story line with
Don Augusto and Doña Magdalena, who live in a villa outside
of Barcelona with their grandson Bernardo, whose parents
died in an automobile accident some years before. Its
thirty-two pages provide a similar counterpoint of the vitality
of nature versus the barren lives of the protagonists, as
Augusto is extremely upset by someone tearing out his geraniums from his garden (he is fanatical over cultivating geraniums) but continues to dedicate himself to writing a useless book about Spain's economic problems. He relates his
anger at his wife to Bernardo, who acts as his confidant,
a mute witness to the conflicts between Augusto and Magdalena. Augusto believes his wife had destroyed his geraniums
purposely to taunt him and wishes his son Julio were there
to take his side against her. Bernardo also acts as confidant to Magdalena and in one conversation with Bernardo,
we discover that Magdalena and Augusta's son Victor (Bernardo's father) died in an auto accident with Bernardo's
mother. (Obviously this Victor is not the same character
we met in Chapter One.) Bernardo listens to Augusto and
Magdalena argue about each other and remains an indifferent,

indolent spectator of their incessant argumentative interludes.
Bernardo does little to entertain himself except to study
some old maps on his bed for diversion. His grandparents
each confide their woes to him, trading "long speeches of
confidences of trusting words about minor problems,"16 for
Bernardo's minimal comprehension.

One "classic" scene demonstrating a complete lack of
communication between the three characters takes place after
dinner. Augusto discusses Bernardo's voracious study of
geography while Magdalena presents him with a geography
puzzle. Augusto sees Magdalena's gift as a means of winning Bernardo over to her side, but the latter merely accepts it and keeps his position as passive intermediary between his grandparents. The chapter ends with Augusto's
vow to cultivate more geraniums, leaving this reader with
an impression that further sociability is impossible for Augusto, Magdalena and Bernardo. Goytisolo presents the
story of two older people with the obvious advantages of financial security, completely immersed in a world of their
own design but recognizing that their youth is gone; he shows
their illnesses, their displeasure with each other and their
futility to break out of their self-created labyrinth.

Chapter Three introduces another character named
Victor, an ex-soldier and factory worker who after a discussion in his car decides to spend one night of pleasure in a
local bar with his war buddy Nacho. Victor believes youth
is synonymous with happiness. He and Nacho order marti-
nis while they reflect on their past and the future. Victor
would like to own a house on the outskirts of Barcelona and
Nacho rambles about the women to whom he would like to
make love. Their conversation is suddenly interrupted by
the shoeshine boy Ciriaco, who was formerly Victor's lieutenant in the war. Ciriaco joins the men for a cigarette
and a drink or two and participates in their conversation.
Ciriaco is ill, tubercular, desperate. He leads Victor and
Nacho through a series of bars, wine cellars, tascas, where
the men continue talking about Ciriaco's imprisonment in
Leningrad, his cough, and his war experiences. Victor and
Nacho witness Ciriaco's abuse of a poor gypsy guitarist in
a local bar. The gypsy criticizes Ciriaco's miserable circumstances but the former lieutenant prefers to disregard
the present, thinking only of his role as a war hero. Victor
and Nacho find Ciriaco's reminiscences and talk of health
depressing, and on some pretext they leave him, driving to
the outskirts of town for some welcome fresh air.

An excellent vignette, this particular episode is principally a conversation among three men. In twenty-six
pages, Goytisolo has successfully captured the loneliness of
old soldiers, the tragedies of illness, the artificiality of the
neon-life of bars and tascas near Barcelona, the suffocating
lives of men who rely on memory and machismo to sustain
them.

Chapter Four is the shortest (twelve pages) and most
depressing in Goytisolo's novel. Domingo and Amelia were
servants on Don Augusto's farm before they married. They
had one son who died during a bombardment in the Civil
War. Now they are old and live in a ramshackle, dark ruin
of a house on the outskirts of the city on government relief.
Except for a small garden in which they cultivate flowers,
Amelia and Domingo do very little. They tend to their
garden and shop in the neighborhood. Like vegetables themselves, they live in cold, rural desolation as city life en-
croaches upon the suburbs. One day, Amelia is hit by a
speeding car while crossing a super highway leading into
Barcelona and Domingo wanders off, distracted after reading a new sign "Land Purchased for the New Municipal
Shelter for the Aged." Goytisolo shows the irony of Amelia's
death and the impossibility of the aged to cope with an advancing, modernized, youth-oriented society which forgets its
aged and causes them to suffer. They are victims of social
injustice and legislative indifference.

Chapter Five narrates the life of the widower Mingo
Cabot, his son Nap, daughter Dineta and how they eke out
their living on their farm on the outskirts of Barcelona.
Mingo represents the stubborn patriarch, the rude, strong
old man who must do things his way, unyielding to correction
or progress. A neighbor of his, Tonio, suggests they col-
laborate and buy a tractor to better cultivate their crops and
take the physical burden of labor off themselves. Mingo,
however, refuses and continues using the "traditional" hoe.
Tonio falls in love with Dineta and Mingo, disliking Tonio,
brutally beats his daughter and throws her out of his house.

Alone with a sickly and deformed son but proud and
defiant, Mingo, the reactionary, continues to farm his land
according to the traditional methods, overwhelmed by fatigue
from his farming labors. This Goytisolo story is much in
the same vein as the social novels of nineteenth-century
Spain, whose themes generally dealt with the triumph of ignorance and brute force over intelligence, education,

technological advances--in a word, progress. Goytisolo
shows that Mingo's children are also subject to social injustices, suffering for the mistakes of their elders. But it is
Mingo's refusal to acknowledge change that makes the story's
last line, "¡Lo de siempre!" (Same as always!), a scalding
rebuke of Mingo's character and an implicit cry for reform
rather than an acceptance of life as it is.

        Chapter Six opens with another character named Ciri-
aco, possibly the husband of Claudina described in Chapter
One. Ciriaco works as a hodcarrier while his wife, Claudina, cares for their apartment and takes in laundry during
the afternoons. Their son Bernardo is obsessed with the
idea that he, like his little brother, will die, burned to a
crisp like a cigarette in a brazier. Although Ciriaco is a
good man who enjoys liquor and sojourns at the local cafe
with his friends, on one particular day he steals some pipe
fittings and sells them. The Civil Guard arrests him, after
Bernardo unknowingly informs them of his father's whereabouts. In the bar below their apartment, where many of
the unemployed and aged take an occasional glass of wine,
an unkempt but compassionate gypsy named Patrach cheers
up Bernardo who is consoling himself with a glass of anise;
Bernardo then goes to see a film at the local movie house.
Claudina's brother offers her his help when Ciriaco is sent
to prison. She hopes that her bad fortune will change. 17

        Though a thoughtless act, placing his family in even
greater jeopardy Ciriaco's theft was motivated by a desire
for money for food and shelter, such thefts a common problem among poor families. Bernardo, although he is called
worse than a Judas for betraying his father, feels no guilt
about causing Ciriaco to be apprehended by the Civil Guard;
judging by his irresponsible actions, he shows little concern
for the welfare of his family. Claudina cannot dissuade
Bernardo from spending money on comic books when they
ought to use it for food. Apparently, Claudina works very
hard to sustain her family. Antonio, Claudina's brother,
remembers what their grandfather used to say about life:
"Ah, when I was young. If I were young. Well [Antonio
continues], now I am young and you see, [I go] from my
house to the factory, from the factory to my house.... To
work in order to eat, to eat in order to continue working
until you're no longer young, until you become old like grandfather and useless, all life passing by like a flash... " (p.
180). On this pessimistic note, one leaves Claudina, Bernardo and Antonio to survive the future. Goytisolo suggests

that life is a useless struggle and only through men and women's helping each other can people succeed to live well.

        The last chapter, Seven, of nineteen pages, begins
with the news that Alvarito, having just finished his examination for the bachillerato, and after enjoying the summer
by himself, playing sports and being bored, goes off to
Barcelona to begin his studies at the university. He receives a gold watch from his father, Victor, the doctor, and
buys a first-class ticket to the city. Alvarito is the youngest protagonist in the entire novel, a señorito without problems, a young man of some financial advantages, with minor
and trivial concerns. This final chapter does not tie up the
great number of loose ends about other characters, the co-
incidences of having similar names or the confusions in sequences of time. Some characters appear old at the beginning and younger at the end of the novel--if indeed, they are
really the very same characters using the same names.
Nora believes

            the reiteration of names throughout the novel is an
            artifice, deliberate and transparent, but not capri-
            cious, rather precisely researched in order to iden-
            tify the destinies beyond the innumerable circum-
            stantial and anecdotal variations. Thus, the Don
            Augustos and Doña Magdalenas are uniform ex-
            amples of the wealthy pre-war bourgeoisie (impli-
            citly leaving themselves in the same constant posi-
            tion of wealth covering their vacuous existence,
            their sordid moral miseries); the Victors are sons
            of such parents, all ex-soldiers and radically frus-
            trated (Chapter One), their triumphs destroyed by
            others (Chapter Three) [and] ... in parallel fashion,
            the Domingos and Amelias ... the Ciriacos....
            [T]he children, the Alvaritos, children of wealth,
            the Antonios, poor but lively, the Dinas and Ber-
            nardos who all acquire conscience in silence,
            mutes or almost mute, are strange, enigmatic
            when facing the not so strange world of their
            elders. 18

                    *   *   *

        Las afueras is an intellectual novel, a social novel,
a negative portrait of the elderly, a pessimistic vision containing little hope for its protagonists, a series of diverse

worlds (seven of them) created by Goytisolo in the realm of
Realism. It is a depressing work conceived in the style of
objective realism and very much the successor both stylistically and thematically to Sánchez Ferlosio's El Jarama. In
each of the seven sections of the novel, Goytisolo follows
an unswerving structure, presenting events, descriptions of
characters, actions and flashbacks until we arrive at the
present again as each protagonist must face a particular
problem with no solution offered. Sobejano calls his style
"objective laconism"[19] with some minor displays of emotion.
Some chapters are written with Realist techniques, such as
the dialogues found in Chapter Three. Bosch characterizes
Goytisolo's style as "hard and not lively, but the novel's sobriety and simplicity make it a very attractive work ... one
of the most interesting books of this age."[20]

   Las afueras depresses its readers because all of its
characters except for one (Alvarito of Chapter Seven) never
realize their ambitions. One critic found Alvarito's "positive" thinking the only hopeful ray of light in the entire work
but considered the ending "stylistically incoherent with the
rest of the work."[21] Each chapter, however, is designed
to show its readers the failures of communication, the social injustices, the blind rages and deafening rancor that
exist among its protagonists, through a terse, sober style
with occasional shafts of poetic prose that do not detract
from the principal themes of each chapter. Just as in El
Jarama, one of the reader's essential problems is that he
would have liked to know more about the characters, their
lives and attitudes. We are confronted once again with a
similar lack of background material. Perhaps this is the
failing of the novelist when he chose to create his novel in
this realist-objective style.

   But equally serious is the artificial construction of
the novel, the confusion among characters, the difference in
writing styles among chapters (some are pure Realist dialogue, others traditional Realist description emulating nineteenth-century models). And like Sánchez Ferlosio, Goytisolo-Gay has taken a particular sector of humanity, circumscribed it according to his idea of Realism and portrayed
these people according to their shared milieu and social
problems; this is typical of the early New Wave writers.
Although Goytisolo did not succumb to Ferlosio's "experimental conceptions" of El Jarama, he committed similar
errors by refusing to state explicitly the failings of modern
Spanish society to cope with the problems of its elderly, to

take care of its soldiers who fought in the Civil War, and to face its own defects, such as its insistence on youth. Yet, unlike Sánchez Ferlosio, Las afueras is redeemed frequently by its important but understated themes and above all by its poetic-Realist and at times objectivist style.

The following atypical passage from Chapter One describes Victor's hunting for rabbits:

> Victor heard the dogs hunting in the stubble. They barked, racing along as if they were harrassing a quarry that was very near. Nevertheless, he didn't call to them, since the land was too wet and they might lose the trail. He advanced slowly, on the edge of the embankment, the slopes of which were covered with tangled grasses. After a little while, a rabbit jumped quickly from the brambles. Victor let it get away up the slope a little further, its tail straight up, its ears tense. The shot sounded when the rabbit rounded the slope above him, straight as an arrow.
>
> Victor found him at the foot of the slope, shuddering, each time more weakly until he closed his eyes. He picked him up by his rump and slapped him on the nape of the neck with the back of his hand; the shuddering stopped. Now those eyes were like rubber, fixed and opaque, covered with dust [pp. 22-3].

This is a marvelous descriptive passage, combined with the traditional Realist style of nineteenth-century writers. It appeals to the reader's imagination because of the author's conjuration of poetic images through his excellent choice of words (best revealed, of course, in the Spanish). Unlike El Jarama, which is basically dialogue with banal thematic concerns, Las afueras abounds in such well-written descriptive passages about life and death and presents as descriptively as possible the backgrounds and decor in which its protagonists move. (See the passage of dialogue to be found in the Appendix, typical of Goytisolo's objectivist-realist style.) And it is clear that Goytisolo-Gay, unlike Sánchez-Ferlosio, prefers to deal with themes of a certain measure of profundity and to use an appropriate Realist style to capture them in his imagination for his readers and for posterity.

Goytisolo has said this himself about the novel and his mission as a novelist:

> The novel is more than a means of transformation of society; it does not just idealize reality on paper but transforms the minds of the readers, making them change their conception of the world. If you believe that this is not possible--that with my work I do not contribute to the readers' consciousness of certain determined aspects of reality and also (although this may be challenged) that I do not fight so that the writer is able to say what he must to be heard--then, of course, I would not write. [22]

Goytisolo's protests made against censorship and Franco's politics have caused him to spend many months in jail. It is a pity that Las afueras, despite its Realism, poetic lyricism and seemingly profound themes, is like El Jarama-- not a true catharsis, not an outspoken portrait of Barcelona's society of the mid-1950's, but a restrained, often depressing work, indicating the perception of a young novelist whose artistry is fettered by the political confines in which he lives.

I have neglected to examine until this moment the meaning behind the particular symbol of las afueras (the outskirts, suburbs, environs) which holds together each of the seven chapter vignettes. For Victor in Chapter Three, the afueras represent a place of tranquility, an escape from city life. For the Victor of Chapter One, the afueras are the countryside where he was born and the land of the carob trees, situated far away from the Café Moderno, his single tie to civilization. Don Augusto and Doña Magdalena of Chapter Two live in the afueras, which for them symbolize an isolated world. In Chapter Four, the afueras represent for Domingo and Amelia a hostile landscape, where people are killed by fast racing cars over the new superhighway, where old people live in desolation and poverty and are left to die, where ironically the government plans to erect a new Home for the Aged. In Chapter Five, Mingo Cabot tills the earth on the outskirts and his land is his life. It sustains his entire family and like the land, Mingo refuses to change in response to it. Claudina and Bernardo of Chapter Six live in a small apartment above a bar in the afueras. For them, the outskirts represent hard work to make ends meet. For the young, middle-class student, Alvarito, of Chapter Seven, the afueras represent a place to live for a short while, to vacation, and unlike the other characters in

the novel, it is a place from which to escape. He will
journey to Barcelona to spend the rest of his life there in
his eventual career as a lawyer. In six of seven cases,
the afueras, Goytisolo's dominant and unifying symbol, spells
defeat for the people who dwell there. They represent, for
his protagonists, an impoverishing of social values "in an
unjust world where indifference, poverty, useless sacrifice,
lack of communication, ignorance, backward tradition and
regression triumph over justice, equality, love and order. "23

        Las afueras is a worthy successor to El Jarama, not
so much for its use of a realist-objectivist style that Sánchez
Ferlosio initiated but because it restores many of the traditional values of Realist writers and serves to renovate the
genre, free it from sheer experimentalism and provide some
measure of authenticity, profundity and art to an otherwise
dwindling, chaotic and at times totally undirected art form.
Las afueras is a Realist novel, despair its central theme,
stylistically imitative of S. Ferlosio but less experimental
and more prudent in its depiction of lives and characters.
Consequently, it displays the genuine artistry of a Realist
writer, not all together "objective," a writer who is more
interested in communicating his themes fully rather than
sacrificing content in favor of style. The novel contains
many flaws of construction and plot, but gives much evidence
that Goytisolo-Gay may emerge as a leader of New Wave fiction should he continue writing in this vein.

THE NOVELS OF LUIS GOYTISOLO-GAY

Las afueras. Barcelona: Ed. Seix Barral, 1958.
Las mismas palabras. Barcelona: Ed. Seix Barral, 1963.

SELECTED STUDIES ON GOYTISOLO-GAY

Cano, J. L. "L. Goytisolo-Gay: 'Las afueras'," Insula,
        no. 146 (enero 1959), 8-9.
Díaz, M. "Las afueras," Nuestras ideas (Brussels), no.
        7 (1959), 99-100.
Prats, A. " 'Las mismas palabras', de Luis Goytisolo, "
        Realidad (Rome), no. 3 (oct. 1964), 123-6.

Chapter 9

ANA MARIA MATUTE and PRIMERA MEMORIA
(First Memories) (1960)

Ana María Matute is probably the most prominent
woman writer in present-day Spain and the best known female Spanish novelist in the United States and abroad.   Much
has been written about her life and works in both English
and Spanish.   The best two studies of her life and work have
been published in America by two extremely talented scholars
of Spanish language and literature. 1   Also, I had the fortunate opportunity of interviewing Matute at her home in Sitges
near Barcelona in the summer of 1968 and will incorporate
my impressions of her into the ensuing portrait of her life
and works.

Ana María Matute was born in Barcelona on July 26,
1926, "the second of five children of a Catalan industrialist.
Her father was the owner of an umbrella factory; her mother
was the 'classic middle-class Spanish wife,' educated exclusively for marriage and motherhood....   The family was
conservative, and the three girls and two boys received a
traditional religious upbringing.   It was a family without
literary or artistic antecedents...."2   Matute was educated
at religious schools during an extremely unhealthy childhood
when many times she was overcome physically by illnesses,
sometimes near the point of death, which required several
long periods of convalescence in the country.

At the outbreak of the Civil War, Matute was confined
to her home where, even under conditions of cultural isolation and lack of formal education, she founded a children's
magazine.   After the war, she briefly returned to school but
in 1941 abandoned all formal education in favor of studying
painting and the violin.   She had no interest in studying
these disciplines at the university and in 1942 published her

113

first short story in a local magazine. Writing thrilled her
so much so that in 1943 she abandoned her violin and painting lessons. Essentially self-taught, she became a serious
writer of fiction. She began Los Abel (The Abel Family) in
1945 and finished it by 1947, when she won the Nadal Prize.
However she considers her official career as a writer to
have begun in 1948, and since then has written a myriad of
novels and short stories.

Fiesta al noroeste (Celebration in the Northwest) won
the Premio Gijón in 1952, the same year she married Ramón
Eugenio de Goicoechea, a poet and writer. In 1954 her son
Juan Pablo was born and she won the Premio Planeta for
Pequeño teatro (Little Theater). In 1958 she ran into censorship difficulties and was forced to rewrite Las luciérnagas
(The Fireflys), which became En esta tierra (In This Land).
Between 1956-1957, she continued writing minor collections
of short stories and in 1958 won the Spanish Critic's Prize
for her novel Los hijos muertos (The Dead Children), as
well as the Miguel de Cervantes National Literary Prize.
She also received a grant of 50,000 pesetas to begin work
on her projected trilogy, "Los mercaderes" (The Merchants)
of which the first volume is Primera memoria (First Memories), published in 1960, which received the Nadal Prize and
is considered by most Spanish critics the best novel of the
trilogy.

In the ensuing years, Matute has grown more prolific,
publishing a variety of novels and short stories for children.
The best known of these in America are El Saltamontés
verde (The Green Grasshopper), Historias de la Artámila
(Tales of the Artamila), Libro de juegos para los niños de
los otros (Book of Games for the Children of Others) and
Caballito loco (Little Crazy Horse). In 1963, when the
English and American editions of Primera memoria were
published simultaneously,[3] Matute separated from her husband and traveled through Europe and to Greece. The following year, she completed Los soldados lloran de noche
(The Soldiers Cry by Night), volume two of "The Merchants"
trilogy, and traveled to the United States, lecturing at several universities about her life and work. In 1965 she won
the Premio Lazarillo, the National Prize for Children's
Literature, for her work, El polizón del "Ulises" (The Cabin
Boy of the Ulysses), became legally separated from her husband, journeyed once again throughout Europe and Scandinavia
and traveled to the United States as a visiting professor of
Spanish literature at several mid-western universities.

On her return to Spain the following year, she continued her lecture tours, and in 1968 established her permanent residence in Sitges in a small white stucco house overlooking the Mediterranean Sea just below the Costa Brava.
It was here I interviewed her in July of 1968. She told me
then she had completed the trilogy with La trampa (The
Trap), published in 1969 (a year in which she returned again
to the United States as a visiting professor and lectured on
her life and career). In the 1968 interview Matute said she
felt she had to "rebel against the literatura de evasión"
currently in vogue, and as a member of the New Wave
whose essence she characterized as "writers who ideally
describe, those who belong to the generation of the Civil
War," she felt many of her contemporaries were writing
"novelas bastante falsas" (essentially false novels). When
asked how the present political situation affected her work,
she replied, "mucho," and warned that "self-censorship is
the fear of every Spanish author, but in spite of it, each
writer has to commit himself to truth which makes it extremely difficult for any author to write." She characterized
Spanish censorship as "subtle, well-organized, powerful" and
spoke out about her difficulties with En las tierras, the re-
written version of the censored original, Las luciérnagas. 4

It is not surprising that in 1971, Matute was fined
50,000 pesetas for her role in drafting and signing the now
famous "Montserrat Manifesto" of December 1970, which
protested the police arrest of clergy, university students and
writers opposing the Nationalist policies of law, order, education and censorship. Matute continues to be an outspoken
critic of Franco and his regime (she refers to el Generalísi-
mo as "la momia" [the mummy]5) and continues to be equally
productive in her literary career as well as her social commentary.

In 1971 she published La torre vigia (The Watchtower),
another novel considered to be "a social variant of the chivalric novel,"6 and is presently dividing her time between
lecture tours in the United States and in Spain at various universities, raising her son in Sitges, and writing novels and
short stories.

*   *   *

Primera memoria (1960) represents a new direction
for the Spanish novel and the New Wave because, unlike its

predecessors, it is the first to encourage a new variant of
style I shall call "subjective Realism." A work of astonishing beauty, Primera memoria is deceptively simple. It fo-
cuses on Matía, a fourteen-year-old girl living with her relatives on an unnamed island (probably one of the Balearics),
who narrates the entire memoir in the first person in the
form of an autobiography. The plot is slender and loosely
constructed. Matía, who resembles physically the author
herself (although Matute has claimed this novel is not her
autobiography),[7] has come to live with her tyrannical grandmother, Doña Práxedes, her aunt Emilia, and Emilia's son
Borja (age fifteen), after her mother, María Teresa, died
and her father went off to the Iberian peninsula to fight on
the Republican side during the Civil War. The island itself
behaves like one of the protagonists--the beaches are afire
with the intensity of the sun, the air vibrates with the violent colors of the earth and sea and the landscape literally
pulsates with character, where most of the "action" in this
tale of children actually takes place.

        Borja and Matía are fond of going to the Descent
(title of the novel's first section) whenever they are saturated with heat, boredom and solitude. On this small, deserted beach, Borja keeps his boats, the "Young Simón,"
and stores his "treasures" of stolen cigarettes, money and
childish paraphernalia of games and costumes. One day,
they find the dead body of José Taronjí "stuck to the side of
the boat like a barnacle," a Jewish Fascist who was apparently murdered or pushed from the high cliffs surrounding
the Descent. Borja and Matía meet Manuel, José's adopted son,
who comes to take the body home and asks Borja if he may
use his boat for this purpose. Borja readily agrees and
Matía feels a special attraction and fascination for Manuel.
She is drawn to him because of his dark skin, his sadness,
his silence, his sensitivity. Borja becomes annoyed when
Matía starts to meet Manuel to play and even more enraged
when he discovers Manuel is the illegitimate son of Jorge de
Son Major, a paralytic and wealthiest landowner of the island.

        In the second section of the novel, entitled "School of
the Sun," Borja and Matía continue to play with other children, particularly Guiem, Toni, Antonio, Ramón and Sebastián, who formed the nucleus of one rival gang, and Juan
Antonio, León, and Carlos, who, along with Borja and
Matía, comprise the other. Matía and Borja smoke cigarettes on the sly, berate and tyrannize their tutor Lauro
(who they nickname "the Chink"), visit Mariné, the local

innkeeper at the Naranjal, and continue to enjoy their summer vacation before school resumes in the fall.

Section Three, entitled "The Bonfires," is symbolic
of the Plaza de los Judíos, where in the fifteenth century
the Jews were burned at the stake, and is also representative of Borja's jealousy and hatred of Manuel's "Jewishness"
and affection for Matía.   On a visit with Manuel and Matía
to Jorge de Son Major's home, who with his homosexual servant Sanamo (who wears a red rose over one ear) provide
drinks to intoxicate the three children, Borja becomes
jealous of the attention that Jorge de Son Major pays Manuel,
especially when the man ignores Borja's idolization of him.
Borja plots to revenge himself of this and break up Manuel's
relationship with Matía.

In the fourth section, "The White Cock," Borja asks
Manuel to deliver "something" in a box to Mariné at the
tavern for safekeeping.   Manuel agrees, not knowing that
Borja has stolen a large sum of money from his grandmother and wants to implicate him.   Under the guise of the
confessional, Borja confides his deed to Monsignor Mayol
and implicates Manuel.   The latter is sent to a reformatory
and Matía, threatened strongly by Borja that she will suffer
the same fate if she utters a single word about his theft,
retreats into silence and cowardice, unable to help Manuel
or herself.

The secondary characters in this novel who represent
the adult world--Emilia, Borja's slightly obese and sybaritic
mother, Jorge de Son Major, paralyzed and decadent, Sanamo, sensual and gay, Malene, an adulterous, beautiful but
suspicious Jewess (Manuel's mother), and Lauro "the Chink,"
sweating and doltish--are all somewhat corrupted by the
languid and sensual landscape while the children and their
world are viewed directly in counterpoint.   The children
move in a chiaroscuro atmosphere of innocence and brightness, an ambience that becomes laden with nuances, and
finally corrupt.

Matute wrote Primera memoria against the background
of a divided Spain, a Spain ravaged by Civil War.   Matía is
fighting a war of her own, between childhood and maturity,
innocence and adulthood, intense friendships and loss of love.
Bored and exasperated in the middle of her summer vacation,
living in an atmosphere embittered by fierce class loyalties,
Matía is forced by a mature recognition of her own "lost

world" of childhood into another world she never wanted.
She is a child who has lost innocence as the secrets of the
world of adults are revealed to her with cruel abruptness,
as children and adults force her to choose between friendship and cowardice, impotence and love. Matía's tragedy
at the end of the novel is that she could not defend nor even
warn Manuel of Borja's treachery. In the closing scene,
she comforts a repentant and crying Borja as the white cock
from Jorge de Son Major's garden shrieks at the breaking
of dawn, proclaiming "some mysterious lost cause,"8 a symbol of Matía's personal defeat which she is unable to articu-
late to herself, a cry representing her transition, and the
knowledge of "lost innocence, lost idealism, lost hope, lost
Republic."9

      Equally fascinating is Borja, who by his childish ac-
tions parallels the adult behavior of his grandmother and
mother, with their senseless cruelty, hardness, moral corruption and hypocrisy. Borja is "hypocritical and Machiavel-
lian, but also a slightly pathetic adolescent [who] probably
personifies the 'perverse innocence' which the novelist has
identified as the theme of First Memories."10 Borja reminds us all of the infamous evil children of literature but
as he causes Manuel to be wrongly punished for a crime he
himself committed, he comes closest to being the male equivalent of Mary Tilford, the malicious and corrupt little girl
who ruined the lives of Martha Dobie and Karen Wright with
her lies and blackmail in Lillian Hellman's classic 1932
American drama, The Children's Hour.

      Doña Práxedes, although having little to do with the
action of the novel is a continual presence whose influence
dominates the entire work. Matute begins her First Memories with an excellent description of her on the first page of
the novel, portraying her as the epitome of grand dame and
ruling matriarch:

> My grandmother's white hair was set in a brist-
> ling wave on her forehead. It gave her a certain
> angry air. She almost always carried a small
> gold-headed bamboo cane, which she did not need,
> for she was as steady as a horse. Looking over
> old photographs I find in that thick, massive, a
> glowing reflection of Borja, and even of me. I
> suppose Borja inherited her gallantry, her absolute
> lack of mercy. I, perhaps, my great sadness.

> My grandmother's hands--big boned, with prom-
> inent knuckles--though not lacking in beauty, were
> splashed with coffee-coloured spots. On the index
> finger and on the ring finger of her right hand
> danced two enormous, dirty diamonds. After
> meals, she would drag her rocking chair to the
> window of her boudoir.... From there, her old
> opera glasses incrusted with false sapphires, she
> would scrutinize the houses of the Descent.... 11

Matía's grandmother is the indomitable force counter-
pointing the weakness found in the personalities of her sybaritic daughter Emilia and her equally morally decaying
grandchildren. "She is at the center of the war on the island (on a much smaller scale than the echoes of the war
that are heard from the peninsula) and her position is to
keep the status quo. "12   War is the largest theme that
Matute discusses on symbolic levels.   Janet Díaz stresses
the war of the "Taronji family (Fascists) against political
undesirables, the war between cousins of the same name--
the Cain theme, war within the family--and the counterpoint
of adolescent 'war' or clashes between juvenile gangs"; and
also points out that "the use of an island, removed from the
main conflict, and of child or adolescent protagonists, may
be seen either as a device to circumvent censorship, or as
a microcosmic, symbolic representation of the national situation. "13

Essentially Díaz is correct since Matute, although an
outspoken liberal to this very day, has had to yield to the
Spanish censors before.   However, her use of the island as
a symbol or microcosm is not essentially a new device.
Jonathan Swift employed the same mechanism for his Gulliver's Travels as early as the eighteenth century and William
Golding used it for his celebrated 1955 novel, Lord of the
Flies.   What is new in Matute's work is her persistent account of Matía's revelations, her psychological anguish, her
nostalgia for her lost childhood, and her presentation through
a subjective-Realist style of Matía's "frustrated rebellion,
nascent love, and the discovery of falseness and sadness. "14
Rafael Bosch, believing this novel to be Matute's best work,
sees four distinct planes of the novel: (1) the war itself,
presented through the immediate events of the assassination
of Manuel's father in relation to what is happening on the
peninsula; (2) a symbolic superstructure, as the battles between the children reflect in their own way the "petty wars"
between adults; (3) the actions and thoughts of Matía with

her relatives, her visits to various places when she was
fourteen years old; and (4) Matía's "pure" thoughts of the
"present," her adult life, that give her actions and thoughts
of the past a perspective and meaning (these thoughts which
are usually found throughout the text in parenthetical remarks). 15

    Janet Díaz establishes a parallel with each of Matute's
divisions of the novel, observing a "discovery" in each section. For example, "The Descent" reveals death, "School
of the Sun" shows us physical love (the "dirty secret of
adults"), "The Bonfires" symbolizes hate and war on various
levels, and in the final section, "The White Cock," we discover the betrayal of Manuel. 16   Certainly, these levels and
discoveries exist for us in the novel. But of supreme importance is the novel's significance which must be sought
through the revelation of Matía's psyche and the tarnished,
bleak reality that Matía unfolds for us by means of her
thoughts both past and present.

    All of Matía's thoughts have an evanescent quality,
an ineffable, intimate nature one cannot categorize precisely.
When she talks in the present, reflecting on her youth, can
we not feel exactly what she means when she says the following words17: "Here I am now, facing this terribly green
glass, my heart heavy. Is it true that life stems from
scenes like this? Is it true that as children we lived our
entire life, in one gulp, only to repeat ourselves stupidly,
blindly, without any sense forever afterwards?" (p. 13-4).
How much of life's experience and suffering she must have
had, to reach this conclusion so early in the novel. "And
later, I was thinking: Have I lost something? I don't know:
I only know I haven't found anything. And it was if someone or something might have betrayed me at some unknown
time" (p. 15). Primera memoria (School of the Sun) is
most assuredly a novel about loss, a lost childhood and
Matía's resistence at entering the adult world which she
senses is sordid and corrupt.

> How foreign is the race of adults, the race of men
> and women! How foreign and absurd we were!
> How outside of the world and even time. We were
> no longer children. We suddenly did not know
> what we were. And in this way, without knowing
> why, face downward and on the floor, we did not
> dare come close to one another. He put his hand
> on top of mine and only our hands touched. Some-

> times I was aware of the curls on his forehead,
> or the cold tip of his nose. And he would say,
> between puffs of smoke: 'When will all this
> end... !' It is certainly true that neither of us
> was sure what he was referring to: if it were
> the war, the island, or our very age [p. 107].

One of the great advantages we have by entering
Matía's thoughts is we may judge for ourselves the validity
of her feelings about herself and her relationships with other
characters in the novel.   Matute permits us, through her
subjective-Realist style, to discover ourselves and our own
reveries of childhood and lost innocence.   We are inside
Matía's world of experiences; we feel her repressed sensuality, we see her vision of this "evil" world that surrounds
her, we retreat with her to those secure places of the mind
and heart that give her stability--her black doll Gorogó, her
cigarettes, her Latin declensions, French translations, her
cardboard theatre. Matía suffers: "What an enormous ache
filled me!   How is it possible to feel so much pain at fourteen? And it was endless pain!" (p. 141).

Primera memoria is filled with true states of feeling,
adolescent emotions of jealousy and excellent, mature writing
about adolescent behavior ("But I had already jumped over
the wall and left Kay and Gerda [her dolls] in their garden
on the rooftop.   ... And at one and the same time, I was
ashamed of the first adult sentiment and I was frightened
and pained at myself, my words, my pity" [p. 157]) that one
critic believes the novel "would deserve its high ranking
solely for its contribution to adolescent psychology.... "18
It is the unexpressed, unnamed aches of growing up which
Matute portrays best: "Something was hurting me so much
that I could not stir.   ... [A]n enormous cowardice held
me fast to the ground.   ...   The outside of my body shiv-
ered, but the cold inside me was even greater ... there
was only one voice shaking me: 'Coward, traitor, coward. '
... I could do nothing else but follow him, like a dog,
breathing my betrayal, without daring to flee" (p. 237-8).

> And suddenly there was the dawn, like a despic-
> able, terrible reality. And I, with my eyes opened,
> as punishment.   (The Island of Never-Never did not
> exist and the Little Mermaid did not achieve an im-
> mortal soul because men and women do not love
> each other, and she was left with a couple of use-
> less legs, and transformed into sea spray.)

Stories now horrible.   Moreover, I had lost
Gorogó... [p. 241].

The outstanding quality of style which endows Primera
memoria with its profundity and novelistic force is Matute's
sensitivity, her response to people, their psychologies and
natures with their various hues, transitions, and nuances.
As a New Wave novelist, Matute has turned her back on the
prevailing style of objective-realism, preferring instead to
cultivate the first-person subjective style of the memoir, to
an astonishing success and international acclaim.

Her background as a violinist and painter surely aided
in the composition of Primera memoria.   Note the beautiful
similies, metaphors, imagery and effects of synesthesia
which she constantly sprinkles through the narrative:

"She looked like a beaten Buddha" (p. 4) referring to
    Doña Práxedes;
"the wings of her nose dilated" (p. 5);
"grandmother searched and scoured the papers for
    news of the red hydra [Fascism]" (p. 18);
"the red balloon of the sun intensified minute by min-
    ute" (p. 30);
"the body of the man was still stuck like a barnacle to
    the keel of Young Simón" (p. 35);
"I tasted violent perfumes on my palate... " (p. 56);
"... and her freckle, which was like a spider on top
    of her lip" (p. 69);
"And I used to bend my head over the darkness of the
    well, down toward the water.   It was like smelling
    the dark heart of the earth" (pp. 100-01);
"and the sun, there outside, lay in ambush like a lion"
    (p. 101);
"the odor of sun lit up the walls, drawing a heavy per-
    fume from the brilliant mahogany of the dresser"
    (p. 120);
"Borja and I had learned to grease the doors of the
    'wild beast's' rooms" (p. 122), referring to
    Práxedes and Emilia;
"I seemed to be breathing inside the haze of a dream"
    (p. 123);
"the odor of the mayor's patio on the morning they re-
    turned from burying José Taronjí came to me and
    so did the sun among the grapevine--like a dazzling
    bewilderment" (p. 125), the odor triggering Matía's
    memory;

"until that moment, I never realized he was a boy [re-
ferring to Lauro]--filled to the brim with the dirty
things of men and women; sunk up to his shoulders
in the world; in that bottomless well into which all
of us were already slipping" (p. 156);

"the red-eye of a cigarette shone in the darkness, like
a one-eyed animal" (p. 164);

"Grandmother's eyes, like two tentacled fish, observed
us crudely" (p. 199);

"I saw grandmother's head detach itself and rise, first
like a balloon floating toward the ceiling" (p. 199)--
a cinematic surreal image worthy of Luis Buñuel's
directorial style;

"it was a horrible gray day, luminous, glowing like
aluminum" (p. 206);

and the closing image of the novel: "there stood the
cock of Son Major, with his angry eyes, like two
buttons of fire.   Straight and luminous, like a
handful of lime... " (p. 242).

In longer, sustained descriptive passages, Matute
demonstrates her skill as a writer especially when depicting
nature:

> We were sitting on the ground.   The almond trees
> covered the land, bordered at intervals with green
> grass, emerald green like the sea.   The almonds
> had already bloomed, and their black trunks stood
> out mysteriously against the pinkish cloud that
> lulled and made the light hazy, like a heavy vapor.
> The olive trees glistened.   Their trunks formed
> faces, arms, mouths.   The seeded earth, recent-
> ly turned over, jutted out in darker squares.   'My
> lord, ' the Chink was saying, 'what rich land'
> [p. 166].

Her sensual nature is revealed in the following passage when
she meets Monsignor Mayol for the first time:

> Monsignor Mayol played distractedly with a bluish
> crystal goblet, beautifully pearled, with opaque
> initials, like light through the rain.   On clear
> nights he drank an orange liqueur, clear as water,
> and Pernod on cloudy nights, because he said
> drinks were directly related to the atmosphere or
> color of sky.   (Amontillado for the glaring light
> of the sun, pristine or melancholy liqueurs for

> twilight.) When he said this, I tasted violent per-
> fumes on my palate and felt a light dizziness
> [pp. 55-6].

Matute's vision of beauty is always intense and personal:

> I shall always remember the rosy light in which
> everything seemed steeped, as in a marvelously
> golden wine. Even if the magnolias were no long-
> er in bloom and the flowers were drying--except
> for the red roses, so dark and deep they seemed
> black, like dried, but still fresh shuddering blood
> --the whole atmosphere was permeated by a poig-
> nant aroma [p. 183].

Although at one point in the novel, Matute feels her own
beauty "was still somewhat nebulous and far off," she, like
her protagonist, believes "beauty, then, [is] the only worthwhile thing one could count on in life" (p. 112), and her life
and career are testimony to these words. It is only on rare
occasions that Matute/Matía, sensitive creatures as they are,
ever seem given to despair:

> The big ribs of the nave, lie a boat submerged in
> the sea, covered with moss, gold and shadows,
> exuded something fascinating and oppressive. I
> feel tired: 'Oh, if only I'd never had to leave
> here [the church of Santa María],' I thought. I
> did not have any desire to live. Life seemed long
> and useless to me. I felt such hatred, such in-
> difference to everything, that even the air, the light
> of the sun, and the flowers seemed foreign to me
> [pp. 233-4].

I have deliberately quoted extensively from Primera
memoria, not only to demonstrate the beauties within the
author's writing style but also to show the consummate skill,
intelligence, artistry and heart with which Matute conceived
her novel. For in writing this work, it seems she has
reached into the very depths of her soul, into her own fragmented experiences of youth, beyond time itself, into the
realm of goodness that makes Primera memoria for us a
masterwork that elevates our appreciation of adolescence and
gives us a poignant, sensitive novel of youthful revelations.

> Then he raised his hand and it fell on mine. He
> pressed my hand against the ground, as if he

wanted to hold me back, so I might not fall down-
ward into the great threat.   Into the thick, blue,
hallucinating vertigo that I could sense from the
tiny plaza where they burned Jews, over the cliff.
As if with Cain, with his hand, with my childhood
which went astray, with our ignorance and goodness, I might want to sink our hands forever, to
nail them in the still pure, old wise earth [p. 136].

If Primera memoria is a novel about moral decay, it
also has enough joyful expectation and kernals of goodness
within it to transcend the bitterness of any unhappy adolescent experience.   Matute's employ of recurrent themes--
e. g. , strange and tortured children, characters with exotic
names--her feeling for fantasy, and her writing technique,
full of introspective monologues, metaphors and lyricism are
positive features of her stylistic innovation.   In an interview
in 1960 which appeared in Insula shortly after the appearance
of Primera memoria, Matute declared: "The novel can no
longer be merely for enjoyment or evasion [of problems].
On a par with a document of our time and with a basis of
the problems of modern man, it ought to wound the conscience of society in its desire to make it better. "19   Matute has invigorated the Spanish novel genre with her unique,
personalized style, which for her is "a variant of the synthesis between reality and art. "20   Her novels, especially
Primera memoria transcend the personal and intimate universe she describes; she is a novelist of a particular world,
exclusive--"an open observer of fantasy, lyricism and en-
cantation. "21

Despite her strong originality and excessive Romanticism, literary critics warn us of the dangers manifest in
her style:

> If in her happy moments the writer reveals her-
> self as a great literary portraitist, the owner of
> a rich palette of shadings, sensitive--in other
> moments that same exuberance and facility may
> push her towards a virtuosity which degenerates
> into a baroque accumulation, a plethora of images
> and in rhetoric. 22

Perhaps these "defects" of style may exist in other
novels by Matute, but Primera memoria is free of them.
Matute's strength as a Realist resides in "her depiction of
the historical and social circumstances that provide the

background of most of her novels and shorter tales; she is
adept at shaping strange moods and bizarre characters, at
enveloping her situation in a lyrical, intimate nimbus, and
at inventing plots of unusual intensity and interest. "[23] Yet
Matute prefers not to be classified as a Realist writer, for
at times, because of the prolixity of her themes, her overwhelming style, her search for symbols and her tendency to
flee reality, her "realism" is converted into a brilliant
"idealism. "[24] Although the majority of her literary works
deal with contemporary Spanish problems (or reality), they
are elevated to a universal level.

      Many critics probably would agree with García-Viñó's
thought that Ana María Matute's subjective style is a kind of
"detour of Realism..., an abandoning of the photographic
technique and the restraining of mere creation, with invented
and conventional passions, with purely literary fictions in
which the fresh air of the imagination clears up the foul atmosphere of daily living. "[25] Matute's arduous battle, her
need to express reality not only beautifully but profoundly
and from all sides has been her constant quest.   Through
different narrative rhythms, diverse shifts in time sequences,
simultaneous actions, distinct points of views of the same action, and fragmented episodes, Matute achieves her reality,
one that is "luminously palpable. " The same critic commented strongly upon Matute's critique of pharisaism or
hypocrisy and her defense of the "absolute liberty of feelings
and inclinations, even the most primal ones" as part of her
artistic vision.   For in Primera memoria, "one cannot deny
that it is a perfect work in which a writer of extraordinary
talent and sensibility has succeeded in realizing a complete
fusion of external and internal elements of her rich novelistic world...." "[Her world is drawn] from a dreadful vision,
including resentment of a youth torn out and the development
of a premature attitude in which hate, foreboding, mistrust,
incomprehension and desperation are so many threads in the
weave that entangles her relations with other human beings. "

            We are in the presence [says García-Viñó] of
            someone who writes with her own blood, with all
            fibres of her being and the trajectory of a tempera-
            mental artist has to be unredeemably so, with
            highs and lows that there is no reason ever [for
            her] to take forcibly any steps backward.

      When I interviewed Matute in 1968, I was very much
aware of her temperament and her sensitivity to color, light,

sound and feelings.   It is this deep sensitivity combined with
a gentle nostalgia that effectively permeates her novels, especially her First Memories.   One critic maintains that
"what is lacking in her novels is theme and a point of view.
After reading them, we are left with a feeling that something has failed to happen, that something impalpable has escaped us, that a more stirring resonance might have
sounded."[26] I could not disagree more.   Matute's precise
strength as a novelist resides in her ability to convey nuances, refined and softened feeling states.   Too many critics feel as Nora does that her writing is "immature, vacil-
lating in its aesthetic orientation, romantically evasive, ingenious in its fictionalized qualities but baroque,"[27] with its
clutter of images.   Nora says her style is

> colored, vibrant, plastic, sensual, rich--to an ex-
> cess, in use of adjectives, abundant in lively
> images--but with images that are superimposed
> and reiterated until they almost cancel out the
> others--in a word, her style is more brilliant
> than it is efficacious--impressionist and expres-
> sionist before simply being expressive. [28]

José María Castellet said of her prose, "it is brilliant as it
is dangerous.   And her danger rides precisely in that very
brilliance, in that fertility for metaphors that cause her to
use and abuse them."[29]

Critics may warn readers of a writer's stylistic excesses, but for me Matute is the only writer up until 1960
who has developed an original writing style and a unique facility to transform her experiences and feelings into an
artistic and subjectively Realistic fictional world.   When
asked about any writers that influenced her career, at first
she said she did not know of anyone and then volunteered
these names--Sartre, Camus, Malraux, Hesse and Knut Hams-
rund.[30] She also felt certain Spanish publishers such as
Lumen, Seix Barral and Destino have furthered her career
since these publishers are particularly against government
censorship.   Also, thanks to the many literary prizes she
has won, she finds there is greater interest in her life and
work, and consequently, she has become prolific as a writer.[31] Matute's consummate skill at avoiding direct questions about her work in no way parallels her unique artistry
as a writer.   Careful not to discuss the war, she feels
Primera memoria is ultimately not a "war novel" but one
about a young girl's adolescence.   Nevertheless, in a chapter

entitled "Children and Adolescents in the War Novel," from
his superb The Spanish Novel of the Civil War, José Luis S.
Ponce de León devoted a large part of his critical study of
Primera memoria to stressing the fact that "Matute was ten
years old in 1936. When she reconstructs the atmosphere
of those days of war, in novels written twenty-five years
later, the authoress shows herself obsessively preoccupied
by one feeling--fear. "32

> Fear is the silence of the islands, in the large
> and shining sea; fear is the silence of the streets
> and the dust and sand lifted by the wind. Fear is
> the port, calm, turbulent, with a slow reflection,
> green and silent under the afternoon heaven, where
> rain shocks and splashes the tiled balustrade with
> dirt. Fear is an enormous funnel, eddying like
> the sea that swallows its ships. I am afraid, and
> Mariné, Jacobo, José Taronjí and Marta are
> afraid; we will always live in fear. 33

Although this excerpt is from Los soldados lloran de noche,
it explains Matute's own nature very dramatically. Fear is
very much a part of her double world of reality--a reality
in which she immerses herself through her writing and one
she also seeks to escape through her memories of youth.

In an interview around the time of writing Los soldados,
she stated,

> the difficult circumstances in which my infancy
> transpired--which I have constantly set down in my
> work--and the deep repercussions that our infan-
> tile existence has on the rest of our lives have
> pushed me to write about these two ages [infancy
> and adolescence]. It has always bothered me,
> why men do not understand each other and I have
> chosen literature as the most proper and effective
> means to communicate my ideas about infancy and
> youth to relate to them my own unshakeable pain
> of living. What I persevere in is to wake up the
> conscience against egoism and injustice, with love
> and charity. 34

If her themes in First Memories are obsessive--Cain
and Abel, the worlds of adulthood and childhood, solitude,
alienation, hypocrisy and loss--Matute attributes this obses-
sion to a troubled and sickly childhood. However in her

maturity, her obsessions (and illnesses) have been replaced
by her art. In Primera memoria, this fictional "autobiography," the colorful images, flowing lyrical passages con-
trasting with violent fragmentary sentences, time convolu-
tions, symbolism, interior monologues, random thoughts
superimposed on the narration have the cinematic effect of
a montage of memory images (as used to expert perfection,
for example, in Alain Resnais' film masterpiece La guerre
est fini). An enormously gifted writer of the nueva oleada,
Matute has great force, great intuition. Like her novels,
she is incomparable, deep, exotic, and fascinating.

     In The Literary World of Ana María Matute, Marga-
ret Jones deals with the author's Weltanschauung in her
Epilogue and provides the best summary of our writer's life
and work in the context of this book:

> Ana María Matute creates [her] literary world
> through the elaboration of a certain number of key
> themes which correspond to an overall vision of
> man's condition, through the use of original charac-
> ter types to express this conception, and through a
> narrative formula which uses special devices to
> convey this vision to the reader. The freshness
> of her approach, her subjective manner of express-
> ing this unique world, and the impression of sin-
> cerity evident in all her writing are responsible for
> the position of prominence she already holds in
> twentieth-century Spanish literature [pp. 120-1].

Janet Díaz, in her Ana María Matute, goes even further:

> While much of the [present] novelistic production
> [in Spain] is mediocre and somewhat downright bad,
> a surprising amount can compare favorably with
> the best written in other periods of Spain's literary
> history. Perhaps a dozen narrators of the postwar
> years deserve to be considered very, very good.
> Few critics would coincide one hundred per cent
> in their selection of the top five or ten, but all
> would include Cela, Delibes and Matute among the
> most significant. If native and foreign Hispanists
> were asked to name the most important female
> novelist of Spain today, the selection of Matute
> would be all but unanimous. ... [A] group of
> critics has begun to suggest Matute as a possible

contender for the Nobel Prize in the not too distant future... [p. 145].

Whatever the verdict may be about her attaining literary greatness in the future, and Matute is probably only
just now entering her most significant period, she surely
now represents the epitome of the true artist, the seeker of
truth, the master story teller, humanity's lover, the nobility
of the soul.

THE WORKS OF ANA MARIA MATUTE

Los Abel. Barcelona: Ed. Destino, 1948.
Fiesta al noreste. Barcelona: Ed. Destino, 1953.
Pequeño teatro. Barcelona: Ed. Destino, 1954.
En esta tierra. Barcelona: Ed. Exito, 1955.
Los hijos muertos. Barcelona: Ed. Planeta, 1958.
Primera memoria. Barcelona: Ed. Destino, 1960.
Los soldados lloran de noche. Barcelona: Ed. Destino,
        1964.
La trampa. Barcelona: Ed. Destino, 1969.
La torre vigia. Barcelona: Ed. Lumen, 1971.

SELECTED STUDIES ON MATUTE

Alborg, J. L. "Los novelistas; A. M. Matute," Indice de
        Artes y Letras, no. 97 (feb. 1957), 30, 38. This
        article appeared in an expanded form in Alborg's
        Hora actual de la novela... (Madrid: Taurus, 1958),
        vol. 1, pp. 181-90.
Cano, J. L. "Los Abel," Insula, no. 38 (15 feb. 1949), 5-
        6; "Pequeño teatro," Ibid., no. 111 (15 marzo 1955),
        6; "Los hijos muertos," Ibid., no. 146 (15 enero
        1959), 8-9; and "Primera memoria," Ibid., no. 161
        (abril 1960), 8-9.
_____. "Una novela de A. M. Matute ['Los soldados
        lloran de noche'], " Insula, no. 214 (sept. 1964), 8-9.
Castellet, J. Ma. "Cuatro novelas con problemas ['Fiesta
        al Noroeste'], " Laye, no. 23 (abril-junio 1953), 119-
        21.
Domingo, José. "Narrative española; Análisis de una so-
        ciedad conformista [A. M. Matute, 'La trampa,' and
        J. Fernández Santos, 'El hombre de los santos'], "
        Insula, no. 274 (sept. 1969), 7.
Duque, A. "Los hijos muertos," Cuadernos Hispanoameri-

canos (Madrid), vol. 42, no. 124 (1960), 148-53.
Hornedo, Rafael Ma. de. "El mundo novelesco de A. M.
    Matute," Razón y Fe (Madrid), no. 162 (1960), 329-
    46.
Izcaray, J.   " 'Los soldados lloran de noche,' de A. Ma.
    Matute," Realidad (Rome), no. 6 (ag. 1965), 109-12.
Martínez Palacio, Javier.   "Una trilogía novelesca de A.
    Ma. Matute ['Los mercaderes']," Insula, no. 219
    (feb. 1965), 1, 6, 7.
Torres Rioseco, A.   "Tres novelistas españolas de hoy [C.
    Laforet, A. M. Matute and E. Quiroga]," Revista
    Hispánica Moderna (New York), no. 31 (1965), 418-
    24.

Chapter 10

DANIEL SUEIRO and LA CRIBA
(The Sieve) (1958)

Daniel Sueiro is one of the most gifted prose writers
of the New Wave generation. Born on December 11, 1931,
in La Coruña, the capital of Galicia where he spent most of
his youth, he studied law at the University of Santiago de
Compostela and later tried his hand at journalism courses
at the University of Madrid. Since changing his residence
to Madrid, he has dedicated himself professionally to journalism and to the arts and is himself a collaborator in the
founding of several new magazines and newspapers.

Sueiro first came to the Spanish reading public's attention when he published a book of short stories entitled
La rebusca y otras desgracias (Garbage and Other Disgraces)
in 1958. This collection was followed the same year by
another group of short stories, La carpa (The Awning), for
which he won the Café Gijón Prize. His next collection,
Los conspiradores (The Conspirators), won the National Prize
of Literature in 1960. On the basis of his prize-winning
short story collections, Sueiro attempted his first novel.
La criba (The Sieve), published in 1961 was one of three
finalists for the Premio Biblioteca Breve (along with Juan
Marsé's Encerrado con sólo un juguete (Locked In with Only
a Toy) and Ana Mairena's Los extraordinarios (The Extraordinary Ones)). No award was given that year, since literary experts could not reach a decision concerning the best
of the three. Sueiro's second novel, Toda la semana (All
Week Long) (1965), was published in Spain and received
minor critical attention. However in the same year, his
third novel, Estos son tus hermanos (These Are Your
Brothers) was, because of its "controversial" themes, published in Mexico. Sueiro also won several literary prizes,
the Premio Juventud among them, for his short story collections.

Turning to the developing art of the motion picture, he collaborated on writing the screenplay for Los golfos (The Hoodlums) in 1958 and Los farsantes (The Jokers) in 1963. He continues to write short stories, newspaper articles, novels and screenplays. His latest novels have been La noche más caliente (The Hottest Night) in 1966, Solo de moto (Only by Motorbike) in 1967, and Corte de corteza (Brain Transplant), published in 1969, won the Premio Alfaguara of 1968 and is considered Sueiro's most ambitious and longest work (it has over four hundred pages). He currently earns his living as a free-lance newspaperman, working for many of Madrid's leading dailies, and is working on a series of essays entitled El arte de matar (The Art of Killing), dealing with the diverse forms of execution for capital punishment throughout the world.

*   *   *

La criba (The Sieve) is a short (186 pages, divided into five chapters), flawed, but fascinating first novel. Its leitmotiv is presented in five lines of prose on the first page: "Each one of these men and each man, in general, is like a sieve: a piece of skin, full of little holes, through which the blood or hope of man pass out uncontrollably. "[1] The action of the novel takes place in Madrid during the early 1960's. The leading character, "he," is unnamed; in fact, the entire novel is written in the third person singular. The protagonist's life and surroundings are unfolded, especially the worlds of journalism, the cafes, the night life of Madrid, the prostitutes and also the people who continually flee from a society that threatens to destroy them. La criba is the story of such a creature, a "poor devil," victimized by his circumstances, moving through the underworld of professional journalists among the "little people" who bring out Madrid's giant dailies each morning.

"He" narrates the daily routines of his life, with neither love nor enthusiasm for life. His wife is pregnant, ready to give birth at any moment. The novel deals with five days within their lives before the "expected" event. However "he" cannot feel love for her or excitement about his impending fatherhood because his life is one of continual tedium, humiliation and desperation. His working day is usually spent at the office. (He works for a firm, Los Milliones, that runs daily lotteries and other contests.) In the evening, he is one of the editors of a new literary magazine,

symbolically and ideally entitled <u>Lauro</u> (<u>Laurel</u>). He needs
these jobs and any other part-time work he can obtain because his wife currently cannot contribute to the family's in-
come.

        We follow "him" through his wanderings around Ma-
drid, between jobs, his local stops at several cafes, dating
and drinking often with his office pals--Rojas, Pons, Prieto,
Calvo, Ignacio, Torrebella, et al. "He" describes his meanderings in and out of a local movie house or along the
streets of Madrid without any particular direction. His wife
has been moved to a private lying-in hospital while they both
await the birth of their baby. "She" is bored, tired, depressed, desperately wanting to give birth. During the hours
he is not with her, "he" visits his girlfriend Carmen, a
prostitute with whom he makes love without really loving.
One of the best passages in the novel occurs in Chapter Two
when "he" accidentally discovers Carmen's diary, which re-
cords her activities with her many lovers (or clientele) and
her daily earnings over the months of December and January.
The narration here uncovers "his" realization that he is referred to as "he": "Es bueno pero nunca tiene dinero. Se
marchó por la noche y ya no salí" (p. 82). (He's a good
lover but he never has any money. He left during the night
and I didn't go out on to the streets.) "El era él. "

        Very little action occurs in the novel. We await the
birth of "his" baby and occasionally listen to the conversations of Sueiro's "little people," protesting about this matter
or that one. There is some humor, for example, when a
new business opens in the building and all the employees are
asked to wear coats and ties but become enraged because
they are not invited to the banquet and protest their exclusion vociferously. There is an undercurrent of protest and
apathy throughout the entire novel. In another chapter, the
employees of the magazine Lauro, wanting to relieve their
frustrations, begin to throw papers, books, folios and pamph-
lets at each other. Another violent incident occurs after the
birth of "his" baby boy (who incidentally is extremely sickly)
when a group of office workers, out on the town, in an "al-
coholic" orgy of gin and vermouth, drink up money saved
for an office mate's recovery from tuberculosis as well as
a flask of "mother's milk" that "he" has just bought from a
local clinic to speed his child's good health. (We have
viewed him buying the flask of milk daily at a hospital dis-
pensary and bringing it to the hospital, where his depressed
wife and sickly son upset him emotionally.)

In the violent delirium of his drunkenness, he fore-
goes his daily preoccupations and responsibilities. The condition of his child worsens; the baby is baptized and then
peacefully dies. He needs some 5000 pesetas to pay the ex-
penses at the clinic and goes to his prostitute-lover-friend
Carmen for the funds. He confesses to her, "I don't have
any friends, nor in truth any kind of job.... There are
people who have money, places where they count bills by
the hundreds ... but I cannot go to them in search of help;
I cannot ask them for anything" (p. 179). After the death
of his son, a strange transference of anxiety takes place.
His wife had been waiting, anxious for nine months with her
pregnancy. Now he becomes disgusted, weary and equally
anxious.

> So that time, those days, had passed, and now it
> was no longer she that was counting and helpless,
> predisposed to whatever occurred in one moment or
> another or in any other instant. That had already
> happened, finally. And he knew that in the same
> moment, the same situation resided in him--the
> counting, the helplessness and the predisposition
> to any and all things that would occur in one mo-
> ment, or another or in any instant or perhaps
> never. One couldn't do anything. Nothing was
> possible any longer. To be already, so alone, to
> permit what occurred or what ought to have oc-
> curred. All the faces that he encountered along
> the way. All the people, all the things were con-
> demned like him, to live out, beyond all counts
> and cares, the nine and nine thousand months of
> anxiety and boredom and to wait for the enlighten-
> ment or death in one instant or another. Without
> intervening, it's clear. [Life goes on] desperately,
> without effort [pp. 185-6].

The novel ends with this pessimistic view after the death of
his child, and life goes on for him, his wife and the greater
population of Madrid.

*   *   *

La criba is more than a novel of violence and protest. It shows how "capitalistic interests with the ingenious
passion of the poor for the lottery put into movement a gigantic bureaucratic machine for the profit of a few."[2] An-

other outstanding feature of the novel is the description of
the daily humiliations of "little people" caught in office routines, their frustrations, their periodic outbursts, their
rage, their fear of the "bosses" who exercise enormous
power over their lives. Particularly memorable and tragically funny is a scene between an insipid radio broadcaster
and an equally silly typesetter when one complains to the
other about certain persons who drop the "p" in "September"
and other similar words.

If one quality persists throughout the entire novel, it
is the profoundly pathetic nature of the human condition expressed in diaphanous fashion, portrayed in powerful, taut,
sober, colorless prose without any elaborations or any pretentious literary artifice or meaning. Perhaps the films of
Ernnano Olmi, The Sound of Trumpets or The Fiancées, or
King Vidor's The Crowd best demonstrate the pathetic atmosphere Sueiro has so accurately captured in his novels. La
criba's protagonist is like so many men,

> minor employees without dignity or character, ser-
> vile or venal newspapermen. ... He is a married
> man without love, a lover without passion, an in-
> different father, a bureaucrat and newspaperman
> out of necessity, a man emptied by a slow, pas-
> sive desperation who sums up all the afflictions and
> degradations of the world which surrounds him. 3

While reading La criba, one feels the basic sterility
of the society in which the protagonist moves. Sobejano
feels the author is trying to demonstrate

> demoralization under the heavy abuse of an ill-
> fated social, political and economic order. Only
> the protagonist, victim of a tearing, indecipherable
> and useless pain seems to endure the major des-
> peration. ... Even with major means, these men
> would not let the wheat of their souls wander
> about the threshing floor across the sieve of time,
> but they would know how to pick themselves up and
> nourish themselves with it. 4

Besides an obvious "grayness" of prose, the novel is also
permeated by an intense feeling of sadness as well as an
implicit spirit of criticism in the mode of the social Realist
novel. It is possible to say Daniel Sueiro suggests critical
atttitudes when he describes the making of careers, corrup-

tion in business, prostitution of political figures and writers, and censorship in the field of journalism. But like other novelists, especially Sánchez Ferlosio and Goytisolo-Gay, Sueiro prefers to give us a realistic vision of his "little world," presenting an abundance of hastily sketched characters revealed through short dialogues that present in functional language the petty concerns of their daily world.

The outstanding quality of style of La criba is its persistent Realism, its unyielding revelation of the thoughts of the narrator, "his" continual reflections. Unfortunately we never are able to conjure a physical portrait of the protagonist. At times, the events (usually a constant interplay between days at the office and afternoons in the café) are not adequately integrated into the narrative and detract from a systematic, generalized development of the protagonist and his thoughts.[5] At other times, with Sueiro's concept of Realism, we lose the novel's continuity because the protagonist lacks a name. Since the narration is conducted in the third person singular, it is difficult to tell when actions are performed by characters other than the protagonist. Gil Casado feels that "this kind of ambiguity causes confusions" and "although the reality and desperation of the main character are easily understood, the manner in which the novel is written causes the narrative to degenerate."[6] Occasionally there are confusions of time (between past and present) and there is a lack of coherence in the prose. Yet in spite of these defects, La criba reads surprisingly well, if a bit monotonous at times. It proceeds convincingly and movingly to its predictable conclusion.

La criba may have certain faults as a first novel, but it is assuredly a realistic social novel describing a petty milieu of Madrid. Its realistic style consists of the alternation of the interior monologue of the "narrator" (who also describes all the physical settings) with the dialogues between the protagonist and his acquaintances. Corrales Egea feels Sueiro's style represents a combination of the Realism of Spanish authors circa 1950 but because of his insistence on the use of dialogue as an exponent of reality (and without abusing its usage), he has created the "novelized dialogue."[7] Sueiro also excels in the use of colloquialisms, slang and popular expressions of Madrid (but not to any excess) which give the novel a feeling of vigor, reality and earthiness. For example, when the narrator goes into a café and meets a friend of his, they talk about their respective offices in somewhat humorous fashion:

--What do you say, bandido [you thug]?, exclaimed
Sánchez laughingly.

--How goes it with you, canalla [you bastard],
he answered joyfully.

. . .

--And that imbecile from Fueyo. Is he with you?

--Yes, I have him pasting telegrams. And that
cretin of a boss, is he still there, 'floating?'

--Like a 'globe,' laughed Sánchez, going with
the wind [p. 68].

One of the best critiques of Sueiro's novel is found in
Rafael Bosch's The Spanish Novel in the 20th Century in
which Bosch calls La criba "one of the master works of the
1960's. " He relates Sueiro's pessimism to the novels of
Kafka and the French Existentialist, Albert Camus. Although one may argue with Bosch's comparisons, he does hit
the mark with the following: "He is a great realistic observer ... he is very Spanish and much more lively than
his creations. His novel is full of vital pulse and besides
an immediate view of life, he gathers a great number of
simple visions but presents them with great subtlety....
His language contains poetic and symbolic force.... "8

As we leaf through Sueiro's novel, we find shafts of
brilliance in perception of the human condition and writing.
Outstanding is Sueiro's attack on the world of business in
the very first chapter:

Business is built on the stupidity of people, and
also on their desire for wealth, that is to say, on
their poverty, on their misery, on their ignorance.
Big business doesn't produce anything for the
country, but it makes one or two people rich, it
gives work to five hundred and entertains five
million people and at the same time, it draws and
quarters them [p. 24].

There are spurts of anti-Americanism:

She showed him her place in the magazine and
said happily:

--Look, one of them is writing a letter of protest about the bullfights.

> He had no intention of writing, although he
> smiled also.
>
> --They published here a report about a bullfight
> and one guy in <u>Wisconsin</u> became furious, she con-
> tinued.   'It's possible that in a civilized country,
> they write about similar barbarous acts,' she read.
> Those people are crazy [p. 11].

Sueiro's description of the personnel who share "his" office
is equally sober, biting and direct:

> Marcial, the draftsman, and the counters, two
> young men, continued doing their jobs, very seri-
> ously, without wanting to find out about anything
> on a par with typists ... that is to say, the typist,
> Miss Raquel, efficient, voluminous and mature,
> without humor, 'indispensable' for being virtuous--
> and the simplistic typist Anita, somewhere between
> being illiterate and foolish--all of them, very young
> and somewhat whorey [pp. 22-3].

Equally sincere and heart rending is Sueiro's description of
the "little people," with their desires and hopes unfulfilled:

> --Don't let the big guys beat me, spit on me,
> insult me, asked Penedo at the beginning of his
> career in journalism.
>
> --Let them receive me amicably and give me
> their hand.   Let them invite me for a drink and
> present me to their wives, asked Penedo.   There
> isn't anything easier for them to do... [p. 45].

The wealthy people in Sueiro's novel are characterized as
vultures; the lower classes are viewed as pathetic, helpless
creatures:

> --I'm sick, you hear?   I have tuberculosis.
> Tuberculosis!
>
> --Okay, okay, but don't get disgusted, Rojas
> cried [p. 54].

Calvo is sick at heart because of his illness and yet his co-
workers can only offer him empty sympathies.   Other workers show their disgust and helplessness before their bosses:

> --There is money to throw away on this entire
> crummy edition because of an error in an article
> that this or that imbecilic writer made about some-
> thing not politic--some stupidity of the kind they
> believe the life of the country and the world de-
> pends on. Imbeciles. For that, there is always
> money. High politics! But I have worked--he
> stretched over the administrator's desk--and today
> begins a new month and I want to get paid for my
> last month's work, do you hear me? [pp. 113-4].

The "little people" are also portrayed as poor, self-righteous,
prone to crass stupidities:

> --... a conspiracy--, he spoke slowly like a
> professor--against the 'p' of September, that is
> going to bring grave consequences. ... Certain
> wise guys on this newspaper have declared war
> against the 'p' of September, séptimo, septentrio-
> nal and septingentésimo, etc., etc., and I let them
> do it, but they disgust me and I have to decide
> what to do about it... [p. 129].

This inane discussion about the "p" continues, counterpointed
by the daily life-death struggle of all workers, living to the
fullest, raising families, bearing children. When "he" thinks
about his own future son or daughter, he confides to himself,
"To have a son is a sad thing, although it may be a handsome well-born son" (p. 150).

The last chapter of Sueiro's novel contains the harrowing birth scene and the death of "his" newborn son. The
protagonist is curiously unmoved, uninvolved. Instead of his
wife's becoming the center of his attention, his thoughts are
curiously directed inward. When his son is born, he receives congratulations with peripheral attention. He is not
a happy man. Faced with the responsibilities of providing
special milk for his son every day, he ducks into a local
cafe one day in a debauched state and gives over the flask
of milk to one of his drunken office pals. The baby dies,
his wife is grief-stricken, ailing, depressed, and "he" is
left with himself.

*   *   *

La criba is a short novel of minor pretensions. Its
"Realism" manifests itself in the author's use of the third

person to delve into the consciousness of the narrator-protagonist as well as a crisp, descriptive prose style that helps the
reader "see" what he sees throughout the narrative. What makes
the novel representative of the New Wave is Sueiro's un-
daunted and singular series of reflections of his protagonist
carried relentlessly through the novel in the tradition of
Elena Quiroga's and Fernández Santos' best introspective
novels. Sueiro's minute examination of the daily world, its
major and minor realities, the protagonist's own mental
angst, the author's "strange portrait of the world, in which
current things and daily miseries are collected in minuscule
relief which makes them stand out like crushing and agoniz-
ing vulgarities in a life full of corruption,"9 is Sueiro's
forte.

        La criba is full of vitality, and like its symbol, the
life described is rushing through the porous skin of daily
existence. Sueiro's words show little or no hope for his
hombre cualquiera--"everyman," or "anyman." However,
he provides his reading public with an extraordinarily stylistically unified, emotionally moving, serious, and sober first
novel, displaying a major talent, replete with the minor
flaws and stylistic ambiguities so typical of a first novel.
Despite its pessimism, La criba redeems itself stylistically
with its occasional poetic prose passages. Especially fine
are Sueiro's lyrical descriptions, especially the ones that
show the "little people" in their individual worlds, victimized,
frustrated, battling against themselves and each other to survive the cruel and corrupt daily fortunes they have been dealt.

THE WORKS OF DANIEL SUEIRO

La rebusca y otras desgracias [stories]. Barcelona: Ed.
        Rocas, 1958.
La Carpa [stories]. Barcelona: Ed. Rocas, 1958.
Los conspiradores [stories]. Madrid: Ed. Taurus, 1960.
La criba. Barcelona: Ed. Seix Barral, 1961.
Toda la semana. Barcelona: Ed. Rocas, 1965.
Estos son tus hermanos. Mexico: Ed. Era, 1965.
La noche más caliente. Barcelona: Ed. Plaza y Janés,
        1966.
Solo de moto. Barcelona: Ed. Alfaguara, 1967.
Corte de corteza. Madrid: Ed. Alfaguara, 1969.

SELECTED STUDIES ON SUEIRO

C[ela] T[rulock], J[orge]. " 'La criba,' de Daniel Sueiro,"
    Cuadernos Hispanoamericanos, no. 139 (julio 1961),
    160-2.
Doménech, Ricardo. "La primera novela de Daniel Sueiro,"
    Insula, nos. 176-177 (julio-ag. 1961), 8.
Domingo, José. "Dos novelistas españoles: Elena Quiroga
    y Daniel Sueiro," Insula, no. 232 (marzo 1966), 3.
_____. "Narrativa española; Anticipación y actualidad en
    una novela de Daniel Sueiro," Insula, no. 270 (mayo
    1969), 7.
Marra-López, José R. " 'La criba,' de Daniel Sueiro,"
    Cuadernos del Congreso por la Libertad de la Cultura,
    no. 58 (marzo 1962), 91.
Núñez, Antonio. "Encuentro con Daniel Sueiro," Insula, no.
    235 (junio 1966), 4.
_____. "Sueiro, Daniel: 'Solo de moto'," Insula, no.
    247 (junio 1967), 9.
S(aña) H. "Corte de corteza," Indice de Artes y Letras,
    no. 245 (15 abril 1969), 40.
_____. "La noche más caliente," Indice de Artes y
    Letras, no. 209 (1966), 43-4.

Chapter 11

JUAN GARCIA HORTELANO and TORMENTA DE VERANO
(Summer Storm) (1962)

Juan García Hortelano was born in Madrid on Febru-
ary 14, 1928, but spent much of his youth in Cuenca, a
small, quiet city southeast of Madrid. He returned to the
capital and received a degree in law at the University of
Madrid. Although he once opposed working, upon finishing
his degree, as a civil servant in the Ministery of Public
Works, he continues to do so presently in addition to his
career as a novelist. He is a family man, married with
several children, and resides in a modern apartment building in one of Madrid's wealthier suburbs. Although he says
he never re-reads anything he has written, he chose Nuevas
amistades (New Friendships) (1961), his first novel, as the
fictional work he likes best, since it also won the Premio
Biblioteca Breve the year it was published. [1] G. Hortelano
had previously written several novels, as yet unpublished,
before Nuevas amistades catapulted him to fame.

His second novel, Tormenta de verano (Summer
Storm) was considered even more of an accomplishment since
with its publication in 1962 he won the celebrated and coveted
Formentor Prize. This literary prize was established early
in 1960 by six publishers from different nations and carried
with it a cash prize of $10,000. Winning it assured G.
Hortelano of an instantaneous international best seller, and
it encouraged as well international interest in new fiction by
young writers, since winning novels would be published simultaneously in thirteen countries and would afford their authors some measure of financial security. Except for a
book of short stories entitled Gente de Madrid (People from
Madrid) (1967), which contains a series of five fictional episodes that neither add to nor detract from Hortelano's stature as a novelist, [2] and a new novel, El gran momento de

Mary Tribune (The Great Moment of Mary Tribune), which
according to Spain's literary critics, offers little new perspective about the author's literary direction and career,[3]
G. Hortelano has not lived up to the literary promise of his
1962 novel and the Formentor Prize.

Nevertheless, his second novel, Tormenta de verano,
is worthy of study since it accurately reflects the kind of
writing occurring in Spain in the early sixties, the social
mores of Spaniards and tourists on the Costa Brava, the
style of neo-objectivism (another off-shoot of social Realism),
and the general international cultural and psychological ambience so accurately captured in the films of that period--
like Federico Fellini's La dolce vita or Michelangelo Antoni-
oni's L'avventura or La notte. It is too bad that, like G.
Hortelano's novel, none of these films has been able to stand
the test of time and now appear, with their ego-oriented
ennui, almost banal, no matter the artistry with which they
were originally conceived.

Tormenta de verano continues the trend begun by Ana
María Matute of narration in the first person, or subjective
Realism.   However the aim of Matute and other New Wave
novelists, including the French practitioners of the nouveau
roman, is to insure intellectual enjoyment in the process of
reading the novel.   This is not the case with G. Hortelano's
Tormenta de verano.   After completing its 323 pages, divided into thirty-four chapters, one comes away with a sensation of despair, boredom, even disgust.   (Perhaps this
was the author's intention--to have his readers experience
the same vacuousness his characters live through, by the
medium of an indictment of affluent, vacationing Spaniards
circa 1960.)   Lacking the "artistic" skill of a work by such
as Matute or Cela, nevertheless Tormenta deserves to be
read since it is certainly the best of the more sensational
best-sellers in vogue at the time.   Some literary critics
have drawn parallels between Tormenta and J. B. Priestly's
An Inspector Calls,[4] Alain Robbe-Grillet's The Voyeur,[5]
and Juan Goytisolo's The Island[6] in plot and social significance.   Hortelano's plot also resembles a real-life mystery
reminiscent of the notorious Montesi case in Italy, where a
nude body of a young woman was washed up on an exclusive
beach resort and attempts were made to identify her and
solve her "murder."

The action of Tormenta de verano is set in Velas
Blancas, an exclusive Spanish beach resort on the Costa

Brava during the summer of 1960. Vacationing there are
(1) Javier, the novel's narrator and leading character, a
forty-ish millionaire, dashing, handsome, forceful, whose
dubious fortune has built this summer colony almost as an
escape from reality; (2) his wife Dora, a cold, puritanical
and dispassionate woman, interested more in the superficialities of living, the petit-bourgeoise personified; (3) Andrés,
Javier's cousin, friend, business partner and neighbor at
Velas Blancas; (4) Elena, Andrés' wife and Javier's long-
time mistress; (5) Angus (short for Angustia), a prostitute
in love with Javier and whom he desires more than either
his wife or mistress, a symbol of his freedom from a
world of deception and moral cowardice; (6) Claudette and
Santiago, Emilio and Asun, Javier's married neighbors, intelligent and affluent socialite friends of Javier and Dora;
(7) Javier's children, Enrique and Dorita; and (8) Andrés'
son Joaquín.

On one beautiful sunny summer morning, a nude female body is discovered on the beach by a group of children
from the summer colony, notably Enrique, Dorita and Joaquín among them. This incident and the identity of the unknown victim soon begins to haunt the imagination of the
entire beach colony. The sheltered but undisciplined children who discover the body have encountered for the first
time the naked facts of life and death; the local townspeople
and fisherman seek desperately to convince themselves that
this is just another shameful crime perpetrated against their
Spain by depraved foreign vacationers in the tent camp on
the outskirts of the colony. Javier himself is compulsively
led to untangle the mystery and for the first time since the
end of the Civil War, he confronts the pointless absurdity
of the life he leads. On several occasions, Javier sees
the cadaver and becomes intrigued with the problem of her
identity. Even his children and Andrés' son, Joaquín, begin to behave strangely. After avoiding their parents, one
day Joaquín is found tied to a tree because he did not want
to reveal the whereabouts of the "treasure" the children had
found on the beach. Another neighbor, Emilio, argues vio-
lently with Javier for having revealed to his son the facts
of life about "female anatomy."

The weather begins to change in Velas Blancas; it becomes rainy; storms brew emotionally within Javier. He is
sick of the vacuous and tedious life he lives with his wife
and mistress. In a local bar, he meets a prostitute from
Madrid. His sensual and consuming affair with her forces

him to probe his own conscience and think about giving up
his affluent life built upon hypocrisy and idleness.   To seek
some new thing, to find purpose in his own life are his
goals.   The police arrest four young fishermen from a
neighboring town.   Javier tries to help them, but the inspector, Don Julio, his neighbors, the townspeople and even
the arrested fishermen themselves cannot understand Javier's
reasons or gratuitous act in trying to save them.

Because Angus realizes the "nobility" of Javier's
thoughts and actions and truly understands his motives to
free himself from all deception, they begin to live together.
But their union is short-lived.   A few days later, a servant
of Javier's brings word that the police inspector wants to
interrogate his children.   Returning home quickly, Emilio
and Javier decide to go to Barcelona, where they succeed
in "pulling strings" to cancel the inspector's interview.
Nevertheless, the inspector calls once again, appealing to
Javier to uncover the truth behind the death of the unidentified "foreign" woman.   The inspector has already discovered
the woman was a French prostitute named Margot or Maruja
who died of a heart attack after imbibing excessive amounts
of alcohol accompanied by three young Spaniards on a sail-
boat.   The three men, frightened by her death, removed her
body from the boat and left her on the beach fully dressed.

Because of this discrepancy in testimony, Javier is
forced to call his children as well as the sons of Andrés
and Emilio to the police inspector's interview.   Joaquín,
Andrés' son, finally admits to removing the woman's
clothes, taking her purse and hiding these things in his
mother's travelling bag.   The mystery is resolved and "the
storm" passes for everyone.   Javier realizes he cannot live
with Angus and renews his affair with Elena.   The people
of Velas Blancas return to their routine patterns of living.
Nothing much has happened in the novel, but, perhaps, for
one final note of deliberate irony: everyone and no one was
responsible for Margo's death, which occurred during a
week-end orgy on the pleasure boat of three wealthy young
Spaniards.

Javier thinks or says very little of worth.   He merely reacts to conversations and thoughts.   However at one
point, he confronts his own crise de conscience when he
answers Elena in a conversation about renewing their affair:

> [I'm] sick to death--you don't know how sick.
> Sick, tired, exhausted, shattered, bored to death.
> Of hearing the same nonsense, inventing the same
> cock-and-bull stories, sick of your husband ...
> even of Claudette who knows the whole thing's a
> lie and puts up with it. I won't put up with it.
> All my life I've got what I wanted, and now I'm
> not going to do without what I want. The last
> twenty years weren't bad. We fought the war, we
> won and we started quadrupling the money our
> families had before the war. But that's enough.
> Quadrupling money, having children, going to
> dinners and parties, acquiring mistresses and put-
> ting up with fools to wangle import licenses and
> contracts at eighty per cent--I've lost sight of
> other things. 7

Tormenta de verano is filled with Javier's somewhat banal
thoughts, which develop in parallel fashion with the "symbolic" oncoming storm.

    Javier is overwhelmed; he desperately wants to extri-
cate himself from the lies, the deceit, the falseness, the
social situation developing around the world of Velas Blancas, but he cannot find a solution. Pablo Gil Casado feels
these people "cannot understand or adjust to the reality of
a social revolution and consequently, their psychological
mechanisms induce them to defend themselves, ignoring the
outside world and what happens in it which is really what
disturbs them, confessing themselves that 'nothing ever happens'. "8   Gil Casado pictures the author's stance as far
away from the narrative (G. Hortelano himself said he could
not identify with Javier9) and completely objective, "exposing
what happens inside this type of society, letting the characters do and say what they like so that the reader may de-
duce [their lives and problems] for themselves. "10 In this
manner, G. Hortelano is very much a practitioner of objective realism in the same fashion as Sánchez Ferlosio but
with one major difference. In El Jarama, we never enter
the conscience of any single character, while in Tormenta
we feel Javier's rage, boredom, and disgust because of the
author's constant reversion to interior monologue alternating
with exterior description and dialogue. Gil Casado maintains that Javier "is the only one who presents a total reality, viewed inside and outside, through what he does, says,
feels, and thinks and also by what people say about and do
with him.... "11

     The brand of Realism attributed to Juan García Horte-
lano has been categorized by most literary critics in Spain
as "objective." Rafael Bosch said this novel suffered from
"the defects of an objectivist and superficial style [although]
the novel's social intentions are good."[12] When I interviewed the author in 1968, he said he belonged to the New
Wave by virtue of his age and that the Spanish novel, as
such, is in a state of major overhauling.[13] Admitting the
influence of the new French novels and their objectivist
forms, G. Hortelano had this to say about Realism: "I believe Spanish reality, through the richness of themes it offers, facilitates the task of the narrator and that merely
choosing [to write realism] already establishes a problem....
In a culturally impoverished milieu, the novelist must force
himself before all else to be faithful to the reality in which
he lives."[14]

     G. Hortelano has interested himself primarily in the
social realist novel and Tormenta is his most important
work from the point of view of style and artistic technique.
"It is a geometric work, minutely constructed, coldly objective, almost frigid in its intensity."[15] Corrales Egea believes Tormenta was written with a carefully balanced
rhythm, slow and repetitive--a basic element that helps to
create a suffocating climate of tedium and triviality. Just
as in El Jarama,

          the conclusion of this work is also pessimistic.
          We find ourselves stagnating inside a society made
          up of people surrounded by material benefits whose
          only interest is enjoyment from the present, people
          who are voluntarily cut off from the rest of so-
          ciety, disinterested, indifferent to all that they
          cannot enjoy ephemerally, their only preoccupation
          being the current moment.[16]

Corrales Egea draws a parallel between the writing style of
Tormenta de verano and Alain Resnais' famous French language film classic, Last Year at Marienbad, declaring that
G. Hortelano's novel is allied with the neo-realist movement
in cinema simply because of the novel's style.[17] The novel
is filled with dialogue, sometimes logical, other times disconnected. Conversations may take place in one locale,
then shift to another suddenly because similar words trigger
responses in different areas of the mind of the narrator
which cause shifts in his own physical and mental setting,
similar to those used cinematically by Resnais with his

famous flashback and flash-forward techniques of Marienbad
and La guerre est fini.

        Pablo Gil Casado, in his excellent book, The Spanish
Social Novel, presents a long but detailed analysis of G.
Hortelano's innovative style which I will attempt to summa-
rize briefly here.   He believes Tormenta de verano concentrates more on development of characters than physical description of protagonists, a tendency contrary to most of the
New Wave writers of the period.   He feels G. Hortelano's
insistence on penetrating the state of mind of his protagonist
is very revealing, but it is his technique of using dialogue
combined with interior monologue that gives the novel its
Realist impact. [18]

        Gil Casado makes much of the fact that certain dia-
logues are incoherent and disconnected; speakers are not
identified; there are lapses in continuity, and unnecessary
transitions.   He selects two important stylistic devices that
G. Hortelano uses throughout the course of the novel to give
it its "Realist" tone: la intromisión, or insertions or interruptions of dialogues by others talking, destroying the continuity of a speech or a series of thoughts, and el supuesto,
or the interpolation or interference of assumptions or hy-
potheses by one or more persons that change the direction
of the dialogue and disorient the reader from the essential
purpose of what is being said.   These two stylistic devices
tend to interrupt the normal flow of what is said or described
and give the novel a "supposed" reality. [19]

        Tormenta is also permeated by descriptions of the
weather and changes in atmosphere which affect the emotional
states of the characters.   Gil Casado documents the "sensual" nature of the author and shows how his characters are
affected by warmth, light, humidity, noises, smells, silence,
tastes, etc. [20]   Although G. Hortelano may have the sensibility of a voluptuary, he is equally adept at creating certain
anti-feelings--boredom, tedium, unwillingness and torpor,
which affect readers in the same fashion as his protagonists.

        Tormenta is a disturbing novel and we must assume
G. Hortelano's intention is not just to satirize the society of
Velas Blancas but condemn it as well although, like many
New Wave writers of the period, G. Hortelano offers little
hope and no solutions to his protagonist's problems.   With
all of the "intended" Realism in which the novel was conceived, certain incidents as well as characters do not ring

true in the narrative. The plot itself is rather dated and
prosaic, and ridden with clichés; it is similar to so many
others in lesser quality detective fiction. Its strength, however, is in its detailed recreation of and implicit condemnation of the Spanish bourgeois life and society. One critic
felt it is not enough just to use the convention of the bourgeoisie to denounce an entire class but to condemn it by virtue of finding a possible solution, which is certainly not
common for novelists of the period.

The problem with G. Hortelano's characters, sketched
somewhat conventionally decadent as they are, is they easily
pass off their worries without reacting. 21 Perhaps this is
because their "problems" are not of great value. In fact,
after finishing the novel, one feels, despite all its qualities
of new Realism, objectivism and sober style, that Tormenta
de verano really has only a very superficial view of the
world it describes and satirizes. G. Hortelano said of his
work and of himself that "to affirm, by means of [my] own
novels, that society is susceptible to variation and to make
it better constitutes [for me] the most intimate root of my
job. " "If, " G. Hortelano has said, quoting Georg Lukács,
'Realism equals the essence of reality that is hidden beneath
the surface,' ... I am not acquainted with any road other
than Realism that the youthful literature of a country may be
able to take, in which the surface of society is--when it is
not a flagstone of granite--an opaque glass, of blind and deceptive reflections. "22 G. Hortelano sees himself as a social critic:

> the novel will cooperate in the task of making so-
> ciety more educated and free. The task of liberty
> and democracy ought not to be hoped for in the
> long years when evidence of the influences of liter-
> ature is delayed. First the writer has to fulfill
> his strictest obligation: true testimony--in its
> several forms--of the society and of the men of
> its time. 23

G. Hortelano also believes the social novel he writes "may
not have found its own esthetic expression and even serves,
in certain measure, as heresy of the great 'traditional
Realism' and it is even possible the novelists may not have
yet been born capable [of portraying society] and in an authentic form of expresssion. "24

We may consider these words of G. Hortelano as a defense of Tormenta and its superficialities. Perhaps the author also lacked the courage necessary to plumb the depths of his world and face the consequences in a society where self-censorship is an imperative for a writer to survive (in the early 1960's as well as now). G. Hortelano remarked about his own fears of censorship and felt most writers of the New Wave in the early 1960's were trying to copy French models since very little stylistically was happening in the Spanish novel. "This [1968] is a time for major reflection since absolutely nothing is happening in our literary world. Spanish literature is currently being improvised, not seriously written."[25] Within this void, G. Hortelano felt his Tormenta de verano, conceived with a certain amount of art, was, despite limited critical praise, one of the best literary efforts of the period.

Gonzalo Sobejano feels, based on style alone, besides the use of symbolic imagery and vigorous objectivism, the outstanding skill in reproducing characters by means of conversations and the "almost Flaubertian impassivity with which [the author] so faithfully reveals the idiosyncrasies of a group shut off in its own descent towards moral idiocy,"[26] that Tormenta de verano ought to be considered an enormously successful work in the realm of "critical-realism." Taking Flaubert's own words,

> [there] was no longer the novel as it had been written by the very greatest, a novel where you were always somewhat aware of the author and his imagination, a novel capable of being classified as tragic, sentimental, passionate, or homely, a novel where the writer's intentions, opinions, and ways of thinking show themselves. It was life itself making an appearance.... [27]

I believe we must re-evaluate Sobejano's words about Tormenta de verano and consider them carefully. For me, Tormenta is not the glowing success Sobejano and a few other critics would make of it.[28] It is merely a capably written novel, now stylistically dated but appropriate for its time, faithfully reproducing the turmoil of Spanish society on the Costa Brava during the 1960's, a fictional work with few grandiose intentions or inventions, but with objectivist stylistic values that, at times, pretend to do more than many literary critics say.

The novel achieves little more than a minor if artistically drawn view of Spanish life, and is certainly less
worthy of renown than the work of G. Hortelano's contemporaries who have written on similar themes, such as Juan
Goytisolo, Ana María Matute, and Juan Marsé. Tormenta
de verano should be read because it does occupy a prime
place in the stylistic transitions taking place within the
Spanish novel genre since 1950 and it is also a good (not
great) example of the author's unflinching use of a new kind
of objective realism.

THE WORKS OF J. G. HORTELANO

Nuevas amistades. Barcelona: Seix Barral, 1959.
Tormenta de verano. Barcelona: Seix Barral, 1961.
Gente de Madrid [stories]. Barcelona: Seix Barral, 1967.
El gran momento de Mary Tribune. Barcelona: Barral Edi-
        tores, 1972.

SELECTED STUDIES ON HORTELANO

Díaz, M. "J. García Hortelano: 'Nuevas amistades',"
        Nuestras Ideas, no. 8 (1960), 102-3.
Domingo, J. "J. García Hortelano: 'Gente de Madrid',"
        Insula, no. 253 (dic. 1967), 5.
Fernández Santos, F. " 'Nuevas amistades,' novela de Juan
        García Hortelano," Cuadernos del Congreso por la
        Libertad de la Cultura, no. 41 (marzo-abril 1960),
Marra-López, José R. "En torno a 'Nuevas amistades',"
        Insula, no. 158 (enero 1962), 20.
_____. "Tormenta de verano," Insula, no. 187 (junio
        1962), 4.
Yracha, Luis. "Intención en la última novela de García
        Hortelano," Papeles de Sons Armadans, vol. 52,
        no. 155 (feb. 1969), 195-200.

Chapter 12

LUIS MARTIN-SANTOS and TIEMPO DE SILENCIO
(Time of Silence) (1962)

Luis Martín-Santos died tragically in an automobile
accident on January 21, 1964, at the age of forty. His career as an author was cut short dramatically. The son of
Spaniards living in Morocco, M.-Santos was born there in
1924 but lived most of his life in San Sebastián, where he
died. A brilliant student, he finished a degree in medicine
at the University of Salamanca in the early 1940's and received a doctorate in psychiatry from the University of Madrid in 1947. From 1951 until the time of his premature
death, he was director of the Psychiatric Sanatorium of San
Sebastián.

Before embarking on a literary career in which he
showed early interest (at the age of nineteen, in fact,) M.-
Santos published (with Seix Barral) one work in 1955 en-
titled Dilthey, Jaspers and the Comprehension of the Mentally
Ill, and in 1964, Liberty, Temporality and Transference in
Existential Psychoanalysis was brought out posthumously by
Seix Barral. Another book to appear posthumously was a
selection of essays entitled Apologues and Other Unedited
Prose Compositions, arranged and edited by the eminent
writer and literary critic Salvador Clotas, once again for
Seix Barral. These three works deal principally with medical problems, psychiatry and philosophy. It is not frivolous
to expect then that this first novel, Tiempo de silencio
(Time of Silence), would draw upon the experiences of his
medical career as well as his extraordinary intellect. But
before we deal with Tiempo de silencio, it is interesting to
note that M.-Santos did publish a book of poems entitled
Cañas gris (Gray Hair) and also received a literary prize
from the newspaper Triunfo for his short story, "Tauro-
maquía" ("Bullfighting"). Time of Silence, his only novel,

was part of a projected trilogy, but because of the author's
untimely death, we will probably never see a posthumous
edition of the long awaited and unfinished manuscript of
Tiempo de destrucción (Time of Destruction) or any kind of
reconstructed manuscript based upon the author's words.
We will have to content ourselves then, with his only published novel, Tiempo de silencio, which won no publishing
awards in 1962 but has become an acknowledged "classic"
of its time and a highly esteemed novel by the New Wave,
renowned for its exciting depiction of character and innovative treatment of reality.

                          *   *   *

        The novel begins in Madrid, circa 1945. Pedro is a
scholarship student working at a research institute in the
heart of the city where he is studying the growth of cancer
in rats.   Unable to finish his experiments because he has
run out of specimens, his laboratory assistant Amador tells
him about some rats that a friend of his called "El Muecas"
(symbolically named for his continual muecas--grimaces)
has bred exclusively for the day the institute would run out
of specimens, with the hope of selling them for a tremendous financial profit. Muecas breeds the rats in his own
house, a slum dwelling that he and his wife, Ricarda, and
their two daughters share. Attracted by the possibility of
securing these new specimens to continue his studies and
wondering how Muecas' daughters have remained immune to
disease, Pedro visits Muecas' shanty and obtains his rats.

        Pedro himself lives in a very modest pensión (board-
ing house) run by a militant widow and her daughter Dora,
who is also the mother of the widow's illegitimate "niece,"
the beautiful Dorita. The widow is making plans for a
marriage between Pedro and Dorita so that his career may
release them all from a life of squalor and penury. M. -
Santos presents a dismal portrait of life in the barrio, how
people barely survive in the chabolas (huts or slum dwell-
ings) where Amador and Pedro visit El Muecas. We meet
the latter, his wife, his eldest daughter Florita (symbolically,
"Little Flower"), and her macho, knife-wielding boyfriend,
Cartucho (symbolically, "Cartridge," deliverer of pain).

        After deciding to buy the rats, Pedro, Amador and
Muecas walk to a nearby café to attend a tertulia (a gather-
ing of literati) on this particular Saturday evening and meet

Matías there, a friend of Muecas. Matías and Pedro, after
a night of drinking and talking end up in a house of prostitution run by Doña Luisa. After an evening of debauchery,
Pedro returns home to his pensión. First fighting then
yielding to his appetite for Dorita, who is sleeping alone,
Pedro makes love to her. At dawn, El Muecas comes to
Pedro's boarding house in search of help; his daughter Florita is hemorrhaging severely. Although Pedro is not a li-
censed doctor, he and Amador obtain some medical instruments to help Florita. Apparently Florita tried to abort
herself of a foetus conceived incestously by her and her
father, El Muecas, but dies despite Pedro's attempts to
save her. Florita's boyfriend, Cartucho, suspects that
Pedro had been having an affair with Dorita, but when he
sees Amador leaving the shanty with medical instruments
under his arm and asks who was responsible for the pregnancy, Amador, terrified of Cartucho's wrath, replies, "It
was the doctor."

Later the same day, Pedro returns to Matías' home,
meets his mother, and discovers that Matías is a man of
intellect, living in virtual paradise compared to himself and
the people of the chabolas. He attends a lecture on philosophy delivered by Ortega y Gasset the following day and during the reception that follows, Dorita arrives to warn him
the police are after him. Pedro seeks out Doña Luisa and
the latter hides him in her brothel. Meanwhile, Matías
(who now has become good friends with Pedro) finds Amador
and begs him to disclose the truth of Pedro's innocence to
the police.

The police finally apprehend Pedro. After several
days in prison, Pedro confesses to performing the abortions
and causing Florita's death; he thus maintains the absurdities
of the situation rather than reveal the truth. In spite of El
Muecas' success in having Florita buried in consecrated
ground (in the eyes of the Catholic church), Florita's body
is exhumed by the police and an autopsy is performed.
Muecas' wife, Ricarda, shaken by the results of the autopsy
and wanting to put her daughter's body to rest, tells the police who was directly responsible for Florita's pregnancy
and abortion. Pedro is freed and returns to work at the
research institute. However, to his dismay, the director of
the institute, despite Pedro's innocence, fires him (and sus-
pends his scholarship). As a result, Pedro is forced to
continue his cancer research privately.

All the same, Dorita and Pedro become engaged and
spend an evening at the theatre to celebrate.   Late at night,
at a verbena (evening celebration on the vigil of a saint's
day), they accidentally meet Cartucho who jealously watches
them dance from afar.   Cartucho still wants to avenge him -
self of Florita's death, supposedly at Pedro's hands.   While
Pedro is buying some churros (a kind of sugar-covered,
fried doughnut), Cartucho approaches Dorita and silently
knifes her in the teeming crowd.

With Dorita dead, Pedro has no recourse other than
to leave Madrid for a rural medical practice in the provinces
of Castille there also to continue his cancer research.   De-
feated in the city in all of his aspirations--his career, his
love for Dorita, the research, everything turned to failure--
Pedro is once again alone, indifferent, condemned to silence
by a society that deprived him of all he wanted.   He could
not even cry out his rage.   It was a time of silence.   A
time to settle in a small town, give prescriptions to the ailing, and play chess in the cafés. 1

                        *   *   *

When Tiempo de silencio was first published, it was
called "one of the most surprising, ambitious, and renovat-
ing experiences that the Spanish novel has come up with
over these last years--a most singular and original work
which constitutes the most surprising literary revelation of
the year...."2   The basic reason Tiempo de silencio has
become so famous is because of M.-Santos' new use of
Realism--that is to say, the author is an excellent observer
of the slum environment of Madrid's lower classes and although objectivism may lend itself more readily to revelation
of this kind of society, M.-Santos has chosen a new dimension he himself calls "dialectic realism" to portray this
world as he sees it.

> Existence is presented as the result of a conglom-
> eration of events, cascading one over the other....
> [T]he author enters into the dance [of life] and
> makes commentaries.   Everything is viewed sim-
> ultaneously from diverse planes: exterior and in-
> terior ... [and there is] abundant dialogue with
> introspection, monologues.   The novel goes from
> dialogue to the descriptive; there is no style, form
> of elocution....   There are grandiloquent passages,

> romantic ones, rhetorical ones. ... The novelist
> finds himself above his material to which he gives
> order and structure from the inside. The result
> of his work is more intellectual, more complex
> than the novels written with objectivist-realist ten-
> dencies. 3

M. -Santos himself used the term "dialectical realism"
in which he meant "to pass from the simple static description of various alienations in order to set-up the real dynamics of the contradictions in actu" (in their performance). 4
One critic considered the novel "an astonishing verbal coin-
ing, a ferociously sarcastic vision of reality";5 another felt
Pedro's psychology is much more complicated and subtle,
and that his future is tied to a project which transcends la
chata realidad (base reality);6 even M. -Santos himself said,
"I fear I have not adjusted to all the concepts of social
realism, but you will see a little adjustment in which sense
I would like to arrive at a kind of 'dialectical realism....'
As you see, I am as pedantic in writing letters as I am in
a simple ordinary conversation. "7 Within the realm of
irony lies M. -Santos' intention to give the Spanish novel a
new purpose and a new direction.

> This irony of Luis Martín-Santos, that habit of
> making fun of the serious in order to confuse the
> hypocrites, constitutes a kind of 'indirect commu-
> nication' that has been one of the methods [he]
> used mostly in order to express the ambiguity of
> truth on the planes of existence found by many of
> the existentialist thinkers, notably by Nietzsche
> and by Kierkegaard. Naturally, that irony consti-
> tutes a prime catalytic element in the dialectic
> of our novelist. ... 8

Irony is certainly one of the keys to the dialectical
realism M. -Santos has created. Another critic, Aquilino
Duque, discusses two different types of Realism in vogue in
the early 1960's (realismo pueblerino o la neopicaresca--
rural or neo-picaresque realism"--and realismo surburbano
--"suburban realism")9 and contrasts them to M. -Santos'
new dialectical realism. For Duque, these kinds of Realism
did not serve the novelist, with their "costumbrista" vision
or premeditated social theories. The great merit of M. -
Santos' novel is that it offers a kind of profound yet subdued
Realist, and contradictory author's vision of the social
milieu as produced by the yet further contradictory vision

of the protagonist. "It is this double contradiction and the
psychological experience of the individual which constitutes
for us the dialectical dynamism of the entire novel. "10
"M. -Santos' dialectical realism does not orient itself exclusively towards the exterior world, but also towards the interior, the conscience, establishing significant and symbolic
relationships. ... It makes reality ironic (in the manner
of Cervantes) and the spirit it projects is of a perceptible
nostalgia for the ideal, for the absolute. "11

On another plane, Tiempo de silencio develops a
temporal, concrete and objective world. One critic warns,
however,

> the novelist does not bring upon himself that char-
> acteristic fetish of objective reality, nor does he
> defy the world of appearances. But neither does
> he underestimate them. What is relevant, in con-
> clusion, is what restores his [idea of the] true
> significance of reality as the road of access to
> other realities, even more complex and contradic-
> tory, and less mechanical. He regains the natu-
> ral dialectic of reality and the objective reality of
> contradiction. 12

Compare Søren Kierkegaard's words (from his work, The
Concept of Irony), "the exterior and the interior do not form
a harmonized unity since the exterior was in opposition to
the interior and only across this refracted angle can [reality]
be understood. " This refracted angle can offer us the best
perspective to understand in what sentiment Time of Silence
is conceived. With M. -Santos, the psychological novel,
undergoing change in the Spanish contemporary novel, approaches or becomes an "existential" novel. Gemma Roberts,
in her excellent philosophical work, Temas existenciales en
la novela española de post-guerra (Existentialist Themes in
the Spanish Postwar Novel), prefers to view M. -Santos'
novel as one of several Spanish efforts containing existential
themes. Her introspective, often moving and challenging
analysis of Tiempo de silencio places M. -Santos' novel on
the same level as Kierkegaard's philosophical treatises.

Much has been written about Tiempo de silencio since
1964. Gemma Robert's brilliant study, cited above, is one
of the best since it contains an excellent discussion of M. -
Santos' "dialectical realism, " a discussion devoted to whether we consider the novel as a social or philosophical

work, to M.-Santos' rebellion against the absurd, to "ironic"
existentialism, failure, Pedro as an existential character,
and other considerations. (Some of the subheadings in
Robert's section on Tiempo de silencio are "Existence,"
"Sex and Love," "Viciousness," "A Symbol of Nausea"--
(exploring Pedro's relationship to Sartrian heroes), "Society
and Liberty," "Society as an Absurdity," "The Essential
Character of Dialectical Realism," "The Function of Irony,"
and "The Ethical and Aesthetics of Dialectical Realism."
Her critical thoughts on that novel are extensive and deep.)

Other critics have written equally seriously (but less
profoundly) about the novel. Ramón Buckley provides an extensive discussion of "the conflict between the anecdotal nature of the novel (events and ambience familiar to the reader) and its themes (a new and surprising focus on these realities). The result of this conflict is irony which manifests
itself throughout the entire work."[13] He delves into various
topics including the cultist and baroque aspects of M.-Santos'
language, the use of scientific and naturalist terminology,
neologisms, subjective chronology, and the novel's leitmotiv.
In Buckley's fourteen pages of intense analysis, he points
out M.-Santos' proximity to Cervantes and the latter's concept of irony as the basis for M.-Santos' view of reality.
Buckley's major point, however, is that M.-Santos has taken
an essentially savage, anti-scientific and trivial reality and
invested it with a scientific, civilized language and a Cervantine irony which elevates the novel's stature as well as
the entire genre.

Pablo Gil Casado, in twenty-four pages of terse
criticism, discusses principally the plot, major themes and
style of the novel in depth and points out the author's evocation and appreciation not only of Cervantes but of Goya as
well as his anti-national sentiments--M.-Santos describes a
bull fight as a spectacle of carnage, a means of escape and
a tradition representative of the national quality of hatred,
not love for king and country.

Carenas and Ferrando devote to this novel some
twenty-six pages of criticism in a chapter entitled "Psychology, Language and Existence in Time of Silence," in which
they discuss sexuality, the language of the poor and the rich,
and Sartrian concepts of heroism and philosophy ("Pedro as
a total man, totally compromised, and totally free").[14] One
of the best critiques of the novel appears in Guillermo and
Hernández' book, La novelística española de los 60, in which

they cover all of the aspects of the novel mentioned previously by other literary critics and add their own vision of M. -
Santos' metaphoric vision of reality, "a palpable reality expressed in order to penetrate a further dimension..., one
with a transcendent purpose."[15] They discuss at great
length the influences on M.-Santos of James Joyce (interior
monologue), William Faulkner (monologues and psychological
aspects), Quevedo (the baroque style), Valle-Inclán (distorted
visions of reality), and Albert Camus (existential philosophy)
--all of whose ideas are present within his novel.

        Thus far, I have attempted to summarize only major
concepts taken from the best criticism about the novel.
Many revealing articles have been written examining some
of these concepts in depth.[16] At this point, however, I
would like to limit myself to a few personal observations.
Regarding the novel's structure, its 240 pages are divided
into sixty-one sections or fragments of varying length. Gonzalo Sobejano's revelation of the novel's internal plan (even
though he miscounted--corrected without comment below) I
am for the most part in agreement with:

            Sections 1-10 narrate the action over several days
            but the action is imprecisely sketched; sections 11-
            24 narrate with perfect continuity the events on a
            Saturday night in which Pedro learns about the
            vanity [of intellectuals], the dizzying [pleasures] of
            the flesh and the horrible presence of death; sec-
            tions 25-50 deal with the following three days in
            which Pedro experiences nausea, literary salons,
            houses of prostitution, prison and eventual freedom;
            sections 51-61 comprise the action of several days,
            again imprecisely delineated but showing Pedro's
            transition from liberty to his final escape. [Sobe-
            jano also remarks] the symmetry between the be-
            ginning of the novel and its end [and comments
            that M.-Santos] may have adhered to Dostoyevsky's
            technique because of the nature of conception of
            the hero, with his continuous intense nature, his
            critical moments of passion, death, imprisonment
            and freedom that make the character renounce his
            difficult career and flee.[17]

        I believe one of the novel's key assets is that it en-
ables the reader to penetrate the continuous flow of thoughts
of the protagonist, which conjure in one's own mind a palpable, almost cinematic reality--a reality that besides per-

mitting the reader to see, lets him explore the conscience
of Pedro and a few other characters in the novel.

On the novel's first page, we see the telephone, the
inside of Pedro's pensión and later, the interiors of a salon,
a shanty, a prison cell--all described in detail. We begin
to feel the oppressiveness, the darkness, the silence and
Pedro's own anguish, despair and ultimate resignation. Just
as with the practitioners of the nouveau roman, the visual
impact of whose prose assaults us, so do Pedro's continuous thoughts assault the Spanish reading audience. It seems
M.-Santos' novel is continually inventive and invented. At
times, the reader supplements what the author has given
him with the products of his own imagination, although we
are always aware that it is M.-Santos who is creating and
stimulating our illusions.

There are many brilliant facets to Time of Silence.
One of the most fascinating sections (number 11) in the
whole novel is M.-Santos' six-point literary interpolation on
the nature of reality and morality as the author questions
Cervantes' aims in writing the Quijote. But Martín-Santos'
most outrageous notion occurs in a conversation Pedro has
with Matías when the former asks Pedro, "¿Pero qué ser
magma?" ("But what is magma?"):

> --Magma is everything. Magma is the preg-
> nant reality of the material which adheres. Mag-
> ma is the protoform of vitality which is born.
> Magma is the resplendent viscosity of the sperm.
> Magma is the rock in its primitive state before it
> degenerates into stones. Magma is the Jews when
> they were still in the ghetto, reproducing among
> themselves indefinitely--18

Another equally important section in the novel demonstrates
how Pedro tries to define his own position in society. He
does not want to be "trapped" by love or sexuality, but

> prefers the building of a new life, remaining on
> the periphery, going further, transcending reality,
> not being identified with the chata realidad [base
> reality] of the city, of the country, of the hour.
> He lives in another world in which a young girl
> does not enter only because she is languid and ap-
> petizing. He has selected a most difficult road,
> at whose extreme is another kind of woman, the

kind not for whom elemental and cyclical exuberance is important but one who is lucid, free and
strong [p. 95].

Pedro clearly lives on the outskirts of society; at times his
flesh weakens although at other moments, his conscience is
strong:

--Do you love me?

--I love you, I love you, I love you, I love you,
I love you.   Pedro feels his mouth continually pro-
nouncing the words, promising, feeling far from
himself, far from her, like some separating cre-
vice in his spirit....

--Will you love me always?

--Always, always, always, always as he goes
staggering through the darkness of the hall full of
familiar objects and of smells which pour through
the opened doors of the bedroom where their bodies,
without the glory of their ancestors, continue expell-
ing breathed-in air at regular intervals... [p. 96].

To reiterate, sex, death and alienation are the three
major themes of Tiempo de silencio.   The novel is full of
interesting but sporadic thoughts on these themes.   However,
there are two sustained passages in the novel that are brilliant tours de force--section 43, which describes Pedro's in-
carceration, and the last section, 61, which narrates Pedro's
departure from Madrid.   M.-Santos prepares us for these
passages stylistically, by having Pedro first characterize his
own and then another person's responses and by letting
Pedro's personal thoughts run completely free in "the spirit
of a Joycean interior monologue with the occasional exercise
(and excess) of Freudian psychoanalysis.... [19]

--Why did I go?

Don't think.   There is no reason to think about
what is already done.   It's useless to try to go
over again the errors one has already committed.
All men make errors.   All men are wrong.   All
men look for this perdition on a simpler or complex road....   You didn't kill her.   She was dead.
She wasn't dead.   You killed her....   Don't
think, don't think, don't think....   You are free
to choose what you want to do because your

freedom goes on existing now. You are free to
draw any drawing or do a straight line on each
day that goes like you have spent the others, and
each seven days a longer line because you are
free to make lines as long as you want and no-
body will stop you.... Imbecile! [pp. 176-80].

In prison, Pedro goes slightly mad, confesses his compli-
city and suffers feelings of complete alienation and nihilism
before the truth is discovered and he is set free:

Not to know anything. Not to know anything. Not
to know the earth is round. But to know the sun
is moving although it seems to rise and set. Not
to know there are three distinct Beings. Not to
know the electric light. Not to know why stones
fall toward the earth. Not to know how to tell
time. Not to know the spermatozoa and ovum are
two individual cells that when fused form a nucleus.
Not to know anything--and to repeat obstinately,
'He didn't exist' [p. 202].

M. -Santos is equally incisive on other themes such as science, sensuality and Pedro's total despair and nihilism:

That science, more than any of the other activities
of humanity, has changed the life of man on earth
is an undisputed truth. That science is the liberating lever of infinite alienation which prevents the
mere concrete existence its free essence is never
refuted by anybody [p. 206].

--How are you? Have you suffered a lot?

I couldn't return her caresses. On her lips, upon
kissing them, I could only feel her teeth ... but I
didn't want to be sensual. Sensuality wasn't important. 'I love you. ' She shuddered, trembled,
oscillated with her entire body around me--'She
loves me, ' Pedro thought. 'Without a doubt, she
loves me' [p. 205].

No, no, no, no. It isn't so. Life isn't so; it
doesn't happen like this. The one that does,
pays... He who gives once, does not give twice.
An eye for an eye ... a tooth for a tooth... [p.
232].

> What's the use.... The bomb doesn't kill with
> noise but with the alpha radiation that is itself si-
> lent, or with deutron rays or with gamma or cos-
> mic rays, all which are more silent than a garrot-
> ing. Also they castrate, just like X-rays. But I,
> I am already gone. Finished, fit for what? It is
> a time of silence.... [I]t will be a time, waiting
> in silence, without speaking to anybody, without
> speaking badly about anybody. Everything consists
> in being silent.... I am despairing of not being
> desperate.... I was silent when they burned pagan
> Torquemadas; ... turn me on this side since I am
> already burning ... and the hangman turned him
> for it was a simple question of symmetry....
> FIN [pp. 238-40].

Tiempo de silencio annihilates its readers at its conclusion,
with its lack of hope, its ultimate despair, its lack of trust
in past history, with its amoral parade of characters gone
by. "It is a pessimistic work, somber, loaded with bitter
reflections, full of hard truths which confront man with his
own smallness, perhaps in order to thrust him into the
search for better roads."[20]

> Nothing ever happens. Only time passes. Time
> which remains outside of my life, between paren-
> theses. Outside of my stupid life. Time in which,
> truthfully, I will live more. Life outside was sus-
> pended with all its stupidities. Time, only time
> fills this emptiness of stupid things and stupid
> people. All has to slip by, slip over me. I am
> not suffering, I am absolutely not suffering at all.
> Whatever you will think, I am not suffering. But
> I do not suffer. I exist. I live. Time passes.
> It fills me; I run on time. Never have I lived
> the time of my life which passes as now that I am
> still, looking at a point on the wall, the black eye
> of the siren that is looking at me. Only here,
> how great it seems to me I'm above everything.
> Nothing can happen to me. I am the one who is
> passing; I live, I live [p. 179].

Perhaps this monologue is M.-Santos' most optimistic statement in the entire novel, whose conclusion is bitter. If
there is any hope left for Pedro, it rests on his decision to
leave Madrid, like Saint Paul, "to seek some new thing."

Tiempo de silencio is really M. -Santos' attempt to
examine the conscience of one man, to stress the absurdities of the experiences that can befall one man in a lifetime, to use a new kind of "dialectic" realism combined with
a new view of the Spanish language in order stylistically to
execute his underlying existential philosophical premises.
Pablo Gil Casado declares the novel's purpose is "to show
Madrid's society with its different strata, seen as a compendium of 'the Iberian man,' its ambience, and its national
character"21 and accordingly divides the strata into three
spheres, the lower class, the intellectual and scientific
middle-class, and high society, composed of wealthy aristo-
crats and intellectuals.   I am not certain if this was M. -
Santos' ultimate purpose, although his vivisection of the
realities of these three spheres of society is nevertheless
magnificent.   But Gil Casado presents a relentless diatribe
on the social aspects of the novel, which, he suggests, demonstrates through M. -Santos' baroque-humoristic style, a
brutal portrait of reality of the chabolas.   Again from the
social perspective, Gil Casado interests us in M. Santos' ideas
about Spain's "national paralysis," the Hispanic caste system.   The Spanish are characterized in M. -Santos' own
words as a "people whose foreheads are so narrow that they
are all stupid.   And to be stupid, there is no remedy."22
The author provides an excellent definition of the true character of the Spanish race, typically using neologisms composed of rarely used words and original combinations of adjectives and nouns:

> Cantehondo, mediaverónica, churumbeliportantes
> faraonas, fidelidades de viejo mozo de estoques,
> hospitalidades, etiquetas, centauros de Andalucía
> la baja, todas ellas siluetas de Elefanta, casta y
> casta y casta y no sólo casta torera sino casta
> pordiosera, casta andariega, casta destripaterró-
> nica, casta de los siete niños siete [p. 129].

This passage was kept in the original Spanish to
demonstrate the stylistic beauties of M. -Santos' often glitter-
ing prose.   Many other examples of his anti-national and
equally corrosive critiques are scattered throughout the
novel, dealing with the church, the bullfight, small towns,
provincial life, the racial composition of Spain, poverty,
misery, the failures of social and scientific progress.   Gil
Casado envisages Pedro as the "living incarnation of destruction, desperation, and resignation felt on the national
plane and doubtlessly, as well, by his creator."23   This

supposition may be true; however everyone in the novel
seems doomed to failure and feelings of desperation. In
fact, despite the heavy employment of stylistic innovation,
most characters in the novel speak exactly like Pedro (or
M. -Santos). Gil Casado makes this interesting commentary
on the author's social motives: "It is curious that a writer
so anti-hispanic as M. -Santos may fall into Spanish-Catholic
vices so excellently--[as in his use of] conceptismo or an
affected style, verbal bravado and perspicacity in Quevedo's
manner. "24 The best example of the baroque nature of M. -
Santos' prose which displays our author's excessive use of
hiperbatón, or inversion of word order, is the following
passage:

> Júpiter-tonante, Moisés-destrozante-de-becerros-
> áureos, Padre-ofrecedor-de-generosos-auxilios-
> que-han-sido-malignamente-rechazados, Virtud-
> sorprendida-y-atónita-por-la-magnitud-casi-infinita-
> de-la-maldad-humana [p. 286].

Other stylistic qualities in his work are neologisms,
metaphor, synecdoche, changes in punctuation, spelling, the
abundant use of scientific and medical terms, made-up
words, interminable run-on sentences, repetitions, confusions, incomplete dialogues, (over)use of parenthetical statement, counterpoint, contrasts, jocular versus painfully serious tones, and irony. If fact, Gil Casado believes one of
the keys to fully understanding the novel is "this contrast
between the fictitious and the excessive, the 'impoverished
reality' as a technique that M. -Santos uses constantly in his
creation of ironic style. "25 Similarly, the author creates a
metaphoric, supposed situation, using scientific language and
jargon, in order to reveal a real situation during the unwind-
ing of the narrative, a device most assuredly reflecting M. -
Santos' medical personality. 40 We also notice that the prose
moves from generalities to specifics, from abstractions to
the concrete and includes real allusions to living (Ortega)
and dead personalities (Cervantes, Goya, Quevedo) in the
quest for palpable reality.

Tiempo de silencio generally received the great accolade it so rightly deserved:

> Differing from that of the companions of his gene-
> ration, the prose in L. M. -Santos' work is sensi-
> tive to the emotion and the force of the word, to
> the profound suggestion of his rhythm. ...   The

language, which marvelously obeys the necessities
and urgencies of the narrator moves from hiperbatón a little less than in the style of a Góngora
[a baroque poet known precisely for his conceited
style] to an almost telegraphic rhythm of cut-off
phrases. If we had to look for some way of syn-
thesizing the diverse qualities of this method of
narration, we would have to ransom the living
word; but not only is the language alive, so are
the characters. Time of Silence is a new and successful invasion of characters in the orbit of the
contemporary novel.... 27

But the originality of L. M.-Santos does not consist so much in the construction [of the work] as
in its style. This is perhaps the most surprising
discovery which entices us to his work. Spanish
contemporary literature is not accustomed to this
search, to this burst of style of the phrase.
... Luis M.-Santos appears as a social writer,
a master of an intellectual style: he narrates for
us that aspiration, that destruction, of his personality with love and with bitterness, but also with
sarcasm and irony, preventing the reader's freedom to dissolve into the indifference of the character, assisting completely so that the reader may
separate himself from the character at the moment
the latter is vanquished.... 28

Renovation of style is certainly one of the major facets to Martín-Santos' success as a writer. Eugenio de
Nora said of the novel,

its ferocity, sarcastic vision of reality, sane critical stance ... deprecatory nihilism, which pulver-
izes not this or that aspect of national or social
life but this one and the other as a lost and rotten
totality without solution, its inconsistency, conventions of human figures 'playing the game' [make
Tiempo de silencio] a master work, a barbarous
work of genius, breaking new ground on whose
eruption it will be possible to construct [a regenerated Spanish novel]. 29

J. Ignacio Ferreras placed Time of Silence alongside the
works of Marcel Proust, James Joyce, Virginia Woolf,
Franz Kafka and Jorge C. Trulock, and feels that M.-Santos

wrote the "anti-novel or dehumanized-intellectual novel or
the novel of degraded realism"[30] but refused to define this
new tendency any further.   Rafael Bosch attributes M. -San-
tos' complex style to James Joyce and William Faulkner especially because of his use of a kind of psycho-pathologic,
incoherent interior monologue and distorted visions of the exterior world ultimately the result of a kind of mental illness.
But Bosch believes M. -Santos' greatest strength is in his
psychoanalytic interpretations of his characters and his Joycean portrayal of a vital, burlesqued and heart-rending reality.[31]   G. Torrente-Ballester compares Time of Silence as
an equal to any of the works of Jonathan Swift or to the
works of the greatest writers of fiction of the Baroque or
the Neo-Classic periods of literature.[32]   One of the techniques persistently used by M. -Santos that gives Time of
Silence its stylistic stature, according to Ramón Buckley, is
the author's use of a peculiar type of terminology (something
scientific) which offers us simultaneously our own interpretations of the anecdote as well as the authors, on a plane of
comprehension superior to even that of the characters of the
novel.[33]   Tiempo has also been called "the invention of an
invective"[34] and both Gil Casado and Sobejano share the view
that this invective is directed principally against the Spanish
bourgeoisie.[35]   Yet within this spirit of condemnation, Felix
Grande believes that "Tiempo de silencio searches for the
liberty of its reader, demonstrates it to him and invites him
severely, under the responsibility of his own possession of
it, to dole out his liberty, making his own destiny. "[36]

        Nearly all critical opinions of Tiempo de silencio
have been on an elevated and laudatory level; I have saved
the worst for the last, to let the reader judge the validity
of these opinions.   Carlos Rojas, a novelist himself, in a
trenchant, fifteen-page article entitled "Problems of the New
Spanish Novel, "[37] presents the dissenting view that "if the
social novel ought to respond to an ever vigilant humanism
whose end is to reveal the human condition of the victims or
the oppressed or ignorant, then the social novel as viewed
by M. -Santos, written with such finality, has been in my
view, carelessly and scandalously betrayed. "[38]

        The most recent condemnation I have read of this
novel is found in José Domingo's La novela española del
siglo XX[39] where it is censured because of its destructive
and tremendously pessimistic nature, its sarcastic and implacable form, its treatment of characters as dolls or grotesque marionettes that are portrayed superficially, never

profoundly.   Even Pedro, according to Domingo "lacks true
being and moves through the events like a somnambulist, almost unconscious. "[40]   Domingo refuses to compare Pedro to
Pío Baroja's characters etched in similar style and considers the

> rhetorical games, ironic adjectivizations which rid-
> icule characters, exacerbated baroque metaphors,
> verbal pirouettes, frequent use of medical terms,
> transpositions of medical and real planes, person-
> alized, intimist prose [to be] destructive of the
> old rhetoric, all part of the measure of a 'great'
> writer whose absurd death crowned a greater frus-
> tration, as if his death put a definitive stamp on
> [M.-Santos'] radical pessimism. [41]

Some recent literary criticism places Tiempo de silencio on the level of Albert Camus' L'étranger (The Strang-
er) and situates it in the fashionable category of "novel of
the absurd" because of possible philosophic and life-style
similarities between Martín-Santos, Jean-Paul Sartre, Albert
Camus and their common existential philosophies.   Although
M.-Santos is a voice closed to us now for eternity, his
single novel, his one truly great work deserves to be read
not only because of its high rank in the evolution of the New
Wave literature, but because of its stylistic and thematic
assets.   It is a major original intellectual exercise on the
highest level, equally intellectually demanding on the reader,
a satiric-ironic, moral novel that reflects the social realities of Spain.   Its "silences" will speak to us for years to
come.

THE WORKS OF LUIS MARTIN-SANTOS

Tiempo de silencio.   Barcelona: Seix Barral, 1962.
Apólogos y otras prosas inéditas [essays].   Barcelona: Seix
        Barral, 1970.

SELECTED STUDIES ON M.-SANTOS

Atienza, J. G.   " 'Tiempo de silencio,' de Luis Martín-
        Santos," Cuadernos del Congreso por la Libertad de
        la Cultura, no. 63 (ag. 1962), 88-9.
Aumente, José.   "Un libro póstumo de Luis Martín-Santos,"
        Insula, no. 220 (mar. 1965), 12.

Chantraine de Van Praag, Jacqueline. "Un malogrado novelista contemporáneo," Cuadernos Americanos (México),
vol. 24, no. 5 (1965), 269-75.

Curutchet, Juan Carlos. "Luis Martín-Santos, el fundador,"
pt. 1, Cuadernos de Ruedo Ibérico, no. 17 (feb. -mar.
1968), 3-18; pt. 2, no. 18 (abril-mayo 1968), 3-15.

Dennis, Ward H. "Luis Martín-Santos; 'Tiempo de silencio,"
Revista Hispánica Moderna, vol. 32, no. 1-2 (enero-
abril 1966), 110.

Díaz, Janet Winicoff. "Luis Martín-Santos and the Contemporary Spanish Novel," Hispania, no. 51 (mayo 1968),
232-8.

Doménech, Ricardo. "Ante una novela irrepetible," Insula,
no. 187 (junio 1962), 4.

_____. "Luis Martín-Santos," Insula, no. 208 (mar.
1964), 4.

Duque, Aquilino. "Un buen entendedor de la realidad; Luis
Martín-Santos," Indice de Artes y Letras, no. 185
(junio 1964), 9-10.

Eoff, H. Sherman, y Schraibman, José. "Dos novelas del
absurdo: 'L'étranger' y 'Tiempo de silencio',"
Papeles de Son Armadans, no. 168 (mayo 1970), 213-
41.

Garciasol, Ramón de. "Un español malogrado: Luis Martín-Santos," Cultura Universitaria (Caracas), no. 92
(julio-sept. 1966).

Grande, Félix. "Luis Martín-Santos: 'Tiempo de silencio',"
Cuadernos Hispanoamericanos, no. 158 (feb. 1963),
337-42.

_____. "Tres fichas para una aproximación a la actual
narrativa española," Margen, no. 2 (dici. 1966), 50.

Ortega, José. "Compromiso formal de Martín-Santos en
'Tiempo de silencio'," Hispanófila, no. 37 (sept.
1969), 23-30.

Werrie, Paul. "La nouvelle vague espagnole," La Table
Ronde (Paris), no. 225 (oct. 1966), 146-52.

Chapter 13

JOSE LUIS CASTILLO-PUCHE and PARALELO 40
(The Fortieth Parallel) (1963)

José Luis Castillo-Puche was born in Yecla, Spain, in the province of Murcia in 1919. Little is known about his childhood or adolescence. However during the years of the Civil War, he spent most of his time at a seminary in Valencia and later at the Pontifical University of Comillas, which he left in 1945. He came to Madrid that year and entered the University of Madrid's School of Journalism, earning a degree in liberal arts. After leaving the university, he worked for the Institute of Hispanic Culture, and traveled through almost all of North and South America while on the job. He has written essays and newspaper articles about his travels throughout the world, but is essentially recognized as one of Spain's leading novelists. He married in 1954 but little else is known about his personal life. Castillo-Puche began writing novels during World War II.

Although Con la muerte al hombro (With Death at Hand) (1954) is considered his first successful fictional work, Sin camino (Without a Road) (1956), although published two years later, is really the author's first novel since he seriously began writing fiction in 1947. (Another novel, entitled Bienaventurados los que sueñan (Fortunate Are Those Who Dream) (1944) has been entirely disowned by the author and literary critics alike.) These novels were followed by others of equal stature: El vengador (The Avenger) (1956), Hicieron partes (They Played Their Roles) (1957), Paralelo 40 (The Fortieth Parallel) (1963), Oro blanco (White Gold) (1963), El perro loco (The Crazy Dog) (1965), and Como ovejas al matadero (Just Like Lambs to the Slaughter) (1971)--this last work initiating a trilogy entitled El cíngulo (The Priest's Girdle), which is yet to be completed. With the publication

171

of these novels, Castillo-Puche profited financially but was
dispirited.   When Con la muerte al hombro appeared in 1954,
he was forced to leave Yecla under duress because of the
townspeople's outrage at his portraying their follies and foibles in such a realistic fashion.   He also won Spain's National Literary Prize and the Premio de Novela Católica
(the Catholic Novel's Literary Prize) in 1957 for Hicieron
partes.

        Apart from his novels, his most interesting collec-
tion of essays may be found in Misión a Istanbul (Mission to
Istanbul) (1954), but the collection, América de cabo a rabo
(America from A to Z), is his most fascinating one since it
is an account of his experiences while making an extended
journey through the Americas.   His critical and biographical
study, Hemingway, entre la vida y la muerte (Hemingway,
Between Life and Death) (1968), is notable because it dem-
onstrates the stylistic effects Hemingway had upon Castillo-
Puche's writing career and his general life style.   Yecla de
Azorín y Baroja (The Yecla of Azorín and Baroja) (1949) and
Memorias íntimas de Aviraneta (Memoirs from Aviraneta) (1952)
also prove our writer's fascination with Azorín, Baroja, and
Aviraneta.

        Although Castillo-Puche earned his literary reputation
essentially because of his early novels, I have deliberately
chosen to discuss Paralelo 40 because it represents the author's views about Americans living in Madrid and is an initial effort by New Wave writers within the realm of Realism
to approach new sectors of Spanish society theretofore not
written about or generally ignored by many of Spain's leading
modern novelists.

                    *   *   *

        Paralelo 40 is a long prolix novel of 477 pages.
Even its title is symbolic of the geographic position of one
of its "protagonists," the city of Madrid, since the nation's
capital lies close to 40° latitude.   But Paralelo 40 is not
the story of all of the people of Madrid (in the style of John
Dos Passos) but rather a cross-section of the northern part
of the city above the Plaza de Castilla called "Korea" by its
inhabitants (famous for its geographical position on the 38th
parallel), where a new class of middle- and lower-echelon
American servicemen and other governmental personnel reside in a somewhat symbiotic relationship with the impover-

ished Spanish working class. The novel is divided into three
parts which include a prologue and an epilogue. In the
book's dedication, to his friends, Castillo-Puche warns us
at the beginning that he lived in this residential section
called "Korea" with several of his fellow newspapermen and
although he did not "escape" the area himself, he feels his
novel is, to a great degree, a documentary more than a fictional work.

At the novel's outset, Castillo-Puche, in an "unnecessary but obligatory prologue" which he also feels is "hardly
useful"[1] somewhat autobiographically recalls moving with his
bride into "Korea" in 1954, into a brand new, modern, lux-
urious apartment but without the services of a butcher,
grocer, pharmacist, or fish peddler, etc. The only estab-
lishments of interest were the great number of bars and
cafeterias which delighted in squeezing the Americans out of
their "sacred" dollar bills. Castillo-Puche felt such a new
geographical and sociological phenomenon like "Korea" should
be written about. He chose to model his protagonist, Genaro,
upon a real "mason" he saw at work one day, a common man
helping to build the new high-rise apartment houses in the
area (which were still in the process of construction in 1974).
Other characters taken from life populate the novel as well,
especially the Air Force and Army personnel of the lower
American social classes. By contrast to fictional prototypes,
the author also chose to use real models of Spanish workers,
people from the district of Tetuán, the closest authentically
Spanish area to "Korea." Our author, however, tells us his
ideas as a writer are not to be found in either set of characters (the real or the fictional), nor does he identify with
them or share their thoughts.

Genaro, the novel's protagonist, is an unfortunate
man, full of hate and resentment. A poor mason, with little
ambition except to marry Elena and live modestly, Genaro
is a symbol of the impotence of most Spanish men, paralyzed
by their poverty, unable to forget their social position, their
bitterness and sterile existences. In contrast to Genaro, we
have Thomas, a young American Negro from Chicago, sta-
tioned in Spain for the past several years, speaking Spanish
fairly fluently and carrying on a love affair with a lovely
Spanish girl, Olympia. Thomas runs the PX in "Korea."
Genaro is the novel's narrator and demonstrates how his life
touches upon Thomas'.

Paralelo 40 is sometimes written with a Dickensian
flair for "realism" (in a traditional style) but with a new
twist.   Castillo-Puche's view is far more vulgar than either
Dickens' or Balzac's or Pérez Galdós' and far less trenchant than the tremendismo of Cela or the naturalism of
Pardo Bazán or Zola.   Castillo-Puche chooses to provide
word pictures of the low-life of "Korea," using intense, colloquial language to suit his images.   The text abounds in
vulgarisms and banalities which also demonstrate the heavy
American linguistic and cultural influence--for example, the
words: el pic-up, el piex, chochazos (when referring to
Cadillacs, etc.).   One of the key themes of the novel is the
constant interplay of Castillo-Puche's (or his characters')
anti-American views joined with his protest for increased
Spanish nationalism and independence from foreign influences.
Genaro, a stone mason, is also a Communist, active in his
local party cell.

We would sum up the structure of the novel accordingly: Part One deals with Genaro's awakening to the American dream, the power of the dollar bill and the building of
a new life where love, marriage, success and money are
the rewards (if he continues to work at the PX instead of at
bricklaying); Part Two demonstrates Genaro's anguish and
conflicts manifested in the figure of El Penca, leader of the
local Communist party block, outrageously anti-American
and plotting Thomas' demise.   Genaro cannot reconcile his
gratefulness to Thomas and to American materialism with
his society's motives, which are to exploit the American
dream but deny its economic and cultural influence.   Genaro
tries to stave off a plot of El Penca's to kill Thomas and
drive an anti-American wedge into United States-Spanish relations.   Part Three demonstrates Genaro's sacrifice of himself, out of friendship (or Christian charity), to spare
Thomas and the Americans of "Korea" the disgrace and confrontation of the entire Communist Party in Spain--and consequently avoiding an international incident.   Genaro is brutally beaten to death by El Penca's henchman.   Unknowingly,
Thomas flies home to the United States while El Penca es-
capes to Morrocco with the party's funds; both find new
lives; and life continues inevitably in "Korea."

This brief résumé is essentially the entire plot of
Paralelo 40.   It is a direct, simple story, never profound
but long on words.   There are a lot of incidents in the
course of the novel, but not much real action since the minor incidents are treated in a very superficial even though

extensive manner.   One feels Castillo-Puche intentionally
prolongs his scenes in restaurants and bars; his conversations between Thomas and Genaro go on interminably without
advancing the major actions of the novel.   Both men understand each other, word for word, concept for concept.
Their repartée is long, verbose but never deep.   Note the
following exchange:

> --Do you want to drink something?
>
> --Who is inviting me?
>
> --When it ends, I'll invite you to have some-
> thing solid.
>
> --What is this "solid"?
>
> --A sardine sandwich or a ham sandwich with
> anchovies or whatever...
>
> --I want to eat something, something, Thomas
> cried, suddenly standing up [p. 71].

The preceding interchange of dialogue takes place in Part
One when Genaro has just won a small fortune at gambling.
He is thankful to Thomas for helping him win and for meeting Thomas' friends.   Although throughout the course of the
novel we never learn in their dialogues about Genaro's feelings, the author on occasion reflects, "He would go with
the Negro Thomas to the end of the world.   He would go
with the Negro Thomas to wherever the latter would take
him.   He would go with the Negro Thomas.... And they
went out into the snow ... " (p. 72).

There is a kind of silent, profound, attitude of masculinity and of mutual rapport pervading the entire novel,
similar to the characters (not story lines) of Ernest Hemingway's better novels.   The men never confide their powerful
or personal feelings to each other.   They even talk about
their women in graphic, vulgar, chauvinist and degrading
terms.   But they never really communicate with each other.
Their masculinity and stoical attitudes are part of their
natural reserve and supposedly enhance their long, emotional
silences which readers may equate to "male strength. "
However, men as well as women in this novel are all weak
character creations.   Genaro and Thomas are also very
"straight," predictable protagonists.   Genaro makes up his
mind about Thomas with the most glaring simplifications of
thought: "Thomas was a 'whole' person ... and loyal.   He
was different from the rest of the Negros that he ever

met ... " (p. 113). Although throughout the novel we are
aware of Genaro's innocent awe and wonder at Thomas, and
the latter's life style, his Negro and white friends, his military and social connections, his sexual prowess, Paralelo 40
is essentially Genaro's story, his transition from innocence
to maturity, from a sterile to a vital life style. But as a
human being Genaro is always a caricature, never convincing us of his motives, his actions, his shifts of thought.
Genaro simply never comes alive, although we see him
clearly at all times throughout the novel. Perhaps this is
one problem with a truly realistic journalistic style, which
captures the milieu more efficiently than the emotional states
of the protagonists.

        Generally, the other characters in the novel are
coldly drawn--equally stereotyped, unassuming presences as
wintery and unrevealing as the dull Madrid weather of December 1960 when most of the so-called "action" of this
novel takes place. We feel some warmth for Emiliano,
Genaro's fellow mason and character counterpart who resists
an offer to work for the Americans and continues earning his
living at bricklaying.

        Did Genaro and Emiliano look like bricklayers?
        Well, no, they didn't since Genaro wore a wrist
        watch. And Emiliano, with a bandaged arm seemed
        more like a day worker temporarily laid off than
        one living off charity. In bricklaying work, the
        majority of the men, who avoided cities and small
        towns, were farmers, people without jobs, even
        miners who took refuge. They earned very little,
        but they kept on fighting [p. 17].

Genaro and Emiliano both take their frustrations out on the
syndicate for not having become successful men. Their
story is of "little people," eking out their existences against
the background of the big, impersonal city, with its highly
efficient corporate structures and social combines in addition to the Americans and their "cherished" dollar bill.
"Me cago en la madre de todos los que hay aquí ... " (p.
35), says Genaro bitterly. Their view of Americans in Madrid, the Spanish prostitute scene, is incisive, vulgar. The
novel is full of street-talk. At one point, Genaro characterizes the city: "There are many Koreans and Madrid is
one more. Korea means, more or less, an occasional
prostitute, adultress with advantages. What a good thing
it would be to sweep away all of this, to empty with one

large hosing all this fucking prostitution!" (p. 77). We discover very little about La Ceci, Emiliano's girl friend, or
Elena, Genaro's mistress. Female roles are subservient
to the male throughout the novel. In fact, El Penca, when
introduced in Part Two, immediately becomes a forceful
character who has the power to manipulate men and to mould
the future destiny of our leading characters. Listen to how
El Penca addresses his friends:

> Anarchy is our major sin. It is a plague one
> hundred times stronger than monarchy, the
> requetés or Catholic Action. It's our greatest
> enemy. We have no other. Anarchy is like a
> nest of vipers in which some of us are devouring
> each other. It's the most destructive thing and
> it's impossible that even in our party there may
> exist some followers that believe their own per-
> sonality has something to do with their unleashing
> the beginning of revolution [pp. 188-9].

Penca's words are dangerous and provocative; he is generally feared by Genaro and Emiliano.

One extremely interesting character is Genaro's
mother, who we meet very briefly in the space of a few
short pages. Genaro visits her when he becomes a man of
means and discovers she is ill, rotting away in a desolate
Madrid slum and finally dies after Genaro tries in vain to
save her. Except for this single, tender scene, it is very
hard to visualize any of the other characters in the novel.
All of the characters are portrayed at the same level of
depth (or lack of it). One cannot build a physical much
less a mental portrait of any of Castillo-Puche's protagonists through their words, deeds or the author's descriptions
of them. Paralelo 40 is rife with superficial action, equally
artificial descriptions and superfluous verbiage.

The best passages following the meager story line
are found at the conclusion when the novel becomes a grade-
B melodrama.

--What are you saying?

--They have sworn that they'll finish him and
they'll do it.

--But why?

--He's fallen into the trap of gambling.

> --But that's not so important... But he has her...
>
> --It's not that easy, Lucy. You see, Thomas loves a Spanish girl... He hasn't done anything bad to her ... he only loves her... But the girl has a boy friend, understand? Jealousy... They'll kill him for that, for jealousy... [p. 393].

Although Genaro is not really telling Lucy the entire truth about Thomas or El Penca's plot to kill the latter, it is this kind of melodramatic interchange that carries us forward to the conclusion of the novel. Genaro intercedes with El Penca to save Thomas' life. Thomas flies off to Torrejón. When Genaro refuses to tell Penca where Thomas is hiding, two toughs beat Genaro to death. It is Genaro's last speech that is the most convincing piece of writing in the entire novel:

> --You see? In such a place, I would like to live with you Elena. ... We have to look for it.... Now that all is ended, now that this persecution by El Penca is over, now that he's been conquered, unmasked.... Didn't I tell you that he was an evil son of a bitch? You see? And you didn't believe me... But you believe me now, don't you? El Penca has gone away by plane... You see? Didn't I tell you so?... Elena, you believe me, don't you? And Thomas has already gone.... You don't have to worry about Thomas.... He's already gone away.... But I couldn't let him die....
>
> Genaro was breathing blood and dust--the last sensations he experienced. He heard many noises, the noises of motors, noises that seemed to him like airplanes whistling as they crossed the sky, but they were really buses, trolleys and trucks that began to move up the avenue... [pp. 466-7].

Genaro dies, a "real" man, unnecessarily sacrificed by others for no important political or personal reason, a mere pawn in the game of life.

In his epilogue, Castillo-Puche ties the loose ends of the novel together. We see Thomas high in his airplane, crossing over Madrid, unaware of the events below, as the Civil Guards place Genaro's badly mutilated body in an

awaiting ambulance as the sound of traffic clamors and clat-
ters from the Plaza de Castilla toward Cibeles, where the
whistling of the ambulance's siren is confused with the noises
of the buses, trolleys, trucks and cars.   Genaro's death is
tragic, sentimental, convenient, purposeless, a pure deus ex
machina, unconvincing in the final analysis but moving, nevertheless.

                        *   *   *

     Apart from heavy fictional considerations of plot,
Castillo-Puche's novel is sprinkled liberally with social commentaries about the United States, the Americans living in
Madrid, the American view of Spain, the race question, the
paralysis of Spanish society--information as stereotyped as
the protagonists, not proceeding from any research, first-
hand knowledge or fact.   Nevertheless, these naive insights
are crystal clear, as Castillo-Puche presents them in his
journalistic prose through the prism of Genaro's "innocent"
point of view and they make interesting, if at times, controversial reading:

> What Genaro couldn't understand either was that
> all these Americans who lived here, in these ele-
> gant houses, were Americans of a 'third' class.
> Just as the United States is a democratic country,
> it classifies its categories of people.   In Madrid,
> there were many Americans also of the second
> and first classes; but these lived in old palaces
> and in comfortable chalets of the residential zones,
> far from the United States soldiers.   The soldiers
> were the ones who lived around here.   And what
> bothered Genaro more was that air of having come
> to teach the Spaniards how to live.   And not only
> the Spaniards!   The American Army was not only
> a combat Army if the occasion ever arose; it was,
> above all, a social army that was going to teach
> the rest of us mortals....   So it could do it, run-
> ning through its dollars.   They were going to teach
> us how to live but if we only had the dollars they
> have--these drunkards... [p. 47].

> Garbage men and Americans--unhappy equals, un-
> happy simpletons.   Some are representatives of a
> world in decadence, others are easy storehouses
> of revolution....   Some through ignorance, others

through ingenuity.   All will be swept away one
day... [p. 100].

Until now it seemed to Genaro that all Negros
were equal.   But Thomas, he could find him
among one thousand others....   Thomas was a
whole, loyal person....   He was different from the
rest of the Negros he saw... [p. 113].

The Americans, undoubtedly, didn't consider the
Spaniards at all.   All had brought to Spain the idea
that it was an absurd and colorful nation, cheap
for them, but poor and backwards.   Spain wasn't
a normal country.   Almost all of the Spaniards
were somewhat crazy.   They didn't understand,
for example, that the Madrileños and even the poor,
miserable people that they came upon with their immense cars always felt like laughing and making
jokes about them.   The American women had a
little more consideration for the Spanish character
and for the national temperament.   Some of them,
above all, the female American tourists, had run
the gamut of the legend of the Spaniard's physical
tolerance for love and their docility on this matter
[p. 126].

The first lesson that Genaro had learned himself
in the first days of [working] at the store was that,
in no way did he have to trust the kindly looks of
the bosses.   When Genaro thought about those
powerful excessively gentle guys, even the least of
whom earned about one thousand pesetas daily, he
felt the terrible urge to spit....   The second thing
Genaro believed he learned was that the majority
of them functioned on alcohol.   No matter how
serious and distracted they seemed, it was because
they were loaded....   The third lesson was still
the most disastrous and intolerable for Genaro.
The Americans lived with the impression that everybody begged from them and that if old Europe existed, it was thanks to the commiseration of the
American people.   According to this theory, they
thought that all people of the ruined West pretended
to live at the cost of American sweat.   'Insufferable efficiency,' when the reality that was 'the defense' of civilization; and the rest of their wealthy
tourists of the world [pp. 154-5].

Interesting insights, but incredibly superficial generalizations.

                              *   *   *

        If we were to describe the kind of realism Castillo-
Puche employs, one critic would call it "dramatic realism,"
that is, our author is "a Realist whose problems reach
great [emotional] intensities.   The ability of style and the
[novelistic] technique of Castillo-Puche consist in concentrat-
ing a maximum of problems into a minimum of materialized
themes--the result being strong, impressionable, almost
deathly novels"; Castillo-Puche is a continuer of the traditional Realist school of the nineteenth century with tendencies
towards writing "intellectual" novels. [2]   Undeniably, Castillo-
Puche is a writer with natural talent.   His language is direct, simple, at times graphic.   His narrative moves efficiently, clearly but somewhat verbosely and simple-mindedly
in Paralelo 40.

        Another critic felt this particular novel was more of
a documentary about Madrid (probably because the author
said so), about the North Americans working at military
bases in Spain and about the Spaniards who move into the
camp of political subversion.   He also viewed the novel as
a "song to friendship--friendship between Genaro, the re-
sented one and Thomas, the United States Negro,"[3] and the
novel as one of protest.   Yet, another critic views Castillo-
Puche's novel as a "balance between the intuitive novel and
the intellectual one."[4]   Regarding his style, it is "served
by direct language--nothing researched, nothing artificial--
perfectly literary and grandly expressive."[5]   As for his
brand of Realism, Baquero Goyanes beels there is "an evident predominance of invention, of creative imagination."
García-Viñó elaborates on this point, believing Castillo-
Puche is selective and "situates himself above the reality
[he writes about] but does not face it directly."[6]

        At a lecture after the publication of Paralelo 40, the
author said of himself: "I am not exactly like any of the
characters of my novel, although some of them may have
borne my own worries and ideas."[7]   García-Viñó believes
part of Castillo-Puche's Realist attitude in his characters is
to destroy conventional ideas, superstitions, and false values,
although his characters, like Genaro are exactly the reverse
of Realists themselves--they're "vegetative, impressionable,

delicate, dreamy, imaginative, maternal, and believe in fantasy, caprices, poetry, lyricism. They are timid, infantile,
melancholic, fraught by memories of the past, in love with
intimacy, sensual, intelligent, intuitive, inspired. "8

These adjectives certainly describe Genaro of Paralelo
40, who seems alien to the Realist milieu created by Castillo-
Puche. Genaro is not a rebel; he is tied to his class by his
mores. Yet ironically, critics consider Paralelo 40 a documentary Realist novel, a novel of protest where "the Americans on their behalf and the terrorist action [of Spaniards]
on their part fulfill a purely functional work. Both ingredi-
ents make visible and unmask at the same time the concrete
allusions of the writer to protest American intervention and
Spanish political cowardice under the guise of Communism. "9
If these were Castillo-Puche's motives in writing this novel,
they certainly did not become apparent to me throughout my
reading of the work. I did not feel Genaro was involved intellectually or politically, only emotionally. He did not experience any tremendous crises of conscience. There were
no remarkable interior (or, mental) struggles within his
thoughts or soul. Quite the opposite: Genaro's actions
were constantly shaped by the influences of the society surrounding him. Castillo-Puche has been called lyrical, poetic, a tremendista writer, a naturalist, a satirist; I would
refrain from using any of these adjectives to characterize
his present literary output. Certainly Paralelo 40 contains
very little of these attributes. What it does contain is the
author's tendency towards caricature and the grotesque.
And his portraits of prostitutes and their language in the
bars, for example, is exceptional.

It is truly difficult to pigeonhole the kind of novelist
Castillo-Puche appears to be and the kind of novels he
writes. Apart from unveiling a distinct class of Realism
in which his protagonists are frequently indecisive and reveal tortuous changes in their mental states while displaying
a constant pessimism, Castillo-Puche's characters search
for a single truth, usually derived from the social situation.
Genaro's problems of conscience are individual ones, not
typifying an entire class. Perhaps the "authenticity" of his
thoughts derive from an autobiographical basis (which Castillo-Puche "refuted" in his prologue to the novel). Consequently, Paralelo 40 cannot really be called a social novel
or a novel of protest despite the author's pretension. Strong
criticism of the United States and Spanish parisitism are in
evidence, but I feel they are the result of the author's ten-

dency to exaggerate scenes and intensify emotions in the
manner of Cela's tremendismo, taking a simple story and
creating with it a strong and at times supercharged, but unconvincing collection of tableaux. Sanz Villanueva has addressed this very point. He says, "if Castillo-Puche would
lend attention to these things, let us say, his excesses, and
if he would decide to insert his plots into a historical dimension and not only one [dealing with] individual problems, he
would be one of our very best, first class novelists."[10]

　　　Castillo-Puche is quite successful at portraying the
conflict of an individual conscience, in this case, Genaro's
conflict with his political party. Although Genaro opts to
sacrifice his life for his personal dignity (in a truly Christian
sense), many literary critics felt Castillo-Puche had become
a leading practitioner of the "Catholic" novel in Spain. Perhaps Brian Dendle shows us why: "Catholic novelists do not
present an entirely uniform approach to the religious question.... Their attitude is mainly defensive. The Catholic
attitude can only be described as one of fear: fear of the
present, fear of the city, fear of alien ideas."[11] These
fears are prevalent in Genaro's character. Gonzalo Sobejano
refutes this conjecture in favor of calling the novel not a
"Catholic" one but a "religious" one, an "existential" work
since "the existential sentiment present derives from a moral
attitude and not intellectual or philosophical positions."[12]
Critics also mistakenly assume the "confessional temper"
of Castillo-Puche's novels derives from his own personal
life and his difficulties in perceiving the truth of real people,
of characters and their situations.[13] To return to the writer as a "Catholic novelist," García-Viñó would say he is
"almost" one and Iglesias Laguna believes Paralelo 40 can
be considered "the most authentic Catholic novel" written to
date.[14]

　　　The issue here is not whether Castillo-Puche is a
propagator of the "Catholic novel genre" (whatever that is).
The key to understanding his novels and their techniques is
his treatment of reality; many critics feel there is an existential dimension given to Paralelo 40 which makes it the
author's outstanding novel. Gemma Roberts expertly studied
the existential view of death found in the writer's 1954
novel, Con la muerte al hombro, and concluded that Julio's
(the protagonist's) death is a kind of complex, self-inflicted
alienation, a type of self-indulgent vocation, a kind of absurdity born out of an anxiety for justice and a frustration
of truth.[15]

I wish I could discover (with Roberts and Iglesias Laguna) the "philosophical" or "religious" or "existential" impact of Paralelo 40 or for that matter, any other Castillo-
Puche's view of reality lies in its excesses, its detailed
portrait of "Korea," its tender relationship between Genaro
and Thomas, its frequent emotional displays, its prolixity
(characters talk too much), its blasphemies, its anti-cleri-
calism, its journalistic style, its graphic descriptions, its
slang.   Although certain critics feel the essential theme of
the novel is hate giving in to love, my feeling is that
Castillo-Puche intended to write a truculent, realistic, prolix novel about daringly new themes--Americans in Spain,
the "color" bar, the resultant problems between conflicting
values in Spanish and American cultures.   Paralelo 40
forms an integral part of our vision of Madrid.   "Korea"
exists and the problems it precipitates are passionate di-
lemmas which may have many national consequences.   Although the narration is fast and lively it is artificial; the
Spaniards are caricatures; the novel is long on talk, short
on meaning.

Nevertheless, Paralelo 40 is worth reading simply
because whether you agree or not with its themes, Catholic
values, or social views, it is a remarkably realistic novel,
striking out into new thematic territory.   Hearing the cry
for regeneration of the novel genre, Castillo-Puche took up
the question of American-Spanish interrelations in Madrid
and his novel, with occasional stylistic lapses into nineteenth-
century Realism, is another step forward in the advancement
of the genre in Spain.   To sum up Castillo-Puche's literary
promise, Eugenio de Nora feels "he has demonstrated (1) a
kind of liveliness and admirable precision in his manner of
observing and describing reality accompanied by a capacity
to objectify intimate experience...; (2) a sincerity and moral
courage to deal with difficult themes...; (3) a constructive
ability to create varying psychological types."[16]   Nora feels
when these qualities harmonize, only then will Castillo-Puche
give to Spain the truly great novel that the country is awaiting from him.   Paralelo 40 is certainly not the best novel
of the author's considerable literary output, but it does show
his willingness to strike out, like other New Wave writers
(as early as 1963) into new thematic directions which enhance the genre and to grasp the "realities" of the social
scene ever-present in contemporary Spain.   We must remember that Castillo-Puche, like Gironella, is a very "popular"
novelist.

His books sell remarkably well and whether or not he has achieved any modicum of artistic success is in my view a moot question. Paralelo 40 is one of the most feeble pieces of fiction I have read by any Spanish writer. However, it does deserve a chapter in this study of Spanish Realism and the evolution of the New Wave writers since it recalls stylistically the anachronisms of traditional Realist nineteenth-century models and is read by a vast segment of the Spanish middle-class which finds its "Catholic" values somewhat inspirational. Paralelo 40, like Los cipreses creen en Dios, is an outstanding commercial success in Spain, but unlike Gironella's novel, it possesses few of the artistic virtues and most of the faults of popular fiction produced by writers whose appeal is to the mass audience.

THE WORKS OF J. L. CASTILLO-PUCHE

Con la muerte al hombro.   Madrid: Ed. Biblioteca Nueva, 1954.
Sin Camino. Buenos Aires: Ed. Emecé, 1956.
El Vengador. Barcelona: Ed. Destino, 1956.
Hicieron partes. Barcelona: Ed. Destino, 1957.
Paralelo 40. Barcelona: Ed. Destino, 1963.
Oro Blanco. Madrid: Ed. Cid, 1963.
El perro loco. Madrid: La Novela Popular, 1965.
Como ovejas al matadero. Barcelona: Ed. Destino, 1971.

SELECTED STUDIES ON CASTILLO-PUCHE

Agulló y Cobo, M. "Escritores contemporáneos: J. L. Castillo Puche," El Libro Español (Madrid), vol. 2 (13 enero 1959), 19-21.
Alborg, J. L. "J. L. Castillo Puche," in Hora actual de la novela..., (vol. 1), pp. 281-303.
Alvarez, C. L. " 'Hicieron partes,' de J. L. C. P.," Punta Europa (Madrid), vol. 3 (1958), 122-3.
          . "Paralelo 40," Blanco y Negro (15 junio 1963), 9.
Arroitia-Jáuregui, M. "Primera novela de C. P.," Alcalá, no. 57 (25 mayo 1954), 14.
Cano, J. L. "Con la muerte al hombro," Insula, no. 102 (junio 1954), 12; and "El vengador," Ibid., no. 125 (abril 1957), 9.
Fernández Almagro, M. "Con la muerte al hombro," ABC (27 junio 1954), 22.
          . "Hicieron partes," ABC (8 feb. 1959), 16.

_____ . " 'Paralelo 40,' por J. L. Castillo Puche, " ABC
            (23 junio 1963), 23.
Hornedo, R. M. de, S. I.   "Hicieron partes, " Razón y Fe
            (1958), 95-100.
Marra-López, J. R.   "J. L. Castillo Puche: 'Paralelo 40', "
            Insula, nos. 200-201 (julio-ag. 1963), 17.
Pastor Mateos, E.   "C. P., Premio Nacional de Literatura, "
            Arbor (Madrid) (1959), 449-50.
Sáinz de Robles, F. C.   "Con la muerte al hombro, " Pano-
            rama Literario, vol. 2 (1955), 58-60.

Chapter 14

JUAN GOYTISOLO and SEÑAS DE IDENTIDAD
(Marks of Identity) (1966)

Juan Goytisolo Gay was born on January 5, 1931, in
Barcelona of Spanish, Basque and French ancestry. As a
youngster, he lived in a small village in the province of
Catalonia during the years of the Spanish Civil War (1936-
1939). His younger brother Luis was born in 1935 and his
older brother, José Agustín (born in 1928) stayed with him
during the war. In that period, his mother, Luisa Gay was
killed in an air raid by the Nationalists in 1938. His father,
a retired chemical factory executive was imprisoned during
the war. At the end of 1939, Goytisolo spent the summer
in a country house owned by his father near Barcelona which
today is used as a school for orphans.

Young Goytisolo showed an early interest in writing,
perhaps derived from his maternal great uncle, Ramón Vives,
a renowned Catalan poet. In 1942, Goytisolo composed a
novel about Joan of Arc (which was never published). His
older brother José began writing poetry and his younger
brother Luis wrote the popular novel Las afueras (The Outskirts) which we discussed in Chapter 8. In 1946, Juan
Goytisolo wrote another (unpublished) novel about cowboys and
indians while taking his bachillerato, which he finally completed at a Jesuit School in 1949. He began to study law at
the University of Barcelona and also took courses at the University of Madrid, but his interests extended primarily into
the literary field.

With Ana María Matute, he founded a literary group
or tertulia called La Turia in Barcelona and published his
first short stories in 1951. The following year, he won the
Premio Joventud for a short story "El mundo de los espejos"
("The World of Mirrors"), which was subsequently censored

by the Franco government and therefore never published.
Also in 1952, he wrote his first novelette, El soldadito (The
Little Soldier) and also conceived his first long novel Juego
de manos (Sleight of Hand), which was published in 1954.
In 1953, he finished his law degree at the University of Barcelona, but writing occupied so much of his time that in the
next two years he completed Duelo en el Paraíso (Sorrow at
Paradise House) (for which he won the Premio Indice in
1955) and Fiestas. Subsequently, he never went into law
practice.

     Because Goytisolo was offered a job by Gallimard
Press in Paris in 1956, he left Spain and decided to settle
permanently there since 1957. He has been instrumental in
arranging French translations for Gallimard of the works of
other New Wave novelists such as Ana María Matute, Elena
Quiroga and Miguel Delibes, for example. While working
for Gallimard, he had the opportunity to travel abroad, to
Cuba and to other European countries, returning home occasionally to Catalonia. During these sojourns, he wrote a
great number of novels and travelogues. He published three
novels, El Circo (The Circus) in 1957; La resaca (The Un-
dertow) and Fiestas in 1958; a travel book entitled Campos
de Níjar (Fields of Níjar) and a collection of short stories,
Para vivir aquí (To Live Here), in 1960; another novel, La
isla (The Island) in 1961; a travel book, La Chanca, and
Fin de fiesta (Holiday's End), a group of short stories, in
1962; another travel book Pueblos en marcha (People on the
March) in 1963; and Señas de identidad (Marks of Identity)
in 1966 and Reivindicación del Conde Don Julián (The Recovery of Count Julián) in 1970, decidedly two of the best
novels ever written in the Spanish language. Goytisolo is
also responsible for two works of literary criticism discussed in an earlier chapter, Problemas de la novela (Problems of the Novel) (1959), and El furgón de cola (The Caboose) (1967), in which he presents his own essays, polemics
and aesthetics dealing with the novel as he uniquely con-
ceives it. Many, many translations of his novels have been
made here in the United States and abroad. Very little else
is known about Goytisolo's personal life except that he remains a bachelor and still lives and works in Paris.[1]

                    *   *   *

     The novel we have chosen to discuss, Señas de identi-
dad (Marks of Identity) was first published in Mexico in 1966.

It created such a stir in the Spanish literary world that it
was subsequently censored in Spain along with several other
Goytisolo novels written before and after the appearance of
Señas.   However with the appearance of Señas, Goytisolo
came to the fore as the undisputed leader of the Spanish New
Wave movement, an outspoken rebel, an extraordinarily talented writer, a revisionist within the novel genre, an incredible inventor of a new type of Realism that we have only
seen barely suggested before in the careers of other leading
New Wave novelists currently residing in Spain.

In 1960, Goytisolo made the following statement to a
reporter for the Paris newspaper L'Express: "In a society
in which human relationships are fundamentally artificial,
Realism becomes a necessity... For ourselves, Spanish
writers, reality however is our only evasion."[2] When Goytisolo first began to compose novels, he did so admittedly
from an infantile, almost tangential point of view, avoiding
coming to grips with a reality as did most of the members
of his generation.   By 1966, and after spending several
years in Paris, Goytisolo was to refute his own "intellectu-
alizations" about the novel genre as well as his own ideas
on Realism.   With Señas de identidad, he became both politically and intellectually engagé.   He commemorates the
past and warns his reading public not to forget what happened in Spain during the Civil War.   "Perhaps someone
will understand what your crime was, what order you tried
to resist."[3]

Goytisolo is the New Wave's leading and most daringly outspoken novelist.   In an excellent interview with Emir
Rodríguez Monegal as reported in the latter's book, El arte
de narrar (The Art of Narration), Goytisolo discusses many
aspects of his novel, Señas de identidad.   Although I shall
only alude to some of Goytisolo's personal remarks about
Señas later on in this chapter, one of his most incisive,
shattering comments concerning reality is the following:

> One of the objectives of the novel is to situate at
> what point we find ourselves.   We live surrounded
> by myths, myths of 1936, myths of 1898; we are
> asphyxiated by these myths and my book is an at-
> tempt to make a tabla rasa, to know where we
> are, because we may not know where we are and
> we may not be able to create a novel; we cannot
> make a valid artistic statement.   In this aspect,
> my novel is a demythification force ... an effort

to situate problems in actual terms....

... an attempt to undo the myths of several Spains
that are acting simultaneously on several distinct
levels today.

One of the objectives of art has always been to
destroy all automatic invention, all which is based
upon myth. In my case, I have proposed to offer
an image of Spain which the reader already knows
about; I have not wanted to reproduce something
that is in everyone's mind but to create a new vision that might destroy the old one.

On all planes of the novel, I have intended to emphasize this painful break (or rupture) between
myth and reality, between the crude reality and
the reality embellished by myth. [4]

To understand Señas, Goytisolo would have his readers
comprehend a series of materials, some from literary
sources, others taken from real life, which he has integrated
into the structure of the novel. Rodríguez Monegal calls
Señas a "collage" and as such, its plot is difficult to set
down. However the highly esteemed critic of modern Spanish literature, Kessel Schwartz, in his excellent book on
Goytisolo, has achieved the best synthesis of a truly difficult
plot outline I have come across in English from which I here
quote liberally.

*   *   *

"Alvaro Mendiola, a member of a conservative and
socially prominent Barcelona family which had supported
Franco in the Civil War, unable to accept their views
went to France in October, 1952, on the pretext of
studying cinematography. In so doing he abandoned his
friends in the midst of a difficult fight for their political rights. In France he had worked sporadically on a
sociological documentary about Spanish emigration and
had indulged in political discussions in various cafes,
especially that of Madame Berger where refugees
gathered to plan reviews and political action which never materialized. Alvaro had tried to help the refugees
at first but ended up by avoiding them completely. Engaging in his somewhat empty existence devoted largely

to smoking, drinking, and getting through the day, he
had met and fallen in love with Dolores, a girl who
lived in his boarding house and whom he had helped
out of a difficult financial situation. She had left her
exiled Republican family in Mexico to travel and learn
about a different kind of existence. Obtaining employment on a French newspaper, he traveled with her
over the world. In early 1963 he suffered a heart attack, and fearing an approaching death, at the age of
thirty-two he returned with Dolores to his family home
near Barcelona five months later, in July. Dolores
was concerned because of his excessive drinking.

"As the story opens in August of 1963, Alvaro sits
listening to Mozart's 'Requiem' and looking through
various family albums, photographs, and letters, in-
dulging in a sentimental exploratory journey into his
past, trying to discover who and what he really is, as
he remembers the events of his life and those of his
family and friends, in a series of temporal excursions
to the past.

"Two days earlier, Professor Ayuso, a liberal professor who had been imprisoned for two years and who
had helped indoctrinate Alvaro and his friends with concern for the dignity of man, had died. Ayuso goes to
an unmarked grave, its occupant still pursued even in
death by the governmental "forces of order." A number of Alvaro's university friends attend the funeral.
Alvaro recalls Antonio Ramírez Trueba, a native of
Murcia, known at the university for his Marxist sympathies. After eighteen months in jail Ramírez had
returned to his home town, patronized at first by the
town's respectable society as the town "Communist,"
but he had been placed under severe restrictions when
he insulted Don Gonzalo, a conservative town leader,
by refusing to associate with him. He had thus freed
his soul, if not his body, through their enmity. Antonio had visited Dolores while Alvaro was in Cuba
covering the Cuban revolution. Alvaro visits his cousin's former home in Cuba and has affairs and adventures with various young ladies. He recalls other university friends: Enrique, a Falangist who felt Franco
had betrayed the revolution; Ricardo and Paco who led
student demonstrations; and the strange, nihilistic
Sergio, with whom he had visited the red-light district.
Ana, Sergio's mother, wanting to share all his experi-

ences, had had a relationship with him which bordered
on the incestuous. She also had aroused Alvaro and
almost become his lover. Later Alvaro visited the
same scenes in Barcelona, after an absence of some
seven years, to try and recover the emotions of the
past. The setting had not changed, but he had. Sergio,
abandoning his earlier bohemian ways, had become a
successful businessman and had died in an automobile
crash in 1955.

"Alvaro had visited the cemetery where his own
mother was buried, thus triggering memories of her
funeral, his feelings at sixteen years of age, that if
he did not cut his family ties he would end up buried
and dissolved back into the elements, to share his
family's absurdity forever.

"One of his recollections concerns his father's assassination in 1936, which he had never been able to
document fully. After the war his family, re-estab-
lished in Barcelona, had also tried to find out the details. Alvaro journeyed to his father's grave to look
up various people who might know something of the
event. The Republic had tried to give the peasants
work, but it was these same hungry peasants, victims
of humiliations and injustices through the years, who
had killed his father. Alvaro remembers his days as
a refugee child and his quarrels with the French
children.

"He recalls his trips to various countries with Dolores, who had helped brighten his grey life, alleviat-
ing momentarily his anguish at his lost identity. In
spite of his love for her, he had forced her to have
an abortion, and for a brief period she had run off
with Enrique to obtain revenge. After nine years they
still love one another, in spite of various brief infi-
delities on his part, including a homosexual episode
which reminded him of his adolescent love for Jerónimo López, one of the former family workers, hired
while he was away at school. Alvaro's ultrareligious
Aunt Mercedes suspected Jerónimo who, it developed,
was a leader of the Maquis and had disappeared one
day. Alvaro continues to recall hundreds of details
and interwoven lives at various periods of his life,
recent and remote, such as the visit of Ricardo and
Artigas with two blond Danish pick-ups.

"Alvaro remembers his grandmother and his visits to her garden, her later loss of memory, and his renewed visits after the Spanish Civil War, when she was living in an old folks' home. Through the pictorial record in the album, he revives the sugar mills and the slaves his great-grandparents had had in Cuba, and their descendants, useless and decorative parasites. He recalls the uniformly grey days at a religious school, which his respectable family had hoped would reintegrate him into the strict, unyielding and dying moral code to which they subscribed. He recollects his even earlier religious exaltation and thoughts of childish martyrdom, encouraged by the vaguely remembered governess, Miss Lourdes. He conjures up his Uncle Eulogio with his youthful studies of astronomy, astrology, and the occult sciences and his enthusiasm for Spengler. He summons up once more the boarding house at which he had lived in France, at the home of a music teacher, Madame de Heredia, and her passionate love for Frederic who, rejecting her, had run off with her son.

"The long vigil ends, and Alvaro, awake all night in his mental retrospection, leaves the sleeping Dolores to drive off, still tired, sick, and on the edge of suicide, to Barcelona, his native city. "5

Señas de identidad is a thrilling, ironic, trenchantly pessimistic, brilliant novel, especially for those who lived in Spain in 1967 and recalled the 25 años de paz slogans plastered on every empty wall throughout the nation, a slogan which had the truth and gave the illusion of Spain as a placid nation rife with tourism, an illusion which Goytisolo attacks. The Señas leitmotiv is presented at the outset when Goytisolo quotes Quevedo, Larra and Cernuda's works respectively: "Yesterday has gone; tomorrow has not come. ... The cemetery is inside Madrid. ... Better yet, destruction, fire" (p. 8). Señas is organized into eight chapters of varying length and is written on a variety of levels. Although it is difficult to impose an order upon these eight chapters because of its juxtapositions of time and space, the following generalizations can be made: Chapter One deals with Alvaro's early youth; Chapter Two, his family and memories of his student days at the university; Chapter Three, his working days in Albacete, Yeste, and the deaths of his father and cousin during the Civil War; Chapter Four, Alvaro's memories of the war, surveillance of his friends

and the political scene; Chapter Five, his exile in Paris and
his role as refugee; Chapter Six, his changing love for Dolores over a period of years; Chapter Seven, his visit to
Cuba; and finally, Chapter Eight, a mixture of all themes
carried through in the seven previous chapters including his
eventual crise de conscience at the conclusion which leads
Alvaro back to Barcelona in a chaotic, oftentimes tormented
search for his own psychological and national identity.

Señas has been called an elaborate puzzle written
perhaps in the same vein as Julio Cortázar's Rayuela (Hopscotch) because of the great alterations and lapses in (1)
chronology (anecdotes are juxtaposed in Alvaro's memory between the years 1956 and 1963), (2) geography (the scene
shifts between palaces and whore houses, university lecture
halls and prisons, from Barcelona to Cuba, to Venice, to
Switzerland), (3) narration (in the first person singular,
first person plural, second person singular, third person
singular, both in objective and personal modes and with use
of the impersonal se), (4) typography (there are long passages with punctuation, without punctuation, broken paragraphs, dialogue, interior monologue in italics, without italics, the use of bold capitals to emphasize ideas) and (5)
language (an extensive use of French, foreign colloquialisms
in Spanish, English, Catalan, German, Arabic, Italian and
Andalusian and Cuban dialects). 6

Goytisolo has successfully fragmented Alvaro's world
(or his own) by means of his use of language and eight distinct levels may be perceived: (1) "the language of 'official
communication,' (2) the Spanish bourgeoisie, (3) the voice of
opposition to present-day Spanish politics, (4) the language
of exiles, (5) juvenile argot, (6) the expression of the poor,
(7) the language of self-awareness of Alvaro and (8) the language of a narrative poem. " Goytisolo manipulates his use
of language carefully in order to give us a full view of his
idea of a vital reality, a reality free of restrictions in which
the novelist presents three types of characters: those
treated generally in a depersonalized fashion; those whose
psyches are somewhat nebulous, undefined but more detailed;
and those whose personalities are revealed entirely. Although one can never really arrive at knowing more than two
characters intimately, completely (Alvaro and Dolores), I
feel nevertheless that Señas is a fierce portrait of modern
Spaniards because of Goytisolo's unique dissection of reality.
This he does to the following: (1) the Spanish and French
bourgeois, "their wealth, hypocrises, support of the Franco

regime, collaboration with the slogan '25 Years of Peace,'
adhesion to order and authority, faith in religion"; (2) Republican politics, the "heterogenous mixture of illusionary
university students, faithful conspirators ... and divided
exiles...; (3) the Franco regime, with its official propaganda,
tourist attractions, exploitation of Spanish myths, censorship,
terror, alliance with North Americans and their adaption to
neo-Capitalism; (4) the Spanish people themselves, revealed
by their virtues and defects (of character), in their passivity,
their complexes and hopes, ... their search for work;
(5) the Civil War from a humanistic point of view in which
all Spaniards were both 'hangmen and victims'; and (6) the
intellectual, both inside and outside of Spain, with their
closed ideas to change, some faithful to incorruptible principles, others totally, vitally interested in the creation of a
New Spain."7

Goytisolo's novel is a work of total desperation, a
pessimistic vision, a novela-testimonio, presenting a startl-
ingly new kind of Realism, but above all, a work of art
faithful to the contemporary narrative and its new conception.
Goytisolo said himself that "this new artistic conception is a
true compromise for the writer who situates himself on a
triple plane--social, personal and technical."8   Goytisolo
feels every Spanish novelist has a distinct social mission--
his is not to let anyone forget what happened in Spain, and
not be silent (like Alvaro) about the repression hidden under
the current popular slogan "35 Years of Peace."

Señas de identidad has been praised internationally.
It has been called "the major effort of his career as a
novelist and the excellence of his work rests jointly on the
richness of its construction and the radical manner of its
examination of conscience."9   "Señas emanates from vital
experiences; it represents a notable and intense effort at national self-analysis, perhaps the most ambitious that may
have been written in the form of a novel."10   The work "ex-
plores historical, geographical, temporal and spatial relationships [using] myth, psychology, poetry, objective and
lyrical descriptions...."11   The critic José Agustín calls it
the "most important Spanish novel of the century."12

On the other side of the coin, Señas has been accused of having flaws, essentially because of the great im-
balance between its themes and real experience, its tendency towards idealizations based on fictions rather than true
knowledge based upon fact (especially with reference to

Spanish political questions), and Goytisolo's imprecise use
of language, replete with errors. [13] Goytisolo has acknowledged there was an excessive concern (or preoccupation)
with portrayal of "vital experiences" rather than directing his
energies towards conceiving a singularly harmonious and truly
artistic work of fiction.   Another critic, Rafael Bosch called
Señas "a pseudo-novel" in imitation of the pretentious subjectivism of Carlos Fuentes (the great Mexican novelist and
critic) and his school; commenting on Goytisolo's career, he
believes "the inclusion of bourgeois prejudices from a stagnant, subjective viewpoint does not pave the way for the future [Spanish novel], neither to scientific or literary advantage. "[14]

        Finally, Goytisolo has been accused, by Nora, of
portraying the world of the Spanish bourgeois from an "irri-
tated, anarchic, violent and almost temperamental point of
view" in which his narrative frequently provides sensations
of unreality despite accurate perception of routine or vulgar
events in the lives of his characters: "Although the novels
of Goytisolo pretend to be Realist ones, they are nothing
but high grade fictions ... since in Goytisolo's very spirit
of authorship, there exists very few cultural and vital elements that he himself energetically is forced to reject or
fight. "[15]   It is clear that with such critical dissention,
Goytisolo's personality and novels are considered controversial matters indeed.   At this juncture, it is necessary to
evaluate Señas de identidad in terms of its achievements for
Goytisolo, the New Wave and the regeneration of the Spanish
narrative.

        Señas is, without a doubt, Goytisolo's most ambitious
fictional work.   According to Ramón Buckley, Goytisolo
tried to resolve the problem between the 'I' and the external
reality.   He feels Goytisolo stated his motives clearly in the
following from the novel: "... to conjugate in a harmonious
manner, one's inner search with objective testimony, the
intimate compresension of your self and the evolution of the
civil conscience of others" (p. 165).   Further, Buckley feels
Goytisolo is not only writing "a literary exercise but is, in
effect, accomplishing a vital necessity: to discuss the justi-
fication of his entire life, the signs of identity that permit
him to be acquainted with himself and to live in society. "[16]
Although Buckley feels Goytisolo's literary motives are
doomed to failure, he considers Señas a worthy, vital, literary experiment towards a literary solution that probably
does not exist.

Throughout his writing career, Goytisolo has been identified as Spain's "angry young man" of the Spanish novel who has written in the tradition of Pío Baroja and Cela. He has always been called a Realist writer, sometimes an objective realist, at others, a social realist. Although he may have, Kessel Schwartz has said, "flirted with objective insistence on reality..., he has not allowed structure and style to overshadow plot nor has he indulged in an over accumulation of details of things observed. ... [I]n the final analysis, Goytisolo is concerned with human and social values... "[17] According to this critic and others, Goytisolo has kept up with literary currents in Europe and America, and feels too deeply the unlimited range of artistic expression to be said to "belong" to any literary movement or to suffer any aesthetic restrictions. And yet, "objectivist," "social-realist," and "neo-realist" are the literary jargon terms associated with Juan Goytisolo's novels. Pablo Gil Casado, a critic of social novels himself, justifiably assumed Señas de identidad to be "the most notable and intense effort at national self-analysis, perhaps the most ambitious ever written in the form of a novel."[18]

Formerly, Goytisolo was a practitioner and believer in the social realist novel, in which he would denounce the absurdities and injustices of the world which surrounded him, inviting the reader, at times, to participate in the moral position of the novelist. His objective style was so engaging that the reality he portrayed was easily self-evident, expressive, very much in the manner of the novels of Ernest Hemingway.[19] And in 1959 Goytisolo felt that to achieve "a complete Realism is impossible: in the modern novel, there are no longer any unappealable judgments or absolute truths but partialities, ambiguities, relativism [and] the novelist admits easily that an event may have a multiplicity of versions."[20] Goytisolo has come a long way since. For with Señas, he believes a complete realism is possible to achieve.

*   *   *

The salient stylistic characteristics of Señas are the author's narrative skill, his creative imagination, the vividness of his language, the successful use of cinematrographic images, a well-constructed, authentically Spanish plot, and a personal, intimate style alternating with interior monologue, realistic dialogue, lyrical passabes with erotic scenes and political action with an analysis of psychological complexes.

Clearly, Goytisolo's main theme is Spain, its past and future. Unlike such writers as Cela, Sánchez Ferlosio and
Fernández Santos, Goytisolo's commentaries about Spanish
politics are courageous and overt denunciations especially
against anti-Franco émigrés, their empty talk, petty intrigues
and political inefficiency. Although many other Spanish New
Wave authors still reside in Spain, Goytisolo has become a
voluntary exile, an outspoken critic of the Franco regime,
a courageous spirit, a writer of the first rank in his never
ending quest for truth and the proper portrayal of reality.
In Señas, Goytisolo comes closest to achieving this goal.
The novel is informative about current events and vital political matters. It attempts to unite living experience with
the fictitious one through experiments with words, with film
techniques, and with temporal arrangement. Kessel Schwartz
recognizes the need for Goytisolo's experimentation and has
said, "The new world needs a new, anarchic and virulent
language...," yet he also points out the even more significant aspect of Goytisolo's work: "Even though he is in a
sense, the most artistic writer of his generation (a fact denied by the defenders of Matute and Aldecoa), which may en-
sure his long-term survival, it is by his refusal to accept
authority in conflict with his moral code which makes him
the leading Spanish novelist of his day." "Although Goytisolo [himself] admits that his own generation has not yet
reached literary maturity, time yet remains for revision of
past errors, re-dedication and re-evaluation."[21]

*   *   *

At this point, several personal commentaries about
Señas de identidad arise. For me, Goytisolo has written a
truly authentic and first-rate novel which breathes reality in
its evocations of Paris and Barcelona and its choice of natural and real physical details to portray the life style of his
protagonist, Alvaro Mendiola. Having lived in Spain and
France myself in the late sixties, the SEU (Sociedad Estudi-
antil Universitaria), No-Do (Noticiario del Día), 25 Años de
Paz signs, IDHEC (Institut des Hautes Etudes Cinématogra-
phiques), the cinema of the rue d'Ulm and Madame Berger's
café are all meaningful and real experiences for me. And
much like the great French novelist, Marcel Proust, in his
A la recherche du temps perdu, Juan Goytisolo has successfully re-created the worlds of Barcelona and Paris with his
unique alternation of action and reflection, between what is
observed and what is thought in order to present an accurate
portrait of reality of the worlds in which Alvaro moves.

Alvaro, like Marcel, is in search of his conscience,
his marks of identity, his self.   Alvaro is particularly concerned with the past (the Civil War and the ensuing years),
while Marcel concentrates on his life in Paris during the
early twentieth century.   Both are susceptible to concrete
stimuli to evoke memory.   Alvaro looks at geography books,
report cards, photos, post cards and other memorabilia and
is receptive to other sensory stimuli.   Alvaro's Fefiñanes
liquer and Marcel's linden tea and petites madeleines
(cookies) produce an evocation of the past, an enquiry into
the nature of time, into the trajectory of their lives, their
physical and psychological identities and their futures.   If I
have drawn parallels between Goytisolo's novel and Proust's,
it is because they are appropriate in theme.   They are certainly not so in degree.   Where Proust's monumental A la
recherche is the product of a lifetime of work and thought,
Goytisolo's is the work of a few short years of mediation
and writing as he indicates on the novel's very last page.
"Havana-Paris-St. Tropez-Tangier.   Autumn 1962-Spring
1966. "   But to rank Goytisolo with Proust seems fitting and
entirely compatible with the writer's view of life, and his
burgeoning talent.   Goytisolo's world embodies a kind of
tough, masculine, brutal, amoral, aggressive, alienated, [22]
even corrupt mystique--unlike the Proustian vision, which is
more feminine, subtle, dilettantish (but equally sadistic and
corrupt).   The comparison of Goytisolo's popular novel to
Proust's immortal one should not be prolonged, but the
parallel as drawn is obvious and should, I hope emphasize
Goytisolo's enormous talent.

Most remarkably, no other writer at this time would
have dared to put the following remarks into print:

> ... the survival of such a regime ... is really
> unthinkable.   It's a scandal in the real meaning of
> the word and the scandal must come to an end....
> We saw Franco on the beach at San Sebastián.
> We were about forty feet away from him and no-
> body searched us....   An assassination seemed
> quite possible....   ...
>
> Our vacation in Spain brought us a little hope, a
> little fresh air.   In [France], at least the word
> freedom means something quite definite.   Here it's
> lost its meaning.   Everyone is thought to be free
> and we live in the worst kind of alienation.   ...

The vicissitudes of the war in Algeria, the dramatic events in Suez, Hungary and Poland were
completely occupying the energies of the group [of
émigrés] while the quixotic struggle of Antonio and
your friend against Spain's obtuse and reactionary
society and its omnipresent guardians was being
asphyxiated in the smoke, mud and lies of your
desolate and useless Years of Peace. ...

There was not the slightest doubt about it: the
police had worked perfectly. Five centuries of vig-
ilance, inquisition and censorship had slowly con-
figured the moral structure of this unique organism,
considered even by its enemies and detractors as
a beacon and model of the many sanitary institutions, that, taking their inspiration from it, are
proliferating throughout the world.... The realm
of Twenty-Five Years of Peace was nothing but the
refined and visible product of an underground effort
of generations, dedicated to the noble and happy
mission of maintaining against the wind and tide
the rigid immobility of principles, the vital respect for the law, the blind and quick obedience to
the mysterious norms that govern that human society arranged into categories and social classes
(each of them representing to perfection its role in
the illusory theatre of life). ...

Nevertheless / in this same environment of burned
earth remote sky impossible birds obsessive light /
during the reign of the Twenty-Five Years of Peace
recognized / and celebrated by all right-thinking
people in the world / armed men had beaten de-
fenseless fellow countrymen with whips / lashes
clubs had vent their fury on them with rifle butts
ropes /guns /men whose only crime had been to
take arms in defense of / their legal government
fulfill their oath of allegiance to the Republic /
proclaim their right to a just and noble existence
believe / in the free will of a human being write
the word Freedom on / walls fences sidewalks
buildings.... 23

Goytisolo is the most daring New Wave writer of his
generation, politically committed to a new Spain, and writing
politics. 24   While reading Señas, one feels the "combative-
ness" of the author's sentiments, although Goytisolo himself

disclaims this. He sees his task of writer as that of dealing with the common experiences of ordinary people. "The
contemporary Spanish novelist must portray Spanish man, in
much the same manner as the picaresque novelists reflected
Spain in the sixteenth and seventeenth-centuries. The novel
must be humanized and show us society, not as it believes
it to be, but as it really is. The writer may not manufac-
ture a reality; he can only mirror it, for the theme deter-
mines the technique. A truly successful contemporary novel
must combine this reality with lyrical elements, a synthesis
which is quite difficult to achieve. Above all, literary creativity must relate to social motivation."25 These thoughts
of Goytisolo's appear in his Problemas de la novela (Problems of the Novel) (1959) but are equally apropos to define
his aesthetics if we consider Señas de identidad the final
product of Goytisolo's "creative system."

     Señas is, undeniably the most powerfully vibrant,
lyrically poetic, experimentally artistic, politically committed novel to come from a Spanish novelist in the last
twenty-five years and it may be one of the greatest, second
only to Cervantes' immortal Don Quixote. Goytisolo himself
has said that "I prefer to live among foreigners who speak
a language foreign to me rather than be in a national setting
which paralyzes me and does not permit me to live nor to
work in peace."26 We cannot consider Goytisolo, however,
one of the many exiled Spanish novelists like Ramón Sender
or Max Aub or Francisco Ayala, since these novelists live
and work primarily outside of the European continent or in
America and elsewhere, and have never returned to Spain.
Goytisolo is ever-present in Paris and frequently travels to
Spain with the permission of the regime; he is always mind-
ful of his nation, its politics, its people and problems. He
does not consider himself one of the rootless, apathetic
Spanish émigrés he so brutally attacks in Señas. Instead,
he, like many of his generation wait, not in silence, but actively engaged in documenting through their fiction the plight
of their regimented Franquista society. Goytisolo has become a one man literary army, proselytizing for the New
Wave, its adherents, its literary slogans--perhaps propa-
gandizing for greater socially-bent streams of fiction rather
than the repressed "experimental" fictions that have preceded
his own work. Whatever direction Goytisolo's novels take,
his influence on other writers has already augured new insights from Spain's new novelists as well as other internationally popular novelists of Latin America and elsewhere.
He continues to be one of the few creative Spanish novelists

working within Europe, demonstrating, disseminating and exhorting the successes (and sometimes failures) of the Spanish New Wave novelists.

THE WORKS OF JUAN GOYTISOLO

El mundo de los espejos. Barcelona: Editorial Janés, 1952.
Juegos de manos. Barcelona: Ediciones Destino, 1954.
El soldadito [novelette]. Barcelona, 1952.
Duelo en el Paraíso. Barcelona: Editorial Planeta, 1955.
El circo. Barcelona: Ediciones Destino, 1957.
Fiestas. Buenos Aires: Emecé, 1958.
La resaca. París: Club del Libro Español, 1958.
Problemas de la novela [criticism]. Barcelona: Ed. Seix Barral,
        1959.
Campos de Níjar [travel]. Barcelona: Seix Barral, 1960.
Para vivir aquí [stories]. Buenos Aires: Sur, 1960.
Chronique d'une ile. París: Gallimard, 1961.
La isla. Barcelona: Seix Barral, 1961.
La Chanca [travel]. París: Librería Española, 1962.
Fin de fiesta [stories]. Barcelona: Seix Barral, 1962.
Pueblos en marcha [travel]. Paris: Librería Española, 1962.
Señas de identidad. México: Joaquín Mortiz, 1966.
El furgón de cola [criticism]. Paris: Ed. Ruedo Ibérico, 1967.
Reivindicación del Conde don Julián. México: Joaquín
        Mortiz, 1970.

SELECTED STUDIES ON GOYTISOLO

Busette, Cedric. "Goytisolo's 'Fiestas': A Search for
        Meaning," Romance Notes, vol. 12, no. 2 (prima-
        vera 1971), 270-3.
_____. "Juan Goytisolo: 'Juegos de manos'," Insula,
        no. 111 (15 marzo 1955), 7.
Castellet, José María. "Juan Goytisolo y la novela es-
        pañola actual," La Torre, no. 33 (1961), 131-40.
Cirre, José Francisco. "Novela e ideología en Juan Goyti-
        solo," Insula, no. 230 (enero 1966), 1, 12.
Coindreau, Maurice-Edgar. "La joven literatura española,"
        Cuadernos del Congreso por la Libertad de la Cul-
        tura, no. 24, (mayo-junio 1957), 39-43.
Corrales Egea, José. "Don Julián y la 'destrucción' de
        España," Cuadernos de Ruedo Ibérico, no. 31-32
        (julio-sept. 1971), pp. 97-101.

Curutchet, Juan Carlos. "Juan Goytisolo y la destrucción
    de la España sagrada," Revista de la Universidad de
    México, suplemento, vol. 23, no. 5-6 (enero-febrero
    1969), 9-14.
Díaz, Martín. "La resaca," Nuestras ideas, no. 7 (1959),
    92-3.
Diazlastra, Alberto. " 'Señas de identidad' de Juan Goyti-
    solo," Cuadernos de Ruedo Ibérico, no. 13-14 (junio-
    sept. 1967), 177-80.
Díaz-Plaja, Fernando. "Naufragio en dos islas; Un paralelo
    narrativo: Goytisolo y Golding," Insula, no. 227
    (oct. 1965), 6.
Domingo, José. "La última novela de Juan Goytisolo,"
    Insula, nos. 248-249 (julio-ag. 1967), 13.
Durán, Manuel. "Vindicación de Juan Goytisolo: 'Reivindi-
    cación del Conde don Julián'," Insula, no. 290
    (enero 1971), 1, 4.
Fuentes, Carlos. "Juan Goytisolo: la lengua común," in:
    La nueva novela hispanoamericana (México: Joaquín
    Mortiz, 1969), pp. 78-85.
Goytisolo, Juan. "Para una literatura nacional popular,"
    Insula, no. 146 (15 enero 1959), 6, 11.
Iglesias, I. "Dos representantes de la nueva literatura es-
    pañola," Cuadernos del Congreso por la Libertad de
    la Cultura, no. 26 (sept.-oct. 1957), 97-9.
_____. "Juan Goytisolo: 'Duelo en el Paraíso'," Cua-
    dernos del Congreso por la Libertad de la Cultura,
    no. 21 (nov.-dici. 1956), 123-4.
_____. "Juan Goytisolo: 'Campos de Níjar'," Cuadernos
    del Congreso por la Libertad de la Cultura, no. 46
    (enero-feb. 1961), 120.
_____. " 'Fiestas' y 'La resaca', de Juan Goytisolo,"
    Cuadernos del Congreso por la Libertad de la Cultura,
    no. 36 (mayo-junio 1959), 114-5.
Marra-López, José R. "Tres nuevos libros de Juan Goyti-
    solo," Insula, no. 193 (dici. 1962), 4.
Martínez-Cachero, José María. "El novelista Juan Goyti-
    solo," Papeles de Son Armadans, no. 95 (feb. 1964),
    125-60.
Nora, Eugenio de. "La obras novelística de Juan Goytisolo,"
    Insula, no. 190 (sept. 1962), 7.
[Rodríguez Monegal, Emir]. "Juan Goytisolo; Destrucción
    de la España sagrada," Mundo Nuevo, no. 12 (junio
    1967), 44-60.
Rosa, Julio M. de la. "Juan Goytisolo o la destrucción de
    las raíces," Cuadernos Hispanoamericanos, no. 237
    (sept. 1969), 779-84.

Schwartz, Kessel.   "The United States in the Novels of Juan
    Goytisolo," Romance Notes, vol. 6, no. 2 (1965),
    122-5.
S[obejano], G[onzalo].   " 'La Chanca' de Juan Goytisolo,"
    Papeles de Son Armadans, no. 97 (abril 1964), 118-
    21.
Torre, Guillermo de la.   "Los puntos sobre algunas íes
    novelísticas (Réplica a Juan Goytisolo)," Insula, no.
    150 (15 mayo 1959), 1-2.
Valente, José Angel.   "Lo demás es silencio," Insula, no.
    271 (junio 1969), 15.
V[ilar], S[ergio].   "Fin de fiesta, de Juan Goytisolo,"
    Papeles de Son Armadans, no. 76 (julio 1962), 106-8.
Zaragoza, Celia.   "Juan Goytisolo: 'Para vivir aquí," Sur,
    no. 269 (marzo-abril 1961), 89-91.

Chapter 15

JUAN MARSE and ULTIMAS TARDES CON TERESA
(Last Afternoons with Teresa) (1966)

Juan Marsé may well be called the true and legitimate
heir apparent of Juan Goytisolo and Luis Martín-Santos,
judging from the kind of Realist novel he writes.   Two years
younger than Goytisolo, he also was born in Barcelona on
January 8, 1933.   Little is known about his personal life except that from the age of thirteen he worked as a machine
operator in a large jewelry store until 1959.   His interest
in writing dates back to 1955 (when Marsé was twenty-two)
in which year he helped to publish a new magazine of theatrical and film criticism (now defunct).   After quitting the
jewelry business, he worked for several newspapers and
movie magazines while pursuing his writing career.   He decided to go abroad and spent two years in Paris (1961-63),
working as a beaker washer in the Pasteur Institute.   Coincidentally, Jacques Monod, for whom Marsé worked, won
the Nobel Prize for Medicine in 1966.

Marsé's critiques for newspapers and magazines led
him into short story writing, for which he won the Sésame
Prize for his first collection in 1959.   However writing
novels interested Marsé most seriously and his first, Encerrados con sólo un juguete (Locked in with Only One Toy),
published in 1960 was so good that it was a finalist for the
Biblioteca Breve Prize.   His second novel, Esta cara de
luna (This Side of the Moon) appeared in 1962 and was fairly
well received by the Spanish reading public, but Ultimas
tardes con Teresa (Last Afternoons with Teresa) which appeared four years later, is his single outstanding work of
fiction to date.   It won the Premio Biblioteca Breve of 1966
in competition with the extremely brilliant novel, La traición
de Rita Hayworth (Betrayed by Rita Hayworth), by the talented Latin American writer, Manuel Puig.   His latest novel,

La oscura historia de la prima Montse (The Dark History of
Cousin Montse), appeared in 1970, confirming Marsé's reputation as a social satirist but still unequal to the success and
fame by his brilliant Ultimas tardes con Teresa--through
which Marsé claims his fame as a continuer of the trends
set by Goytisolo and Martín-Santos. Marsé presently lives
with his wife and young son in Paris and dedicates himself
fully to his writing.

                              *   *   *

          Ultimas tardes con Teresa's 334 pages are divided
into three principal parts with roughly eight or nine chapters
in each, totalling twenty-five, including a somewhat literary
prologue referring to Charles Baudelaire's famous poem
L'albatros (The Albatross). Every chapter is also preceded
by a literary leitmotiv, choice quotations from the pens of
renowned poets and novelists such as Espronceda, San Juan
de la Cruz, Pedro Salinas, Rimbaud, Apollinaire, Góngora,
Virginia Woolf, Lionel Trilling, Balzac, and Shakespeare,
and other lesser known Catalan sources such as Lorrenç
Villalonga and Jaime Gil de Biedma. One critic calls our
immediate attention to the "ironic effect" of the use of these
quotations throughout the novel because of their heterogeneity,
their discrepancy with the text and the singularly distinct
tone which follows. (The "three strophes of Baudelaire's
L'albatros establish a hilarious dissonance throughout the
novel."1) It is possible Marsé intended to use these quotations as a means of criticizing their authors for their pedantic concerns and pointing out the schism that has occurred,
between literary ideals and the "reality" of suffering humanity. Nevertheless, sarcasm, cynicism, satire and parody
are the chief literary elements of Ultimas tardes con Teresa
and they define the novel's general parameters with respect
to the kind of "social" novel it reportedly is.

          Ultimas tardes con Teresa is essentially the story of
Teresa Serrat and her love affair with Manolo Reyes, nick-
named Pijoaparte. Part One is concerned with their meeting
through Teresa's maid, Maruja, and Manolo's ingratiating
and degrading amorous relationship with the latter. Part
Two relates the love idyll between Teresa and Manolo as a
consequence of an accident which Maruja suffers, forcing the
pair together. The final section, Part Three deals with
Manolo's "last afternoons" with Teresa from which the
novel's title is derived. The majority of the action in the

novel takes place in Barcelona and at the nearby beach resort of Blanes. Two worlds of Barcelona are carefully
counterpointed: the one of the neighborhood of El Caramelo
--of thieves, prostitutes, gangsters, con artists, pretty
boys (chulos)--and the other of San Gervasio, a rich suburb
with exclusive domains, populated by the very rich, who are
insecure, and anxious personalities, replete with strong emotions and vain illusions. These two worlds are placed face
to face--the El Caramelo of Manolo and the San Gervasio of
Teresa.

        The action of the novel takes place within a period of
one year and three months with a coda, after the passage of
two years. As readers we are mainly interested in the
summer months in and around Barcelona and Blanes.   Manolo (or Ricardo de Salvarrosa, his real name) is from
Murcia, a gitano (gypsy or immigrant), a petty thief of
motorcycles.   Consequently the language he uses is colloquial and exuberant, a rich baroque mixture of modern Spanish, Catalan and Caló or gutter Spanish. The narrative is
in the third person although Marsé includes some interior
monologue in both first and second persons. At one point
in the novel, he even identifies himself as one of a group of
student activists (circa 1956) vitally interested in the social
scene. Apart from linguistic and stylistic considerations,
the essential worth of Ultimas tardes con Teresa lies in its
simple plot, vaguely reminiscent of the 1950's American
film The Wild One (with Marlon Brando) because of its "at-
mospheric" similarities. We must remember Manolo is
ignoble, a poor, petty motorcycle thief associated with an
equally petty gang, but a social climber, nevertheless.
Manolo is anxious to enter the bourgeois world of San Gervasio and in Part One, he daringly party crashes a high
society gala, meeting both Maruja and Teresa. Mistakenly
believing Maruja to be part of the wealthy aristocracy, he
seduces her, realizing later she is only a servant in the
house when the light of dawn exposes her maid's uniforms
casually strewn about her room in the Serrat country house.
Realizing his error is perhaps the most grippingly narrated
section in Part One. Maruja, however, an "experienced"
girl of many past sexual escapades falls hopelessly in love
with Manolo, who uses her as his stepping-stone to meet
the lady of the house, Teresa Serrat.

        Teresa is a beautiful, wealthy, nineteen-year-old
blonde, a politically engagé student at the University of
Barcelona, intellectually gifted, spoiled, supposedly in love

with Luis Trías de Giralt, her intellectual and societal equal.
Teresa and Manolo do not meet for many weeks, since he
is furtively having a nightly affair with Maruja in her rooms.
One sunny day, Teresa and Maruja go walking on the local
pier near the Serrat estate and Maruja slips and falls, bang-
ing her head.   When they arrive home, Maruja decides to
rest in her room.   She falls into a deep coma and is discovered in this state by Manolo as he makes his usual noc-
turnal appearance through Maruja's window.   Manolo seeks
help and "officially" meets Teresa for the first time.
Maruja is rushed to the local clinic for treatment.   Her
condition improves slightly.   Meanwhile Manolo and Teresa
have made "contact. "   She mistakenly feels he is a political
activist with much influence at the university.   He leads her
into his world of bars and broads at El Caramelo.   They
have a turbulent love affair.   The usual clichés of fast
motorcycling, hot-rodding, bar-hopping permeate the novel,
including the obligatory sex scene on the beach reminiscent
of Burt Lancaster and Deborah Kerr in From Here to Eternity (very 1950's).   At one hilarious point, Teresa thinks
of herself as Teresa (Jean) Simmons, perhaps reacting to
Manolo's image of Marlon Brando.   Perhaps Marsé himself
was influenced by Samuel Goldwyn's film Guys and Dolls
(1954), which starred both Brando and Simmons, when he
was casting his characters for this novel.

        The trysting of Manolo and Teresa degenerates when
Maruja dies suddenly, unexpectedly.   Having little in common, Manolo and Teresa stop their daily visits to the clinic.
Teresa begins to realize the vast intellectual gulf between
herself and Manolo, and Manolo's and her friends, especially Luis Trías de Giralt, but is still highly attracted to
Manolo sexually.   Manolo, however is running out of money
with which he wines and dines Teresa.   He tries to negoti-
ate a loan from El Cardenal, leader of a petty theft ring
but refuses to work for him again.   Meanwhile, Teresa's
parents, Oriol and Marta Serrat, now aware of Manolo's
existence, feel he is a threat to their family and to Teresa's
social standing.   They take steps to isolate their daughter
from Manolo, believing any relationship between them, much
less marriage, would never work.   Teresa sends Manolo a
desperate note to liberate her from her parent's designs.
Having already settled some debts with El Cardinal by selling his own motorcycle and refusing to steal again, Manolo
pleads with the gang leader for a cash loan and some
"wheels" to reclaim his lost love.   El Cardenal refuses and
Manolo runs off angrily, stealing a motorcycle from the

gangster. As is the case in such novels, an old girl friend
of Manolo's in El Cardenal's employ (this time, it is Hortensia, who is by chance El Cardenal's niece) denounces
Manolo to the Civil Guard. Manolo is arrested on his way
to join Teresa.

Two years pass. Manolo returns to a local bar in
El Caramelo after spending time in prison. He meets
Teresa's ex-boy friend, Luis Trías de Giralt, drinking scotch.
Luis tells Manolo that Teresa "personally" came down to the
bar to find out why Manolo did not show up to free her from
her parents. When Teresa found out Manolo was arrested
for stealing a motorcycle, she burst out laughing and according to Luis, "she is still laughing about it." Reminiscent of the eternal bitch Eulalia who continues laughing in
Rubén Darío's famous modernist poem, Era un aire suave,
Teresa too takes on the qualities of Darío's famous golden
girl, bitch-goddess, always bewitching but unattainable. As
we read the last portion of the novel, we realize that on
those last afternoons with Teresa (and despite the foreshadow-
ing of the title), the intellectual and societal gulf between the
two was a greater breach than either of them could overcome.
When Luis tells Manolo of Teresa's brilliant academic career, her "intellectual" relationship with the wife of a notable intellect who is now living with an artist, Manolo feels
further alienated and isolated. The novel ends in bittersweet fashion: " 'Yes, it was fun,' remarks Luis. 'What
do you intend to do now?,' he asks Manolo. 'I'll see,' replies Manolo. 'Goodbye.' And with a half turn, with hands
in his pockets, el Píoaparte left...."[2]

*   *   *

Ultimas tardes con Teresa is a bitter novel, a depressing and corrosive but predictable one. Much in the
same vein as Juan Goytisolo's demythification force, Marsé
uses Spain as his background to expose the post-Civil War
social realities, the problems of a new class of youth living
in opposing worlds, each idealizing his or her own, exposing
their realities and finally destroying the "ideals" or "myths"
of the world they inhabit. Marsé views the youth of today
as a leveling force against the old prejudices and conventional mores--a new wave caught up in the growing phenomenon
of advanced modernization, heavy industrialization, international tourism, the Europeanization of Spain, the advent of
the Common Market, student activism, and changing social

and intellectual patterns of Spanish society since the Civil
War.   As a novel, Teresa has been viewed as representative
of a new kind of fictional work, utilizing the themes of
suburbia as its essential motif. 3   Madrid and its environs
has been the subject of many novels, but Barcelona and its
surrounding suburbs, with its "immigrants" like Manolo,
has become Marsé's pretext for examining new Spanish
sociological problems.   One critic felt this novel was "the
study of an inferiority complex inherent in the sociological
situation" and that Marsé also applied a documentary approach (estilo testimonial) to demonstrate these sociological
implications of plot, using language typical of the lower
classes to capture this particular kind of reality.   He even
felt Marsé attempted a kind of super-naturalism on the descriptive level, a critical misinterpretation with which I
must disagree. 4

        Clearly, Juan Marsé is concerned with a type of re-
ality in which he defines himself as a novelist of great personality, independent of the work of others, in which he develops a world of critical ideas effectively. 5   Marsé has
said of himself and about his novelistic art:

            To describe reality without falsifying it is the
            first thing that should be imposed on all novelists.
            ...But besides this, among other reasons, writing
            novels for me is to always defend some cause.
            Like the majority of writers of my generation do,
            I intend to clearly denounce today's Spanish so-
            ciety, calling attention to the structures that have
            to be revised or those that must be put down as
            unworkable.   In this critical aspect of my work,
            I, as denouncer hardly have any merit: the same
            reality cries out for transformation.   The writer's
            merit is, in any case, in his effectiveness at ex-
            position and his artistic success [at portraying re-
            ality].... Reality is here and there is only one
            way of examining it--with veracity.   ...Funda-
            mentally, my mission will not change: to reflect
            the real without falsifying it is to follow a pro-
            gressive road, so that reality, in itself, is always
            a progressive quantity.   My only mission, today
            and tomorrow is to try to be truthful.   ...The
            modern novel however does not have as its mis-
            sion to agitate the social structure but to go in
            search for something more intimate that resides
            within man.   The documentary type of novel

> [novela-testimonio] bores me and subjectivism
> does not interest me when it does not go beyond
> the [usual] inventory [of feelings]. I believe that
> the values of society have changed and that the
> modern novel, while wanting to be socially-oriented
> and useful, runs the risk of becoming nothing. I
> don't think my own works will have contributed
> anything. I want to believe they will. Since I
> was a worker and since I spent the major part of
> my youth in a vile factory where they paid me
> badly, my position towards society when I write
> can be no other than one of criticism and denunci-
> ation. However, neither in the selection of
> themes nor in the treatment of them do I see a
> direct influence of all this [background] on my
> work. That is to say, I don't know--if we sup-
> pose my social origin were different--what would
> have been my constant theme. But I would like to
> believe it would have been the same thing [i.e.,
> criticism and denunciation of Spanish society]. [6]

Although Marsé himself declares his literary output
to be socially oriented, Pablo Gil Casado, in his book La
novela social española, resists placing Ultimas tardes con
Teresa within this framework of "social novel" because of
its "ironic" framework although it creates a social situation
which may undoubtedly exist in certain university circles,
where a predisposition for social revolution and student activism may be found. [7] Although Marsé himself might argue
with Gil Casado's thesis, the author has essentially written
a Realist novel with social pretensions.

"Teresa is not a novel with major emphasis on dialogue, but it is more thoughtful, meditative, constructed in
the opposite direction to the one utilized by the New Wave
and even opposite to Marsé's earlier works. It goes from
the inside to the outside instead of the reverse. That is, it
presents from the beginning the complete portrait of the
characters without our having to guess about their behavior
patterns. ...Marsé's novel reconciles two methods of narration: objective realism and psychological realism. "[8] We
fully experience the worlds of El Caramelo and San Gervasio
through the objective and psychological attitudes as one
critic has pointed out. But the author's goal is not to alert
our social conscience. Marsé prefers to ridicule the characters of the novel and use irony to denounce the mores of
Teresa, Manolo and their comrades.

Keeping to Marsé's own statements about composing novels and his notion of reality, he has succeeded in doing what he set out to do. However, some literary critics thought Teresa represented a step backward (after Martín-Santos and Juan Goytisolo), since Marsé's tendency to use irony and ridicule eclipse the social intent and forceful denunciation the novel might have had. 9 Nevertheless, Marsé's censure of the Spanish bourgeoisie, its intellectual snobbery and his support of student activism are felt, somewhat indirectly but everpresent, nevertheless. Spanish literary critics have frequently compared Marsé's Teresa to Goytisolo's Señas de identidad and Martín-Santos' Tiempo de silencio-- they are comparable, suggests Sobejano, because of their "cultural virulence, the vast panorama of society, the skill at composition and the opulence of their means of expression."10 At times, Manolo's attempt to rise socially is reminiscent of Julian Sorel, infamous hero of Stendhal's The Red and the Black, but this parallel is of little value since Manolo is so authentic a Spanish personality of the 1950's, romantic like Sorel but more cynical. Nevertheless, Marsé does not renounce certain elements of plot or conventions common to nineteenth-century Romantic-Realist fiction such as Manolo's Don Juan-machismo attitudes, the illness and sudden death of Maruja, Hortensia's betrayal of Manolo at a "critical" moment of the narrative, and the jealousies of various men and women throughout the course of the novel. 11

One of the new elements found in Ultimas tardes con Teresa is Juan Marsé's use of indirect critiques of current novels. Juan Goytisolo's Duelo en el Paraíso, another by Blas de Otero entitled Pido la paz y la palabra, a novel of Simone de Beauvoir's and one of Jean-Paul Sartre's are also mentioned. Students discuss capitalism, socialism, and Castellet's opinion of nineteenth-century Spanish novelists, among a wide variety of subject. Marsé himself appears in the novel as a character (in perhaps a bit of self-parody), describing himself in a conversation with student activists as "a short, dark guy with curly hair and always walking with his hands in his pockets" (p. 256)--reminiscent, perhaps, of our hero Manolo at the novel's end. Spanish critic Gonzalo Sobejano's view is that Teresa is itself really "a parody, a sarcastic parody of the social novel on two levels --a testimony to the suffering of the Spanish people and testimony of the decadence of the bourgeoisie" and he rebuts Corrales Egea by saying the novel is "not objective but rather indirect, subjective, expansive, satirical, angry."12

In their excellent essay on Ultimas tardes con Teresa,
Guillermo and Hernández touched upon many points outlined
here and that have also been dealt with by other literary
critics. They have carefully singled out, however, some interesting stylistic devices Marsé used such as innovative
composed words (e.g., automóvil-rica-muchacha-cha-cha),
the repeated use of adverbs, effective similies and images reflecting the typical cultural complexity of the twentieth-
century, an enormous vocabulary referring to automobiles
and motorcycles, an over-use of gerunds, and an injection
of fantasy. The note also that the novel is full of "gutter"
Spanish. Words like marmota (sleepy-head), raspa (slang
for female servant), chalao (to be nuts), jilipollo (chicken-
livered bastard) are found sprinkled throughout the text.
However Guillermo and Hernández agree that quite apart
from his linguistic and stylistic contributions to the New
Wave, Juan Marsé is really a great story-teller. "His ability to relate creates a palpable reality upon opening the book
to any page. The action flies by rapidly, lively, with agil-
ity. "[13]

Perhaps Juan Marsé received his greatest accolade
from Latin-American writer Mario Vargas Llosa (known primarily in the United States for his novel, The Green House),
who believed Marsé's novel "would irritate everybody. In
many areas--principally three, literature, sociology and pol-
itics--the book exudes a kind of aggressiveness so wounding
and corrosive that it's reason for being, one would say, is
exclusively for purposes of provocation. " Vargas Llosa
then paid Marsé the ultimate compliment: "When a character is lifted from the flat and calm literary reality and nulli-
fies the conscience of the reader and replaces it with his
own and makes his spirit contagious and that magic possession between man and ghost is consummated, the novelist
then, is a true creator and his work, an authentic novel. "
For Vargas Llosa,

> while reading Ultimas tardes con Teresa, I had the
> impression of being present at the most minute and
> impeccable preparations of a suicide that is about
> to culminate one hundred times into a grotesque
> hecatomb and which is always frustrated at the last
> instant by that dark, uncontrollable and spontaneous
> force which animates words and communicates
> truth and life to all who touch it ... and which
> constitutes the highest and most mysterious human
> faculty: the power of creation. Few times in life

> has an author reunited such varied and effective
> resources in order to write a novel about evil and
> for that very reason, such a notable and astonish-
> ing victory has resulted from the powers of his
> reason. The book, in fact, not only is good, but
> perhaps is the most vigorous and convincing of the
> writings to come from Spain these last years.... 14

After finishing Juan Marsé's novel, I found myself ill
at ease because of some of the lofty praise it received in
contrast to my own feelings. Essentially, Ultimas tardes
con Teresa is a celebration of youth on the whirlwind of life,
a confusion of white sport cars, bikini-draped bodies bronzed
by the sun, wild parties, student-activism, illicit sexual encounters, fast motorcycles, anti-bourgeois sentiments, social
climbers, the generation-gap. All this comes in the mode
of Françoise Sagan's Bonjour Tristesse, Juan Goytisolo's La
isla, García Hortelano's Tormenta de verano, Federico Fellini's La dolce vita and François Truffaut's Jules et Jim,
but is executed in the disciplined style of a pessimist-turned-
writer with a very real, deep metaphysical problem that
transcends the mere romance of the protagonists. Despite
Manolo's multi-faceted journey through the novel touching on
different social strata and different lives, we find at the
novel's conclusion that he has arrived at the point where he
began, "fulfilling that concept of 'eternal return' pointed out
by the old teachers of Greek Philosophy"; for Manolo,
"everything is the same..., everything has ended, but it was
as if it had never occurred, each person in his position,
doing his thing, under the indifference of the stars...."15
Marsé's novel is a bitter, sarcastic condemnation of Spanish
society, its bourgeois and low life inhabitants, its anarchists
and intellectuals. After reading the novel, one feels he
cannot go against "the system." We learn in the last chapter that Teresa married a playboy and her student-activist
friends were absorbed into the existing society as industrial
pirates or intellectual decadents. Marsé says they were a
lost generation from the very beginning, they were fated to
be part of the Spanish bourgeoisie and their activist years
were frustrated attempts to go against the grain of a society
they had come to accept with the passage of time.

If I were to try to identify a parallel in literature
that gives an equally bitter, catastrophic vision of society, I
would choose the one of Louis Ferdinand Céline. 16 His
Journey to the End of Night (1932), the story of a romantic
wandering soldier-hero, anti-war, pessimistic, bent upon

self-destruction, is reminiscent of Manolo's pessimism, desperate humor and cyclical journey to nowhere. As Vargas Llosa has said, "... it is difficult to speak of influences [on Marsé]. But there is something shared between both authors [Marsé and Céline] ... a kind of secret fraternity."[17]

Despite all comparisons, however, Ultimas tardes con Teresa stands on its own as a tour de force, a Realistic novel written in the mode of the New Wave. Above all, it is singularly authentic in its portrayal of characters and society. For this reason alone it should be hailed, not only as a sarcastic explosion in the modern Spanish novel but as a genuine contribution to the ever-developing novel genre still very much in search of itself. Teresa, like Señas de identidad, is another fictional effort attempting to open the Spanish novel to life (reality), drawing from the juices of every-day living its own particular indictment against the Spanish bourgeoisie and prevailing political regime. Judging from the number of student strikes in Catalonia and work-stoppages by miners in Asturias and elsewhere in Spain since 1966 and the recent bombing murder of Spanish Premier Luis Carrero Blanco allegedly by ETA (Basque Liberation and Unity Party) terrorists in Madrid in December 1973, peace in Spain is a mere illusion and the novels reflecting societal agitation and political frustration (especially apropos of Teresa and Señas) are far more relevant as documents in light of their historical context. Teresa then, represents not only an occasional "sarcastic explosion" or parody in the modern novel but is a telescopic sighting lens, poring over a repressed Catalan society, revealing then and now the chinks within its armor, the imperfections of Spanish society on the surface and sometimes below the depths, predicting the possibility of future eruptions.

THE WORKS OF JUAN MARSE

Encerrados con un solo juguete.   Barcelona: Seix Barral, 1960.
Esta cara de la luna.   Barcelona: Seix Barral, 1962.
Ultimas tardes con Teresa.   Barcelona: Seix Barral, 1965.
La oscura historia de la prima Montse.   Barcelona: Seix Barral, 1970.

SELECTED STUDIES ON MARSE

Corrales Egea, José.   " 'Ultimas tardes con Teresa' o la
      ocasión perdida, " Cuadernos de Ruedo Ibérico, no. 9
      (oct. -nov. 1966), 108-13.
M[arra]-L[ópez], J. R.   "Juan Marsé: 'Encerrados con un
      solo juguete, " Cuadernos del Congreso por la Liber-
      tad de la Cultura, no. 52 (sept. 1961), 89-90.
Santos Fontenla, F.   "Marsé, Juan: 'Encerrados con un
      solo juguete', " Insula, no. 172 (marzo 1961), 8.
Vargas Llosa, Mario.   "Una explosión sarcástica en la
      novela española moderna, " Insula, no. 233 (abril
      1966), 1, 12.

Chapter 16

IGNACIO ALDECOA and PARTE DE UNA HISTORIA
(Part of a Story) (1967)

Ignacio Aldecoa was born on July 24, 1925, in the town of Vitoria in the Basque provinces. Very little is known about his youth except that he studied at the University of Madrid for a liberal arts degree and thereafter dedicated himself to journalism, working for several of Madrid's leading newspapers. His newspaper articles served him well as an apprenticeship for later work as a novelist, short-story writer, and poet. His first published works, however, are two collections of poems, entitled Todavía la vida (And Yet, Life) (1947) and Libro de las algas (Book of Algae) (1949). Between 1947 and 1956, he was heard weekly on the radio station, "Voice of the Falange," wrote for political magazines such as La Hora, Alcalá, Juventud, and such leading literary journals as Correo Literario, Clavileño and Revista Española. His production of short stories steadily increased. Collections of them are numerous and appeared at intervals throughout his literary career: Vísperas de silencio (Evenings of Silence) and Espera de tercera clase (Waiting Room--Third Class) (1955), El corazón y otros frutos amargos (The Heart and Other Bitter Fruits) (1959), Caballo de pica and Cuaderno de godo (A Gothic Notebook) (1961) Arqueología (Archaeology) (1962), Neutral Corner (1963) and Los pájaros de Baden-Baden (1965).

His novels, for which he is best known, are few in number despite his twenty-year literary career. They are El fulgor y la sangre (The Brightness and the Blood) (1954), Con el viento solano (Along with the Sun-Drenched Wind) (1956), Gran Sol (Big Sun) (1957)--for which Aldecoa won the Premio de la Crítica in 1958--and Parte de una historia (Part of a Story) (1967), Aldecoa's last novel, written shortly before his death. Aldecoa died on November 15, 1969,

217

of a heart attack, at age forty-four, leaving only his wife,
the writer Josefina Rodríguez.   When I visited Aldecoa at
his Madrid apartment in June of 1968, he told me he was
plagued with health problems (about which he did not elaborate) and the color of his face was an ashen gray.   Nevertheless, he spoke sharply, decisively, about his life, career,
and future projects.   Several of his comments are reproduced in this chapter.   One posthumously published work,
Santa Olaja de acero y otras historias (Saint Olaja of Steel
and Other Stories) (1968), contains an anthology of Aldecoa's
short fiction, probably chosen by the author himself before
his death.

                         *   *   *

          Aldecoa's reply on June 26, 1968, when I asked him
which literary work of his he considered best, was ironic:
"the latest one," he said, which in this case, happened to
be his last one as well.   After finishing Parte de una historia, Aldecoa told me, he never re-read it, nor did he re-
read any of his other completed novels.   He had begun work
on another novel, tentatively titled Años de crisálida (Years
of Transformation), in which he uses the symbol of the pupa
as a creature of metamorphosis, transforming itself into
nothingness which, as Aldecoa emphasized, is a symbol of
the political and intellectual vacuity of present-day Spain. 1
It is unfortunate that Aldecoa's first highly political, polemi-
cal, metaphorical but incomplete work of fiction will never
be published.   One can only suspect it might contain the
rhetoric of a politically-engagé social writer-critic similar
to that in Luis Martín-Santos' unpublished, posthumous and
fragmented second novel, Tiempo de destrucción (Time of
Destruction).

          Like Martín-Santos, Aldecoa is essentially a social
realist writer, but without reformist tendencies.

          What is purely social, perhaps, is the level from
          which Ignacio Aldecoa takes his creative material--
          those impoverished people of Spain; what is pecu-
          liar, more humane than anything else, is the
          treatment to which he subjects them.   That kind
          of Realism, ambivalently cruel and tender, is
          seen without the paternal sentiment characteristic
          of bourgeois portraiture ... and without ideologi-
          cal tendencies ... or political response.   Aldecoa

never wrote from a political-ideological point of
view but from a humanist's passion, or from an
author's real compassion--suffering with his character creations. 2

Parte de una historia deals with a cross-section of Spanish
life--fishermen and their families. Aldecoa describes their
daily routines, "their fishing jobs, visits to the lighthouse,
climbing the local mountain, sales of camels, the ambience
of the local town store and its assiduous discussions, the
council of old men, the stupidities of Carnival time, the in-
communicative loneliness of the Atlantic Ocean and the 'much
work for nothing' attitudes of the people. "3 It is against this
background that Aldecoa unveiled the plot for his short, 219-
page, twenty-two chapter novel.

*   *   *

The setting is Isla Graciosa, one of the small islands
of the Canary archipelago. After four years of living in the
city, the unnamed narrator-protagonist arrives there to spend
some time, anxious to find himself in a real, down-to-earth,
pulsating society. His host is Roque, owner of the local
town store. Our narrator stays with Roque, his wife Enedina, their children and through all of them, he meets their
neighbors, the local fishermen. He goes out on their boats,
participates in their daily fishing tasks and their conversations in local bars. Aldecoa created several interesting
"characters" like the vocal and vulgar raconteur Mateo el
Guanache, who holds forth at the local bar. Except for
Mateo and others like him, life for the fisher folk is monotonous and lethargic until the accidental sinking of an American yacht called the Bloody Mary during a violent storm that
lashes the island for two days. No one is killed when the
yacht founders but the islanders are introduced to a group
of Americans--Bobby, Gary, Jerry, Beatrice, David and
Laurel. The American visitors live in a world of moral decay and dissipation; they drink excessively and view their
adventure on the island as an "injection of erotic energy. "4
The Americans spend several days on the island and together
with Roque and his family, they celebrate Carnival, witness
a display of fireworks and go off for a midnight swim in the
ocean. All return from the sea except Jerry, who is lost
during the highlight of the carnival celebration. His body is
recovered the following day and the entire island population
witness his burial at the Great Dune. Several days of wind

and rain follow before the Americans can return to Isla
Mayor, the largest island of the archipelago. Roque and
our narrator leave them on the main island, only to return
to their small Isla Graciosa (ironically named), whose
people are beginning to recover from the shock of this
tragedy and resume their monotonous daily life style.   It is
at this point the narrator realizes there is nothing left for
him to do but leave the island forever.

                    *   *   *

        Perhaps one of the principal reasons Aldecoa was so
revered by the New Wave is that he remained a true "Realist" author, continuing to write about a certain Spanish
theme untouched by his contemporaries since the nineteenth
century--the life of the Spanish worker, viewed as an individual, a humble figure, fighting desperately each day to
earn a living in a world that is hostile to his needs and to
his dreams.   Roque is Aldecoa's most ardent portrait conceived in this vein.   His character is presented by means
of simple, natural dialogues and brief, simple descriptions,
both of which Aldecoa handles with consummate expertise.
Aldecoa wrote, it is said, a kind of "faithful testimony, in
a style of costumbrism that is updated, without resorting to
excessive picturesque qualities or [colloquial] vulgarities ...
and in an admirable [realistic] style. "[5] His portrait of contemporary Spain is only vaguely reminiscent of Fernán Caballero's La gaviota (The Sea Gull) and Pereda's Sotileza, two
fascinating costumbrista novels of the nineteenth century.
Aldecoa, however, departed from these authors by revealing
his elemental world to us "slowly, dallying stylistically
while outlining the things he sees, using adjectives excessively and making verbs of nouns, creating at each step, with
scrupulous skill, the proper sound, "[6] for what he sees.

        In Parte de una historia, which is highly visual in
character, Aldecoa's descriptions, although apparently simple,
natural and dynamic, representative of fishermen and their
life of constant struggle, are in reality labored reworkings
of his conscious effects of style.   Aldecoa described things
well, "purifying his adjectives, rejecting the showy mode of
expression, looking for the original movement of the phrase. "[7]
The critic Díaz-Plaja also believes that in his descriptions of
fishermen, seamen, and townspeople, Aldecoa was looking
for a different profile, one that accentuates individual qualities, and that he arrived at a certain kind of "deformed"

stylization in the mode of Ramón María de Valle-Inclán, especially in his characterization of the environment. When I asked Aldecoa which major writers exerted their major influence on his work, he replied, "Valle-Inclán, because of his pleasure in using words, and Pío Baroja with his sentimental views of landscape and his immersion into city life."[8]

The cardinal point in considering Aldecoa's entire fiction-writing career is that every novel or short story of his gives the reader an impression of rigorous stylization-- writing that rejects imprecision. His writing was labored, edited and re-edited. His language reveals a most refined and penetrating psychological vision of his characters, and with it Aldecoa was able rigorously to inspect the very souls of his protagonists. Parte de una historia was undoubtedly written/edited in similar fashion; it succeeds in capturing descriptively the island, its inhabitants, and their colloquial language (which is, I am told, at times difficult for even the most seasoned Spanish intellect to comprehend). However this last novel of Aldecoa's, for all of its labored style, never seems to lift itself out of the clichés of its artificial plot, not to deepen its superficial views of Americans, who are portrayed largely as one-dimensional characters. Nor is the climax unexpected or thrilling; it is rather casual.

What the author has succeeded very well in doing is suggesting the life of mariners and the island's physical ambience and etching permanently in our memories the characters of Roque, Enedina and Mateo el Guanache. (His narrator-protagonist still remains, perhaps intentionally, anonymous and elusive.) However, Parte de una historia is consciously stylized and rigorous; it is a cold work of art, probably one of the faults of "excessive" stylization, in my opinion. One critic felt that Aldecoa took material for a very short, simple story and because of his attempts to extend it, negated what possible emotional depth and interest the novel could have had.[9] Another critic felt the reason for the novel's "chilliness" was that the protagonist himself was not of flesh and blood. It is also possible to say the novel's coldness stems from Aldecoa's use of the sea itself as a protagonist, despite the juxtaposition of such "warm" erotic elements as camels, sand dunes, intense sun, and hot winds. The loneliness of the narrator-protagonist has a chilling effect even on the warmth of the island's inhabitants. Another critic felt that although Aldecoa's novel showed a "lack of invention" and an "excessive fidelity to a conception;

which tended to limit a number of important narrative elements that the author may have felt were merely semantic
accessories, he nevertheless was "perhaps more gifted than
any other [Spanish] contemporary writer in the creation of
ambiences. "10

It is generally agreed by most critics that in Parte
de una historia, Aldecoa's writing style had arrived at its
maximum perfection, "unsurpassed by today's writers because of its concision, expressive sobriety, functional tenses
and poetic softness in its description. ... It adolesces
[i.e., is short of maturation], however, in its excessive
superficiality, one of the most powerful sins of objectivism. "11
Despite Aldecoa's realist-objectivist style, most critics,
again, agree that Parte de una historia (apart from superficially depicting the Americans) presents a world of flesh and
blood, one seemingly lived by the author himself; the world
of Roque, his family and their neighbors on Isla Graciosa.
Perhaps what most endeared Aldecoa to the New Wave writers was his sharing of their stylistic attitudes of "formal
perfection [in the] scrupulous organization of his novels and
short stories, severely circumscribed by an exacting sense
of time and space and [in his] clear prose, with neither
highs or lows but always limpid.... "12 Aldecoa, however,
was not personally concerned whether his Realist writing
style coincided with the New Wave's principles or not. Although he felt he did belong to some group "post-ismo, " and
probably this one, he generally renounced active participation, considering his own "distinct realism" a product of his
own "angle of vision" of the world; "there are many different
kinds of Realism, utilized with different ends in mind. "13

Aldecoa's work, then, does not fit perfectly into that
of the New Wave group. His objective-realism, tinted with
costumbrism, is distinct from the styles of his fellow writers. Also, he did not identify with his characters--that is,
their conflicts of duty and conscience were far from his own
circumstances. As for social interests, Aldecoa preferred to
write about the poor, humble, individual Spaniard (placed in
the context of the nation), without moralizing. He was an
individualist endowed with an extremely personal sense of
style. His works contain neither express political motives
nor outspoken attitudes toward the improvement of Spanish
society; he merely wrote in the context of his personal vision. Eugenio de Nora felt that Aldecoa was addressing
"universal, humane elements" through his almost "classical,
documentary and professional style, " which seemed imbued

with a "Franciscan spirit of love and humility"; Nora suggests the author had returned "to the old Cervantine traditions that views life in all of its facets. " Nora also notes
that Aldecoa's "classical" style is relatively sober, "not ex-
tremist either in his themes or his approaches, but above
all, [giving] an impression of firmness and strength. "14 No
one can deny, after reading Parte de una historia, Aldecoa's
unique sensibility, the extraordinary richness of his prose,
and his classical simplicity and condensation.

    I will return here to the author's conception of him-
self as a writer and his view of Realism.   Aldecoa has said
himself:

> To be a writer is, before anything, an attitude
> towards the world.   I have seen, I see continually,
> how the poor people of Spain are.   I do not adopt
> either a sentimental or a tendentious attitude
> towards them.   What moves me, above all, is the
> conviction there is a Spanish reality, cruel and
> tender at the same time, that goes almost unex-
> pressed in our modern novel.
>
> ...   [I may want to describe] the life of an 'au-
> thentic' man--a real and concrete man above all,
> without social pretensions, no matter what may be
> the social preoccupation of the writer [i. e. , my-
> self].   Because the tender and painful humanity of
> my characters is precisely the fundamental marrow
> of all my stories. 15

This preference of Realism, for the humble and simple
people, "for writing about their intimate tragedies that almost never burst forth into spectacular dramatic episodes,
gives all of Aldecoa's stories and novels a tonality of smooth
colors, of subtleties.... "16

    Gaspar Gómez de la Serna presents, in an excellent
critical work, Ensayos sobre literatura social (Essays on
Social Literature), the most systematic, critical treatise (in
twelve chapters) on Aldecoa's career to date, examining his
work as a "pure" writer, his apprenticeship and idealism,
the themes of humor, pity, work, dereliction, love, and social literature, Aldecoa's interpretation of Spain, his short-
story telling, his art of writing novels, and, finally, his
literary transformation of reality.   Gómez de la Serna's
view of Aldecoa's use of language per se as the chief

conveyance of the author's view of Realism is most accurate.
Summing up his ideas on Realism, this critic gives in the
following excerpts[17] perhaps the most eloquent, critical
statement offered about an author and his ideas on Realism
and style:

> "Aldecoa presents his kind of reality with a technique
> that is objective at the same time as it is malleable,
> describing the hidden realities within the lives of his
> characters, revealing them, intensifying their thoughts
> without separating them from their world, rendering
> them more effective fictional creations. . . .

> "Aldecoa takes the material of reality directly into
> his hands, and with an unusual credibility, objectivity
> and an almost scientific precision, then uses his enor-
> mous reservoir of technical terminology in accurately
> describing the world in which his fictional creations
> move. Thus, in his novels about the sea, for example,
> a large amount of material referring to machines, the
> characteristics of boats, etc. , is recorded.

> "Having accumulated this 'material' of reality, Al-
> decoa selects and applies the transforming filter of his
> sensibility and the chief instrument of his literary oper-
> ation: the art of language.

> ". . . Aldecoa's vision of things is . . . a kind of
> Realism that transcends first appearances and penetrates
> into the intimacy of the essence of things. . . .   Aldecoa
> makes things themselves visible to the eyes of the
> soul. . . .   He reveals their beauty, their quality, their
> sentiment, their true role in the world of his narra-
> tion, giving them a significance with which they can
> operate intensively and effectively. . . .

> "In reality, Aldecoa lived all his literature, con-
> suming to excess his own existence and precarious
> health and giving his time too generously participating
> in and penetrating personally all the climates and am-
> biences that interested him. . . .

> "For Aldecoa is a writer and all that he does, all
> in the process of creation which results from his mode
> of experience--what he perceives, selects, uses sensi-
> tively or transforms--is in his domain and is conceived
> within the material of language.

"And the language of Aldecoa is ... a poetic one,
transforming reality, powerfully expressing by itself
the most important human pursuits, the most creative
forces of literary beauty. The aesthetic of the ugly,
the tremendista cut of Realism, was not his style. On
the contrary, he submerged himself on the most humble
level ... into the crude ambiences where one prances
with blood, sweat and tears--the epic of the working
man--and also where the impoverished struggle for life
continues in the eternal picaresque Spanish life. Aldecoa's contact with all that heterogeneous society and
what we call his 'Realist world' is at the same time
redeeming, salvational, because he wanted to preserve
the tender face of reality for those who are also immersed in all the cruel hardness of that other side of
life, the bitter and the terrible, as necessary compensation for them to go on living. "

These comments of Gómez de là Serna are empassioned ones, raining praise on the memory and talent of the
recently deceased novelist. They alude to the total literary
output of Aldecoa and accurately embrace some of the values
found in the novel under discussion in this chapter. Turning
to Parte de una historia itself, perhaps a few short passages
and comments will bring into focus some of Gómez de la
Serna's comments and Aldecoa's intensely personal ideas on
Realism. Above all, one must consider Ignacio Aldecoa an
individual stylist and Realist. That is to say, he was a
literary aesthete, interested primarily in the beauties (and
uglinesses) of life and in portraying these aspects through
equivalent uses of the Spanish language. His preoccupation
with language was so great that at times, he was accused
of fashioning "baroque" conceits or euphemisms, [18] which to
my mind is not justified. As were the "pure poets"--Juan
Ramón Jiménez, Jorge Guillén and the like--Aldecoa could
be accused of (overly) polishing his work, all to brilliant
effect however. For example, although the element of fantasy is rather slim in Parte, a nebulous if intimate sense
of the sea pervades the entire novel. (The plot of the book
is hardly relevant or even important.) What is outstanding
is Aldecoa's palpable sense of the reality of the mariners,
their Isla Graciosa, their daily combat with life and death.
A good example of his descriptive style is the following passage:

> Del clorfílico cielo, de la amanecida, sobre el
> perfil del acantilado, pende un nubarrón orondo,

cárdeno y frutal.   Desprendido rodaría por las
laderas, machucándose y esparciendo zumo, hasta
las playas de nuestra isla.   El río de mar, en la
turbiedad de la penumbra, parece canecido y mate.
Las mujeres vierten los bacines en las aguas sin
despertar de La Caleta, donde mora las falúas; y
corren niños madrugadores, camaradas de perros,
hacia el espigón del muelle, repuluznando a algún
gato tránsfuga y alborotando a las gallinas, que
picotean pulcramente en las basuras de la baja
marea.   Cantando hermosos quiquiriquíes y ahue-
cando las alas, el muecín de los gallow convoca a
sol desde el alminar de una roca solitaria, domi-
nante.   En la vacilación de la mañana van a llegar
las barcas de la pesca nocturna. 19

Another example of Aldecoa's sensitivity is the following passage relating the narrator's sensibility to life:

Camino despacio hasta la playa de la caleta y me
siento junto a una barca.   La atención engaña
creando imágenes y sonidos.   Tenue y preciso oigo
de pronto el motor de la falúa.   Son las sensaci-
ones de la espera.   Y de pronto abandono esta
vigilancia.   Estoy aquí junto a esta barca, hume-
deciendo las manos en la arena.   Estoy otra vez
en la isla y de huída.   ¿De quién huyo?   No
sabría decírmelo.   Todo es demasiado vago.
¿Tengo alguna razón?   ¿Por qué y de qué?   No,
no sabrí decírmelo.   ¿Y estoy aquí porque es aquí
donde puedo encontrar algo?   No sabría decírmelo.
Huir acaso explica la huída.   Y estoy aquí junto a
esta barca, solo en la noche.   ¿Y, estoy como esta
barca, rumbo al vacío y para siempre? [p. 35].

Aldecoa deals with nature, creation and their mysteries:

En el rayo de sol que flecha por la contraventana
hay un tobogán de arena iridiscente.   Ondas, nubes,
multitud.   Creación y descreación de formas en un
calidoscopic enloquecido.   Contemplarlo es acer-
carse al caos.   Variación permanente, metamorfo-
sis infinita, continua construcción destruida.   Inter-
rumpo con la mano la luz de la vorágine [p. 38].

At times, the author is concerned with the feelings of his
narrator:

> Entro en las preocupaciones de la isla, me deshago
> un poco de mí mismo pensando en las posibilidades
> de mañana, participo de la inquietud despertada por
> el riesgo de los que están en la mar o están en
> puerto o se han quedado entre las olas para
> siempre [p. 45].

When the shipwreck of the Bloody Mary occurs at the
beginning of Chapter Five, the novel loses its interest and
intensity, and becomes rather banal.   The only serious sections that lift it out of its sorry state are the narrator's descriptions of his feelings about Roque, the sea and as always,
himself.

> Ahora rememoro, encontrando una suerte de com-
> pasión gozosa, todo lo que ha sido encastillado
> desastre y orgulloso cansancio de mí mismo.
> ¿Hasta dónde el orgullo puede desarraigarnos?
> Ahora rememoro, estando a muchas millas de
> mar, a muchos quilómetros de mi tierra, la ciu-
> dad de desasosiego que he abandonado.   Aquí en
> esta isla, y en esta mañana bruñida, comienzo a
> comprenderme distanciado de la imagen que tengo
> de mí, allá, lejos, como en una historia sucedida
> a otro.

> Apacible y ensimismado siento discurrir años
> náufragos, meses delirantes, semanas llenas de
> gemas empolvadas, días de estiércol y aún horas,
> minutos, segundos, milésimas de segundos o
> simples fulguraciones de mi vida, que no sé si
> alcanzan a ser contadas en tiempo.   Pero en todo
> solamente hay amargura e insolidaridad [p. 64].

The narrator gives us the impression he remains apart from
the "realities" of the novel's intrigue, that he is, at times,
part of the sea itself:

> Estamos junto al mar, en una naturaleza en la que
> el hombre lleva una vida artificial, como si la isla
> no fuera un definitivo asentamiento, ni una patria
> pequeña, sino lugar de paso que cualquier día
> abandonará por algo mejor.   Arena, falta de agua,
> vegetación de desierto, incomunicación, soledad de
> supervivientes [p. 95].

Our narrator's life is filled with a spiritual presence as was

the famous Andalusian poet García Lorca, whose life and
talent were endowed with that mystical substance called
duende (spirit). This feeling occurs to the reader, perhaps,
only when he reads one of the most beautiful poetic prose
descriptions Aldecoa ever created, at the beginning of Chapter Thirteen (see the explication de texte in the Appendix) as
well as several others that are found disseminated throughout
the novel. When the narrator himself refers to his own
sense of reality as desmayada, or "swooning," I feel we as
readers are caught up in a unique, personal type of Realism
that exists apart from the novel's banal plot, a kind of unreality or unrealness (irrealidad) which Aldecoa constantly
saw in nature:

> Acumulo extraños datos--sorprendiéndome a di-
> stintas épocas de mi vida--, instauro objetos signi-
> ficativos, que me abruman con su permanencia en
> el tiempo y no logro armonizar esta desmayada
> realidad con el emanante recuerdo que, turbio y
> cálido, me anega. Busco, durante extensos minu-
> tos de fuga y rememoración, lo que este ámbito y
> esta hora tienen de sutil vínculo con el pasado, y
> me fatigo y nada encuentro. Pero alguna como
> chispita o lucecilla delirante debió de encenderse
> en un momento para que yo iniciara mi viaje a la
> memoria y que ésta me transmitiera la sensación
> de estar lejos de aquí y de mí en otro día
> [pp. 134-5].
>
> . . .
>
> Por las linternas de la cupulilla entra una luz
> mercurial y la iglesia es un espejo viejo, donde
> se retratan movimientos y figuras que pertenecen
> a la irrealidad [p. 187].

Perhaps Aldecoa did his best writing when he was suggesting
certain "truisms" or thoughts he discovered in his own life,
and putting them in the mind of the narrator:

> Todo está lleno de sorpresas. Nadie sabe dónde
> va a morir--y pienso que mis palabras son banales
> para el dolor, la emoción y el amoroso don que
> tiene por las criaturas [p. 182].

At times, Aldecoa's protagonist suggests that his own internal struggle is as difficult as the writer's and sometimes
there is a clarity of vision in his soul as is reflected in

Aldecoa's portrait of another dawn:

> Después de dos días de lluvia y viento, después de
> dos interminables días de crisálida, que he dividido
> entre la alcoba y la cocina, entreviendo, desde las
> ventanas, un paisaje bañado en permanente luz
> crepuscular, hoy ha amanecido un cielo despejado,
> sólo con algunas nubes pesando sobre el horizonte
> de la alta mar del oeste [p. 200].

But the singular resonance in Aldecoa's personal life that
impresses most readers of this work is the narrator's final
decision to leave the island:

> Mañana, poco después de amanecer, la escuadra
> bombardeará, en sus habituales ejercicios de tiro
> de esta época del año, el roque del Este, el más
> despegado del archipiélago. Mañana, poco después
> de que amanezca, dejaré la isla [p. 219].

Aldecoa was clearly an artist who, by virtue of his sensibility and talent, stood apart from the society in which he
lives. He was, like his protagonist-narrator, the receptacle
of experience, the artistic interpreter of life, the lonely,
sensitive hero always in search of knowledge, truth and himself.

When I asked Aldecoa what he thought of his own
novels, he said he preferred to write "unconventional end-
ings, open-ended stories because they are more real than
reality."[20] Most of Aldecoa's shorter fictional works, like
"El autobús de 7:40" ("The 7:40 A.M. Bus"), are open-
ended, quizzical, enigmatic stories, providing psychological
resonances of physical reality. Parte de una historia, at
its conclusion, suggests we have come to the end of this
particular section of the narrator's story, implying we already know something about the enigmatic narrator, and
possibly that more is yet to come. Unfortunately, Aldecoa
died in his prime, at the height of his stylistic maturity, a
voice never to be heard from again.

> Todo está lleno de sorpresas.   Nadie sabe dónde
> va a morir ... [p. 182].

Although Parte may fall into the category of novel as
described by the astute critic, Gemma Roberts ("problematic
content ... and a moralist orientation ... leading to a search

for significance"21), I feel any existential significance in the
novel is lost simply because of the lack of originality of the
plot and the transparent character of the protagonist. I do
believe it was Aldecoa's intention that his narrator emerge
at the end of the novel intact, and helpful of our own better
perspective. If Parte de una historia succeeds in art and
life to have accomplished one goal, it has documented the
narrator's (and possibly the author's) loneliness, which
Roberts feels is both painful and liberating and which recalls
Miguel de Unamuno's words: "Leave me, then, so that I
may flee society and that I may take refuge in the peace of
the countryside, searching in the middle of it and inside of
my soul for the company of people."43 These implicit ideas
of fleeing, taking refuge and searching for one's identity are
perhaps, the underlying literary and philosophical motifs of
Parte de una historia, ideas that give this novel an elevated
importance, even a transcendence of the Spanish literary
world and substance and of New Wave ideologies and themes.

THE WORKS OF IGNACIO ALDECOA

El fulgor y la sangre. Barcelona: Planeta, 1954.
El mercado [novelette]. Madrid: Ediciones Cid, 1954.
Espera de tercera clase [stories]. Madrid: Ed. Puerta del
        Sol, 1955.
Vísperas de silencio [stories]. Madrid: Taurus, 1955.
Los pájaros de Badén-Badén [stories]. Madrid: Ediciones
        Cid, 1955.
Con el viento solano. Barcelona: Planeta, 1956.
Gran Sol. Barcelona: Editorial Noguer, 1957.
El corazón y otros frutos amargos [stories]. Madrid:
        Arión, 1959.
Caballo de pica [stories]. Madrid: Taurus, 1961.
Cuaderno de Godo [stories]. Madrid: Arión, 1961.
Arqueología [stories]. Madrid: Arión, 1962.
Parte de una historia. Barcelona: Editorial Noguer, 1967.
Santa Oleja de acero y otras historias [stories]. Madrid:
        Alianza Editorial, 1968.

SELECTED STUDIES ON ALDECOA

Arce Robledo, C. de. "I. A.," Virtud y Letras (Bogotá),
        no. 17 (1958), 105-13.
B. "Preguntas a Ignacio Aldecoa," Indice (Madrid), no. 132
        (enero 1960).

B. B. R. "Con el viento solano," Indice de Artes y Letras, no. 93 (sept. 1956), 20.

B. P. P. "Una novela del mar," Papeles de Son Armadans, no. 26 (mayo 1958), 235-6.

Blanco Amor, José. "Ignacio Aldecoa: El corazón y otros frutos amargos," Sur, no. 273 (mayo-junio 1960), 72-4.

Cano, José Luis. "Sigue el auge del cuento. Ignacio Aldecoa: Caballo de pica," Insula, nos. 176-177 (julio-ag. 1961), 12-3.

Castro, F. Guillermo de. "Ignacio Aldecoa: Entre el alcohol y el mar," Indice de Artes y Letras, no. 260 (15 dic. 1969), 28-30.

Díaz, Janet Winecoff. "The novels of Ignacio Aldecoa," Romance Notes, vol. 11, no. 2 (1969), 475-81.

Domingo, José. "Ignacio Aldecoa, Santa Olaja de acero y otras historias," Insula, no. 267 (feb. 1969), 5.

_____. "Parte de una historia de Ignacio Aldecoa," Insula, no. 252 (nov. 1967), 4.

_____. "Narrativa española," Insula, no. 267 (feb. 1969), 5.

Duncan, Bernice G. "Three Novelists from Spain," Books Abroad (Norman), vol. 39, no. 2 (1965).

Fernández Almagro, M. "[Sobre: Con el viento solano]," ABC (Madrid), 9 julio 1956.

Fernández-Braso, M. "Ignacio Aldecoa levanta acta...," Indice de Artes y Letras, no. 236 (oct. 1968), 41-2.

Fernández Santos, Jesús. "Ignacio y yo," Insula, no. 280 (marzo 1970), 11.

García Pavón, F. "Semblanzas españolas; Ignacio Aldecoa: novelista cuentista," Indice de Artes y Letras, no. 146 (1961), 4.

Garciasol Ramón de. "Ignacio Aldecoa: Vísperas de silencio," Insula, no. 115 (julio 1955), 6-7.

González López, Emilio. "Las novelas de Ignacio Aldecoa," Revista Hispánica Moderna, vol. 26, no. 1-2 (1960), 112-3.

Marra-López, José R. "Ignacio Aldecoa: El corazón y otros frutos amargos," Insula, no. 156 (nov. 1959), 6.

_____. "Lirismo y esperpento en la obra de Ignacio Aldecoa," Insula, no. 226 (sept. 1965), 5.

R. P. "Gran Sol, de Ignacio Aldecoa," Cuadernos del Congreso por la Libertad de la Cultura, no. 33 (nov. - dic. 1958), 111.

Rosa, Julio M. de la. "Notas para un estudio sobre Ignacio Aldecoa," Cuadernos Hispanoamericanos, no. 241

(1970), 188-96.
Senabre, Ricardo. "La obra narrativa de Ignacio Aldecoa,"
    Papeles de Son Armadans, no. 166 (enero 1970), 5,
    24.
Torres, Raúl. "Ignacio Aldecoa: 'Parte de una historia',"
    Cuadernos Hispanoamericanos, no. 219 (marzo 1968),
    623-6.
Tudela, Mariano. "Reflexión ante dos libros de narraciones,"
    Cuadernos Hispanoamericanos, no. 70 (oct. 1955),
    114-6.

Chapter 17

JUAN BENET and VOLVERAS A REGION
(You'll Probably Return to Región) (1967)

Juan Benet Goitia was born in October 1927 in Madrid. During the Civil War period, Benet and his family lived in exile for many years. In fact, his father died during the first days of the war. Upon his return to Spain sometime in 1939, Benet studied for his bachillerato in Madrid, which led him to an advanced degree (which he finally completed in 1954) and into a career as a highway and construction engineer. Between 1954 and 1964, he lived outside Spain's capital, dedicating himself to his profession and the building of public works, spending much time in the rural zones of León (probably the physical setting for many of his novels).

About his writing career, Benet has always maintained that he continued to write fiction and other things since his student days. Reflecting on his infancy, youth and student days, he had the following comments for Antonio Núñez in a recent interview: "I believe the single thing which influenced me most was the Civil War which surprised me at nine years of age ... to see oneself separated from one's parents, to live in two Spains.... " About his education as a colegial, Benet believed there was not any "real education" going on in the classroom at this time. His student days were spent in "absolute enmity of the teacher"[1] and as a recourse, he trained himself to write. Happily married with four children and currently residing in an apartment building on Madrid's famous Calle Serrano, Benet has somewhat softened his view of education and educators, believing now one does not have to be in constant combat with teachers in order to learn.

Benet's first book of short stories, Nunca llegarás a nada (You Will Never Become Anything) (1961), went virtually

"unnoticed" by Spain's reading public as did his critical essay, La inspiración y el estilo (Inspiration and Style) (1966),
until the publication of his first novel, Volverás a Región
(You'll Probably Return to Región) (1967), which caused a
major sensation in Spanish letters.   Since the success of his
first novel was overwhelming in Spain, Benet has since published a second one, Una meditación (A Meditation) (1969),
which won the Biblioteca Breve Prize for 1970, as well as
another critical essay entitled Puerta de hierro (The Iron
Door) (1969).   During this productive year, he ventured into
the Spanish theatre and wrote his first play, Agonía confutana
(Confused Agony), which was unsuccessful.   Returning to the
novel, Benet recently completed his third, Una tumba (A
Tomb) (1971), dealing with his perennial theme, the Civil
War.   Benet continues to live and work as a writer in Madrid, and occasionally contributes articles to leading Spanish
periodicals while continuing with the creation of serious fiction.

                          *   *   *

        Volverás a Región was written between 1962 and 1964
and has four main chapters with a total of thirteen pauses
throughout the novel, including five footnotes, one of which
extends to three full pages.   The novel is mainly an exercise in excessive narration, mostly monologues with few
limited occasions for dialogues.   "Región is a 'mythical'
place, like the Yoknapatawpha County in the novels of William Faulkner or the Macondo of Gregorio García Márquez...."[2]   Into this mythical place of almost impenetrable
mountains several men escaped after the Civil War, among
them, a doctor, Daniel Sebastián, and his protégé, who was
sentenced to death.   Dr. Sebastián now lives a decrepit existence, buried alive in the isolation of Región, in an impoverished, decaying, clinic-residence.   His major preoccupations are alcohol, and memory, and caring for a young
boy who is somewhat deranged because he was left with the
doctor by his mother who subsequently disappeared forever,
yet he continues to await her return.

        Dr. Sebastián is visited by a woman who was former-
ly the mistress of his protégé.   In several long passages in
the novel, the woman discloses intimate secrets of their affair and how it represented for her "complete fulfillment."
She has now returned to Región after the war, in search of
her lover in order to recapture the ecstasy that was once

theirs.   The doctor, after hearing her story, is also stirred
by his own powerful and painful memories of a love affair
he had experienced (possibly) with a woman named María
Timoner, whose son he educated and protected in his role
as godfather.   After their mutual "confessions" of respective
intimacies, the woman leaves.   The young boy in Dr. Sebastián's household mistakenly believes that the woman was
his real mother who had come back to reclaim him, but once
again had disappeared.   In his delirium, the boy fatally
shoots Dr. Sebastián and the novel ends with all of its leading characters either destroyed or ruined, fulfilling the tragedy already evident in each of their destinies. 3

        Structurally, the novel is singularly unusual.   A very
extensive first chapter, some ninety pages (or almost one
third of the novel) describes the geological, physical and historical attributes of Región and presents some of the initial
clues to the "plot" and characters which in later chapters,
become confused and lost as the narrative continues.   The
three remaining chapters consist of a series of monologues,
speeches alternating between the doctor and the woman who
has come to visit him--she, in search of hope (her lover),
and he, after extensive researches into memory, suspecting
he will soon die.

        The novel itself has no real plot.   There are, how-
ever, the three main characters that weave the threads of
meaning in the aggregate: Dr. Sebastián, the woman who
visits him and the Nationalist Colonel Gamallo (also a re-
puted lover of the elusive María Timoner, the doctor's supposed mistress).   Each of these characters reveals his intimate history intertwined with the tale of war and the presentation of the physical and social geography of Región.
Except for María Timoner, the doctor's mistress who is
referred to but never plays an active role in the narrative,
all other characters are delineated through the pronouns
"he" or "she," or by common nouns such as "the doctor,"
"the woman," "the lieutenant," "the gambler," "the colonel,"
and so on.

        There are also two anecdotal themes that run through-
out the novel, sometimes parallel, other times criss-cross-
ing: one is the Civil War, the other is the adventure of a
clerk who owns a magic coin and always wins at gambling
when he possesses it.   Fortune and ruin play the biggest
thematic roles in the development of the novel.   Most critics
admit that because of the narrative structure of the novel,

interpretation of it is extremely difficult. Structurally, the
first part dealing with Región, its physical and historical
profile and the Civil War is narrated by a neutral voice in
the third person. The second, third and fourth parts are
supposedly a dialogue between the doctor and the woman who
visits him, which apparently establishes little or no communication between the characters, but these sections really
are two parallel discourses that in their intermingling comprise the so-called plot of the novel.

        Admittedly, Volverás a Región is an extremely diffi-
cult novel to read. Most Spanish critics would perhaps
agree that Benet has accomplished "a mythical transfigura-
tion of reality" but some say that although he may use social
themes combined with objectivist techniques in his efforts to
create a new vision of Spanish fiction, he really has created
nothing so terribly new. Several of the major difficulties
in reading Volverás a Región are attributed to the novel's
fragmentary form, numerous changes of point of view, impersonal narrations, self-indulgent monologues, incessant
repetition of motifs, pedantic use of literary quotations, imprecision of characters' names and events in which they participate, inappropriate comparisons, use of foreign words,
long, intellectual discourses on time, reality, conscience,
and virginity, which appear hermetically sealed off from the
realization or development of their character-proponents.
"The characters speak in an uncharacteristic manner, not
faithful to their psychology but to the same manner of the
author, or in a language of long and subtle sentences, always 'literary,' poetic on occasion, pedantic at times,
vaguely related to the ramifications and arabesques of a
Marcel Proust."[4] Perhaps the language of Volverás a Región is the greatest single problem for the reader of this
novel since it is an unnatural, wild, complicated, and sophisticated language normally beyond the capacities of its
audience. Volverás demands a thoroughly intellectual approach and a serious reading; it is demanding, dense and
truculently literary.

        Equally demanding is Benet's notion of reality. It
has been said that Benet's position on reality represents the
most distant and extreme view facing "traditional" Spanish
Realism, from which it radically departs. Benet's notion
of reality, like many of the newer Latin-American authors,
notably Mario Vargas Llosa and Gregorio García Márquez,
displays renewed interest in the fantastic and magical motifs
in his quest for transforming reality. In fact, and somewhat

paradoxically, reality is the real protagonist of Volverás--
the geographical, historical and psychic reality of Región
converted into a character within the framework of a "fantastic" work of art. [5] Through this brand of stylistic Realism, one is permitted to enter the asceptic, introverted,
meditated world of the doctor and the primitive, impetuous,
psychological world of the women, worlds which in turn revealed them as confused people who digress, hide facts, lie,
falsify deeds and events, hide feelings, contradict themselves
and offer a very "subjective" version about everything they
narrate. Each individual is isolated in his or her own
trauma and is as incapable of communicating effectively with
others as understanding his or her own problems. [6]

        Benet's notion of reality in this particular novel makes
heavy use of stylistic ambiguities, obscured prose, and a
vague overall outline, which leads to frustrations for the
reader and renders almost impossible any comprehension of
the very subject of the novel. "The structure of the novel,
its plan of development, its execution, all these play an effective role, transmitting a crushing, demolishing sensation
of absurdity, confusion and chaos. "[7] One simply cannot
read Volverás a Región in the traditional manner; its organization defies logical perception. Because of the author's
over-reliance on the magical, fantastic, unreal, and fragmentary, the reader's pursuit of the characters and their
ideologies often goes astray.

        It is even difficult to place the novel in its proper
chronological setting. Perhaps it takes place in the 1960's
although certain years such as 1925, 1939 are cited frequently but with little effect on the reader. There is never a
clear sense of time. It is almost Proustian in its scope
when memory is linked with the events that, by themselves,
become confused in the minds of the protagonists in their
re-telling of incidents. Besides memory, there is a great
insistence on psychology--on the revelation of feelings, fear,
and instincts combined with reason to reveal certain prime
motifs of sexuality, guilt and penitence. Man is viewed in
this novel primarily as in a constant struggle, where the
fortunes of gambling and war are the two forces of destiny
that circumscribe the protagonists. The world, for Dr. Sebastián and the women he encounters is a trap, a labyrinth.
Their vision of life is a pessimistic one--violent, nihilistic,
desolate, chaotic. For them, war represents complete rui-
nation. It is only the individual that can win against the
struggles in society. But Spanish society, for Benet, is

rife with evils. Benet rails against the falsity of societal
conventions, the perverseness of materialism, the false notion of family ties, the paralyzing effect of religious education, the construction of a bureaucratic-dictatorial society.
Critics Guillermo and Hernández have extricated these aforementioned societal critiques from the "juxtaposed, dispersed
narrative elements which appear in a verbal forest that
seems impenetrable. "[8] In fact, the principal fault of the
novel is its arduousness and single-mindedly intellectual
thrust that the very same critics, including myself, found
"asphyxiating. "

        Volverás a Región appeals to a limited public. Its
references to Faulkner, Nietzsche, Andrés and others only
corroborates Benet's access to complex visions of the world,
visions he himself complicates with experimental cinematic
and film-documentary techniques. [9] Volverás was conceived
by a vivid imagination, by a writer who intended to fuse art
and life, persistently overwhelming the reader with confusion,
but stimulating him as well. Like reality, Benet's vision of
Región manifests itself in a complete confusion of present,
past and future; characters come and go, united and separate; no one can control his destiny. Paradoxically, Benet's
physical world of Región is clearly defined, but the emotional life of his protagonists is so vague and confused that it
creates an atmosphere in the novel of "going beyond the
frontiers of reality"[10] as we know it.

        I believe as long as there are authors writing novels,
there will always be a New Wave of writers, seeking to
create in their genre something new. Whether Benet has
done what he set out to do, regenerate the novel genre in
Spain, is certainly one of the prime questions of most
Spanish literary critics. Benet has become a target for
those who feel the spirit of his writing is not New Wave but
Contraola or "against the wave. " Corrales Egea views
Benet's novel as the new product of a decline in the neo-
realistic style of writing of traditional Realist writers who
had followed the path of "mimesis" and have now scrupulously substituted the norms and narrative formulas of the
French nouveau roman movement. The Contraola, or
counterwave embraces William Faulkner as its principal
idol although Pedro Gimferrer, in a recent review of Volverás a Región recounts the following influences on Benet
as well: Kafka, Proust, Hardy, Martín-Santos, James,
Stevenson, Sterne, Melville, Conrad, Lowry and the Latin-
American writers Vargas Llosa and García Márquez, no
less than twelve authors besides Faulkner. [15]

In an extensive analysis of Benet's style, both Gimferrer and Corrales Egea conclude, because of the nearly
complete absence of dialogue, the conglomeration of curvi-
linear sentences (long, unmarried zig-zagging sentences interrupted by circumlocutions, parentheses, subparentheses,
with a profusion of "buts," "althoughs," "rathers" or "perhaps's," creating a kind of hypothetical and labyrinthine
rhetoric), that Benet's style coincides precisely with the
most accursed, identifiable qualities of the nouveau roman:
the protagonist's attitude of suspicion and his environment
in the labyrinth. [12] As a consequence, Benet's style is depersonalized, negative, and pessimistic, with neither the
ideological nor the rational contexts of the Contraola, since
the earlier type of Realism before the advent of nouveau roman embraced an optimistic vision of life, where the writer
believed in his social mission.   For Benet, it is not having
something to say of thematic value that is important, rather
how it is said, which, in turn is the guiding principle of the
objective realism of the practitioners of the nouveau roman.
Benet has rejected the classical manner of describing characters, rational chronology, and the logical and grammatical
use of language.   What was conventionally represented by
writers before Benet has now been viewed as a turning point,
leading to the portrayal of an inanimate world, a world of
things, reducing all emotions and meaning to the level of
"objects," reducing everything to their essences.   Corrales
Egea suggests there is no longer a New Wave and concludes
that a counter-wave exists, believing Benet's novel represents the turning point, showing the transition between the
mimetic character of Realism of the neo-realists and the
new objectivist style of the practitioners of nouveau roman.
Gimferrer and Corrales Egea have noted the extensive use
of gallicisms, Benet's reliance upon the second person singular (note the title), and many other stylistic innovations directly attributible to the nouveau roman and too numerous to
recount here.   However, what was originally a simple
"plotted" novel has now been turned into a maze by Benet
as a consequence of his conscious use of the nouveau roman
style.

Volverás a Región is not a novel for the general
reading audience but rather for the select intellectual or university scholar.   Corrales Egea notes continual references
to mythology, cultisms, Latinisms, Italian and Gallic
phrases, Germanic and Gaelic themes, the influence of
Gide's Los alimentos terrestres, in short an increasingly intellectual burden placed upon the reader which demands not

just a talent for languages and literature but a wide, cosmo-
politan view of life as well.   Apart from these intellectual
requisites, the reader must be able to grasp, as Gimferrer
calls it, Benet's "collective vision of collective catastrophe,"
a world leading itself to the inertia of its own ruin.   "Volverás is one of the most violent and nihilistic works ever
written.   ...   It treats the implacable and systematic process of self-destruction, corresponding to the interior of the
work, to the fatal process of individual and collective self-
destruction which constitutes its theme ... everything unites
in nothingness, in total ruin, in the final silence that follows
a single solitary shot in the mountains of Región. "13

When asked about Volverás a Región in a recent interview, Benet said, "It is a very boring work. " However,
when discussing the contemporary Spanish novel, he stated,
"I believe the novel of today, yesterday and the day before
is one that lacks imagination and that the Spanish writer has
not extricated himself yet from a certain kind of blunt costumbrism.   ...   In this country, there has not been, since
the nineteenth century a novel of adventure, mystery, of the
sea, with the exception of Baroja nor a novel of the imagination ... nor a novel of passion. " Acknowledging the influences of Melville, James and Stevenson on his work,
Benet spoke in that interview rather pessimistically about
his own novels (perhaps reflecting the nihilistic spirit of
contemporary Spain so apparent in Volverás and its 1969
prize-winning successor Una meditación, admitting to a
"prolix narrative, with great analytical pretensions which
makes the work a rather confused volume. "14

                    *   *   *

My first impression upon reading Volverás a Región
was one of extraordinary confusion, because of its seemingly
impenetrable nature, its complex and varied prose style,
the visual and mental fatigue it induced.   Sanz Villaneuva
felt that only upon re-reading Benet could "the accomplish-
ments of this search for a new ambitious novel, far from
the realms of crude Realism"15 be appreciated.   This critical view raises grave doubts in my mind concerning (1) the
mission of the new Spanish writer, New Wave or Counter-
Wave oriented and (2) the state of the novel sui generis
(two subjects that will be discussed in the concluding Chapter 22).   Needless to say, Volverás a Región is a novel of
great imaginative power and Benet, "independent of the

classic traditional novels, has chosen the most difficult road,
which is a ruptura or breakthrough, but also the one that
would supposedly acredit, with major eloquence, his role as
narrator. "16

   In analyzing Benet's imaginative powers, Cárdenas
and Ferrando, in their excellent article, "El mundo pre-
ceptivo de Volverás a Región," consider the roles of time,
memory and perception and conclude that perhaps through a
"diachronic-semantic analysis of Benet's style would a precise determination of information about the characters, their
mysteries, their personal psychology, be revealed to us to
help illuminate certain stylistic techniques of the author. "17
In another fairly recent interview, Benet succeeded in mystifying his public rather than enlightening them about his life
and work.   When asked if the "boom" of Latin-American
literature was a direct result of the decadence of Spanish
literature, Benet answered: "... there may be no true
decadence of Spanish literature but rather a complete decadence of Spanish life which reflects itself in the thought,
politics, science, in the streets, in its architecture and in
its women ... not only spiritually, but morally, physically.... "18   In the same interview, Benet admitted to having
little interest in his contemporaries, especially in Camilo
José Cela and Miguel Delibes.

   If we were to judge Benet's novel itself on the basis
of its own prose style and notion of reality, we would discover a much cited auto-critical passage, another confused
set of words, in which Benet promises to involve us but instead only frustrates us

> ...esa mezcla de deleite e intriga que al especta-
> dor procuran con esos cuadros de tema mitológico,
> bíblico o devoto y cuyo asunto no conoce cabalmente
> ... en la que toda índole del argumento se centra
> en una liviana y lejana figura al fondo de un
> escenario exuberante; y de la misma forma que
> en tales cuadros la ignorancia estima caprichosos
> ciertos acontecimientos que se desarrollan en otros
> planos que, de otra forma, están ligados a aquella
> enigmática figura por un vínculo que sólo puede
> descifrar una erudición ausente o la clave de un
> lenguaje esotérico que el artista utilizó para hacer
> manifiesta una creencia prohibida. 19

Perhaps one "new facet" of Benet's work is his revival of the

conscious stylistic technique Cervantes used to fine effect in
Don Quixote--that of "orden desordenada" (disordered order)
or as Don Quixote says himself, "La razón de mi sinrazón
que a mi razón se hace...." Perhaps Benet is becoming a
neo-Baroque stylist and his novel an exercise in baroque be-
haviorism. By transcending reality and abandoning the laws
of logical perception, Benet consistently substitutes illusion
for disillusion, the illogical for the logical. And very much
like Cervantes, "he has a vigorous capacity for the vivid
visualization of very different people in very varied situations, for the vivid realization and expression of what
thoughts enter the minds, what emotions fill their hearts
and what words come to their lips."[20] Benet's characters
express their respective idées fixes within the framework of
reason without logic, and create such ambiguities that it is,
at times, impossible to understand them, their world or
their notion of reality. At least, Don Quixote's monomania,
to revive knight-errantry, was clearly evinced by Cervantes,
who also made clear the multiple perspectives from which
Don Quixote was judged. I would not equate Benet's novel
with the Cervantes masterpiece in any sense, except to say
where the latter transformed reality through a sense of
Baroque style, producing both wisdom and entertainment,
the former relies heavily upon behaviorist techniques, evinc-
ing an overwhelming sense of confusion through a tortuous
style whose total effect, because of its fragmentary nature
and multiple and illogical perspectives, produces frustration
and despondency in its readers. (See the explication de
texte in the Appendix.)

    Even Pedro Gimferrer admits, despite drawing paral-
lels between Benet and Faulkner's Absalom, Absalom and
Malcolm Lowry's Under the Volcano (both distinctly behaviorist novels), "there are some passages that are gradually developed later, others in which you are destined to confuse
and lose yourself." At times, I thought perhaps Benet himself was "out of control" when he wrote the novel, that he
had lost the thread of his plot. Gimferrer contests this
opinion vigorously, believing, "the symmetry and inter-
changeability of the events, the chronological confusions,
the dark points, the fluctuation of names and references ...
are the result of an implacable and systematic process of
self-destruction ... corresponding to the fatal process of individual and collective self-destruction which constitutes its
theme."[21]

Clearly, Juan Benet is the mouthpiece of the new
New Wave of Spanish novelists (or the Counter-Wave) and
his later novels seemed to have confirmed this. Benet is
the adversary of Pérez Galdós and in a recent article, "Re-
flexiones sobre Galdós," he reconfirmed his rupture with
traditional Galdosian Realism as well as neo-realism and its
multi-faceted forms right up to the time of publication of
Luis Martín-Santos' Tiempo de Silencio. 22 Benet sees himself as a behaviorist-objectivist author, and of course as an
experimental writer. His "trilogy" now already completed,
with Una meditación and Una tumba following closely on the
heels of Volverás a Región, it is significant to note that his
narrative pattern is becoming clearer, easier to follow, less
ambiguous although the same long, winding profoundly organic
paragraphs dominated by a kind of poetic irrationalism, and
propensity for fantastic and subconscious thought still exist. 23
As other critics have noted, Juan Benet is also a master of
the "put-on." What may pass for stylisticly brilliant behaviorist-objectivist prose may also be considered confused,
artless verbal meandering. As access to Benet's world becomes increasingly easier, Benet himself, despite certain
simple-minded, laconic replies at interviews and an occasional feigned lack of information about the Spanish literary
scene, remains a perpetual promise. 24 His work is clearly
"transitional"--a question--and Spanish letters still awaits
an appropriate opportunity for his evaluation.

Benet has already been singled out as a promising
author who has supposedly precipitated the stylistic innovations found in Camilo José Cela's San Camilio 36 (1969),
Miguel Delibes Parábola del náufrago (1969), and Juan Goytisolo's Reivindicación del Conde don Julián (1970). Although
Volverás a Región augurs well for new directions, to me it
is a disappointment because of its heavy intellectualism, its
conscious eclecticism à la the French-inspired nouveau roman, and its prolix, inaccesible style. But, as a transitional work, it breathes new life into the Spanish narrative
and gives impetus to young, aspiring authors seeking recognition for their narrative skills. One can only hope for future models of renovation in a completely Spanish vein that
are in keeping with the high intellectual spirit of the nation.

THE WORKS OF JUAN BENET GOITIA

Nunca llegarás a nada [stories]. Madrid: Ed. Tebas, 1961.
La inspiración y el estilo [criticism]. Barcelona: Ed. Seix

Barral, 1966.
Volverás a Región. Barcelona: Ed. Destino, 1967.
Una meditación. Barcelona: Ed. Seix Barral, 1969.
Puerta de hierro [criticism]. Barcelona: Ed. Seix Barral,
1969.
Agonía confutana [drama]. Madrid: Ed. Col. Libros de Textos,
1969.
Una tumba. Barcelona: Ed. Seix Barral, 1971.

SELECTED STUDIES ON BENET GOITIA

Carenas, F. and Ferrando, J. "El mundo pre-perceptivo de
'Volverás a Región'," La sociedad en la novela de
postguerra (New York: E. Torres, 1971).
Gimferrer, Pedro. "En torno a 'Volverás a Región'," In-
sula, no. 266 (Jan. 1969), 14-5.
Guillermo and Hernández. La novelística española de los
años 60 (New York: Eliseo Torres, 1971), pp. 127-
51.
Marco, Joaquín. "Las obras recientes de Juan Benet,"
Nueva literatura en España y América (Barcelona:
Ed. Cruen, 1972), pp. 143-55.
Núñez, Antonio. "Encuentro con Juan Benet," Insula, no.
269 (April 1969), 4.
Parra, Sergio G. "J. Benet: La ruptura de un horizonte
novelístico," Reseña (Madrid), no. 58 (9 Oct. 1972),
31-2.
Tola de Habich F. and Grieve, P. "Entrevista con Juan
Benet," Los españoles y el boom (Caracas: Ed.
Nuevo Tiempo, 1971), pp. 25-41.

Chapter 18

MIGUEL DELIBES and PARABOLA DEL NAUFRAGO
(Parable of the Drowning Man) (1969)

As noted in the last chapter, a new stylistic approach, beginning late in 1967, definitely Contraola (or, "counter-wave"), was barely perceptible in the works of several young, new and exciting Spanish novelists. Not until 1969 did this neo-Baroque, highly intellectual, objectivist style, somewhat imitative of the French nouveau roman, reach its culmination in Spain (possibly thereby forecasting its own decline or decadence). What is especially surprising to the Spanish public is that Miguel Delibes, a mature and widely renowned Spanish novelist, embraced the Contraola, seizing the "new" techniques created by younger, less well-known writers and using them in his latest novel, Parábola del náufrago.

*   *   *

Miguel Delibes Setién was born on October 17, 1920, in Valladolid, in northern Castille, the third of eight children. He is the son of Alonso Delibes Cortés, a native of Santander and professor of mercantile law at the Valladolid School of Commerce, and María Setién, a native of Burgos. His grandfather was a French engineer from Toulouse working on the construction of the railroad between the towns of Reinosa (Santander) and Torrelavega where he met and married Saturnina Cortés. Delibes' grandfather was also the nephew of the famous French composer Léo Delibes, known for his ballet music, especially the world famous Coppélia. With this unusual heritage, young Miguel grew up in and around Valladolid, received his early education from Carmelite nuns and in 1927 moved to Lourdes where he received his high school education. When the Civil War broke out in 1936, Delibes had already completed his bachillerato, but

could not enter the university since it was closed. Consequently, he began to take courses at the Mercantile School
in Valladolid and afterwards, enlisted in the Nationalist Navy
aboard the cruiser Canarias in 1938. "Those post-war
years of political effervescence and economic hardship should
have powerfully influenced the character of young Miguel,
who became withdrawn and very pessimistic. "[1]

     In 1941, Miguel returned to Valladolid and began
working at the Banco Castellano. During this year he met
Angeles de Castro, his future wife, and afterwards began
work on the Valladolid newspaper El Norte de Castilla while
studying for a degree as an intendente mercantil as well as
one in law. After spending some time in Madrid taking in-
tensive journalism courses, he finally passed his doctoral
examinations in law in 1943 and in 1945 obtained the cátedra,
or chair, of mercantile law formerly occupied by his father
in the Valladolid School of Commerce. In 1946, he married
Angeles de Castro and began to write novels.

     His first novel and first child (a son) appeared simul-
taneously, although publication was delayed until 1948 of La
sombra del ciprés es alargada (Long is the Cypresses'
Shadow), which won the Nadal Prize. Because of this sensational success, Delibes followed with his Aún es día (Still
It Is Day) (1949), after spending some time in North Africa
and Southern France. While his first two novels may be
considered pessimistic, his third, El camino (The Path)
(1950), is a light-hearted, happy work and was received by
the Spanish public with enthusiasm.

     After a long period during which Delibes suffered
from a small cystic tumor, and even during his confinement,
he began work on his fourth novel, Mi idolatrado hijo Sisí
(My Adored Son Sisí) (1953), and became one of the directors
of the newspaper El Norte de Castilla. Delibes' reputation
as a novelist began to grow in the mid-1950's. His first
book of short stories, La partida (The Departure) (1954),
based upon his navy days, was an instantaneous success, as
was his next novel, Diario de un cazador (Diary of a Hunter)
(1955), which won the Miguel de Cervantes National Prize
for Literature. In that year, Delibes also journeyed to
South America (Chile) and consequently published his first
book of travel notes entitled Un novelista descubre América
(A Novelist Discovers America) (1956). After short trips to
Italy, France and Portugal (where he was a lecturer), in
1957 he published Siestas con viento sur (Siestas with the

Southern Breeze), a group of four novelettes for which he
received the Fastenrath Prize, and in 1958, Diario de un
emigrante (Diary of an Immigrant) in which he continued the
life of Lorenzo, the hunter of Diario de un cazador.   In
1958 he also became the (chief) Director of El Norte de
Castilla and began to undertake a campaign in favor of the
Spanish farmer for agrarian reforms.

Delibes' new preoccupations appear in La hoja roja
(The Red Leaf) (1959), Las ratas (The Rats) (1962; it won
the Critic's Prize in 1963), and later in Cinco horas con
Mario (Five Hours with Mario) (1966).   In 1960, he traveled
to Germany, where he was known primarily by translations
of his works, and subsequently published another travel book,
entitled Por esos mundos (Round About the World).   Delibes
culled his memory for further travel impressions of 1963
and came up with Europa: parada y fonda (Europe: Stops
and Inns); in that year, too, he was forced to resign the
directorship of the newspaper because of his "socialist"
leanings.   In 1964, Delibes left Spain and became a visiting
professor at the University of Maryland where he lectured
on the contemporary Spanish novel.   Meanwhile, three of his
books appeared, on the theme of hunting and rural life: La
caza de la perdiz roja (Hunting the Red Partridge) (1963),
and El libro de la caza menor (Small Game Hunting) and
Viejas historias de Castilla la Vieja (Olden Tales of Old
Castille), both in 1964.   Also, with the collaboration of his
eldest son, Miguel, Delibes translated into French Alegrías
de la caza (The Joys of Hunting), the original Spanish version of which he published in 1968.   During the period 1965-
1966, Delibes traveled through the United States and in 1966,
USA y yo (The USA and I) appeared, containing Delibes' observations of North American life.

Another fine novel, Cinco horas con Mario (Five
Hours with Mario), also appeared (in 1966), in which Delibes
began to embrace the interior monologue and other techniques of the behaviorist novels he became acquainted with
in America.   Having kept up his journalism since 1933, in
1968 he brought out Vivir al día (Living from Day to Day),
a compilation of his best newspaper articles written between
1933 and 1967.   Also, La primavera de Praga (Springtime
in Prague), another travel work, was published that year
after Delibes' sojourn in Czechoslovakia during its Russian
occupation.

In 1969, Delibes published his second symbolic-
realist work, Parábola del náufrago (Parable of the Drowning Man), following the new techniques he initiated in his
earlier novel, Cinco horas con Mario. Parábola stirred
much controversy in Spain and its evaluation is still in the
offing. In 1970, Delibes returned to the short story and
published a collection entitled La mortaja (The Shroud),
reminiscent of his pessimistic style of the period 1948 to
1963. His latest collection, Con la escopeta al hombro
(Shouldering the Gun) (1971), is another work in the hunting
genre and contains related articles and memoirs. Un año de
mi vida (1972) is yet another collection of a series of articles in which Delibes comments on diverse aspects of his
life as a writer. Currently, Delibes is working on an anti-
war novel and continues to enjoy a solid international reputation.

Miguel Delibes' literary career has spanned several
generations and he is considered, like Cela and Matute, one
of the most fecund writers of his time. Janet Wynecoff Díaz
in her excellent book, Miguel Delibes, gives the following
accurate appraisal of Delibes' life and works:

> Thus, before reaching the age of fifty, Delibes had
> produced at least half a dozen novels worthy to be
> counted among the best of this century, several of
> them with excellent chances of outlasting the pre-
> sent era and enduring among the classics of the
> language. The novelist is now at the height of his
> creative powers and can yet be reasonably expected
> to surpass these successes in the years to come. [2]

At this point, it is necessary to evaluate Delibes' most controversial novel, Parábola del náufrago, to judge if it is indeed worthy of his talent and if it is one of the "enduring
classics" to which Díaz alludes. But before entering into a
discussion of Parábola itself, I would like to discuss, in
general terms, Delibes' earlier stylistic approach in order
to dramatize the trajectory of his past works and his revolutionary rupture with his former style, the New Wave and the
critics.

*   *   *

Delibes has been always considered a major novelist
whose career is constantly developing, growing in quantity

and quality, and becoming more prestigious because of his
consistent use of Realism and his attachment to rural
themes, which display a variety of character types. Delibes is also known as a conscientious practitioner of his
craft, always seeking some new theme and new means of
novelistic expression. Yet several critics like James R.
Stamm feel "Delibes is not an exuberant novelist, has not as
yet approached a grand theme or found a striking point of
view, but all of the equipment of a major novelist is there:
imagination, sensitivity, a genuine feeling for language that
is both intuitive, and sophisticated."[3] Critics acknowledge
his skepticism, pessimism, reactionary vision of nature,
his love for the man of instinct, of nature in contrast to a
"civilized" product, in short, his negative view of progress
and "civilization," his black humor and cold intellectualism.
William Faulkner, John Steinbeck, Albert Camus and Marcel
Proust are seen as possible influences upon his work.[4]

Most critics would agree that despite Delibes' international travels, his true artistry lies in the works that retain Castillian settings and themes. Delibes is a sharp observer of daily life, with refined sensibilities and an enormous capacity to capture within his writings the essences of
nature by means of his starkly Realist style. When he first
began his writing career, his works appeared unconvincing
and the reading public were unreceptive; however, his novels
gained in veracity over the years because of a progressively
purer or refined style. Most critics affirm that his latest
novels are his best ones. In them he combines humor,
tenderness, nature and tragedy in a harmonious manner, reviving the theme of nature as a literary element indispens-
able to the human condition and portraying this harmony
through his extremely personal style.[5]

Ramón Buckley, in his excellent critical work Problemas formales de la novela española contemporánea devotes
fifty-seven pages to Delibes' "selectivist" style, first examining the Delibean ideology behind his novels (or thematic
content) and then, the two distinct stylistic epochs into which
Delibes' novels belong.[6] Buckley categorizes the novels in
the following manner: those which relate stories, in which
events of fictional value occur, and those which do not relate stories, in which nothing really happens (where there is
no real plot).[7] Buckley's analysis is inclusive of Cinco
horas con Mario. However if we were to insert Parábola
into one of his categories, it would fit most decidedly into
Buckley's second one, with Delibes viewed essentially as a

fableist, a teller of tales, parables, whose stylistic devices
(interior monologue, chronological subjectivity, objectivism,
ironic, comic and explicative interventions) are substituted
for traditional plot outlines and routine storytelling. Buckley
views Delibes' switch in style (his transition from one epoch
to another) with a comparison between Delibes' earliest and
latest novels, realizing that Delibes' stylistic changes reflect an intimate personal problem of the mature author "who
is in full possession of his technical faculties. "[8]

Cinco horas con Mario marks the decisive turning
point in Delibes' writing career, as it stylistically departs
from everything written before it, demonstrating the revelation (through its three hundred pages of interior monologue)
of story and characters in a Proustian or Joycean manner,
whose psychic meanderings break all ties with chronological
time and physical space (as we know them) in fiction.
Delibes' characters move "in a world with neither maps nor
watches, in one where the place and time can atomize,
cross over, dilute or reconstitute itself with the most freedom possible. "[9] Cinco horas is "a pessimistic novel, painful, bitter, written in a compact structure that attains artistic fullness in its foundation and form of execution. "[10]

When Cinco horas con Mario appeared in 1966, three
years before Parábola, Delibes had made some major statements about the state of the Spanish novel and his own mission as novelist, statements which have a direct bearing on
the genesis of his latest novel, Parable of the Drowning Man.
As early as 1963, Delibes considered himself apolitical,
faithful to his own conception of art, but justified in denouncing hypocrisy, oppression and injustice, an artistic position
incumbent upon the social novelist. Delibes found the necessary freedom of expression and independence from political
ideologies or pressure groups to function fully as an artist.
He hoped his writings would contribute to the opening of the
eyes of those who did not obstinately stay blind to the "realities" of daily life. He chose themes and writing styles
appropriate to this hope. "The desire for originality, the
simple thirst for change creates forms of art only apparently 'new' but do not really answer an [artistic] necessity that
remains ephemeral [for the Spanish novelist]. "[11] However
Delibes was also keenly aware of the intellectual paralysis
and political censorship, two causes which played havoc
among Spanish novelists, depriving them of a literary and
spiritual conscience within their own generation. For Delibes, the modern Spanish novel (up to 1963) has been

> a sober exercise in which one can appreciate the
> economy of adjectives [in which] descriptions are
> spare [and in which] the writer insensitively, with-
> out any ostensible preoccupation, creates an at-
> mosphere which imprisons the reader.... [D]e-
> scription in today's Spanish novel is naked and is
> supported by indispensible elements far from the
> old [style] of prolixity. From this, we deduce
> that, in our time, to write literature does not con-
> sist in expounding words, using adjectives exces-
> sively or digressing but simply 'suggesting'.... 12

When asked about his own novels, Delibes said, "for me,
the essential thing in a novel is the characters. That they
be living or lifeless depends upon the quality of the work.
A well-developed character can make the most absurd of
stories convincing...."13

> The writer [according to Vásquez and Kosoff]
> ought to be a man forewarned against the dark and
> irreparable rebellion of words. There is nothing
> so upsetting, unstable and slippery as a word.
> The written word is something like soap in the
> bathtub. The rebellion of words ambushes the
> writer when he wants to pretend that he saw more
> than he saw or to pretend to give a petulant meta-
> physical death to daily minutiae. Truth defends
> itself with its claws just like a growling cat. 14

As a novelist, Delibes places great faith on the
written word and the creation of characters. Although he
may dislike the current state of the Spanish novel, he "is
not impatient or bitter enough about what he finds around
him to have a violent desire to reject and destroy forms as
they are and move on to bold experimentation. He advances
by testing and trying. There also seems to be a trend
away from instrospective analysis, toward apparent objectivity."15 When asked if he felt the Spanish novel found itself (1970) currently in a state of crisis, Delibes replied:
"It is too soon to judge; ... to blame government censorship alone for its decline would be an excessively simple solution.... I believe the novelists today write better than
Galdós although they may not have his capacity for storytelling ... but perhaps it is the need for a 'climate of freedom'...."16 When asked by César Alonso de los Ríos in
1971 in one of their conversations about the state of the
Spanish novel, Delibes admitted his respect for Sánchez

Ferlosio's El Jarama and Martín-Santos' Tiempo de silencio,
believing the authors to be authentic geniuses, while for Juan
Goytisolo he had less praise concerning the latter's Señas de
identidad, primarily because of Goytisolo's use of the literary innovations of recent Spanish-American writers. [17]
While Delibes has read his contemporaries widely, he is
hesitant to express critical judgments about their novels,
preferring to talk mainly about his own.

Perhaps the most valuable statement about novels and
writing novels should serve us as the lietmotiv of Delibes'
entire literary career: "All novels should have at least
three elements: a man, a setting and a passion." If my
previous digressions have served only to confuse the reader, it is to be noted sometimes that Delibes himself deliberately sets out on that very track, to confuse, mystify,
elude his interviewers, his readers--his public. While I
have chosen to introduce his most controversial work,
Parable of the Drowning Man, with a longer than usual pre-
amble to Delibes' own feelings about the novel genre and the
course of his career to date, I have done so with a jaun-
diced view that the author's own statements may or may not
hold true any longer, simply because, as he says, "I know
what I am not: an intellectual. To pontificate about what
is or is not literature annoys me. And on the other hand,
it doesn't suit me."[18] After reading many critical works
and interviews about Delibes, I conclude that he is, himself,
that "slippery soap." He is certainly a talented intellectual
who refuses to be pinned down, whose intellectual positions,
despite their rigidity, have a tendency to change as the political or literary climate varies. In Parábola, he has conceived the true manifestation and expression of his ideosyn-
crasies.

*   *   *

A parable, as the dictionary says, is a short, simple
story from which a moral lesson may be drawn. The "parable" as Delibes has conceived it is a 236-page novel with
no chapter divisions, a rather complicated story but from
which several lessons, moral or otherwise, may be drawn.
Essentially, the novel is a critique against technological advances when they enslave man and subvert his notions of justice and liberty. For Janet Wynecoff Díaz,

the book represents the total crushing of the individual by the collective, dehumanization and the
loss of liberty as a result of the progressive en-
croachment by the state upon areas of the personal
conscience and beliefs. Two symbolically dehumanized individuals undergo physical metamorphoses
(representing spiritual degradation) as a result of
punishment received for daring to question the om-
niscience of an all powerful bureaucratic organization, appearing to be economic in nature, but later
proving more complex, probably representing the
totalitarian state. [19]

The society as we envisage it appears to be a big
business whose owner (or ruler) is Don Abdón, a mixture of
man and woman, "the most maternal father of all our fa-
thers, "[20] who is adored and venerated by all his workers.
While no name as such exists in the Spanish language, its
lexical origin is interesting: don means "gift" and the pre-
fix "ab-" signifies "taking away"; its combination may con-
note the Biblical connotation of God--"he who gives and he
who takes away. "[21] Whoever desires to question or investigate the nature or mission of Don Abdón's enterprise is
thoroughly degraded and returned to his natural state (and
usually killed). As the novel opens, one character named
Genaro (later shortened to Gen or "ordinary man") has been
demoted for putting personal concerns before the interests
of the organization. He is chained nude in a dog house and
treated like a hound, eventually acquiring many canine habits
and physical characteristics. He finally becomes a dog and
is later killed grotesquely by a gardener while pursuing a
female cocker spaniel. Genaro's only friend is Jacinto San
José, a calligrapher who also one day questions the reasons
behind his own work. Jacinto adds figures the entire day,
figures without significance, mainly zeros. Jacinto is a
timid man, a lover of nature, flowers, with a definite sensibility that induces him to worry about the problems of humanity. One of his chief goals is to bring the world closer
together through language and he becomes an avid promoter
of Esperanto. Jacinto also thinks about his friend Genaro
and his fate, deducing that Gen's demotion was because of
"thought crimes. " During the novel, Jacinto becomes obsessed with Genaro's fate, his metamorphosis into a dog
and his eventual death. Besides, Jacinto cannot refrain
from "thinking" despite the fact it may bring about his own
metamorphosis (in this case, into a ram) and his eventual
doom (suffocated or "drowned" to death by a hydra plant).

One day, Jacinto becomes ill while adding an endless
series of zeros. He is advised by Darío Esteban, a Gestapo-
like foreman of Don Abdón's "enterprise," to forget what the
sums represent and cure his vertigo. Still dizzied by writing zeros repeatedly, Jacinto is sent to a remote cabin retreat and is instructed to plant a group of seeds. The re-
sulting plant grows rapidly, out of control, converting Jacinto's cabin hideaway into a prison. Jacinto finds himself
trapped by the ever-encroaching hydra-type plant, fighting
with all his physical and mental power, futilely, to escape.
He begins to tunnel under the miniature jungle but is trapped
by roots and creepers. Frantically, he uses his gasoline
supply (intended for fuel to heat his cabin) to destroy a portion of the hedge and open an escape route. Like an octopus
with a million tentacles, the hydra persists as Jacinto fights
vainly against it with homemade bombs, the cabin's furniture,
etc. Physically and emotionally exhausted, Jacinto begins
to nibble at the hydra and feels a desire to walk on all
fours while a light wool begins to cover his body. Jacinto's
metamorphosis is complete. By the novel's end, Jacinto
has become a ram, suitable for breeding, saying no more
than "baaa."

During his transformation, Jacinto imagined himself
to be a sailor, trapped in a sinking ship slowly filling with
water. Realizing he is doomed, he clings to life, swimming
desperately as "water" fills the cabin. This is Delibes'
parable of Jacinto's fight for survival. Jacinto is fighting
to preserve his life in this almost hopeless situation. At
one point, Darío Esteban, Don Abdón's foreman, flies re-
conaissance over the hedge-engulfed cabin. As Jacinto spies
him above in his plane, he believes he will survive the
"drowning." A team of flame-throwers, part of a rescue
mission that finally cuts through the engulfing hedge, find
Jacinto "survived," but turned into a ram. Jacinto can
only answer, "baaa, baaa," to the rescue team's queries
about his complete metamorphosis.

*   *   *

Parable of the Drowning Man has been widely interpreted by many literary critics as a parody of modern
man, [22] alienated from society because of its technology, [23]
a satire of the present Spanish government (Don Abdón bears
a remarkable resemblance to General Francisco Franco), [24]
a literary experiment in the imitative realm of the nouvelle

vague, an imitation of Franz Kafka's Metamorphosis or Eugene Ionesco's Rhinocerous,[25] a burlesque in the style of Valle-Inclán's esperpentos, exaggerating the grotesque elements for comic and tragic effects,[26] an exercise in black humor,[27] an adaptation of Spanish American literary innovations,[28] an exercise in artistic ideosyncrasy.[29]   Never has a novel stirred so much controversy among Spanish critics and readers alike, as well as internationally; not just because of its intrinsic thematic worth, but because of its possible "political" resonances.   It may be "an indictment of the Spanish government with its abrogation of individual liberties and rights and its vast bureaucratic structure, conflicting with local traditions of exaggerated individualism and separatism."[30]   It may also represent the universal struggle of the individual "dominated by that monstrous Leviathan of the modern State, calling itself Fascist, Neo-capitalist or Socialist."[31]   It certainly echoes many of the pessimistic, dehumanized sentiments expressed in George Orwell's 1984, Aldous Huxley's Brave New World, Samuel Beckett's Waiting for Godot and Ferdinand de Céline's Journey to the End of the Earth, but as Janet Díaz puts it, "Parable is a lesson, a warning and perhaps a cry for help, help in saving that which is most human in humanity."[32]   If we place Delibes' work in the same frame of reference as Orwell, Huxley, Céline or Beckett, we immediately notice his singular stylistic departure from the others of this group.

*   *   *

        At the outset, I must state that Delibes' work is one of the best novels to come from the New Wave (or Counter-Wave), properly crowning the 1960's with its fresh experimental design within a genre becoming stale through reliance upon out-moded intellectual models, stereotyped plots and imitation of other literary schools.   That the New Wave has been sustained and reinvigorated by a writer not really placed in its generation is both alarming and gratifying at the same time.   I cannot agree with critics such as Professor Entrambasaguas, who claims Parable "is one of the most boring novels I have read in these times, lacking all of Delibes' former literary devices or those of any other good novelist,"[33] or José Domingo, who cannot make up his mind if Parable is either a "good parody or a bad joke,"[34] or Francisco Umbral's insinuation that Delibes' Parable represents the "frustration, wasted effort and failure of the author to criticize the society and [that] the novel is a grotesque

attempt, a collection of jokes, sketches, gossip that reflects
the author's (or the novel's) complete degeneration. "35

      For once, I am on the side of the angels: Gonzalo
Sobejano declared Parable to be a "great literary creation...,
a new advance in height and profundity" of the Spanish
novel36; Sanz Villanueva remarked that "Delibes is a true
wit, a genius of the macabre with an extraordinary capacity
for satire"37; Joaquín Marco believes Parable is a "transcendental experiment within the framework of the Spanish
contemporary novel. "38 The case may be made (usually by
José Corrales Egea) that Parable is a Counter-Wave novel,
going against the postulates of the French nouveau roman,
with its heavy use of interior monologue and its strange lack
of punctuation. 39 However, unlike its predecessor, Volverás
a Región, Delibes' novel is accesible, decidedly not labyrinthine, overly intellectually demanding, or hermetic.   It
does not suffer from the faults of Volverás but rather,
through its unique style and simple plot, projects an equally
harrowing but far more intelligent, humorous (black humor,
that is) and devastating probe into man's degeneration and
ruin.

      Delibes' point of view, however, may no longer be
that of the Spaniard but of Everyman.   In fact, there are few
(if any) intellectual or geographical ties in the novel where
the reader might conclude the "mythical" country or enterprise Delibes describes is really Spain or any Spanish-
speaking country.   Delibes has raised his sights to the universal human condition.   Most critics do not doubt the ser-
iousness or honesty behind his thematic intentions, for they
envisage Delibes as a responsible intellectual who is moved
deeply by man and his spiritual problems.   When asked about
the genesis of Parábola, Delibes remarked in a newspaper
interview: "What I have tried to do in this book is to syn-
thesize my own nightmares. "40 In an interview with the
critic Alonso de los Ríos, he said, "I have not needed to
study Freud (of whom I've read very little) or Marcuse
(whom I have hardly understood) but to look back at any dic-
tator who tried to transform his subjects into sheep, which
is the gist of my nightmare. " Asked in that same interview
why he used Max Horkheimer's statement, "the principal
feeling is fear, " as the leitmotif to open his novel Delibes
replied, "... because of my own deep fear ... of intransi-
gence, nepotism, autocracy, violence, the tyranny of money,
the power of organization, the Atomic Bomb..., the deifica-
tion of technology, torture, anguish.   ... My novel ... is

a song to love, to justice, to liberty. "[41] Delibes admits the genesis of the novel was in Prague in 1968 where he noted the crushing effects of Russian Communism, stifling the very sentiments of freedom and justice. But it is only an imponderable as to what effects this Czechoslovakian experience might have had on the composition of this novel. [42]

As for the novel itself, it consists of a witty barrage of verbal and stylistic pyrotechnics that left this reader both amazed, delighted and dazzled. On page one, Delibes begins with a series of conventions replacing normal punctuation (as we know it) which is indeed, revolutionary for the reader. For example, he transcribes phonetically the signs of punctuation: "Behind the fence comma was the little house of Genaro open parenthesis who was now called Gen colon Here, Gen! close parenthesis comma ... " (p. 10). This technique serves Delibes well although he has stated, "I never plan a book technically first before having a theme. I believe the theme itself imposes the conditions (of the novel). I'll tell you something else: if I could not summon another theme tomorrow, I would not write again. I cannot work on demand.... "[43]

As I said before, Parable is not divided into chapters like all of his previous works, nor is there any progressive continuity of the narrative thread along traditional Delibean lines. The novel is written mostly in the third person but there are sections (usually in italics) when Jacinto's conscience speaks (as he looks into a mirror or sees his image reflected elsewhere) which are narrated in the second person singular in the form of an interior monologue. Within these monologues and general texts, there are elliptical thoughts, changes of time, interpolations of different themes, onomatopoeia, repetition, details deliberately selected to reinforce thought patterns, an extended use of syllabification and capital letters, apocopated words in Spanish used to form the new language of "the contract. " No translation into English of this work could do it justice for its cleverness, intelligence, and witty style would probably be lost. Delibes' novel is a refreshing exercise in the intelligent use of the aforementioned stylistic techniques, which help to evoke the philosophy, parody, satire, black humor and grotesqueness inherent in Delibes' principal thematic concerns. While E. Entrambasaguas denounced Delibes for "trying something new ... but not hitting the mark, "[44] José Domingo credits him, like Cervantes, for writing the best book about Spanish society of the future, satirizing the genre with the same

breadth and depth as either a Cervantes or a Voltaire. [45]
Another critic felt that

> Parable is more of a satire of the nouveau roman
> than a simple imitation. ... If Delibes has appro-
> priated certain techniques and characteristics of the
> nouveau roman, he has done so in the same spirit
> of satire and irony which typify so many of his
> other works and not as a serious imitator of that
> school. ... Perhaps, in the tradition of Cer-
> vantes, he has produced a particular type of novel
> by producing an excellent example of that genre.... [46]

*   *   *

If we dare to perceive any "structure" as such in the
novel, we might say it exists on two separate levels where
different tenses are utilized: on the first, Delibes uses the
present tense, narrating Jacinto's adventure in the cabin,
gradually being overtaken by the hydra, giving us the actual
sensation of life as the events occur; on the second, he employs the past tenses (imperfects and preterites), which relate the causes of Jacinto's illness, facts about his work,
home, the city in which he lives, themes handled such that
the impression is given that something has already occurred
and something belongs to the past. [47] Apart from the notion
of structure or style, Delibes develops his characters and
themes in extraordinary fashion, embracing or escaping the
totally crushing philosophies which appear to us in the realm
of impersonal and sometimes cryptic, ironic and paradoxical
slogans: Sumar es la más notable actividad del hombre
sobre la tierra (To add is the most noble activity of man on
earth); Hablar de deportes es aún más saludable que practi-
carlos (To speak about sports is even healthier than to play
at them); Eludir la responsabilidad es el primer paso para
ser felices (To avoid responsibility is the first step toward
happiness) (p. 21); Orden es libertad (Order is liberty)
(p. 25); Respirar por don Abdón o no respirar, he aquí la
opción (To breathe [live] for Don Abdón or not to breathe,
that is the question) (p. 35); Por la mudez a la paz (Through
dumbness, peace) (p. 76); La palabra no sólo es voluble sino
un instrumento de agresión (Words are not only fickle but
are instruments of aggression) (p. 84); Ni retórica ni dialéctica: Todo intento de comprensión por la palabra es una
utopía (Neither through rhetoric nor dialectics: All intentions of understanding by words is a utopia) (pp. 100-1); El

seto es la defensa de los tímidos (The hedge is the defense
of the timid) (p. 164). Most amusing is Delibes' playfulness
with the Spanish language (using a lack of punctuation and
then a super-abundance of it) to achieve within his characters (and readers) their mental confusion, so that we may
feel the confused and disoriented sensations of Jacinto.

Janet Díaz believes Delibes also achieves another purpose beyond showing the disintegration of the personality, by
creating a language invented by Jacinto, "to satirize certain
modern literary theories involving the breakdown and destruction of language."[48] Note the following transcription of
the earlier slogan, "Ni retórica ni dialéctica; todo intento de
comprensión por la palabra es una utopía," and the breakdown of language: "Ni retora ni diala; todo into de compra
por la pala es una uta"--an explosively comic linguistic utterance but tragic in its intent since it indicates a thoroughly conventionalized, regimented society, bereft of all naturalness and spontaneity. Delibes presents many examples of
Don Abdón's society, its crushing effects on language, personality, but never a more depressing statement on personal
communication as voiced by Jacinto: "(a) It is not rational
that man expends all his force through his mouth, (b) the
word, until today, has hardly served but as an instrument
of aggression or exponent of stupidity, (c) with words,
people build inaccessible paradises and (d) the fewer words
uttered, the briefer will be the aggressiveness and stupidity
floating in the world" (pp. 99-100).

There are certain hilarious episodes that are etched
in Delibes' uncanny "black" humor. One is Jacinto's long
discussion with his doctor at the onset of his illness, that
his daily writing of zeros causes him vertigo while the doctor who interviews him seeks to find some "physical" symptoms and discover any irregularities in Jacinto's sex life as
a possible cause (perhaps Delibes is lampooning here the
short-sightedness of medical doctors). Another exhilarating
episode occurs later between a psychiatrist and Jacinto, the
former trying to discover reasons for the latter's dizziness
through a confusing but funny discussion about zeros and the
shape of eggs. Yet another is a devastatingly funny reunion
of Esperanto linguaphiles, talking in their synthetic language,
excessively theorizing while coming to no conclusions. Delibes himself, like the "technicians" of Parable, felt many
practitioners of the Spanish novel theorize excessively and
reportedly said: "We overload ourselves with theories and
forget the practice. Today our aesthetic ideas occupy more

than a technical experiment.   There is no room for sentiment. "⁴⁹   From these words it is also possible to conclude
that "various formal characteristics of Parable can thus be
partially explained as Delibes' ironic reactions to contemporary experiments with structure, technique and language. "⁵⁰

        Perhaps the most moving section of the novel occurs
near its conclusion when Jacinto realizes he is a prisoner of
the hydra and vainly tries to send messages for help but to
no avail.   In one of his interior monologues, Jacinto discusses the meaning of reality: "The world neither sees, nor
hears, nor understands, because the blind do not see and
the deaf do not hear and no one can understand what one
does not see nor hear" (p. 194).   Jacinto has been reduced
to the most elemental level of communication in his struggle
for survival, a struggle he eventually loses.   Delibes presents the reasons for Jacinto's downfall early in the novel in
a capsulized biography: "In May, 1966, he has shown an unhealthy curiosity about the reasons behind his work.... He
mistrusts words ... and trusts only in man and in his goodness.   (Under observation by the State)" (pp. 66-7).   When
Jacinto the man becomes jacinto the metamorphosized ram,
Delibes even reflects these changes in the spelling of his
name.   When Jacinto or (jacinto) cries out for help, the
echoes of his words create a dialogue for the solitary drowning man:

                    -- ¡Malditos!

                    -- ¡Itos!

                    -- ¡No me la mientes!

                    -- ¡Entes!

                    -- ¡Me cago en la madre que te parió!

                    -- ¡Arió! [p. 209]

        At this point, one can only hope the reader will di-
vest himself of all of the controversy and criticism surrounding the novel and take up the original text or a translation
in order to discover the brilliance of Miguel Delibes' imaginative fiction.   For every critical view of the work that applauds it--such as the words of Vintila Horia: "Parable is
the greatest novel of this Spanish writer and one of the most
significant of the Spanish contemporary novels, "⁵¹ or those
of Isaac Montero: "Jacinto San José ... is of the same
lineage as Samuel Gulliver, Robinson Crusoe and Don Quixote

... all visitors to absurd and impossible worlds where daily
events seem surprising and monstrous to them, who because
of their innocence, do not understand the motives of their
original deformation,"[52]--there will always be one that will
crucify it for its snobist stylistic techniques, its supposed
imitations of Kafka or Ionesco, the nouvelle roman or other
literary fads.

One cannot help wondering about Delibes' reasons for
completely breaking stylistically and thematically with his
former literary production (his neo-realism in favor of extreme subjectivism), unless he finds Parábola will have
greater historical and literary relevance for him and his
fellow Spaniards.   Personally, I found Parable a refreshing
novel, one of the worthiest efforts of the New Wave, but depressing since perhaps Delibes believes Jacinto is drowning
just as our whole civilization is.   In one of the longest
studies written about Delibes, Leo Hickey, while not taking
into account the author's Parable and preferring to disprove
(somewhat unconvincingly) the theory that Delibes is not essentially a Catholic novelist, states that while our author "is
not a partisan of the theories of pure objectivism, behavior-
ism or other stylistic devices of the nouveau roman, at
times, one finds some of the qualities of these techniques in
his works.   In general, he is master of his character creations and does not deny telling us their most intimate thoughts
and emotions in the manner of James Joyce."[53]   Whereas
Joyce totally revolutionized the English novel with his use of
interior monologue and original use of language (in Ulysses
and Finnegans Wake), Delibes must certainly be considered
a pale successor by Spanish standards.   Although there is
nothing so terribly new in the thematic or stylistic realms
of Delibes, if we consider his novels in comparison to international literature, we nevertheless find that unlike many
such similar practical works by his contemporaries (or predecessors), Parable is a novel that deserves to be read and
bears re-reading.   For it is a novel to mull over, not only
for its thought content, but for its style.   As one critic put
it, "Parable is a plethora of intellectual content, whose technique is overshadowed by its theme."[54]   It is a book one
cannot forget and one that is basic to the development of the
novel genre in Spain as well as a key work in understanding
the revolutionary turnabout in thinking and artistic accomp-
lishments of Miguel Delibes himself.   It may very well be
the pace-setter for the "New" New Wave of the 1970's.

THE WORKS OF MIGUEL DELIBES SETIEN

La sombra del ciprés es alargada. Barcelona: Ediciones
        Destino, 1948.
Aún es de día. Barcelona: Destino, 1949.
El camino. Barcelona: Destino, 1950.
Mi idolatrado hijo Sisí. Barcelona: Destino, 1953.
La partida [stories]. Barcelona: Luis de Caralt, 1954.
Diario de un cazador [non-fiction]. Barcelona: Destino,
        1955.
Un novelista descubre América [travel]. Madrid: Nacional,
        1956.
Siestas con viento sur [4 novelettes]. Barcelona: Destino,
        1957.
Diario de un emigrante. Barcelona: Destino, 1958.
La hoja roja. Barcelona: Destino, 1959.
Por esos mundos [travel]. Barcelona: Destino, 1961.
Las ratas. Barcelona: Destino, 1962.
La caza de la perdiz roja [non-fiction]. Barcelona: Lumen,
        1963.
El libro de la caza menor [non-fiction]. Barcelona: Destino,
        1964.
Viejas historias de Castilla la Vieja [stories]. Barcelona:
        Lumen, 1964.
Cinco horas con Mario. Barcelona: Destino, 1966.
Vivir al día [journalistic anthology]. Barcelona: Destino, 1968.
La primavera de Praga [travel]. Madrid: Alianza Editorial,
        1968.
Alegrías de la caza [non-fiction]. Barcelona: Destino, 1968.
Parábola del náufrago. Barcelona: Destino, 1969.
La mortaja [stories]. Madrid: Alianza Editorial, 1970.
Con la escopeta al hombro [non-fiction]. Barcelona: Destino,
        1970.
Un año de mi vida [memoir]. Barcelona: Destino, 1971.
El príncipe destronado. Barcelona: Ed. Destino, 1973.

SELECTED STUDIES ON DELIBES

BOOKS

Díaz, Janet W. Miguel Delibes. New York: Twayne, 1971.
Hickey, Leo. Cinco horas con Miguel Delibes.... Madrid:
        Editorial Prensa Española, 1968.
Martínez, Luis L. La novelística de M. Delibes. Murcia:
        University of Murcia, 1973.

ARTICLES

Alonso García, Manuel. "Sobre la última novela de Deli-
   bes," Cuadernos Hispanoamericanos, no. 57 (sept.
   1954), 392-5.
Arroitia Jaúregui, M. " 'Mi idolatrado hijo Sisí'," Correo
   Literario, no. 3 (1 nov. 1953).
Bayo, Marcial J. "La última interpretación de Avila,"
   Cuadernos Hispanoamericanos, no. 72 (dic. 1955),
   327-34.
C[aballero] B[onald], J. M. "M. Delibes: 'Siestas con
   viento sur'," Papeles de Son Armadans, no. 17 (1957),
   209-11.
Cano, J. L. "Los libros del mes," Insula, no. 30 (julio
   1938), 4-5.
_____. "Tres novelas," Insula, no. 49 (enero 1950), 4-5.
_____. "Miguel Delibes: 'El camino'," Insula, no. 63
   (marzo 1951), 4-5.
_____. " 'Mi idolatrado hijo Sisí '," Insula, no. 97 (enero
   1954), 6.
_____. " 'Diario de un cazador'," Insula, no. 114 (junio
   1955), 6.
Castro, F. Guillermo de. "M. Delibes: Un narrador re-
   alista," Indice de Artes y Letras, no. 64 (30 junio
   1953).
Díaz, Luis A. "La promesa de nuestra desesperanza,"
   Información Latinoamericana, no. 221 (4 enero 1971),
   45-8.
Domingo, José. "Crónica de novela," Insula, no. 245 (abril
   1967), 5.
_____. "Narrativa española: Una parábola de Miguel
   Delibes," Insula, no. 277 (dic. 1969), 7.
Gullón, R. "Carta de España: Dos novelas recientes,"
   Realidad (Buenos Aires), vol. 4, no. 10 (1948), 75-
   80.
I[glesias], I[gnacio]. "Miguel Delibes: 'La hoja roja',"
   Cuadernos del Congreso por la Libertad de la Cultura,
   no. 40 (enero-feb. 1960), 111-2.
Marra-López, J. R. "M. Delibes: 'Diario de un emi-
   grante'," Insula, no. 149 (abril 1959), 6.
_____. " 'La hoja roja'," Insula, no. 160 (marzo 1960),
   10.
_____. "El tiempo joven," Insula, no. 189 (mayo 1962),
   4.
_____. " 'Las ratas,' de Miguel Delibes," Cuadernos del
   Congreso por la Libertad de la Cultura, no. 64 (sept.
   1962), 92-3.

Ponce de León, Luis. "Miguel Delibes: 'Siestas con viento sur'," Cuadernos Hispanoamericanos, no. 94 (oct. 1957), 115-6.

R. V. " 'La hoja roja,' de Miguel Delibes," Nuestras Ideas, no. 7 (dic. 1959), 97-8.

Villa Pastur, J. "Miguel Delibes: 'Diario de un cazador'," Archivum, no. 2-3 (mayo-dic. 1955), 9-11.

Vivanco, José Manuel. "El premio Nadal 1947," Cuadernos Hispanoamericanos, no. 7 (enero-feb. 1949), 222-4.

Chapter 19

ALFONSO GROSSO and GUARNICION DE SILLA
(Troop of Cavalry) (1971)

As the decade of the 1970's began, despite the attempts of the late sixties to reinvigorate the novel genre,
very few Spanish authors were stimulated to try something
"new" and as a result, the genre showed symptoms of boredom, tiredness, inertia, a lack of fresh spirit because of
continual thematic monotony, giving the impression that
Spanish contemporary literature was constantly repeating itself. Nevertheless, there were a few new writers who did
not conform to the thematic or intellectual paralysis sympto-
matic of most new Spanish novels of the early seventies.
These "new" New Wave writers--such as Alfonso Grosso,
Antonio Ferrés, Jorge Trulock, Luis Berenguer, Antonio
Palominos, Francisco Umbral, Ana María Moix, Manuel
Vázquez Montalbán and José María Carrascal--have written
perhaps two or three novels and are presently engaged in
revamping the old formulas of social or critical Realism,
expanding their terrain, choosing new points of view and
themes (sometimes germane to Spanish life), writing of their
experiences outside of the Iberian peninsula in their fiction
or using experimental stylistic approaches to themes pertain-
ing to their daily life at home. Such is the case with Alfonso Grosso's Guarnición de silla (Troop of Cavalry) (1971),
which decidely broke with all past stylistic conventions of the
New Wave of the late 1960's and became the first, really
authentic and worthwhile novel of the 1970's of Spain's
novísimos (newest) authors. It is one of the few works,
like Juan Goytisolo's Marks of Identity, to have broken new
ground with its incorporation of those particular literary
tendencies deemed "international," a novel that caused a rupture within Spain and made Grosso one of the newest nationally and internationally known writers.

*   *   *

Alfonso Grosso was born in Seville in 1928 of Italian-
Andalusian heritage. Little is known about his youth or adolescence, although, like most Spaniards, he suffered many
hardships during and after the Civil War. He held many un-
skilled jobs during the 1940's and 1950's and finally burst
upon the literary scene with his first published novel, La
zanja (The Trench) (1961), which was also a finalist for the
Nadal Prize of 1960. La zanja was a social-realist novel
portraying the life of the ignorant peons of Southern Spain
caught in the throes of civil war. Its plot centers upon the
construction of a trench, symbolic of the separation between
social classes. Un cielo difícilmente azul (A Stubbornly Blue
Sky) (1961) followed shortly, repeating the same style of social Realism, dealing this time with truckers in Southern
Spain and their difficulties in transporting shipments of coal
near the región of Las Hurdes. It also analyzes the barbar-
ic practices of caciques against a small group of Andalusian
farmers.

In 1963, Seix Barral brought out a short novel or
novella, Germinal y otros relatos (Germinal and Other
Stories), that had originally won the Sesame Prize in 1958
(note that Emile Zola's great 1883 Naturalist novel of French
miners and their lives was titled Germinal), as well as
Testa de copo (Cotton-head), dealing with the lives of Italian
tuna fishermen living along the Mediterranean. El capirote
(The Hooded One), although originally written in 1961 was
also published in 1963 in Mexico. It treats of the pathetic
life, death and passion of a poor day worker (jornalero),
hired to carry one of the floats during Holy Week procession
in Seville. Up to this point, Grosso had been considered a
social Realist and another undistinguished novel, Los días
iluminados (Lighted Days) (1966) bears this out. However,
his next two novels, Inés Just Coming, subtitled "Compás de
espera de un ciclón en el Caribe" ("Interruption of a Cyclone
in the Caribbean) (1968), and Guarnición de silla (Troop of
Cavalry) (1971) are considered his most ambitious works, in
which he broke with social-realist patterns and turned to a
new, baroque, rich, and elegant style.

Grosso had traveled to Cuba in 1966 as a winner of
that country's National Prize for Literature. His observations of life on the island during his sojourn there are the
basis for the somewhat "sociological" and human study he
wrote, Inés Just Coming, conceived in his new "baroque"

style, utilizing interior monologue and other literary innovations. Inés is a vast narrative trilogy of three persons,
Dionysis, Helen and Melanie, whose lives collectively describe the particular society of La Habana in revolution--em-
battled, besieged by numerous moral outrages.

*   *   *

Guarnición de silla (Troop of Cavalry), which won the
Premio Nacional de la Crítica in 1970, distinguishes itself
primarily as a continuation of Grosso's new baroque style,
surpassing the narrow limits of his former use of critical
and social Realism.   Decidedly a very popular author with
many critics, Grosso appears as one of the most fecund and
vigorous in contemporary Spain.   His books have been translated into French, English, German, Italian, Norwegian,
Danish, Russian, Czechoslovakian and Chinese.   Although he
has also written three travel books in collaboration with
other authors, only one has appeared: Por el río abajo (Up
the River), published in Paris in 1966 and written with Armando López Salinas, another social novelist.   Another as
yet unpublished work, En romería (Picnicking), supposedly
will complete the trilogy he intended to write (entitled A la
izquierda del sol (To the Left of the Sun)) beginning with
Testa de copo and El capirote.   But this too, has not been
published.   Nevertheless, Grosso currently lives in an apartment house in the Barrio Blanco of Madrid with his wife and
adolescent son.   He works in publicity to earn a living but
would prefer to dedicate himself exclusively to his career as
a writer.

*   *   *

Most of Alfonso Grosso's literary career has been
spent in writing about social problems.   Although certain
Spanish literary critics believe he has written some master-
works before 1966,[1] others feel he has difficulty in individual-
izing social problems or that he "has not ever resolved the
novelistic condition between class and individuals and therefore opts for a multiplicity of characters."[2]   Some critics
feel Grosso is a social-Realist who has compromised his
points of view in favor of his fictional premise.   To understand Grosso and his notion of reality is imperative at this
point before we can comprehend his post-1966 stylistic turnabout into a kind of baroque Realism, part of the new trends
of "cultural revisionism" prevalent in the early 1970's.

When Grosso first began writing in the late 1950's,
he felt, like other writers of his generation, that there was
faith in progress and believed in the solidarity of humanity.
His works, then, took on this kind of vital idealism.   And
like other writers, he pretended to awaken the Spaniard's
political conscience by means of denouncing those phases of
society which proved repellent to him: "I am adopting an
attitude of denouncement and from now on engagé...,"[3] "to
give testimony to the 'black days' which my country and her
people have lived through...."[4] Grosso always sought an
international audience, hoping Spanish problems portrayed
through his social-realist style would be given international
attention, sympathy and perhaps, aid.   He felt his own role
as a writer in exposing these problems had precipitated a
widening of the breach of omniscient Spanish censorship and
the Spanish proletariat would someday achieve the liberty it
so rightfully deserved.   In terms of his own style and technique, "they have nothing to do with [his] political posture.
The themes..., the problems of [his] region Andalusia, are
those that interest him, preferentially those about the farmers."[5] Grosso also claims his travel works have had social
significance, since he was able to present an accurate picture of Andalusian reality and the real problems of the Andalusian people.   "I continue alternating novels with travel
literature, with the hope that I will be more fortunate with
the Censorship Bureau."[6] Like so many other writers before 1966, Grosso cries out for the liberty necessary to
write as he would like.

After a trip to Cuba, and with the publication of Inés
Just Coming, Grosso had changed his "peninsular" orientation
to one of international perspectives.   In June of 1970, Grosso
initiated a huge polemic in the Literary Supplement of the
newspaper Informaciones (Madrid), denouncing in characteristic fashion the "new" Spanish-American writers as bluffers
and charlatans.   However beneath this attack of the booming
Latin-American novel, Grosso had much to say about the
Spanish novel and its current practice of "self-absorption" in
its pursuit of 1970's Realism.   "The Spanish Realist novel is
no longer socially oriented.   The Spanish novel is self-con-
suming, in a state of crisis."[7] Because of the recent publication in Spain of Peruvian novelist Mario Vargas Llosa's
latest work, Conversations in the Cathedral, and the general
acceptance of the "boom" of Latin American literature in
Spain and elsewhere, few new Spanish writers have come to
the forefront.   Grosso also attributes the greatness of Latin-
American literature to the influence of William Faulkner but

Alfonso Grosso

269

sees its rise mostly as a "commercial" phenomenon. About
the Spanish novel itself, Grosso had the following to say:

> I believe Spanish literature really has not had any
> major importance; I don't think in Spain there may
> have been an authentic Spanish novel ... one can-
> not speak about a Spanish novel (in which there was
> practically nothing until after the outbreak of the
> Civil War) except in isolated cases [such as] Cela,
> who was capable of suggesting something that there
> was in the tradition of the great Spanish novel....
> [Currently] I think we are all attending the cere-
> mony of confusion and I do not know where it is
> going to end. The experiments they are doing
> right now confirm it, for example in the case of
> Benet's Una meditación, which appears to me a
> novel but does not bring anything new to the genre.
> ... But in some way, if my own literature is
> parallel to Latin American literature, it is because
> Andalusia and [South] America are temperamentally
> very close. ... One already observes a mimetic
> situation.... The influence of Latin America is
> exercising itself on the young writers stylistically;
> also William Faulkner's influence is felt in the way
> young writers are now approaching their portrayal
> of character. [8]

It is clear that Grosso has undergone a transition in
thinking. Among his own generation of New Wave writers,
he felt Sánchez Ferlosio's El Jarama was the first work of
importance. Later with the contributions of Matute, Aldecoa
(who for him was a great Spanish writer), Martín-Santos,
Fernández Santos, he considered these writers, and himself,
foremost in developing a type of social Realism (the School
of Barcelona, as he called it) that is now history. He feels
he began to write in the now popular "boom" style way back
in 1953 or 1954 and cites his story, "La bolichada" ("The
Bowling Match"), as a prime example of the mimetic prowess of these New World writers. "The Latin Americans
didn't create; they re-created what was already there.
Cortázar is a buffoon and doesn't interest me. García
Márquez is a bluffer. Vargas Llosa is very confusing and
has not discovered anything. ¡Ya está bien de la novela
latinoamericana! [Enough already about the Latin American
novel!]"[9] Grosso later declared about his own work during
the late 1960's:

> I am married to stern Realism only in a circum-
> stantial manner. To the so-called 'critical' school
> of Madrid, my first novels sounded South American,
> a very deprecatory comment for those years and it
> remained invalidated precisely because of my styl-
> istic preoccupations. My novels are too well
> written, and to write too well is very dangerous
> for a novelist, Juan García Hortelano told me
> once. ... Even José María Castellet, the pontiff
> of Realism, refused to include me in the nomina-
> tion of the selected few [Spanish Realists], although
> the reading public believed the contrary because
> my novels were translated by Gallimard or Seuil
> into French. [10]

Grosso would be made fun of as Spanish-American by some
of his fellow novelists on another occasion (those who were
more faithful to social Realism) when his Inés Just Coming
appeared in 1966 with its insistence on "Cuban" themes.
Alfonso Grosso has always been considered a highly polished
writer, a practitioner of the "expressive baroque style, ...
a very elaborate, complex technique of writing in accord
with the most modern procedures, converting him into a decided renewer of the genre. "[11]

His latest novel, Guarnición de silla, another extremely well-written and highly baroque styled work is a thoroughly Spanish novel to the core, in the framework of its style
and themes. Its intelligence, execution, techniques and
brilliance might mistakenly be labeled a recreation of
Spanish-American stylistics but the novel is unmistakenly
and purely a Spanish tour de force. Grosso may be erro-
neously thought of as Latin-American, or Italian (because of
the spelling of his name), or a passionate, gesticulating,
heavyset, slightly-balding, Latin epicurean (see his recent
photographs on the dust jackets of Inés or El capirote) but
he is unmistakeably a revisionist Sevillian, a "modern" baroque stylist whose "sumptuous style is apt to reflect all
the sensations that in some moments make us think of that
artful expression that was Gabriel Miró's. "[12]   As world
famous poet Jorge Guillén said of Alfonso Grosso's style,
"His literary expression constitutes a spiritual conquest,
that in its last term [or on its highest level] is [the best]
of authentically Spanish aesthetic creation. "[13]

*   *   *

Guarnición de silla, Grosso's seventh novel, is perhaps the most representative of his newly developed creative
style, begun with Inés Just Coming.   It is essentially an experimental and exploratory novel; it is cast in a new approach to render contemporary experience more exciting,
stylized because of its splendidly verbal baroque character,
with its use of cultisms, time shifts, neologisms, incorporation of foreign words and expressions, interior monologue
and other technical devices.   The novel's six chapters
stretch over some two hundred pages in a rich and varied
prose style that is at times brilliant and at times difficult,
even inaccessible.   Grosso begins his novel with a quotation
of the last two lines of a very famous John Lennon-Paul
McCartney song ("She's Going Home") from their Ser-
geant Pepper's Lonely Hearts Club Band record album:

> ...For so many years.   Bye, bye.
> She's leaving home.   Bye, bye.

Though he states the theme of the novel, that of departure
(for most of the characters), in this original fashion, Grosso
barely alludes to the lyric or dramatic situation of the song,
much less use it as a part of the novel's slim plot line
(see p. 188 of Grosso's novel for the only other reference
to it).   The novel is also written on several levels (mostly
physical and emotional) that reproduce the thoughts of the
protagonists and depict the Andalusian and Castillian countryside in its brilliant celebration of nature.   Grosso has a
particularly fertile imagination, matching the virtuosity of
his style.   "His same prose can as well describe a countryside as a state of mind, as well a reference to the past (with
that nuance of lithographs of the epoch) as a dynamic attitude
of the present.   It is one of sensibility, sensuality, sonority."[14]
Through Grosso's heavy baroque prose, a slender outline of
a plot may be discerned.

Ignacio sets out in his red sports car with foreign
license plates for an unnamed Andalusian city.   Having spent
many years in exile, he has now returned to Spain in order
to transport the body of his brother Leonardo to his family's
mausoleum.   Leonardo was killed during the first days of
the Civil War and was buried in a common grave.   Ignacio's
arrival coincides with Claudia's psychological trauma.   Claudia is a prioress at a local convent and at the present moment
of her life, she deliberates about her past, how she has

"buried" herself in the convent because of Leonardo's death
and remonstrates with herself because of her frustrated,
unconsummated love for him.

Many other characters enter the mainstream of the
novel. Begga, the present female owner of a castle, under
her aunt's (Lady Victoria's) leadership continues to hold afternoon parties, tertulias and soirées for the "golden" youth
of yesterday (Claudia and Leonardo) and today (Jaime, Elisa
and Miguel). She is continually advised by her friend Elisa.
The "events" of the novel, taking place both in present and
past time, are viewed on several levels: we witness the
successful Ignacio at Lady Victoria's castle in his youth as
counterpointed to his present plight--to bury his dead brother.
We live through Claudia's youthful memories of the castle,
her gilded youth, her lonely present, through Begga's evocation of the past. We are privy to the activities of Jaime,
Elisa's son, who maintains a "relationship" with Miguel,
thirty years his senior, a successful landowner and secretary of the local craft's guild. On another level, we are
present during the journey of an anonymous truck driver,
careening with his huge petroleum van cross-country, from
the mountainous Cantabrian north to the southern climes of
Andalusia where destiny will be meted out to four of the
novel's protagonists. The ultimate tragedy ends with the
unifying of the invisible threads of the protagonists' lives,
whose particular actions merge in an ironic twist. 15

In a somewhat confusing and indirect prose, we learn
on the novel's last two pages of Jaime's death in an auto
accident, Miguel's death (he was riding with Jaime in his
Land Rover), Claudia's natural death and Ignacio's fateful
accident (the shocking collision of his little red sports car
with the petroleum truck from Cantabria). One of the major motifs throughout the novel is expressed in the French
refrain, partir c'est mourir un peu (leaving is like dying a
little bit), and at the novel's denouement, except for one
major character, Elisa, all others are victims of destiny
(or the fate Grosso assigned them in a somewhat Pirandel-
lian or Unamunian fashion). Our writer has the ability to
give "fictional" life and take it away. And so he does, as
he reveals ever so slowly, through his tenuous, sumptuous
prose, the history of the Andalusian city, the genealogical
branches of importance of the characters, the flux of aristocracy, culture, traditions momentarily interrupted by the
Civil War, the aristocratic "refinements" of life and the
eventual cultural decadence of post-war Spain. One critic

felt the reporting of the death of Leonardo had so many
stylistic and historical reverberations with the sad demise
of famous Spanish playwright-poet Federico García Lorca
during the early days of the war that the coincidence was
neither astonishing nor accidental. [16]   Apart from Lorca's
(Leonardo's) and Pilarito's (an eighteen-year-old girl to
whom the novel is dedicated) death, Guarnición de silla has
no other grasp on tangible reality.   Clearly, Grosso succeeds in arousing our intellects first because of his fertile
imagination and second because of his brilliant style.

Grosso is essentially preoccupied with nature, architecture, genealogy, and the cultural mores of the society he
portrays through the thoughts of his protagonists.   His external descriptions of the castle, the food people eat, the
clothes they wear, and their patterns of conversation are
especially delightful.   Note the following pile-up of images:

> Las pasteleras cornisas, las churriguerescas
> fuentes, los goyescos gestos, las silbadas eses tan
> falsamente moduladas; las enyesadas medianerías,
> los lóbregos portales, los banales cocteles, las
> sonrisas quebradas a flor de labio, los arcos tri-
> unfales, los mentirosos espejos, los pelones di-
> vanes, la lacustre vacuidad de los artificiales
> lagos.... [17]

This description displays the very prissy, effete sensibility
of Grosso and at the same time, it indicates the sharp perception of an astute social critic.   Here Grosso is forever
attacking the vacuousness of Spanish society.   Notice how he
succeeds again in the following passage, through his unique
view of those essential surfaces that reveal the hollow artifi-
cialities of Spanish life:

> Dispuesto a enfrentarse con la muerte aunque ame
> la vida. ¿O no la ama?   ¿Puede amarse acaso la
> vida sin bohemias y sedosas melenas, sin panta-
> lones acampanados que mantienen el eduardino
> cuadrito, sin chemises Lacoste, sin tabardos de
> viejo lobo de mar, sin polos de cachemire y
> foulard rutilante, sin pendentifs, sin cinturones de
> color malva ... sin una motorcicleta Harley-
> Davidson, sin una caricia materna y una sonrisa
> paterna, sin siquiera un beso? [p. 176-7].

Apart from his virtuosity at exterior description, Grosso

also reveals his particular view of reality to us through his
unique use of interior monologue, which usually appears in
italics throughout the course of the novel. But the key to
Grosso's notion of reality is found in this rather curious
passage:

> Dos zonas de atención. Una para los ojos, y otra
> para los oídos. Una para las fosas, las tumbas,
> las lápidas, los resales, los lagartos y otra para
> la cancela entreabierta y el rumor de las conver-
> saciones de los grupos que discurren tras ella
> [p. 115].

It is clear that Grosso's appeal and orientation to us is on
a level in which sensation and intellect are coordinated.
Like most gifted contemporary writers, he combines his
sensuality with the presently popular concept of nostalgia,
fusing them to evoke his own sense of reality:

> No caben las nostalgias, pero inevitablemente se
> halla de nuevo instalado en ella. El pasado y el
> presente se confunden hermanados en un solo
> bloque circundado de brumas contra las que es
> imposible luchar y por las que, voluntariamente,
> se deja arrastrar sin fuerzas [p. 60].

Besides the evolution of a conscious style, Grosso is also
concerned with time and harmony. "The [most beautiful]
prose the harmonic disposition of its structure, the certain
revelation of his characters, the sharp introspection, the
naturalness of monologues ably differentiating correctly
among the personalities of each protagonist, all have a tendency to make this novel a definite advance on the road of
incorporating our (Spanish) narrative into the new tendencies
of the international novel. "18

    The key to Guarnición de silla, as with its predeces-
sor, Inés Just Coming (in spite of their common baroque
style), is that it is a description of a society in an accele-
rated and pathetic evolution, in obstinate conflict, out of
joint with its physical settings (Castille, Andalusia) and besieged by its own terrible moral defects. As a social critic,
Grosso depicts his society through the long monologues of
Ignacio, his leading character. (We follow the trajectory of
Ignacio's thoughts as well as other characters in monologues
that permit the author to include idiomatic popular and
cultist language for both lower and aristocratic classes.) All

this is captured by Grosso's constant creative effort in a
"tense" prose, adorned with images, obstinate in its search
for syntactic effects, including new vocabulary, all geared to
express an almost poetic tension. [19]   In this stylistic vein,
it is possible to say the Spanish novel is entering upon the
same route that had begun to characterize the Latin American narrative of Alejo Carpentier, Mújica Láinez or García
Márquez.   If we should also select any of Grosso's splendid
descriptions (see p. 160 of his novel), in which each word,
each observation, each adjective and each verb are chosen
in compliance to our author's heavily demanding sense of
literary creation, we would discover a great deal of rhetorical knowledge below the surface, placed in discreet opposition
to his burgeoning mental posturing.   Grosso's accumulative
aesthetic is so indefatigably demanding of the reader that, at
times, it is unbearable--unbearably brilliant and difficult at
the same time.   He calls to mind the best in the style of
Racine, Théophile de Gautier and Rubén Darío, because of
his own classical coldness, his sculpted images and his
modern revival of Parnassian-symbolist surfaces to reveal
contemporary realities.

                    *   *   *

    Summing up my impressions of Alfonso Grosso's
Guarnición de silla (I still cannot assign any significance to
the title unless the characters represent cavalry or chess
pieces moving across the board until they meet their fate),
it is an extremely imaginative novel, stylistically elaborate,
carefully written, difficult in its researched style, obfuscating in its baroqueness (which may create havoc for Spain's
reading public if Grosso continues to write in this stylistic
vein, as one critic has already suggested)[20] but nonetheless
fascinating.

            Guarnición de silla presents the immediate history
            of Spain, of the times of the First Republic to our
            days, across the family histories that coincide with
            an (unexpected) automobile accident.   But it does
            not present it in a lyrical or descriptive manner,
            but with abrupt, brusque leaps in time.   In reality,
            the novel is nothing but a series of instantaneous
            impressions, of flashes that reach the minimal in-
            dispensable elements for its reconstruction, while
            it gives us only the facts so that the reader has to
            keep on composing and recomposing [the plot] in

order to successfully understand the sentiment behind the narration. 21

One of the great problems with Guarnición de silla is the
reader must constantly work at interpreting the sentiments
of the characters and the events of the plot, much in the
same way as a jig-saw puzzle. This facility for interpretation must depend upon the intellectual gifts of the reader as
well as the accessibility of Grosso's prose. Another problem is Grosso's insistence that characters (somewhat play-
fully) constantly return to the past at a moment's notice during the narrative and interrupt the reader's logical grasp of
its present-time action. These flashbacks are triggered by
the sight of an object or the sound of a tune or the utterance
of a word which stimulates memory (very Proustian) and is
both glorious (rewarding) and obfuscating (illogical) for the
reader. One of the novel's weaknesses is its apparent lack
of clarity. And yet it is a diaphanous work, shot full of
brilliant poetic passages, written with a style that simply
demands reading and re-reading. At this point, we wonder
if Alfonso Grosso's "social Realism" will continue to find
expression in this same baroque stylistic direction or find a
new, perhaps even more creative yet simpler direction.

THE WORKS OF ALFONSO GROSSO

La zanja. Barcelona: Ediciones Destino, 1961.
Un cielo difícilmente azul [stories]. Barcelona: Seix Barral,
        1961.
Germinal y otros relatos [novel and stories]. Barcelona:
        Seix Barral, 1963.
Testa de copo. Barcelona: Seix Barral, 1963.
El capirote. México: Joaquín Mortiz, 1963.
Los días iluminados Barcelona: Palabra e Imagen, 1966.
Por el río abajo [travel]. With Armando López Salinas.
        París: Editions de la Librairie du Blobe, 1966.
Inés just coming. Barcelona: Seix Barral, 1968.
Guarnición de silla. Barcelona: EDHASA, 1970.

SELECTED STUDIES ON GROSSO

Núñez, Antonio. "Grosso, Alfonso y López Salinas, Arman-
        do. 'Por el río abajo,'" Insula, no. 236-237 (jul. -ag.
        1966), 19.
_____. "Encuentro con Alfonso Grosso," Insula, no. 232

(marzo 1966), 4.
Santos Fontenla, F. "Grosso, Alfonso: 'La zanja', " Insula,
    no. 180 (nov. 1961), 9.
Tovar, Antonio. "Review of 'Guarnición de silla', " Novela
    española e hispanoamericana (Madrid: Ed. Alfaguara,
    1972), pp. 192-5.

Chapter 20

JOSE MARIA CARRASCAL and GROOVY (1973)

Groovy is the very American colloquial title of Spain's
latest literary sensation, which won the 1972 Nadal Prize in
competition with 104 other works for its author of forty-four
years, José María Carrascal. It is his second novel, but
the first to achieve national and international prominence.

Carrascal was born in 1930 in the El Vellón section
of Madrid in 1930. Little is known about his early years.
He was a consistently good student whose major interest was
the sea. As a young adult, he completed a degree in philosophy and maritime studies at the university level and
worked on many Spanish cargo ships. His first novel, El
capitán que nunca mandó un barco (The Captain Who Never
Commanded a Ship), was published in 1972 and narrates the
adventures of sailors aboard a Spanish freighter. We may
suppose a great deal of Carrascal's own sailing adventures,
imagined or real, are reflected throughout the course of
this novel. Besides the sea, Carrascal has also been active as a newspaperman and writer of short stories, and at
one time he even held a post as an official in Spain's mer-
chant marine.

Carrascal is also a nomad of sorts. Before 1966,
he lived in Berlin as Spanish correspondent for the newspapers Diario de Barcelona and Pueblo. He spent the next
seven years in the United States, residing mostly in New
York City, the setting of his prize-winning second novel,
Groovy, which is principally about the world of Manhattan
hippies living in the Greenwich Village area. He continued
work as a journalist while writing Groovy. Carrascal, now
married, spends several months a year in New York City
and occasionally returns to Spain once or twice a year. He
has finished a new work, USA Superstar, a collection of es-

says with a sociological premise, published in Barcelona by
Editorial Destino in early 1974.

José María Carrascal is one of Spain's newest New
Wave writers. Consciously searching for new roads for the
Spanish novel, Groovy is a reaction to the invasion of Spain's
literary scene by Latin American writers and represents the
conscious launching of a new group of Iberian peninsular
author-competitors, striking out in new and unique thematic
directions. However, because Groovy is not strictly about
Spain or Spanish society, it may cause literary critics both
here and abroad to speculate about evaluating it as an "authentic" Spanish narrative. (Antonio Ferré's En el segundo
hemisferio (In the Second Hemisphere) (1970), for instance,
also published by Seix Barral, deals with multi-racial problems in the state of Kansas, but was written by a Spanish-
born professor of Spanish literature residing in the American
mid-West, in the style of social Realism that is common to
the Spanish New Wave). A detailed examination of Carrascal's writing style should make it evident that Groovy, despite
its international themes of rebellious youth and the generation gap, falls technically within the realm of the Spanish
novel, which is itself still within the throes of an "experimental" phase because it displays many of the stylistic attitudes common the the novísimo authors such as Alfonso
Grosso, Francisco Umbral, Ana María Moix and Manuel
Vásquez Montalbán, attitudes which will be discussed in ensuing paragraphs. Presently, Carrascal has taken up residence in Madrid and continues his journalism while writing
novels.

*   *   *

Groovy is the story of a young girl from New Hamp-
shire, Pat Hulton, her family, her adventures in New York
City's hippie community situated in the East Village, her
mode of survival in the metropolis and her ultimate despair.
Although there are frequent interruptions within the framework of logical chronology, the novel, however, begins somewhat traditionally. Pat lives in an apparently average American home, enjoys the usual freedom of teenagers her own
age and falls into the prescribed view of the "good" American life--a world of studies, the usual normal mixture of
good boy and girl friends, contemplated marriage with a boy
of her own social and economic status, in short, the "good
life." Pat's mother "keeps up with the Joneses," believing

not only in the "American dream" of success, but in keeping
up appearances and conformity on all levels. In fact, her
parents force Pat's unmarried and pregnant sister Rose out
of their home in compliance with the appearances of the
Puritan ideal of chastity, yet Pat's father, Dan Hulton, is
permitted to reside in their home, even when Pat reveals to
her mother his affair with her schoolmate, Eve.

        Dan's character is also primarily a stereotype of the
middle-aged American male who is very much aroused by
"erotica," the Madison Avenue idea of "flower children," the
hippie culture, searching for the "fountain of youth" as he
slips gently into his early fifties. Sleeping with Eve gives
him a sense of being young again. In fact, he says at one
point in the novel, "Pat. You know Eve and I are lovers?
Yes, Eve and I, lovers since last year. I cannot resist it
anymore. I had to tell someone. ... What can I do? Divorce your mother? ... You know, something strange happens to me [with her] ... it seems that I am the youngest
and you are all older...."[1] Eve, on the other hand treats
her "affair" with Dan as so much "impersonal" sexual experience. She is cynical, hard-boiled, a true "flower child,"
but devoid of the philosophy of love. She has been hardened
by life's bitter experiences.

        Like Eve, Pat's story is also one of disillusion and
corruption. We watch her proceed into an hallucinatory
world of New York low life, riddled with sex, drugs, alcohol, while her own adolescent past is exposed through mem-
ory--her first sexual encounter in the back seat of a Ford
Mustang, her first excursion into pot, hashish, cocaine and
the rest. Disenchanted with the hypocrisy that is rife in
her home town, wanting to evade her familial responsibilities, Pat runs away, takes off for the "big scene," searches
for her friends, her "soulmates" in New York's East Village.

        The remainder of the novel's ten-chapter, 336-page
format is a reconstruction of New York's hippie world. Pat
becomes part of several movements in vogue--the "drug"
scene, anti-war marches, feminist movements, anti-establishment modes of behavior, the "folk" scene, the "pop"
world, the "flower children" communes, the "topless" bar
scene. Without money, she works and moves her way from
one "party" to another, one bed to another, one philosophy
to another, constantly disillusioned, disenchanted, barely
surviving. The novel reproduces a great deal of the New
York clichés and linguistic phenomena of the preceding "in"

groups--the jargon of hippies, flower children, motorcyclists,
ex-Vietnam veterans, college dropouts, Bowery drunks and
hustlers, East Side prostitutes, Greenwich Village homosexu-
als and the rest of New York's demimonde.

Pat discovers life for herself and participates willing-
ly in the communes, the world of grass, acid, heroin, and
sex and begins to steal and to commit other major crimes
in order to feed her "habits" just to survive.   She holds a
wide variety of jobs--from babysitting for a dog (the proud
"mother" is an eccentric millionairess) to working for a
Feminist group to serving drinks in a "topless" bar where
she receives the token salary of one dollar per night but
makes her "real" wages in "tips. "   Against this panorama,
Carrascal presents a wide variety of characters: besides
Pat's family and Eve, there are Pulga (Flea) (Pat's first
New York friend), Jack (Pat's first seducer), Rafe, Michael,
Mr. Bell, Mario, Ro, Olga, Karenga (Pat's African lover)
and a wide variety of Greenwich Village types.   None of the
characters are really presented in depth.   However when
placed in the context of the incidents of the novel (and there
are virtually hundreds of scenes we can visualize through
Pat's narrative odyssey), each character assumes his or her
proper stereotyped position.

Groovy is a bitter novel, full of graphic incidents
leading us further into the depths of Pat's despair.   At the
novel's conclusion, Pat is asking herself (at age seventeen)
why she is so bored, why can't people ask for what they
really want instead of running roughshod over her life and
spirit.   On the very last page of the novel, Pat winds up a
prostitute, being treated for venereal disease at a local free
clinic.   Her parents, frantically worried by her disappearance, had set the New York City Police after her.   They
finally track her down but Pat eludes the law once again.
As she enters a taxi, the driver asks, "Where do you want
to go?" Pat answers, "Nowhere. " And the driver sarcasti-
cally and pitifully replies, "Okay, I'm going nowhere, too"
(p. 336).

*   *   *

Groovy is a bitter novel, depressing because of its
central characters, total disillusion and desperation, but im-
pressive because of its accurate views of life through a collection of hundreds of incidents of New York living circa

1970. Carrascal has chosen to portray, in a verbal mosaic,
the hundreds of varied incidents that make up the novel
through a kind of nervous, journalistic style, held together
principally by the narrator (who sometimes confusingly tells
her story in the third person singular). In the frame of social Realism and as part of the "experimentalism" now in
vogue within the Spanish narrative, Carrascal utilizes interi-
or monologue, abrupt shifts of time between present and past,
frequent alternations of dialogue with exterior descriptions,
retrospective recall, breaks in the logical narrative pattern,
a fragmented, erratic presentation of the novel's bare plot
outline instead of a logical, flowing, linear approach.
Stylistically, Groovy is certainly part of the new Spanish
1970's narrative stream. Apart from its themes--the "generation gap," rebellious youth, the corruption of a young teenage girl, the "drug" world, student and feminist movements,
the "anti-establishment" ethic, folk and pop music scenes--
Groovy is in every sense sensational to Spaniards reading
the novel for the very first time since these themes never
have been attempted by a Spanish writer before nor have they
been executed so graphically. What Juan García Hortelano
and Juan Goytisolo may have suggested in their respective
novels, Tormenta de verano and La isla, in their portraits
of corrupt youths living in a decadent society is in no way
repeated in Groovy. Groovy is an excellent example of a
complete panorama of jaded youth, corruption "American-
style," and Carrascal has reproduced New York society
splendidly.

     Groovy has a kind of sincerity and naturalness of
tone, a living presence, because Carrascal is successful in
presenting the feelings as well as the idiom of his characters (no matter how short lived in the novel). There is an
intense feeling of palpitating life throughout the novel. You
can visualize each character (and there are dozens of them),
feel them breathe, watch them act out their roles in the
vast panorama that is the East Village hippie scene. Carrascal is a particularly good observer of life. In short,
quick prose passages, he captures the entire soul and portrait of his "types" as an Impressionist painter captures his
images on canvas with flecks of color. At times, Carrascal uses an almost photographic sense, literally reproducing
snapshots of New York life, brief clear scenes accurately
and sharply portrayed. A native New Yorker myself, I can
vouch for Carrascal's accurate depiction of the city, both
its physical locales and its human beings as Carrascal envisages them. Carrascal is even particularly sensitive to

the New York slang used throughout the novel.   In fact, one
can compile a short dictionary of popular argot (with their
proper translations into Spanish) which would make for an
amusing lexical exercise.   Note common Anglicisms and
their Spanish equivalents such as ¡Wau!, Bai-bai, Jai.   Note
also the great quantity of Spanish slang such as joder, coño,
perra, pedazo, hijoperras, etc.

And yet, for all of the novel's incidental character,
accuracy of idiom, perception into the drug scene, and excellent exterior descriptions of New York City and environs,
Groovy comes off curiously as a superficial work, cold, objective, without heart, essentially because of our lack of
sympathy for Pat Hulton and her life style.   Perhaps I personally have little in the way of sympathy or commiseration
for this new "lost generation of the 1970's," but I particularly feel the novel is overly artificial since there is only
the author's presentation of actions and surfaces as he sees
them.   Perhaps interpretations of actions and incisive perception into the characters by the writer are needed as well.
Groovy is a good novel in some sense, since it does not
openly moralize.   Carrascal does not permit any emotional
outbursts or utterances of ridiculous scruples.   It is a level-
headed novel, objective, cold, almost like a documentary
film.

Although I do not agree with José Domingo's mild suggestion that Groovy is essentially an anti-American novel, 2
nevertheless Carrascal has presented a most revealing, un-
complimentary and indeed, accurate view of our contemporary
society.   It is difficult to comprehend, though, why this particular novel, in competition with 104 others, would win the
Nadal Prize since it deals with American themes not necessarily germane to the Iberian peninsula.   Nevertheless, the
Nadal jury felt Groovy deserved first prize because of its
"audacious innovations, its extraordinary technical perfection
and for its depth and transcendence of the problem it presents."3   Pat is seen as "a symbol of the immature idealist,
in search of her own identity, a new archetypal romantic
heroine of disillusion, incapable of realizing in the abject
and decadent world that surrounds her, a utopian ideal for
a better, purer and more beautiful life."4

During my reading of the novel, its "audacious" innovations and technical perfection seemed omnipresent.   However, regarding the matter of depth or transcendence,
Groovy contains little if any insights that really matter.

The only genuinely moving speech our heroine makes takes
place at the conclusion, when Pat asks herself, "What's happening in this city? ... Why are so many people leaving
it? What do they do? What are they looking for? I'm fed
up with looking, tired of searching, tired of everything,
bored. ... I haven't felt this tired, to be so painfully
bored in a long time, to know that I'm going to rest, to
stop ... nothingness, nothing ever happens...." (p. 335).
Pat's last words reflect her complete disillusion with her
present life and her past experiences. At age seventeen,
she sounds like a potential suicide, depressed, lonely,
burnt out. I never thought of her as a "utopian idealist"
looking for a better life, but generally as an immature and
passive spectator, shaped by the society with which she
comes in contact, a malleable, formless, transparent being,
with little emotional or intellectual stamina left except to escape her family and run loose in the savage city.

Carrascal's strength as a writer of fiction lies in his
ability to capture incident and incidental character. However, given the chance to present a single character in depth,
the author certainly spared us from profundity. And maybe
that was precisely his intention. Pat Hulton is a vapid, immature teenager with little of her own style or character
coloring. Carrascal is particularly good however, in con-
veying to us her immaturity as well as the flavor of the
"original" characters he has created, capturing the precise
imagery, idiom and English vocabulary of the hippie world
which is certainly a daringly different and risky theme for a
Spanish novelist, somewhat alien to the United States and its
customs. Carrascal's seven years of New York living obviously helped him achieve the depressing portrait he paints
of Manhattan but it is his gifts of observation, his sensorial
orientation and unique writing ability that has made Groovy
a popular success in Spain during the 1973-1974 literary
season.

Strangely enough, as sales for the novel increased in
Spain, displaying a marked interest by the country's reading
public in themes other than Spanish ones, here in America,
interest in the hippie movement dwindled very quickly.
What began with Mario Savio and the ferment of student
movements at Berkeley, California, in the early 1960's,
with all its nuances (the flower children of San Francisco's
Haight-Ashbury or descendants of the James Dean Rebel Without a Cause 1950's rebellion of youth or the Hell's Angels'
motorcycle rampage emanating from the 1950's vision of

Marlon Brando's Wild One or the drug scene given popularity
through Jack Kerouac's novels of the beat generation, On the
Road or The Subterraneans) has mysteriously died a slow
death in the American mythologies and artistic works of the
seventies. The sixties and early seventies in America were
tumultuous times for youth because of the Kennedy assassi-
nations, Vietnam war protests, perceived ecological crises,
gay and women's liberation movements, Third World ascendancy, and Watergate. Curiously, the American novel was
rarely affected by these themes to any great extent. However in the motion picture, Peter Fonda's and Dennis Hop-
per's cyclist portraits in their production of Easy Rider,
Peter Boyle's electric performance as Joe (unmistakeably
resembling Pat Hulton's father Dan) in the film of the same
name, and Haskell Wexler's serious, semi-documentary
Medium Cool, about student riots, come to mind, along with
more pretentious Hollywood efforts such as Jack Nicholson's
portrait of a dropout in Five Easy Pieces, Elliot Gould's
engagé graduate student in Getting Straight and Bruce Davi-
son's disillusioned student in James Kuen's Strawberry State-
ment--all of which show the heights and the depths of America's artistic preoccupation with its own subcultures of drugs,
hippies and student movements.

	It is curious that the Spanish are only now beginning
to take an interest in America, circa 1973, in what was a
passing show in our social mores some five years ago.
However, contemporary Spanish society is besieged very
much by the same problems that beset us several years ago.
Carrascal has capitalized on this fact and has written a commercially successful novel with a terrifically catchy title that
ably points out the newest trend of writing among Spain's
novísimo authors. However is it proper to include Carrascal in this collection of New Wave Spanish writers? Is
Groovy to be considered a real, legitimate, authentic contribution to New Wave writing or is it a pale imitation of the
kind of novels so commonly written by Americans like John
Updike or James Purdy? When Spaniards like Antonio Ferrés
or Alfonso Grosso or Spanish exiles like Ramón Sender and
Francisco Ayala left the Iberian peninsula, did they run the
risk of losing their interest in Spain or making vital contributions to Spanish life and culture by exploring subjects out
of the peninsula, beyond the frontiers of Spanish society?
Are novels like Groovy valid contributions because they deal
with themes important to the Spanish nation?

I shall digress momentarily to discuss another famous, popular Spanish novelist in exile, Juan Goytisolo. Although Goytisolo has lived out of Spain some ten years and occasionally returns to visit friends and relatives, he never really "leaves" Spain because Spain is the major preoccupation of his novels. His latest work, Count Julian, recently translated here in America, is banned in Spain and yet, Goytisolo still writes of an emotional love-hate relationship with the country of his birth. Is Groovy, then, just as legitimate a contribution, although it deals with American themes?

One easily concludes Goytisolo is a major novelist, a major talent with major preoccupations. I would place Ferrés, Grosso and Carrascal also as major writers with uniquely varying talents but perhaps with fewer major preoccupations than those of Goytisolo. Ferrés, Grosso and Carrascal are currently caught up in Spain's literary movement of "cultural revisionism" and they exhibit in their fiction the same fervor of cultural confusion taking place among Spain's novísimo writers, a confusion that manifests itself in a wide variety of experimental styles and choice of new themes. Groovy is a facile, commercial product of this revisionism, confusion and commercialism. It is an authentic Spanish literary creation as is Goytisolo's Count Julian simply because it deals with new themes and is written in colloquial Spanish by a new writer in the popular styles of the moment.

As an American reading Carrascal's novel, I may have found it somewhat talky, stereotyped, even banal in stretches because of its accurate reproduction of character types and dialogue I have seen and heard for many years as a resident of the New York metropolis. But my own attitudes should not discourage the Spanish reader with fresh vision from entering the East Village scene of New York's hippie world, a scene that is certainly completely alien to mine and to the way of life of many Spaniards. Sometimes I may dare to speculate that when a jury of critics makes a literary award for excellence (e.g., the Nadal for Groovy), it is based really on the "commercial" possibilities of the novel rather than its intrinsic literary worth. Carrascal's Groovy causes me to speculate a bit further about the whole idea behind literary prizes and their real value to the Spanish publishing world. Do juries of critics ideally choose the novelistic work that also contributes most to the evolution of the genre? Whatever our own conjectures may be at this

moment, Groovy is certainly the undisputed winner, maintaining the Nadal Prize tradition of "measured equality, new
experiences [not letting itself be dragged into the experimentalist trend now in vogue], discreet judgment and public
favor.   Where it is possible to guess which novels will receive awards from other publishers, the Nadal Prize also
conserves its tradition of truly being a welcome surprise to
author and public alike. "[5]   In this case, I trust Groovy's
commercial possibilities were already prejudged.   Groovy is
a good second novel for Carrascal and aptly displays the preoccupations of contemporary Spanish authors and publishers
alike.   It truly deserves its accolades.   However its success
leads me to wonder about the novel genre in Spain and its
near future.   One can only pray for a real burst of creative
energy in the Spanish nation that will hopefully dispel the
Orwellian prophesies of 1984 or the Delibean "parable" discussed in an earlier chapter.   After all, we are but ten
short years away from the age of Big Brother and hopefully,
mankind will fare better than that.   We can only rely on the
individualist nature of the Spanish character for intellectual
regeneration in the arts.   "It is because nations tend to
stupidity and baseness that mankind moves so slowly; it is
because individuals have a capacity for better things that it
moves at all. "[6]   Only with great faith, then, in the Spanish
intellect and in individualist writers who are divorced from
the political exigencies of a decaying dictatorship, will
Spanish letters have the opportunity, the ability to flourish
and bask in the glory of their nearly new-found freedom. [7]

THE WORKS OF JOSE MARIA CARRASCAL

El capitán que nunca mandó un barco.   Barcelona: Ed. Des-
       tino, 1972.
Groovy.   Barcelona: Ed. Destino, 1973.
USA Superstar [essays].   Barcelona: Ed. Destino, 1974.

SELECTED STUDIES ON CARRASCAL

Díaz, Janet W.   "Spanish Literary Prizes, " Hispania, vol.
       56 (Sept. 1973), 723-4.
Domingo, José.   "Narrativa española: La rueda de los
       premios, " Insula, no. 318 (May 1973), 7.

Chapter 21

SUMMARY:
MAJOR TRENDS AND WRITERS (1950-1970's)

1974 was, perhaps, the best year for all Spanish
writers, old wave, New Wave or novísimo. Spain's reading
public was particularly attuned to the novísimo authors,
Francisco Umbral, Ana María Moix, Vásquez Montalbán and
the like. However, Spain's older, well-established writers--
Cela, Fernández Santos, Juan Benet and Juan Goytisolo--are
providing much distraction and entertainment for their intellectual audiences with their latest fictional works as well.
If we were to examine the formidable list of authors reviewed in this volume, it is evident that Cela, Martín-Santos,
Benet and Goytisolo are the four principal revolutionaries
who have done most to regenerate the Spanish novel. Fernández Santos, Sánchez Ferlosio, Marsé and García Hortelano have also made and continue to provide formidable contributions to the genre.

Supportive of these two categories of writers are the
steadily productive novelists of major talent but whose writings have shown only occasional sparks in restoring prestige
and fame to the Spanish narrative. They are Matute, Aldecoa, Delibes, Quiroga and Gironella.

The next group of contributors, whose careers are
somewhat fragmented by their erratic, though solid literary
production, are writers of merit whose occasional novels have
exerted some force on the Spanish reading public and subsequent revival of interest in the genre. They are Sueiro,
Goytisolo-Gay and Castillo-Puche.

Finally, among the experimentalists and younger group
of novelists whose works show considerable promise, we consider Grosso, Ferrés, Carrascal, Umbral, Hernández,

Vásquez Montalbán, Moix to be the best as well as a host of
other novísimo authors who have yet to make their mark on
the Spanish literary scene.

What we have noticed until this point is that chronological age or reputation or the maturity of a writer has
little or no bearing on his or her impact or quality as an
innovator within the framework of the genre. For example,
Cela may be one of the oldest, most mature and steady contributors to the Spanish novel and other genres, but his
tremendismo cannot compete with the youth, excitement and
ability of Juan Goytisolo's fictions of demythification and cultural revisionism. Nor should it. However, at this point I
should like to consider the progress of the Spanish novel as
I see it from 1950 to 1974, taking into account Realism as
a style and the many shapes it has taken over the past
twenty-five years as well as review the major writing styles
(from Cela to Carrascal) and include a fairly sketchy, if
rounded portrait of each writer's career (for example, Cela
from 1950 to Cela of 1974).

Giving credit where credit is due, we must acknowledge Camilo José Cela as the first great innovator of the
post-Civil War Spanish novel, especially because of his philosophy of tremendismo and the extremely naturalistic, realistic writing style he initiated in 1942 with the publication of
his best seller, The Family of Pascual Duarte. Although an
occasional novel attempted to match Cela's inventiveness and
creativity within the genre between 1943 and 1950 (I may cite
Carmen Laforet's psychological novel, Nada (1945), Miguel
Delibes' realistic work, La sombra del ciprés es alargada
(1948), and Elena Quiroga's regionalist work, Viento al norte
(1950), as most representative) by in large, the Spanish narrative reached a standstill. Its main practitioners were the
former greats of the Generation of 1898 such as Pío Baroja,
Unamuno and Azorín (whose fictional works during these
years were very undistinguished), or the exiles who wrote
realistic novels about their fictional or real experiences
within the Civil War. Such writers as Max Aub in Mexico
(his Campo cerrado and Campo abierto are deservedly famous
works), Serrano Poncela in Argentina, Francisco Ayala in
New York, Ramón Sender in New Mexico and Arturo Barea
in Buenos Aires are justly famous among other exiles for
their war novels.

Spanish critic José R. Marra-López has documented
the influence of these and other Spanish exiles in his thorough

critical work, Narrativa española fuera de España 1939-1961
and gives special attention to the writers cited previously in
several chapters written in depth about them as well as many
other novelists such as the well-known scholar, philologist,
and essayist of Oxford fame, Salvador de Madariaga, and the
young Spanish professor of literature, and poet-novelist currently residing in the United States, Roberto Ruiz.

Thus, with only occasional bright moments and attempts by newer authors, such as Ana María Matute (Los
abel, 1948), Gironella (Un hombre, 1946) and Luis Romero
(La noria, 1952), to write about themes other than the Civil
War, the war itself was nevertheless the major preoccupation of many established Spanish novelists such as Rafael
García Serrano (La fiel infantería, 1943), José Suárez Carreño (Las últimas horas, 1950), and Mercedes Formica (La
ciudad perdida, 1951) and would continue to be so for many
years.

Even Cela returned to the theme of civil war in his
San Camilo '36 (1970) and other writers, such as Gironella
(with his trilogy), Juan Goytisolo (Duelo en el paraíso, 1955
and Señas de identidad, 1966), Angel María de Lera (Las
últimas banderas, 1968), Matute and her trilogy, Ignacio
Agustí (19 de julio, 1965) and Juan Benet (Volverás a Región,
1967), have built thriving, successful writing careers upon
the single most traumatic incident in their lives--the Civil
War of 1936.   Nevertheless, it is not until La colmena (The
Hive) was published in 1951 that Spanish writers were aware
of a new orientation which would lift them out of the pessimistic, naturalistic, horrific philosophy of Cela's tremendismo
and away from his crudely realistic writing style into the new
world of objective Realism and the creation of a New Wave
of Spanish writers and writing.

It was Cela who introduced objective Realism into
the Spanish novel (in a social context) (see Chapter 3) and
the genre has not quite yet recovered from the shock of his
innovations.   As Cela departed from the nineteenth-century
Romantic-Realist traditions which characterized the Spanish
narrative between 1940 and 1950, with his use of photographic
techniques in prose, interior monologue, clinical objectivity,
fragmentation, use of colloquial language and visceral character portraits, so Gironella retreated to the traditional,
nineteenth-century Galdosian Realism in his portrait of Spain
in the throes of civil war in his 1953 novel, The Cypresses
Believe in God.   As Cela is the first daring experimenter,

leader of the New Wave, Gironella represents a more conservative approach to his writing, blending fact, fiction and
autobiography into a vast panorama in the tradition of nineteenth-century Realism.   Spanish readers loved Cypresses
and made it one of the best selling novels of all time in
Spain despite its retrogressive style, hampering further development of the genre (and perhaps because of its optimistic
philosophy of life and its reawakening of Catholic values).
Its real contribution to the New Wave is that Spaniards could
now treat in Spain themes formerly forbidden by the Spanish
government.   Cypresses was a clear breakthrough against
government censorship (see Chapter 4).

          Elena Quiroga, a writer certainly more courageous
than Gironella, advanced the New Wave and the genre on
several fronts.   First, she paved the way for recognition of
female novelists and with this accomplishment, increased our
knowledge of feminine psychology.   Secondly, she added to
our notion of Realism a poetic lyricism in her prose and a
feminine delicatesse, as she also deals with contemporary
problems of Spanish women (through her use of interior mon-
ologue--see Chapter 5).

          Interior monologue became quite fashionable as a
writing technique for most Spanish novelists to create their
"new" kind of Realism.   Most Spanish novelists would acknowledge their debt to William Faulkner; however some,
such as Jesús Fernández Santos, have used this literary device to a limited extent, preferring to rely on the tested
techniques of nineteenth-century Realism common to the Regional novels of that period.   Los bravos is ideally a Regional novel, social in theme but psychological and cinematic in
style, combining the best of nineteenth-century Realism and
twentieth-century innovative techniques (see Chapter 6).
Fernández Santos has followed Cela's lead and continues the
objectivist style of writing with a greater propensity for
cinematic, psychological and behaviorist techniques, as well
as drawing upon the traditional Realist values of solid plot
construction and ample descriptions.

          By 1956, the Spanish novel reached a turning point
when Sánchez Ferlosio's El Jarama (see Chapter 7) was published.   Objectivism reached its apogee in this tightly written,
slice-of-life, highly controversial novel.   It is also one of
the first "experimental" novels written "almost" according to
the French concept of classical unities of time, place and
action, perhaps imitating the nouveau roman of Michel Butor

and Alain Robbe-Grillet, but is still a frustrating novel because it "objectively" pretends to reveal much about Spain's
lower middle classes but does not dare to openly criticize
the society. Similarly, Luis Goytisolo's Las afueras (see
Chapter 8) is also about Spanish society, obliquely critical
of old age, the bourgeoisie and the perils of encroaching
modernization. Sánchez Ferlosio and Goytisolo-Gay both
offer differing social portraits of contemporary Spain, something daringly new for the genre with their objective but laconic views. Both writers are social Realists; however they
do not protest too vigorously for reform of contemporary
living conditions. Unlike Sánchez Ferlosio, Goytisolo-Gay
introduces a poetic lyricism into his prose and frees the
genre from a completely "experimental" mode which Cela
initiated and Sánchez Ferlosio continued.

    In 1960 came a turn from objective to subjective
Realism with the publication of Ana María Matute's Primera
memoria (see Chapter 9). Matute is the great female novelist of the twentieth century, unafraid of government censorship, aware of the novel genre as an artistic medium, a
brilliant stylist, wholly subjective (and somewhat autobiographical) in her treatment of characters and their interior
worlds. Matute has consciously turned her back on an objective-realist style and has successfully cultivated the sub-
jective-neo-realist style memoir. Interestingly enough, very
few New Wave writers have followed Matute's lead and consequently other novelists, such as Daniel Suerio, author of
La criba (see Chapter 10), returned to social themes translated into objectivist stylistic forms and combined with interior monologue in the best tradition of Elena Quiroga's or
Fernández Santos' best introspective novels.

    Following the objectivist trend combined with social
Realism, García Hortelano celebrated, with his neo-objectivism (another off-shoot of social realism) the corruption and
decadence of contemporary Spain, in his novel Tormenta de
verano (1962) (see Chapter 11), using, however, ample subjectivist modes, as his protagonist narrates the entire novel
in the first person singular. As with El Jarama, its view
of modern Spain riddled with ennui is materialistic, pessimistic, and pathetic; the novel may also be part of the
critical-realist spirit that began taking hold with El Jarama.
But it is assuredly Martín-Santos' Time of Silence (see
Chapter 12) that has truly revolutionized the Spanish novel
with its "dialectic realism," its portrayal of the author's
world from diverse planes. Silence is a rhetorical, intellec-

tual, psychologically complex novel with existential, ironic and pessimistic views of society envisaged on many levels. In short, the author's only published novel is compared today on a grand scale with the greatness of Joyce, Faulkner, Valle-Inclán, Quevedo and Camus and seeks to show through its "dialectical realism" the absurdities of experience that may befall one man in his lifetime. Time of Silence is an x-ray of Spanish society, stylistically conceived in a baroque, affected, highly intellectual and literary style. It is a great novel, incredibly creative and continually fascinating.

Such "peaks" of creativity are usually followed by a return to normalcy or even lower literary standards. I deliberately singled out Castillo-Puche's novel Paralelo 40 (see Chapter 13) as a compromise effort since it sought to reinvigorate the Spanish novel by its choice of themes theretofore uncommon to Spanish writers, themes mildly critical of United States political and social attitudes, but stylistically traditional, harking back to nineteenth-century Realism and the traditional Catholic values in an effort to present a balanced, realist and optimistic picture of contemporary Spanish life circa 1960. Four years later however, another literary "peak" was achieved when Juan Goytisolo's Señas de identidad (see Chapter 14) was first published in Mexico; later, in 1970, his Count Julian also astounded literary critics internationally. Both novels are part of the New Wave's "cultural revisionism" movement in which Goytisolo acts as a demythification force, replacing the old myths or images of Spanish society with new ones as seen from Goytisolo's own autobiographical perspectives. Señas de identidad has been called neo-realistic, existential, mythical and an experimental venture of incredible social proportions. Goytisolo himself feels he has achieved a complete kind of Realism that will illuminate a "new" reality based upon the fusion of personal experiences, emotions and ideas.

Juan Marsé is Goytisolo's heir apparent in dealing with the "new" reality as Goytisolo sees it, and in destroying the ideals or myths of a false society. His Ultimas tardes con Teresa (1966) (see Chapter 15) however lacks the same spirit of denunciation and clamor that enhances Goytisolo's Señas and Count Julian. Marsé sees himself as a social realist, much in the same vein as García Hortelano and Goytisolo of the "early fifties," however, he too, has added irony (following the direction of Martín-Santos) and sarcasm in an effort to draw fictional premises from the juices of every-day living.

Going against the trend, but returning to the aesthetic
values of a conscious style and cultivation of beauty in language, Ignacio Aldecoa's Parte de una historia (1967) (see
Chapter 16) is a novel of social Realism, however devoid of
reformist denunciation tendencies, but with nineteenth-century
Regionalist qualities. Not subject to the "explosions" of the
New Wave or the experiments of the younger generation, Aldecoa has always written Realist novels on smaller themes
that demonstrate a consciously cold, artistic, highly stylized
art and unique sensibility and sensitivity to the Spanish language. He is a twentieth-century Realist whose protagonists
have existential resonances.

Another landmark for the Spanish New Wave appeared
in 1967 when Juan Benet's Volverás a Región (see Chapter
17) is published and challenges Spain's reading public. Admittedly, it is a long, difficult, highly complex and intellectual novel, defying logical perception, sometimes absurd,
generally confusing and most chaotic. It is the turning point
for the New Wave or Counter Wave and represents for us
the decline of neo-realism. Volverás has its genesis in the
French nouveau roman, whose influence it manifests greatly
in its labyrinthine arrangement. It adds the philosophical
aspects of nihilism and self-destruction to the coffer of innovative themes and is indeed a breakthrough from Marsé's
previous style of writing, with its neo-baroque, illogical,
confusing, fragmentary and disillusioning prose.

Within the framework of experimentation, Miguel Delibes advances the genre in 1969 with his Parábola del náufrago (see Chapter 18) also going Counter-Wave and seizing
the new techniques of less experienced writers (like Benet),
conceiving a parody of modern man with satirical, political
and tragi-comic overtones. Parable may be considered science fiction, or a satire of the nouveau roman or simply an
imaginative, entertaining, vital novel, innovative in its use
of language, devastating in its predictions of "things to
come. "

As of the very early seventies, very few Spanish
writers have achieved the unabashed success of Goytisolo,
Martín-Santos, García Hortelano, Matute, Delibes or Cela.
The genre suffered a decline until publishing houses begin
launching a new commercial and literary offensive with their
introduction of the novísimo authors. Among the "newest, "
Alfonso Grosso is one of the most successful because, as
he indicates in Guarnición de silla (1971) (see Chapter 19),

he broke with the New Wave and consciously became part of
the novísimo group of the 1970's.   Grosso was essentially a
social realist.   But unlike the writers who are caught in a
state of experimentation or confusion (characteristic of the
early seventies' writers), he discovered his own notion of
reality but portrayed it through a baroque style.   It is as
baroque stylists of Social Realism that Grosso and other
writers like him are achieving national and international
prominence.   Grosso is also a practitioner of the interior
monologue and fragmentary narrative as is José María Carrascal, whose Groovy (1973) (see Chapter 20) won the Nadal Prize.   Where Grosso and others (such as Palominos,
Umbral, Moíx and Vásquez Montalbán) have preferred to
limit themselves thematically to the Iberian peninsula, other
writers like Carrascal and Ferrés have chosen new geographical locales, new paths to portray the "social realities"
in their novels about New York or Kansas (as the case may
be), using the "new" writing techniques currently in vogue
with the novísimo authors.

     As of 1975, the Spanish novel is in a highly experi-
mental state, its direction still somewhat undefined.   Nevertheless, over the past twenty-five years or so it has passed
through several discernible stages of development: from
tremendismo to objective realism, with occasional retrogres-
sions into traditional nineteenth-century realism and regionalist tendencies, to behaviorist or psychological realism to
pure experimentalism to subjective realism to novels of social realism, utilizing behaviorist and objectivist techniques,
to neo-objectivism to critical realism, to the dialectical
realism of Martín-Santos, to the cultural revisionism of Goytisolo with its demythification tendencies, to the Counter-
Wave tendencies of Benet--with its nouveau roman influences,
nihilist, existential philosophies, ironic tone and neo-Baroque
style--to Counter-Wave experimentalism, utilizing neo-baroque
stylistics, commercial values, themes other than Spanish
peninsular ones, and finally, to a state of cultural confusion,
most newly expressed by the novísimo authors.

     To sum up the aforementioned literary currents:
Cela, through his use of tremendismo, began to show Spanish
life as it is, graphically, crudely, with great detail, not just
with two-dimensional "realistic" portraits of it.   His post-
war novels are

          based upon the discontinuity of Spanish life and
          they are the only cultural manifestation which

recognizes sufficiently the rupture [between life
and art]. Cela led the resurgence of the post-war
Spanish novel into three new phases: first, the
denunciation of the discontinuity [of Spanish life because of the war], second, the treatment of new
social sectors of Spanish society independent of
history, politics and culture through objectivist and
behaviorist stylistics, and finally, the totally objective novel, showing exactly what is, but without
interpreting or evolving ideas about the social and
cultural development of our society. 1

Cela subscribes, in La colmena, to the Unamunoist point of
view, writing novels about the society of masses. It is the
best novel of social dislocation produced in Spain after the
Civil War. Cela opens the path for the novel of political or
social thesis.

Other 1950 authors under Cela's and William Faulkner's influence (chiefly because of their insistence on interior monologue), such as Fernández Santos and young Juan
Goytisolo, substitute "character" and "destiny" in their objectivist novels for "situation" while describing their primi-
tivistic, rural societies. Las afueras and Los bravos are
good examples of primitivist novels, elemental objectivist
works describing the base, crude reality of Spaniards of the
early 1950's. In trying to create a new vision of reality,
objectivist authors were sometimes carried away by reducing
their novels to mere studies of objects (a distinct quality of
the French nouveau roman). Most literary Spaniards, however, think of objectivism not merely in terms of the vision
of the object perceived but also from what point of view the
object is seen.

García Hortelano's Tormenta de verano represents
this objectivist trend, using brand names, Anglicisms, etc.,
in order to put us into direct contact with the decadent ambience of which he writes. Combined with objectivist frame-
works, novelists frequently include behaviorist traits. Behaviorist writers such as Sánchez Ferlosio and García Hortelano deal principally with the interior life of their characters
and their psyches. For example, El Jarama presents a picture of objective reality based upon the worlds of the protagonist interacting with the human dynamics of the group of
weekenders; Tormenta de verano tries to show, through interior monologue, Javier's moral crisis and his guilt. These
novels border on social novels, since they try to show the

injustice and inequality of social conditions, but do not have
the courage for overt criticism.

Writers like Martín-Santos, Juan Goytisolo and Miguel
Delibes have moved in the direction of presenting a "global
vision, reflecting the reality of an epoch, a society, a
people."[2] All three writers have discovered for themselves
the meaning of Spanish Realism in its total complexity and
have completely immersed themselves in their writings.
Where formerly the relationship of the Spanish writer to his
society was somewhat oblique (possibly because of government censorship), new writers like Martín-Santos, Goytisolo
and to a lesser extent, Miguel Delibes are totally involved
in their fiction, taking complete responsibility for their visions of reality, participating in the world of ideas.   Stylistically this engagé attitude leads us into subjectivism, or an
author's striving to reveal himself, to identify himself
(Matute's Primera memoria and Goytisolo's Señas de Identidad).   Subjectivism and self-analysis combined with objectivist style may provide us with various levels of reality.
For example, Martín-Santos' writing style is unlike the per-
sonalist-subjective attitudes of a Matute or a Goytisolo.   He
delves rationally into the intellectual levels of "reality,"
searching for a public truth but remaining coldly distant
from his characters and the events he creates.   His use of
a scientific style to describe true "medical" realities and
others has already been noted in Martín-Santos' attempt to
create a "dialectical realism," the reality of ideas and the
intellect.   Martín-Santos and Goytisolo are both revisionist
writers, tending to reconstruct the Spanish novel through
their cultural, intellectual and technical innovations in the
genre.

Some writers like Delibes and Grosso follow the
Flaubertian principle of writer as God and supreme creator:
"An author ought to be in his work like God is in the universe: present everywhere but visible nowhere." As we
scan the long list of novels of the fifties and sisties, we
return to Sueiro and Delibes, writers who have anticipated
the alienation themes in social novels about the masses and
have returned to the novels of scientific anticipation, such
as Corte de corteza (Sueiro) and Parábola del náufrago (Delibes), which also tend to denounce, in a somewhat oblique
fashion, the mechanized society of the 1980's.

Turning finally to the novísimo authors, Grosso, Carrascal, Umbral and the rest, we note the heavy use of a

neo-Baroque style. In Fernando Morán's excellent essay,
"Dilema y perspectivas de la novela española actual" (from
which I have been quoting in this chapter), in which he perceptively traces the trajectory of the Spanish novel from
1940 onwards, Morán concludes the novísimo authors are
utilizing the new Baroque style of writing in their pursuit of
reality simply because they have run out of steam. He envisages the Spanish novel presently (i.e., 1970) to be in a
complete state of inertia; the baroque style currently manifests the writer's craft in order to hide the lack of dynamism and the weak capability of contemporary writers to
create something new. [3] Written between 1967 and 1970,
Morán's ideas are currently borne out by the scarcity of
novels of ideas. (Morán feels that the Spanish novelist's
only hope to regenerate the genre would be the reinvigoration
of the society, the bettering of its economic and political
phases so that Spain again may become dynamic with "ideas"
--in whose novels, then, would be reflected the prosperity,
health and intellect of a proud nation.) It had been Morán's
sociological premise that the Spanish novel is in a state of
semidesarrollo (partial development) as a consequence of the
country's own political, economic and industrial backward-
ness (citing Irwin Rostow's theories) and somewhat pessimistically, this situation is irreversible (citing Costa Pinto's
words), but it does offer some real alternatives. [4] Spaniards
cannot alter the fact of late industrialization, late economic
propserity, the Civil War and its resultant interruption in
the lives and cultural cycle of the country. However, from
the tensions caused by these social and economic developments, it is possible that a true "drive for maturity" (politically and economically) will be reflected in the novel
genre in the late 1970's or early 1980's.

                    *   *   *

        By way of a short statistical analysis, if we examine
the careers of the eighteen writers dealt with in this volume,
we find that ten of them have published novels in the 1970's.
These writers, Cela, Gironella, Fernández Santos, Matute,
Sueiro, García Hortelano, Goytisolo, Marsé, Benet and Delibes, continue to be the most prolific contributors to the
genre. Two of them, Martín-Santos and Aldecoa have died,
the former after a terribly brief but brilliant career that left
us one completed novel and another fragmented one, the
latter after a moderately productive career with a few peaks
in his artistry. Four writers, Quiroga, Sánchez Ferlosio,

Goytisolo-Gay and Castillo-Puche, have either retired or--
as in the case of Quiroga--produced only one or two novels
or have reduplicated their artistic efforts so thoroughly that
they have run out of creativity.   Interestingly enough, in
1973 Quiroga had a new novel published, Presente profundo
(The Deep Present) (1973), another of her open-ended psychological novels treating the lives of two Galician families,
one rural, the other urban, both trying to avoid communication and their responsibilities to Spanish society.   It is another "introspective" novel; Quiroga arrives at no definitive
conclusion about these people or their lives, but asks the
eternal question, "What is the truth?"[5]   About the two
novísimo authors, since their careers are still taking shape,
we cannot make any decisive judgments as yet, concerning
their contributions to the genre.

But what are the quality of contributions made by our
most prolific Spanish novelists? Although Cela's most recent work, El tacata oxidado (The Rusty Starter) (1973), is
really a compendium of short stories and essays about his
trips to the United States and his Oficio de tinieblas (5 Crafts
of Darkness) (1973) is a thesis novel to be sung by a chorus
of sick people, his last truly major novel, San Camilo 1936
(1971), made a great impact on the Spanish reading public.
However somewhat retrogressively, Cela deals with the
Civil War and has carefully researched the facts to present
an historically accurate account of the principal events of
the week the war actually began (July 18, 1936).   But San
Camilo is Cela's boldest and best work since La colmena.
It recapitulates the stylistic devices already employed in La
colmena, but to finer effect.   One critic thought "Cela's
newly demonstrated mastery of Spanish prose and his idealistic concern for his country in San Camilo 1936 ... may
move him into serious contention for the Nobel Prize."[6]

José María Gironella continues to write in his popular journalistic style in the same tradition of nineteenth-
century Realism he introduced in his The Cypresses Believe
in God as in his latest novel (in two volumes), Condenados
a vivir (Condemned to Live) (1971), which won the Planeta
Prize the year it was published.   Gironella has begun another cycle of novels about the Civil War, this time about
the Vega and Ventura families of Barcelona and their problems from 1939-1967, in his attempt to create another vital
tableau (or panorama) about still another sector of Spanish
society somewhat different from that of the Alvears of Gerona in his highly praised trilogy.

Matute, Sueiro, García Hortelano, Fernández Santos
and Delibes have all written novels in the 1970's but have
received very little in the way of critical acclaim. Matute's
La torre vigía (The Watch Tower) (1971), which was described as a "social variant" of the chivalric novel, proved
unconvincing and unpopular with the Spanish public. So did
Daniel Sueiro's Corte de corteza (Brain Transplant) (1969),
which proved too intellectual and experimentally dense.
Nevertheless, Corte won the Alfaguara Prize of 1968 and although its setting was New York, it was a stylistic return to
traditional Realism with social pretensions (the alienation of
the individual from society). Its theme was daringly imaginative (a brain transplant and its social and moral consequences), but its great length and alternation of exterior descriptions with interior dialogue proved confusing to readers.

Fernández Santos has contributed three new fictional
works in the decade of the seventies. Trailing behind the
triumph of his prize-winning novel of 1969, El hombre de los
santos (winner of the Critic's Prize of 1968), which dealt
with the monotonous, gray life of a shipper of Roman fres-
coes working at a small church in the Pyrenees and written
in the picturesque style of Pío Baroja, Las catedrales (1970)
continued Fernández Santos' panorama of a similar provincial
life style also viewed in the shadows of the churches. His
most recent work, Libro de las memorias de las cosas[7]
(1971) (which won the Nadal Prize the same year), is a further continuation of religious themes, dealing essentially
with a community of Protestants in Spain and the growing
problems of their rebellious youth. Fernández Santos' newest, most remarkable work to date is Paraíso encerrado
(Sheltered Paradise) (1973), whose protagonist is Madrid's
famous Retiro Park. Through his genuinely personal style,
the lives of the people who work and play at El Retiro are
revealed to us, subjectively, intimately, psychologically.
Realist visions of character alternate with poetic-prose
images of Spain's nostalgic past (including the Civil War) as
seen through the people of the Retiro. José Domingo calls
it "a brilliant exercise ... oscillating between an almost objective realism and a subjective intimacy which places this
novel on a really extraordinary level, [demonstrating the author's] constant faith in the novel genre."[8]

Unlike Fernández Santos, García Hortelano's latest
novel in two volumes, El gran momento de Mary Tribune
(1972), his third novel (and fourth published work), was a
total literary disaster and did not add any luster to his

career or enhance the genre accordingly. Mary Tribune is
a long novel, "notable for its efforts at linguistic creation
and synthesis of conversation ... as well as its tedium and
vacuousness [in portraying] the Spanish life of the 1960's."[9]
It revisits the Barcelonan society García Hortelano represented so well in his earlier success, Tormenta de verano,
and its themes and prose style seem almost an anachronism,
even lacking the spirit of critical realism evident in the
early Juan Goytisolo novels of the 1950's, which Mary Tribune resembles markedly.

     Miguel Delibes has produced one new novel after
Parábola del náufrago (1969)--he also did a group of short
stories in 1970 under the collective title, La mortaja (The
Shroud)--but El príncipe destronado (The Dethroned Prince),
as it is titled, was published in December 1973 (Barcelona:
Ed. Destino) and had not by this writing been reviewed by
Spanish critics or reached the United States. One guess is
that it is something new in the style of novísimo authors,
José María Carrascal and Alfonso Grosso. While Carrascal
is still basking in the success of Groovy, Grosso however
has produced a new novel, Florido de mayo (1973), which
won the Alfaguara Prize that year. Grosso continued his
neo-Baroque style in depicting the decadence of a Sevillian
family of Italian origin, the Gentiles and, very much in the
same vein as Guarnición de silla (1970), the novel is a fragmented, somewhat confused work written on several levels,
with multiple unidentified narrators, again adding to the
frustration of the reader.[10]

     I have deliberately left three writers, Marsé, Benet
and Goytisolo (in ascending order of importance) for these
last paragraphs to give analyses of their latest literary efforts. Marsé's La oscura historia de la prima Montse (1971)
(The Dark Story of Cousin Montse), is written in the mode
of his first success, Ultimas tardes con Teresa, using sarcasm, in the spirit of critical realism, to expose the vices
(and virtues) of the Catalan bourgeoisie. However, stylistically speaking, Marsé's sarcasm becomes overly exaggerated
and the expressed desires for social justice become so bla-
tantly caricaturized that the novel suffers from a kind of
corrosive aggressiveness which, at times, overwhelms the
reader. Nevertheless, written very much in the spirit of
critical realism, Marsé once again shatters the myths of
Catalan aristocracy, burlesquing their false codes of humor,
satirizing their mores, ridiculing their very life style.[11]
Montse is a thoroughly cynical vivisection of a sector of

today's Catalonian society. About Marsé's most recent novel, Si te dicen que caí... (If They Tell You I Fell...) (1974), it was reported that it won the Premio de la Novela Internacional México ($10,000) for the author, although the novel and its reviews have yet to appear in the United States. 12

Within the framework of critical realism, Juan Benet's 1971 novel, Una tumba (A Tomb), adds little to his prestige. It is, once again, a history of Región (the mythical setting of his first novel, Volverás a Región) during the days of the Civil War. However, apart from Una meditación (1970) (a novel discussed briefly in Chapter 15), another novel, Un viaje de invierno (1972), which won the Premio de la crítica that year, an interesting collection of essays entitled La inspiración y el estilo (1973), a group of short stories entitled Cinco narraciones y dos fábulas (1973), and a volume of dialogue entitled Teatro (1971), Benet's newest, most controversial novel is entitled La otra casa de Mazón (1973) and follows the trend of his Teatro, conceived mostly in dialogue (five scenes, in fact) which is held together by a prologue and the tragic narrative of one of the novel's protagonists. Following Juan Goytisolo's trend of demythification of the Reconquest, the war in Morocco, the Civil War and ensuing post-war years, Benet's human characters discuss jealousy, sexuality, and vengeance as related to their own psychic realities and those of the nation. Benet's view is often skeptical, always pessimistic, and his vision of Spain as a nation constantly masking her true feelings behind the shadows of her past history is paralleled with the kind of hermetic, airless, confusing, obfuscating style in which Benet continues to write. La casa de Mazón tells of the twilight and eventual fall of the Mazón family and its narrative and dialogue are permeated with the tragedy and biting sarcasm so typical of Benet's novels. All of Benet's literary works are generally puzzling. He, like Goytisolo is a fecund creative force, but unlike Goytisolo, he is "lacking in vision and clarity of intellect to come to terms directly with his ideas. Benet may be a practitioner of the 'new novel of ideas,' but his intellectualism and hermeticism make him a prisoner of his style. "13

Perhaps the most creative and free spirit in Spanish literature today is Juan Goytisolo. His Señas de identidad is an acknowledged masterpiece, brilliant and accessible (see Chapter 12). His latest novel, Reivindicación del Conde don Julián (Revindication of Count Julian) (1970), is perhaps his most brilliant work to date, discussion of which I have deliberately saved for the conclusion of this chapter.

Written in the same spirit of critical realism which
Goytisolo established in his early novels of the 1950's,
Count Julian is a definite successor to Señas, setting out to
destroy the myths that have paralyzed the national conscience
and life of contemporary Spain.   Hence, like Señas, Count
Julian is a powerful, courageous work, an attempt to liberate
Spain from the myths which suffocate it and keep it from
achieving its real glory.   The key event of the novel is
present-day Don Julián's investigation of the original (historical) Count Julián's treachery (circa A.D. 711), when the
latter let the Moors invade a decadent, down-trodden Spain,
victim of centuries of Visigothic conquests.   The contemporary Don Julián lives in Tangiers, the setting of Goytisolo's
novel.   His locura or madness consists of destroying the
myths of a supposedly glorious Spain as compensation for
his namesake's "original" treason who, according to Goytisolo, later caused the expulsion of Jews and Arabs which
brought Spain to its knees as a nation, both culturally and
intellectually.   By arousing the bitterness of the reader,
Goytisolo attempts to destroy the myths of the Christian
knight, virginity, innocence, religion, the bullfight, mysti-
cism, stoicism, the greatness of the Generation of 1898
writers, the Royal Academy, the very language of Spain itself.   Conceived on several planes--psychological, imaginative, dream-like--the end result of the novel is the complete
fusion of history and myth and their total destruction.   It is
a novel of great fantasy and realism, always stirring and
continually fascinating the reader.   "Goytisolo fuses real and
imaginative action in an incomparable form.... This fascinating work is a display of narrative engineering.   With
Count Julian, Goytisolo has consecrated himself definitely
as the first writer of our narrative."[14]

Other critics have been equally laudatory.   Claude
Roy of Le Nouvel Observateur said:

> Goytisolo's Count Julian is to Spain what Joyce's
> Leopold Bloom is to Ireland, and what Malcolm
> Lowry's Consul in Under the Volcano is to Mexico.
> I am fully aware of the dangerous implications of
> comparing this work to such masterpieces, but
> Count Julian strikes me as fully worthy of such
> comparison.   It is a strong book, full of fire,
> anger and humor, of subtle intentions fully realized.
> Each new Goytisolo work is more interesting than
> the last.   Count Julian, his most recent, is nothing
> less than superb.[15]

Screenwriter Jorge Semprun stated, "with Count Julian, Goytisolo has succeeded in giving us a meticulous and clear-
minded account of a descent into hell.... A brilliant book,
full of salutary laughter," in a recent review in L'Express.
Vargas Llosa, the Latin American novelist, in his review
in Le Monde, said Count Julian is "the most moving of Goytisolo's works, but also the one most full of despair....
This book is a crime of passion ... an attempt at purifica-
tion through fire. An epic work, to be read and re-read."
The dean of Spanish critics, José María Castellet said, "it
is my firm belief that many of the most brilliant and savage
pages of this masterpiece should be made obligatory reading
in the classrooms [of Spain]." Mexican philosopher and poet,
Octavio Paz said, "in the long history of Spanish heterodoxy,
Count Julian is the moment in which rational criticism becomes the pawn of mockery, and mockery turns into poetic
invention."

        Although there has been much controversy over this
novel here and abroad, the most cogent, fair, brilliant and
accurate review I read of the novel comes from the pen of
Mexico's prolific (and prophetic) critic and novelist, Carlos
Fuentes. Fuentes declares,

> Count Julian is a shout from the heart and the
> belly of a modern Spaniard against the triumph of
> all that killed the promise of freedom and love and
> joy in Spain. It is a fierce answer to the Spanish
> decadence that began in the instant of Spanish
> glory. ... [Goytisolo] has wreaked the vengeance
> of the expelled Jews, the vanquished Arabs, the
> silenced writers, the repressed lovers. Count
> Julian is the most terrible attack against the op-
> pressive forces of a nation that I have ever read.
> Nothing that black has written against white, or
> woman against man, or poor against rich or son
> against father, reaches quite the peak of intense
> hatred and horror that Goytisolo achieves in this
> novel. That he does it with magnificent beauty
> and perfect craftsmanship only adds to the power
> of his invective against his 'harsh homeland.' It
> is quite a feat and quite a risk for the novelist
> works with words, yet he is conscious that 'vio-
> lence is mute.' ... Goytisolo's book is the most
> beautifully cruel requiem written by a Spaniard for
> his native land. [16]

Count Julian is a brilliant novel, written in the perspective of cultural revisionism, which seeks to revindicate
its protagonist through its author-"mythoclast" who is searching for a second truth (another reality) behind the masks of
present-day hypocrisy. The novel itself is the mirror and
as Fuentes puts it, "an acid mirror, dissolving the features
of a worn-out hag. Spain is the hag."[17] Count Julian represents the force of language, an explosion of words wielded
against the base reality of contemporary Spain, to explode
the myths of the past.

In Manuel Durán's excellent review of Count Julian,
he believes much of the difficulty in reading Goytisolo is because the writer claims he has no single style, while in actuality, he coordinates and orchestrates a large variety of
stylistic devices; Durán enumerates them thus: (1) the use
of literary or historical texts similar to epigraphs or col-
lages in the style of Braque or Picasso; (2) the style of
parody and caricature or patent sarcasm; (3) objectivism in
the mode of the nouveau roman; (4) the style of objective
collage consisting of newspaper ads, announcements, anonymous inscriptions, etc.; (5) normal subjective observations;
(6) mixtures of subjective observations, descriptions, physical acts, objective views of the country; (7) Goytisolo's "delirious" style, the "critical nightmare," the "sexual grotto";
and finally (8) the complete fusion of all of these into a
concrete present, a sarcastic, critical and comical vision of
that present, a wild, delirious imagination which forms a
total novel that embraces us on a multiplicity of levels.[18]

For those who find the language and structure of
Count Julian a devastating task to read in the original Spanish, an excellent translation by Helen R. Lane published in
1974 by Viking Press is available. Most assuredly it is
Juan Goytisolo, a frequent exile yet the best representative
of Spain's intellectual promise, who has provided the most
creative energy of the New Wave's most aggressive attempts
to reinvigorate and regenerate the Spanish novel of the
1970's. "This scathing indictment of a country, and by ex-
tension, of hypocrisy and cant wherever they exist, stems
from an exile's thwarted love for the land that bore him,
the culture that formed him, and the language that gave him
tongue. [Ironically,] if it is perhaps the most anti-Spanish
novel ever penned, it nonetheless is one that brings us back
to the real Spain, that of Goya, Picasso and Buñel."[19]

Chapter 22

THE SEVENTIES: CRITICS, EXILES, NEW WRITERS,
THE "BOOM" AND PREDICTIONS

Within Spain itself, there are many other writers and
critics that are worthy of inclusion in this volume, whose
works, although major in creativity and promise, have not
had the thunderous national and international accolades of a
Matute, a Delibes or a Goytisolo. Dividing these writers
into four categories, I will discuss (1) those literary critics
who are novelists in their own right, residing in Spain and
still contributing to the genre, (2) other important resident
novelists, a discussion of whose careers and novels I will
attempt to briefly capsulize, (3) a very brief summary of
the exiled writers and their present contributions to the
Spanish novel, and (4) the newest resident writers, the
novísimo authors, their novels and the latest trends of the
seventies. Finally, I will treat cursorily the Latin American
"boom" of novels, novelists and their influence on Spain.
Also, by reappraising the current political and social situation of Spain in 1974-75, I shall make some predictions
about the new and future directions for the genre and the
nation.

Influential Novelist Critics

There are some twenty-five prominent literary critics,
the majority of whom are residing in Spain; a few of these
have made their mark as novelists as well. Only a handful
of them have written truly influential novels in the early
1970's, fictional works that have received widespread acclaim. One of the leading author-critics in Spain today is
Gonzalo Torrente Ballester (born in 1910) whose last three
novels, Don Juan (1963), Off-side (1969), and especially his
immense La saga/fuga de J. B. (The Saga-Fugue of J. B.)
(1972),

have earned him instant recognition as one of
Spain's finest novelists. In three long chapters,
corresponding to the divisions of a fugue, he tells
the story [saga] of J. B. and his search of identity. The book is destined to arouse continuing
critical interest for its vigorous realism, ... its
irony, its flowering prose..., its imaginative
recreation of experience, ... its invention of language and other techniques.... 1

    Vying for publishing honors with Torrente Ballester
is the younger and equally talented Francisco Umbral (born
in 1936), whose last three novels, Memorias de un niño de
derechos (Memoirs of a Principled Young Boy) (1972), Diario
de un snob (1972), and Retrato de un joven malvado (Portrait
of a Young Evil-Doer) (1973), have had a fair amount of success with the reading public. Memorias is part of the current international trend towards nostalgia, and this particular
novel is concerned with life after the Civil War, but deals
with it through a ''humorous treatment of the material, indicating a change in attitude toward the war and its events.''2
Diario continues Umbral's somewhat autobiographical memoirs,
using interior monologue to penetrate the narcissistic
thoughts of its protagonist and to re-create an epoch. Retrato continues Umbral's penetration into the present, portraying ironically and somewhat graphically, the life of Madrid, its world of people, cafes, pensiones, while the writer
searches for his own identity. Umbral vivisects the myths
and the realities of Spain's famous capital while evolving his
portrait of the artist as a young man. Umbral is also
known as a sensualist, a writer who had begun his novelistic
career in the terrain of eroticism but whose ideological
roots were sometimes meshed with ''existential'' philosophies.3

    Carlos Rojas (born in 1928 in Barcelona) is mainly
known in Spain for his historical novels, especially Auto de
fe (1968), which is an ambitious, historical reconstruction
of the epoch of Charles II but conceived in a Baroque, plastic style, and also his latest novel, Azaña (1973), for which
he won the $35,000 Planeta Prize of 1973. ''Azaña is a
story related by the president of the fictional Second Spanish
Republic. The narration includes dialogues with many fictitious and historical personalities and reflects the wide range
of the author's interests in literature and art.''4

    Francisco García Pavón (born in 1919 in Tomelloso),
like Carlos Rojas, is a practitioner of the historical novel

and deservedly won the Nadal Prize in 1969 for his Las
hermanas coloradas (1970), which is more of a humorous
work than a historical one, written in the vein of imaginative detective fiction. [5] Like García Pavón, Manuel García
Viñó (born in Seville in 1928) also deals with mystery fiction. Primarily known as a critic, he recently published
his seventh novel, La granja del solitario (The Recluse's
Farm) (1969), which indicates his leaning towards the newer
literary experiments going on in Spain--the recreation of
magic-realism but in the style of Franz Kafka. The plot of
Granja concerns a young woman who discovers herself in
mysterious circumstances which almost force her to lose
hope in her life, in herself.

        Of the few leading literary critics in exile, Segundo
Serrano Poncela is one of a minority who has continued his
production of novels. His El hombre de la cruz verde (Man
with the Green Cross) (1969) is written in the tradition of
Carlos Rojas and Torrente Ballester, a historical novel
about the Inquisition at the time of Philip II, "conceived in
a dense ambience of eroticism and terror, pulsating with
historical figures.... This first historical work of our author ... shows his intellectual probity, critical spirit, domination of expressive nuances which [help us to] cultivate our
genre. "[6]

        Only very brief mention should be made here of sev-
eral Latin American critics, among them the novelists Mario
Vargas Llosa, Gregorio García Márquez and especially Carlos Fuentes. The latter, however, has had the most to do
with regenerating Mexico's novel (his La región más transparente (1959) is his most famous fictional work) and influ-
encing Spanish peninsular criticism (his critical work La
nueva novela hispanoamericana[7] is best known because of the
essay in which he discusses Juan Goytisolo as the single
Spanish novelist most responsible for international recognition of Spanish letters).

Novelists with One or Two Major Works

        Along with the literary critics cited in previous para-
graphs, there are many, many novelists who deserve mention
in this chapter simply because they have produced one or
two outstanding works of merit in a sometimes erratic career, novels that have had considerable influence on the
genre, but never achieved the heights or accolades of the

eighteen authors to whom we devoted a single chapter each
in this volume. Except for a few novelists who have produced only one novel or have either retired or not written
any fiction in the 1970's, I shall briefly capsulize the writer's life and his (or her) most widely known novel in Spain
and abroad, writers who have differentiated themselves from
the novísimo authors of the seventies, with no attempt at
chronological, alphabetical or any other kind of order what-
soever.

Living in Spain today, there are several novelists in
this category who have produced only one or two works of
fictional and technical brilliance. José Caballero Bonald
(born in Jérez de la Frontera in 1926) is one of these writers whose only novel, Dos días de septiembre (Two Days in
September) (1962), won the Biblioteca Breve Prize of 1961.
Dos días tells the story of two days in the life of a worker
in the vineyards of southern Spain (Andalusia) and is written
in a style reminiscent of the nineteenth-century Realism-
Regionalism of Vicente Blasco Ibánez' La bodega (The Wine-
cellar). Boasting similar social themes, it up-dates and
modernizes the eternal clash between workers and land own-
ers because of Caballero Bonald's acute sensitivity and brilliant techniques of dialogue and retrospective recall. Although Caballero Bonald has not continued to write novels,
he does use his talent as a screenwriter and submits occasional articles for magazines, usually on the theme of
Spanish folklore.

Another award winner, Luis Romero, a Catalan (born
in Barcelona in 1916)--according to Ana María Matute) helped
regenerate the Spanish novel of the early 1950's. His work,
La noria (The Water-Wheel) (1952), won the Nadal Prize in
1951 chiefly because of Romero's technical ability to link
some thirty distinct and simultaneous episodes about life in
Barcelona through the revolutionary use of an omniscient author, interior monologue and dialogue in a convincing, ami-
cable and colloquial style. [8] Unfortunately, his later novels
have never attained the same quality or technical skill as
La noria. But worthy of mention are El cacique (The Chief-
tain) (1963), a social novel outlining contemporary Spanish
problems for which he won the Planeta Prize of 1964 and
Tres días de julio (Three Days in July) (1968), a historical
novel returning to the throes of the Civil War, documenting
the first three days and the eruption of the war with a great
amount of historically accurate details and documentation in
the mode of José María Gironella. (Note by comparison the
title of Cela's San Camilo 36 (discussed in Chapter 21).

Receiving tumultuous praise in the early fifties was another novel which garnered the Nadal Prize in 1950, José Suárez Carreño's Las últimas horas (Last Hours) (1950). Suárez Carreño is a native of Guadalajara, Mexico, and was born in 1914. After becoming a Spanish resident, he received a law degree from the University of Valladolid and has continued to live in Madrid. He is a practitioner of the "existential" novel and his Ultimas horas deals with the social conditions of post-war Madrid, its problems and people but written very much in the style of Albert Camus. The worlds of the Spanish bourgeoisie and lower classes (el hampa madrileño) are portrayed realistically, almost "with tones of a picaresque etching"[9] of the Renaissance. Unfortunately, Proceso personal (1955), his second and latest novel to date, did not carry forth the promise of Ultimas horas because it dealt with a minor, but interesting theme on the level of detective fiction and had a tendency to moralize about corrupt Madrid society, although it did display some of the competent techniques of good fiction writing previously displayed in his first novel.

Along with the male writers, there are three female novelists worth noting who have produced some interesting fiction over the past twenty-five years. Carmen María Gaite has earned her reputation primarily on three novels: El balneario (1954), Entre visillos (1957), and Ritmo lento (1963). A native of Salamanca (born in 1917) and the wife of Sánchez Ferlosio, she won the Nadal Prize in 1957 for Entre visillos (Between the Blinds) doubtless because of its style, its interplay between evasion and reality, its lucidity and technical brilliance. "Entre visillos is a prodigious work of nuances and critical sensibility, an indictment of Spanish provincial life because of its sordidness, narrowness and limited horizons."[10]

Dolores Medio, a native of Oviedo, born in the early 1920's is a very popular but lesser known writer of distinct talent. Her most influential work is a social novel, Nosotros los Rivero (1953), dealing with the lower middle class of Madrid and their problems. Although that work suffers several defects, notably an insufferable air of idealism and excessive romanticism, Medio's novels generally maintain her popularity, as her latest fictional effort, Bibiana (1967) certainly proves. Medio is well-acquainted with Madrid and especially its lower-middle class and presents an evocative tableau in terms of dialogue and colloquialisms of contemporary Madrileños participating actively in their society.

Finally, there is Concha Alos, who besides Matute
and Quiroga is the only other female to attain great prominence in the late sixties--for her novels Los enanos (The
Dwarfs) (1962), voted the Planeta Prize that year, Los cien
pájaros (1963), Las hogueras (1964), for which she won another Planeta prize, El caballo rojo (1966), La Madama
(1969) and Rey de gatos (1972). Her best of these is undoubtedly her first Los enanos because as a social or sociological novel, it accurately depicts in terse, realistic prose
the problems of a group of people living in a small hotel,
enslaved by their own pessimism without any glimmer of hope
for the future.

Several leading male novelists in the decades of the
fifties and sixties worth citing as influential writers are the
following: (1) Manuel Arce, born in 1928, a native of Santander known primarily for his social novels, Testamento en
la montaña (1955), Oficio de muchacho (1963), Anzuelos para
la lubina (1962), and, most recently, El precio de la derrota
(1970). Precio, his latest novel, is considered his best in
one's critic's view because "it describes the contradictions
of a generation caught in conflict between the indirect effects
of the Civil War and economic prosperity. A well planned
and executed novel, it is a positive step on the ascending
road of a good novelist."[11]

(2) From Barcelona, Ignacio Agustí (born in 1913) is
noted for his continuing use of traditional Realism in his projected and incomplete pentalogy, "La ceniza fué antes árbol"
("The Ash Was a Tree Before"), beginning with Mariona Rebull (1944), followed by El viudo Ruis (1945), Desiderio
(1957) and 19 de julio (1965). A social critic, Agustí denounces the corruption of the middle class, its anti-intellec-
tual attitudes, its vacuousness and demoralized value system.
Although many critics believe his first of the series, Mariona
Rebull, is his best work, Agustí's 19 de julio was awarded
the Premio Nacional de la Crítica, perhaps with the expectation of the completion of his pentalogy.

(3) From Galicia, Alvaro Cunqueiro (born in Lugo in
1911) has cornered the market on what is known as "magical
realism" or portraying reality from the creation of a unique
and personal world. "A shadowy world of sirens, dolphins,
ships crossing from one side of the stream to the other ...
a world of dreams, baroque language, fables, fantasy, wild
imagination, myths ... [a world that] exalts the aesthetic
whose sole function is beauty, enjoyment, so that the reader

may enjoy or evade reality with the 'magic' of Cunqueiro's
poetic material. "12 Most of Cunqueiro's novels represent
an escape from objectivism, anxiety, the absurd, or experimentalism, and treat of antiquity, the Middle Ages, pagan
legends, or Greek and Roman mythology. His entire writing
career has been a reaction to the Realism of the New Wave,
as some of the following and well-known titles will suggest:
El caballero, la muerte y el diablo (1956), Merlín y familia
(1957), Las mocedades de Ulises (1960), and finally the 1968
Nadal Prize winner, Un hombre que se parecía a Orestes
(1969), among many other titles.

(4) From Baides, Angel María de Lera (born in 1912)
has achieved renown for his best novel, Los clarines del
miedo (1958), about bullfighting, and more recently, Las
últimas banderas (1967), winner of the Planeta Prize, dealing with the Civil War. These are the two perennial thematic
concerns of the Spanish novel. Lera excels in his gift for
presenting natural dialogue but his works suffer because of
excessive melodrama and intense egoism that detract from
his achieving the success, let us say, of a Gironella, although his novels, because of their honesty and documentation, are not without interest.

(5) From Madrid, Jesús López Pacheco (born in 1930)
wrote only one novel, entitled Central Eléctrico (1958). A
social novel, it is well known in Spain because it was the
first to present the proletariat as its protagonist. The novel
primarily deals with the construction of an electric station
in Aldeaseca (note the pun, "dry town") and in the tradition
of Naturalism (e.g., Zola's Germinal), the novel documents
the flooding of the valley, and numerous and unnecessary
deaths of townspeople and workers.

(6) Also from Madrid, Armando López Salinas continues his concepts of social realism very much in the same
style as López Pacheco. His best novel, La mina (1960),
was conceived in the best tradition of Zola or Richard
Llewellyn's How Green Was My Valley. It is a thesis novel,
demonstrating the conflicting interests of capitalists and
workers, miserable working conditions and the need for
unionism; it is written in documentary fashion. His second
and latest novel, Año tras año (1962), which won the Ruedo
Ibérico Prize that year, continues López Salinas' preoccupation with the proletariat, their penury and suffering after
three years of civil war.

(7) From the Basque provinces (Vizcaya), Juan Antonio de Zunzunegui (born 1901), a lawyer and resident of Madrid and member of the Royal Academy, continues his remarkable writing career (begun in the early twenties), publishing a wide variety of novels. Among his best in the style of traditional nineteenth-century Realism are El supremo bien (1951), La vida como es (1954), Una mujer sobre la tierra (1959), and Un hombre entre dos mujeres (1966). All of his best novels deal with Madrid's middle-class citizenry and are considered thesis novels with a heavy dosage of moralizing. Many critics feel Zunzunegui (rather than Gironella) to be the most likely candidate as the "Pérez Galdós" of our times because of his ability to vivisect the social nexus of Madrid and re-create on many levels, with accuracy, the ambience of contemporary Madrid.

(8) From Palencia, Tomás Salvador (born in 1921) has achieved a great deal of popularity in Spain during the 1950's especially since he revived the adventure novel and the novel of manners and customs, and began working at writing psychological and Realist novels with social themes. His most famous ones are Cuerda de presos (1952), Cabo de varas (1958), a Realist novel about the Spanish penal colony in Ceuta during the nineteenth-century, and El atentado (1960), which won the Planeta Prize. Salvador also writes good science-fiction, but not at the high quality of the aforementioned novels.

(9) From Bilbao, Ramiro Pinilla (born in 1922) has written only three novels, the most famous of which, Las ciegas hormigas (Blind Ants) (1961), winner of the Nadal Prize of 1960, revives the Costumbrista novel of the nineteenth century, as it deals with the sufferings of a Basque family trying to collect coal from a sunken barge in the Cantabrian Sea. Ramón Buckley cites Pinilla's myths of "liberty and primitivism" and his use of linguistic subjectivism that gives added stylistic luster to this important novel. [13] His second novel, written in the style of detective fiction, En el tiempo de los tallos tiernos (1969), sings the praises of the Basques, their lives, passions and crimes, and is a compromise between costumbrista fiction of the nineteenth century and the detective fiction of our era.

(10) From Montalbos (Albacete), we have Rodrigo Rubio (born in 1931), who writes novels about the human condition--sentimental works, with lyrical prose. His best known novel is Equipaje de amor para la tierra (1966),

which won the Planeta Prize and deals with the problems of
Spanish immigrant workers in Germany. Rubio's later novels
also describe the lower classes and find their popular appeal
among middle class readers.

One last writer, José María Sanjuán, born in 1937
in Barcelona and died in Pamplona in 1968, is worth brief
mention among the preceding list of prize winners simply
because of the four novels he produced. His Requiem por
todos nosotros (1968), which won the Nadal Prize, is probably the best of its type, written in the vein of critical
Realism, examining the dolce vita of contemporary Spanish
society. His posthumously published works have confirmed
his talent as an astute observer and moralist, but unfortunately his untimely death cut short his promise. He wrote
of both Spaniards and the tourists with their peculiar moeurs
who invade the Iberian peninsula every year.

The Newer Writers

The next group of writers listed below are the ones
who have made their major impact on Spanish letters during
the late 1960's and the decade of the seventies. Some are
novísimo authors (the newest ones), and any penetrating analysis into their lives and careers will be, at this point,
deliberately sketchy.

Antonio Ferrés is probably the best known of this
group of New Wave writers. Born in Madrid in 1925,
Ferrés, now a professor of Spanish literature at a mid-
west university in the United States, is primarily known for
his naturalistic work, La piqueta (1959), written in the gutsy
Zolaesque style of traditional Realism. However his writings span at least two distinct phases of the New Wave
movement. Los vencidos (1962) returns somewhat anachron-
istically to the theme of civil war, as does Con las manos
vacías (1964), another thesis novel seeking to redress the
injustices of the Spanish judicial system. But between 1968
and 1969, En el segundo hemísfero, a novel dealing with
racism in the United States (Kansas, in fact), opened the
way for other Spanish novelists to treat themes other than
those of the Iberian peninsula. His latest novel, Ocho,
siete, seis (1972) continues this new trend of extending the
thematic considerations of the Spanish novel beyond the
peninsula, once again dealing with North American themes.
Ferrés himself has formally changed residence and now
lives in Mexico where he continues to teach and write novels.

A contemporary of Ferrés, Angel Palominos, published his first novel Zamora y Gomorra in 1968, criticizing and satirizing the provincial mode of life in the Spanish city of Zamora. Written in the vein of humor and portraying colorful customs, this novel is in direct opposition to his latest work, Torremolinos Gran Hotel (1971), which satirizes the tourist trade along the Costa del Sol and makes for a biting work in the category of social realism.

Aquilino Duque, a native of Sevilla (born 1931), also lives outside of Spain and continues writing fiction in reaction to the trenchant Realism and recent experimentation of the New Wave. A writer of historical novels, Operación marabú (1966) and Los consuladores de más allá (1966) for example, Duque's latest works, La rueda de fuego (1971) and La linterna mágica (1971), reveal his fertile imagination, his gift for fantasy and innovative technique in the style of supra-realism that makes him the heir apparent of Alvaro Cunqueiro and one of the most promising, interesting and gifted novelists of the moment.

Another young novelist, Ramón Hernández (born 1935) is well known in Spain and elsewhere because of his first novel, Palabras en el muro (Words on the Wall) (1969), in which he describes prison life in realistic detail, using the latest techniques of good fiction--excellent character development, interpolation of past events within present time, narration in first and third persons, penetration into the psychological motives behind the actions of the protagonists, and dislocation of events, thus breaking up the flow of the narrative with jarring effects upon the reader. His latest two novels, Ira de la noche (1970), which won the Aguila Prize that year, and El tirano inmóvil (1970), confirm his reputation as a novelist and as a continuer of social realism.

Of the same generation as Duque and Hernández, Jorge C. Trulock (born in Madrid in 1932) is best recognized in Spain and abroad for his short novel, Inventario base (1970), a realistic work written in the best tradition of the nouveau roman, with, however, "humanity and tenderness."[14] Dealing with the lives of three humble families, nothing much happens in this novel. There is neither an ending nor a beginning. Events and people repeat themselves, leading us into a sterile cul-de-sac.[15]

Among the writers born in the late thirties or in the forties, Jesús Torbado (born in 1943) from León is probably

316 Spain's New Wave Novelists

the best known disciple of Goytisolo after Juan Marsé in the realm of critical realism. His first novel, Las corrupciones (Corruption) (1965), which was awarded the Alfaguara Prize, deals with the preoccupations of Spanish youth circa 1960, their "ye-ye," hitch-hiking life-styles, their cynical attitudes about love, God and themselves. Torbado continues his pessimistic view of Spain's youth in La construcción del odio (1968) and describes the hippy life style on the island of Formentera in his latest work, Moira estuvo aquí (1971), worthy of consideration as a forerunner to Carrascal's 1973 award-winning novel Groovy.

A unique stylist, Luis Berenguer, won the Alfaguara Prize in 1972 for his latest novel, Leña Verde (Virgin Wood) (1972). It is a strange work, a reaction to New Wave Realism in which Berenguer turns the clock back to the time of the Middle Ages, recapturing the idylls of knights and sheperdesses but with a uniquely modern view of the revelation of modern personality. It is all done in the manner of his English counterpart, John Knowles, who revitalized England's Victorian era in his classic, The French Lieutenant's Woman. Written in a beautifully exquisite prose style, Leña Verde is a welcome change of pace for the writer (and his reading public) from his earlier novels. His first novel, El mundo de Juan Lobón (1966), dealing with hunters and landlords and their respective rights, and his second novel, Marea escorada (which won the National Prize for Literature in 1969 because of Berenguer's excellent treatment of life and problems of mariners), were both written in the earlier style of social realism.

Among the younger novelists, Antonio Beneyto's first novel, Los chicos salvajes (1971), written in a surrealist style has demonstrated he "possesses excellent qualities as a novelist [and] it is possible to relate him with Kafka, Borges and Cortazar. "16

The Best of the Novísimo

In the group of novelists that esteemed literary critic José María Castellet dubbed novísimo authors, the best known are (1) Ana María Moíx (born in Barcelona in 1947), whose novels Julia (1969) and Walter ¿ Por qué te fuiste? (1973), demonstrate great poetic gifts and a sincere understanding of humanity; (2) Manuel Vázquez Montalbán (born in 1939), whose novels, Recordano a Dardé (1969) and Yo maté a Kennedy (I Killed Kennedy) (1973), are regarded as "political" fiction,

written very much in the same style as Richard Condon's Man-
churian Candidate or Carlos Rojas' Azaña; apart from recon-
structing President Kennedy's assassination, Vásquez Montalbán also displays a good sense of satire of American customs
and humor common to the traditions of the U. S. political arena;
(3) José María Vaz de Soto, whose Realist and poetic novel,
Diálogo del anochecer (1973), a continuation of his first fictional autobiographical work, El infierno y la brisa (1970),
shows his promise as a young author of quality and talent,
a gifted writer with a unique prose style; (4) Federico López-
Pereira, an Andalusian whose first novel, La verdadera
patria (The Real Country) (1964), won the Elisenda de Mont-
cada Prize and whose latest work, La última llave (1973),
which treats the novel as "a happening, a nostalgic interlude
and an investigation,"[17] shows remarkable gifts as a novelist
because of his careful prose style and his use of modern
writing techniques; (5) Ramón Carnicer, another "new"
novelist, whose works, New York, nivel de vida, nivel de
muerte (1970) and También murió Manceñido (1973), confirm
his notable sense of humor and wisdom as an observer of
the social scene.   (6) Finally, we have the Jesuit Germán
Sánchez Espeso (born in 1940) whose latest novel, Laberinto
levítico (1973) is the third of a series of a projected pentalogy entitled "Pentateuco" and whose earlier style in Experi-
mento en Genesis (1967) and Síntomas de éxodo (1969) recalls remarkably the best traditions of the nouveau roman
carried forth into the decade of the seventies.

The Interesting and the Promising

At this moment, the new novel of the seventies is
suffering from an excess of experimentation, profusion of
themes and confusion in styles.   It is possible this critic
may have overlooked many new writers in this category or
other categories of New Wave writers.   For example, I neglected to cite among the critics Ricardo Domench, José
María Pemán, and Francisco García Pavón; among the fifties
novelists, Ramón Nieto, Carmen Laforet, Manuel Pombo An-
gulo, Mercedes Formica, and Concha Castroviejo; among the
sixties novelists, Victor Alperi, José Luis Martín Vigil,
Manuel Vincent, Ramón Solís, Juan Mollá, Luis Manegat,
Luis de Castresana, and Rodríguez Rubio; and in the late
sixties and early seventies, novelists such as Gabriel G.
Badell, Juan Jesús Rodero, Gonzáles Torrente Malvido,
Manuel Barrios, Mercedes Salisachs (whose Adagio confi-
dencial won the Planeta Prize of 1973), Carmen Kurz and
Antonio Molina among others.   Keeping up with the "stream"

of fiction being written in contemporary Spain is an impossible task. Other novísimo writers (authors of first novels) such as Javier del Amo and his La espiral (1973), Javier Fernández de Castro and his Alimento del salto (1973), Carlos Trías and his El juego del lagarto (1973), and Vicente Molina-Foix, whose Premio Barral-winning novel, Busto (1973) deals with survival in an atmosphere of horror, are all interesting first works of promising young writers which reflect the current trends of experimentalism and confusion, and deal with themes like eroticism and the social system but do little else in establishing a discernible trend in today's world of Spanish fiction. Having also neglected certain short story writers, such as Julián Ríos, Laura Olmo and others who have also published longer works (novellas and novels), at this time, I would like to re-examine one category, the Spanish exiles and their influence on Spain's peninsular literature of the 1970's.

The Exiles

Today, the most prolific writer of the Spanish exiles is Ramón Sender (born in Huesca in 1902), who began writing fiction with his novel, Imán (1930), and has published works of considerable merit over the last forty years, especially the famous Crónica del Alba (Before Noon) (1942). Sender's influence on the Spanish narrative is considerable and since the relaxing of censorship in the late sixties, his last four novels have been published there. Among them, En la vida de Ignacio Morel (1969) won the Planeta Prize that year and deals with the life of a young man in contemporary Paris and his search for identity. As is often the case in Sender's novels, Ignacio Morel is a blend of fact and fiction in an effort to try to reproduce reality as it is. Sender is a practitioner and continuer of traditional Realism.

Two other Realist writers, Max Aub (who died in Mexico in 1972) and Arturo Barea (who died in London in 1957), emulated the same kind of historical Realism found in Sender's works. Their steady stream of fiction (Aub is noted mainly for his series of six novels about the Civil War, among them, Campo abierto (1943) and Campo de los almendros (1965); Barea is noted for his famous trilogy, La forja de un rebelde (1941-1944)) gave the Spanish novel a great deal of stability, purpose and international fame because of their tenacious portrayal of history and their personal traumas concerning that single event--the Civil War.

Besides Sender, Francisco Ayala, Manuel Andújar
and Roberto Ruiz are the only exiles who have published
works of fiction in the 1970's in Spain and whose influence
is felt keenly among the new novelists.   Ayala's latest novel,
El jardín de las delicias (The Garden of Delights) (1971),
won the Premio de la crítica that year and has since been
filmed by Spanish director Carlos Saura.   It is an excellent
novel depicting, through modern techniques of interior monologue, flashback and flash-forward, the disintegration of a
man's mind, his tenuous hold upon reality and the conniving
efforts of his family to wrest his fortune away from him.
Unfortunately, the protagonist and his "healthy" family all
become cripples (surrealistically roaming about the garden
in wheelchairs) at the novel's conclusion.   A breathtaking
work of fiction, full of theatrical and cinematic techniques,
even utilizing the principles of participation in Julian Beck's
and Judith Malina's Living Theater, Ayala's novel displays
a dazzling amount of artistry that peninsular authors have
found unrivalled.   Equally thrilling is Manuel Andújar's Los
lugares vacíos (Empty Places) (1971), a novel similar to
Luis Goytisolo-Gay's Las afueras, dealing in a symbolic
fashion with the illusions, disillusions and failures of its
protagonists. 18

Finally, among the exiles living in the United States,
Roberto Ruiz (born in 1925), a Spanish professor at Wheaton
and Middlebury colleges, continues to impress his readers
through his excellent sensibility, revealing (somewhat autobiographically) through fiction his own experiences in a concentration camp in France in El último oasis (1964), his anti-
militaristic attitudes in Plaza sin muros (1966), and his
pessimism about the futility of war (especially civil war) in
Los jueces implacables (The Implacable Judges) (1970).

The "Boom" in Latin America

If the exiled Spanish authors have had some influence
upon the "peninsular" narrative, undoubtedly, so has the
latest "boom" of novelists in Latin America.   The word
"boom" is synonymous with the eruption of the New Wave
of Latin American writers that occurred in the mid-1960's
and continues into this decade.   Many novelists have contributed to the "boom" (a descriptive word used by publishers
to market their new products).   "Boom" is the Latin American novelist's answer to Realism which manifests itself in
"the capacity to encounter and to raise up [through the

Spanish language] the myths and prophesies of an epoch ...
paving the way for a new concept of reality. [To these writers, the novel is essentially composed of] myth, language
and structure."19 Because of the limitations of space, I
cannot delve more deeply into the Latin American "boom"
itself, but will say its chief practitioners are essentially
Borges, García Márquez, Carpentier, Donoso, Cortázar,
Puig, Lezama Lima, Cabrera Infante, Onetti, Vargas Llosa,
Rulfo and Fuentes. Coming from different Latin American
nations, all have reinvigorated the Spanish language and
novel genre through their highly individual and unique fictional works. (We noted before that Carlos Fuentes included
Spain's Juan Goytisolo and his Señas de identidad in his evaluation of the new Spanish American novel, believing Goytisolo "understands the most urgent task of the Spanish writer
--to destroy the old language (and myths) and create a new
one, making the novel the proper vehicle to create this kind
of reality."20)

Novels like One Hundred Years of Solitude (G. Mar-
quez), Paradiso (L. Lima), Three Saddened Tigers (C. Infante), The Obscene Bird of Night (Donoso), Hopscotch (Cortázar), The Green House (V. Llosa), The Lost Steps (Carpentier) and The Betrayal of Rita Hayworth (Puig) have had infinite repercussions on the Spanish novel. Rafael Bosch, in
one of his extremely pessimistic predictions about the Spanish novel foresees an "iberoamericanization of the Spanish
peninsula ... unless Spanish writers begin to develop an
elite-ist and equally sensational kind of literature. ... The
Spaniard ought to break through the cultural barriers imposed
by centuries of ignorance...."21 Another critic, Guillermo
Díaz-Plaja, pleads that Spanish writers, through the example
of Latin American novelists, begin to consider seriously new
horizons of literary creation and not to be content with "the
indolent dalliances of our local purisms."22

Critical opinions vary about the effect of the "boom"
on Spanish literature. When in 1969-70 Fernando de Tola de
Habich and Patricia Grieve interviewed eleven of the Spanish
novelists discussed in this volume, along with two poets and
one publisher, recorded these interviews in their book, Los
españoles y el boom, they encountered divergent opinions as
to how they see and think about the Latin American New
Wave writers. (Some of these opinions have already been
stated in individual chapters dealing with Benet, Cela, Delibes, F. Santos, G. Hortelano, Goytisolo-Gay, Grosso,
Marsé and Sueiro.) Perhaps, Latin American influences can

best be summed up in terms of the "magical realism" (previously attributed to the works of Cunqueiro, Sender and Rojas) that has become the vogue of Central and South American writers. The success of the "boom" has served as an inducement to peninsular writers to find their own voices, create their own myths, renovate their own genre, innovate with the Spanish language. However very few except Juan Goytisolo have sought to break with the heavy burden of Spanish reality and enter the realm of "magical realism" or fantasy. Except for Goytisolo, then, the influence of the Latin American "boom" has been a great disappointment and minimal in its influence on the novel genre in Spain.

The Current Political and Social Situation in Spain

Perhaps an updated view of Spain's political, social and economic situation may help in appreciating the reasons for the relatively minor growth within the artistic genre of the Spanish novel, which in itself is (or should be) a genuine reflection of the mores of Spanish society. 1974 has been a target year, full of political, social and economic stresses for the Spanish nation. If we analyze a brief sampling of the events that took place in that year and during the early seventies, we note a wide variety of extremes and several areas of expansion in Spanish politics throughout the entire Iberian peninsula.

The following headlines of articles by leading reporters appeared between 1970 and 1974, revealing the progressively mounting tensions and preoccupations of a nation in perpetual conflict: (1) "Spanish Joke: Franco declines the gift of a baby tortoise because it will live to be only 100 and he can't bear to see a pet die," (2) "Spain Appears to Resist Liberalization in Full Role in Europe," (3) "University Administration Quits in Spain After Protest," (4) "The Unsolved Problems of Succession," (5) "A Spanish Anarchist, 26, Is Executed by Garroting," (6) "Retrogression in Spain," (7) "Ten Basque Workers Acquitted," (8) "(Portuguese) Coup's Echo in Spain," (9) "Spain Eyes Portugal," (10) "A Miracle Coming to an End," and finally (11) "Spain on the Brink. "23

These headlines sum up the stresses and strains of a regime controlled by an eighty-five year old potentate whose harsh, totalitarian attitudes are occasionally relieved by their suspension and tendency to go to opposite extremes--from

harsh oppression to almost complete relaxation of laws and
full liberalization. As the headlines suggest, Spain's major
preoccupations are still to enter the Common Market, pick
a successor (probably Franco's designate, Prince Juan Carlos de Borbón) if Franco should die, suppress student rebellion and the separatist tendencies of Basques and Catalonians,
and allay political tensions on the Iberian peninsula caused
by Portugal's recent independence from a longtime repressive
dictatorship. The Portuguese change has been reflected in
the Spanish nation's swing back to liberal tendencies in the
arts and an extraordinary relaxation of governmental censorship.

       In late 1974 Madrileños were lining up at their local
theatres to see a new Carlos Saura film, La prima
angélica (1974), another motion picture about the celebrated
Civil War but also dealing with a young boy's sexual awakening and containing many satirical scenes about the Falange
(Spain's one and only political party) of the 1930's. A film
such as this was forbidden in Spain until this sudden relaxation of press and cultural censorship. Also the Ministry of
Information has repeated frequently, through press releases,
that only one publication was censored this year (1974) versus
the eighty or so that were prohibited from publication last
year. Apparently, the Spanish press, for the first time in
thirty years, gave full coverage to the recent Portuguese
coup, which indicates a liberal Spanish press, but not necessarily a free one. Most Spaniards also realize that one-man
governments, like those of Salazar and de Gaulle (or Franco)
cannot survive and most politicians in Spain want change for

              everybody knows we are at the end of an era.
              ... Both government leaders and the conservative
              establishment prefer some 'liberalization' while
              [Franco] is still at the head of state. Otherwise,
              they fear, his death and the sudden absence of au-
              thority would create greater upheaval and more
              democracy than they care to contemplate. That is
              why censorship has been relaxed, and why ... the
              change in Spain is mostly in the name. 24

       Whatever today's outward political appearances--i.e.,
that of completely relaxed censorship--may be, "Spanish
writers are faced with the same problems in 1974 as in
1954 and 1964. That is to say, unless there is some enormous and unexpected transformation of the present political
situation, [we] writers will find [ourselves] condemned to

the same sad and interminable masochistic trap [of writing
in an occupied language]. " Juan Goytisolo, perhaps the
greatest living Spanish writer today and in 1974-75 a visiting
professor of Spanish literature at City University of New
York, recounted, in the 1974 guest article for the New York
Times, quoted from, above, the ups and downs of the "see-
saw" of Spanish censorship, reviewing the Ministry of Information's practices from the 1940's to the present. Goytisolo
is searching for an end to posibilismo--"the act of writers
adapting themselves to censorship ... with all the usual consequences: self-censorship, elliptical prose, allegory,
vague illusions and so forth. " Spanish readers should not
be subject to "decoding allusions" or "reading between the
lines" or be prisoners of this "oblique style" of writing
which results in "moral atrophy. " Goytisolo feels the se-
verest side of government censorship produces in its writers
"a perpetual feeling of guilt ... which is difficult to overcome and ... our Spanish language ... is constantly being
mutilated by the Fascistic mind which controls the government and, by exercising a covert violence in the virtual significance of words and meanings, mutilates the possibilities
of expression. "[25]

Goytisolo is one writer whose literary works in Spain
over the past ten years have been outlawed, who refuses to
be intellectually castrated, whether residing in or outside of
Spain. He feels, however, the best writing, the most innovative techniques used to revive the novel genre, are presently taking place outside of Spain and that besides demanding the abolition of censorship (which may be a long, long
time in coming) on the peninsula, the best route for Spanish
intellectuals interested in preserving their creativity and integrity is to publish outside of Spain, "creating works as
free as possible and as powerful as possible ... that by
their very existence, make censorship die under the blows
of the most efficient army: ridicule. "[26]

We can judge at this point the truth behind Juan Goytisolo's statements about the "repressed" writers living in
the Spanish nation if we examine, for example, the Nadal
Prize winner of 1973, El rito (The Rite) (1974), by José
García Blásquez. García Blásquez is virtually unknown in
the United States. He received a doctorate in 1940 at the
University of Madrid, has worked and taught in England,
published a study about Oscar Wilde as well as two or three
novels in Spain since 1966 before achieving recognition with
this latest one, El rito. His earlier novels, Los diablos

(1966), No encontré rosas para mi madre (1967) and Fiesta
en el polvo (1971), are well-known in Spain--especially the
latter, since, like Carrascal's Groovy, it deals with the
world of youth, sexual promiscuity, electric guitars, drugs
and hippies, themes in direct contrast to the superior ones
of purity, loyalty and love that are found in his Diablos, or
to the neo-tremendismo of No encontré rosas, where the protagonist is a non-conformist, incapable of belonging to any
group in his society. Fiesta goes one step further and re-
introduces the popular sixties theme of la dolce vita into the
Spanish novel, the amoral life occurring in the world of film-
making. Apart from its neo-tremendismo, treatment of
prison life, homosexuality and psychological penetration into
its protagonists, Fiesta is a novel whose fragmented and disconnected style goes against the fluid portrayal of men and
women abused by their interior ghosts.

        García Blásquez is very successful at portraying
pathological types. In El rito, a novel much like Fiesta, he
deals with a man obsessed so much by his past that he denies the real world and retreats into his youth through the
delirium of his imagination and is later seduced into magic
rites and rituals of infantile games in which he is most
happy. Written in a style similar to Fiesta, El rito is
Spain's newest example of a novel whose oblique style cor-
rupts the essences of truth and renders the novelist and his
themes impotent and unimportant. Some critics may heap
praise on El rito for a multitude of reasons. However it is
just another novel in a series of Spanish "experimental"
works in the genre that is limited by its "baroque" style,
its own lack of freedom, the cultural restrictions of its
milieu, its fear of censorship, its constrictive use of language, its vagaries, its lack of creative facility, and its
self-mutilation. Goytisolo would view this novel as one of
the clichés or stereotypes of language against which he is
rebelling. Writers like García Blásquez (or others living
within Spain's borders) have unconsciously fallen into the
myths and mental prisons Goytisolo is actively seeking to
overthrow.

        Where I had hoped the 1974-1975 literary season
would offer a glimmer of hope for the Spanish novel's complete regeneration, it is with regret and dismay that I must
share Goytisolo's pessimism about the genre. But not his
cynicism. For Spain is still one of the few countries where
life is effervescent and perhaps some of the novísimo authors
or their successors may be able to unlock the mental prisons

of Spanish writers, freeing their perceptions to give forth
brilliant, brave and free works of art that would regenerate
the nation intellectually as well as politically and philosophically. And the novel is the only area left in the nation
where citizens have this opportunity to create powerful works
that may use ridicule or employ critical realism as the basis to demonstrate their author's imagination.

     In a very recent article in Spain's leading literary
publication, Insula, astute literary critic Ramón Buckley re-
appraised the Spanish novel over the past thirty-five years.
He divides its course into three principal parts: first, the
existential and tremendista trend, concluding in the late
forties, which opened the way for the new novels of "social
realism," such as La colmena, La noria and Las últimas
horas; second, the "dialectical realism" of Martín-Santos
with his publication of Tiempo de silencio, yielding to the
"neo-realistic" and "critical realist" novels of Delibes' Cinco
horas con Mario, Goytisolo's Señas de identidad and Count
Julian, Marsé's La primera historia de la prima Montse and
Grosso's Guarnición de silla; and third, the fantastic and
purely imaginative novel, typified by Delibes' recent Parábola
del náufrago, Rafael Pinilla's Seno and the recent novels of
Rojas, Cunqueiro and Sender, probably as a consequence of
the Latin American "boom" and its insistence on "magical
realism" as a new writing style. [27]

     Buckley's perception of the transitions of the Spanish
novel, largely from "social realism" to "dialectical realism"
to the imaginative values of "magical realism" is a fairly
accurate view. In accordance are José María Castellet,
Pere Gimferrer and Julián Ríos, critics and novelists themselves in search of the trends in the New Spanish novel.
However all these critics agree that in the seventies, a
"new sensibility" has arisen, one opposed to those writers
born after the Civil War. New Spanish novelists reject the
leading authors of the past from the "Generation of 1898"
through the mid-1940's. They are the children of the forties
and fifties, writing in an anti-Spanish tradition. The novels
published between 1966 and 1970 by Goytisolo and Benet display this new sensitivity--the "poetic personality" of the
novelist, according to Castellet. [28] Their attention to "history" and their "poetic" attitudes are clearly illustrative of
the new inroads in Spanish fiction writing. Goytisolo is the
best known example of the Spanish novelist who has redis-
covered the imagination, eroticism, humor, and vitality within the Spanish language. However, except for Goytisolo (and

possibly Benet), the "new sensibility," appearing among
youthful Spanish authors of this new generation, has not yet
produced the "new" literature they speak of. This "new"
generation of 1950 authors, unlike their predecessors, shows
traits of cosmopolitanism as manifested in their greater capacity for studying languages other than Spanish) and foreign
travel and scholarship in other literatures. They show a
new sensibility towards life that has been absent from Spain
for many years, combined with a great optimism for the
future of the novel genre--heretofore unexpressed by novelists and critics alike.

Publishing a first novel in Spain is still part of a
young writer's Utopian dream, since the possibilities to do
so are rife. Publishers and critics alike are anxious to
award literary prizes to promising young novelists and since
the 1960's, there has been a proliferation of awards of all
types. In his fairly thorough study of the Spanish novel,
Martínez Cachero discusses the cash prizes[29]--the Bullón,
the Alfaguara, the Aguila prizes (all carrying a 200,000
peseta award) and the more prestigious publishing awards,
such as the Nadal, Miguel de Cervantes, Planeta, Biblioteca
Breve, and Fastenrath, the critical prizes like the Pardo
Bazán, and the internationally financed Formentor Prize,
which carries a $15,000 cash award and simultaneous pub-
lishing of a fictional work in eleven countries. Joaquín
Marco, in his new book of criticism, Nueva literatura en
España y América,[30] also discusses the "award" situation
in Spain with special reference to the novels ("Genre in
Crisis?") of 1970 and 1971, Delibes' "experimentalism,"
Matute's trilogy, Cela's San Camilo 36, Marsé's Prima
Montse and the latest works of Juan Benet exclusive of Casa
de Mazón. Unlike Martínez Cachero's volume--which encompasses the novel genre pre- and post-1936, the dark
forties, the sluggish fifties from La colmena to Tiempo de
silencio (1962), and renovation within the genre (from 1962
to 1969)--Joaquín Marco's study is dispersed generically and
geographically. Mostly a collection of essays, he reserves
two chapters for the Spanish contemporary novel, one each
for Latin American and Catalan literature, one for Spanish
poetry and the other, a catch-all for miscellaneous essays.
Although Marco's view is wider than Martínez-Cachero's,
since he sees the obvious positive influences of the Latin
American "boom" on the Spanish novel, he is not as pessimistic about the "award" situation as critic Isaac Montero,
who considers the literary prize "false evidence" of thirty
years of "fecundity."[31] Acknowledging the "new sensibility,"

even novelist Daniel Sueiro's pessimism for the fate of the
Spanish novel is abundant in his views of "silence" and
"crisis" for the genre. [32]   As has been noted throughout this
book, there are partisans for opposing sides of any issue
and in a world as timorous as literary criticism and the
writing of "imaginative" fiction, a world where shifting positions, balances and counter-balances are always in abundance,
there is always dissension.

Conclusion

        As we come to the end of this study of the Spanish
novel, its principal practitioners and the evaluation of Spanish Realism over the past twenty-five years, we must never
forget that the duty of each author (in the largest sense) was
to present some facet of reality, by allowing characters and
events to appear "real" in their works, to deal with large
subjects in a comprehensible way, offering their works
principally as a means of communication among men.
Whether a writer intervenes himself (or herself) in his (or
her) narrative art or not, whether or not he uses a symbolic, objective, dialectical or critical style, in his most
elementary guise the novelist must present "reality" through
the people he observes, in an effort to "transcend actual reality, by interpreting it, helping to improve it, humanly,
socially, historically. [Writing Realist novels] is not an
art enclosed in the pride of its autonomy, but a [communi-
cative] art centered on integral reality, concentric with it. "[33]

        Presently, a new Realism, a "new conscience" among
Spanish novelists concerning their styles, language, forms
of writing, and overall structure is in the offing.   Consequently, a search for new literary methods will bring about
new themes, new stylistics and new relationships within the
genre itself.   At this point, one cannot foresee the direction
the Spanish novel will take.   We can only hope that the
literary conception of Realism will be a central factor (whatever the direction) in the continual creation of fiction since
it is ingrained in the Spanish character.   We must hope, too,
that our own sensibilities as readers will bear witness to
the best creative efforts among our new authors.   For
wherever there are writers, as Jorge Luis Borges said,

        it is our duty to help these future benefactors to
        attain that final discovery of themselves which
        makes for great literature.   Literature is not a

mere juggling of words; what matters is what is
[sometimes] left unsaid, or what may be read between the lines [e.g. , the case for the Spanish
novel between 1950 and 1962]. Were it not for
this deep inner feeling, literature would be no
more than a game, and we all know that it can be
more than that. 34

The fate of the Spanish novel is now in the hands of
the novísimo writers. Whether they will revive the tenets
of the past (objective, historical, naturalistic, melioristic,
socialistic or new Realism) or, with their "new" sensibility,
create something different stylistically, aesthetically, and/or
ideologically we cannot say; in part, whether we reach the
truth of man and of being is now their dilemma. Theirs is
the pleasure and the task. We can only pray the efforts of
the novísimo will bear fruit in the future and bring Spain
even greater esteem, built on the courageous but slowly
fading glory of the Spanish New Wave.

CHAPTER NOTES

CHAPTER 1

1. Federico Carlos Saínz de Robles, La novela española en el siglo XX (Madrid: Ed. Pegaso, 1957), p. 227.

2. New York Times, July 15, 1972, p. 3.

3. Ibid.

CHAPTER 2

1. José María Castellet, "Veinte años de novela española," Cuadernos Americanos, vol. 22, no. 126 (1963), 293.

2. Ibid., p. 292.

3. Alain Robbe-Grillet, For a New Novel: Essays on Fiction (New York: Books for Libraries Press, 1970), pp. 8-17, passim.

4. Ibid., p. 134-40, passim.

5. Jacques Siclier, Nouvelle vague (Paris: Ed. du Cerf, 1961), p. 1.

6. Ibid., p. 2.

7. Thrall, Hibbard and Holman, A Handbook to Literature (New York: Odyssey Press, 1960), pp. 397-8.

8. Juan Luis Alborg, Hora actual de la novela española (Madrid: Ed. Taurus, 1958), vol. 1, pp. 23-40.

9. Excerpts in this paragraph from Ibid., p. 32, 45 and 50.

10. Ibid., pp. 53-81; the excerpts following are from this essay, passim.

11. Rafael Bosch, La novela española del siglo XX (New York: Las Américas, 1970), p. 17.

12. See Bosch, pp. 24-50 and 71-98, for his ideas on the development of Spanish Realism; the excerpts in this paragraph

are from pp. 80 and 86.

13. Ibid., p. 98.

14. Ramón Buckley, Problemas formales en la novela española contemporánea (Barcelona: Ed. Península, 1968), p. 16.

15. Ibid., pp. 28-9.

16. Juan Carlos Curutchet, Introducción a la novela española de postguerra (Montevideo: Ed. Alfa, 1966), p. 120.

17. Castellet, "Veinte años," 120.

18. Juan Ignacio Ferreras, Tendencias de la novela española actual (1931-1969) (Paris: Ed. Hispanoamericanas, 1970), p. 201.

19. Excerpts in this paragraph from Ibid., pp. 203, 219 and 18.

20. Carlos Fuentes, La nueva novela hispanoamericana (Mexico: Ed. Joaquín Mortiz, 1969), p. 18.

21. Ibid.

22. Juan Goytisolo, Problemas de la novela (Barcelona: Ed. Seix Barral, 1959), p. 29.

23. Juan Goytisolo, El furgón de cola (Paris: Ruedo Ibérico, 1967), p. 2.

24. Kessel Schwartz, Juan Goytisolo (New York: Twayne, 1970), pp. 133-4.

25. José Angel Valente, "Lo demás es silencio," Insula, no. 271 (June 1969), 2.

26. K. Schwartz, Juan Goytisolo, pp. 135-6.

27. Julio Ortega, "Juan Goytisolo: hacia Juan sin tierra," Plural, vol. 25 (Mexico, Oct. 13, 1973), 5.

28. M. García-Viñó, Novela española actual (Madrid: Ed. Guadarrama, 1967); following three excerpts from pp. 16, 229 and 221.

29. M. García-Viñó, "La nueva novela española," La nueva novela europea (Madrid: Ed. Guadarrama, 1968), pp. 220, 52.

30. Gil Casado's new edition of his work published by Seix Barral in 1973 adds two new categories: "The conquered" and "demythification" as well as considering the Spanish novel from 1920 to 1971.

31. Pablo Gil Casado, La novela social española (Barcelona: Ed. Seix Barral, 1968), p. 301.

32. Antonio Iglesias Laguna, Treinta años de novela española (1938-1968) (Madrid: Ed. Prensa Española, 1970), vol. 1, p. 305.

33. J. R. Marra-López, Narrativa española fuera de España
     (1939-1961) (Madrid: Ed. Guadarrama, 1963), pp. 64-5.

34. Eugenio de Nora, La novela española contemporánea (1927-
     1960) (Madrid: Ed. Gredos, 1962), vol. 3, p. 285.

35. Domingo Pérez Minik, Novelistas españoles de los siglos XIX
     y XX (Madrid: Ed. Guadarrama, 1957), pp. 343 and 347.

36. Federico Carlos Saínz de Robles, La novela española en el
     siglo XX (Madrid: Ed. Pegaso, 1957), pp. 228 and 230.

37. Gonzalo Sobejano, Novela española de nuestro tiempo (Madrid:
     Ed. Prensa Española, 1970), pp. 16-7; excerpts that fol-
     low are from pp. 212-3, 220 and 423-60, passim.

38. See note 37.

39. G. Torrente Ballester, Panorama de la literatura española
     contemporánea (Madrid: Ed. Guadarrama, 1965), p. 558.

40. Carlos Rojas, "Problemas de la nueva novela española," La
     nueva novela europea (Madrid: Ed. Guadarrama, 1968),
     pp. 125 and 135.

41. E. Guillermo & J. A. Hernández, La novelística española de
     los 60 (New York: Eliseo Torres, 1971); the two excerpts
     in the following paragraph are from pp. 36 and 40.

42. See Chapter 21 for an analysis of the three newest works of
     literary criticism on the Spanish novel by Martínez-Cachero,
     Joaquín Marco and F. Morán.

CHAPTER 3

1. R. E. Chandler & K. Schwartz, A New History of Spanish
    Literature (Baton Rouge: Louisiana State University Press,
    1969), p. 40.

2. Camilo José Cela, La colmena, 11th ed. (Barcelona: Ed.
    Noguer, 1971), p. 9. All page numbers in this chapter
    given for quotations from La colmena are to this edition.

3. Thrall, Hibbard and Holman, A Handbook to Literature (New
    York: Odyssey Press, 1960), pp. 318-9.

4. Ibid., p. 323-4.

5. D. W. McPheeters, Camilo José Cela (New York: Twayne,
    1963), p. 86.

6. David W. Foster, Forms of the Novel in the Work of Camilo
    José Cela (Columbia: University of Missouri Press, 1967),
    pp. 63-5.

7. McPheeters, Cela, p. 101.

8. See Foster, Forms of the Novel, p. 80.

9. Ibid., p. 65.

10. Ibid., p. 68.

11. Ibid., p. 69.

12. McPheeters, Cela, p. 101.

13. John J. Flasher, "Aspects of Novelistic Technique in Cela's 'La colmena'," West Virginia University Philological Papers, 21 (Nov. 1959), 30-43.

14. Foster, Forms of the Novel, p. 70.

15. Ibid., p. 71.

16. Ibid., p. 75.

17. Ibid., p. 80.

18. Ibid., p. 154.

19. Ibid., p. 78.

20. Ibid., p. 157.

21. Ibid., p. 154.

22. Ibid., p. 13.

CHAPTER 4

1. For an extended discussion of Un hombre, see Ronald Schwartz, José María Gironella (New York: Twayne, 1972), pp. 38-50.

2. Ibid., pp. 41-3.

3. J. M. Gironella, Los cipreses creen en Dios (Barcelona: Ed. Planeta, 1953), pp. 870-1; the translation is my own from the original Spanish text. All page references given in parentheses in this chapter are to this edition.

4. R. Schwartz, Gironella, pp. 51-69.

5. Ibid.; I cite the words of Julián Marías here.

6. Ibid., pp. 174-7.

7. Ibid.

8. Ibid., pp. 51-69.

CHAPTER 5

1. Elena Quiroga, Algo pasa en la calle (Barcelona: Ed. Destino, 1954), p. 81. All page references in parentheses in this chapter are to this edition.

2. Eugenio de Nora, La novela española contemporánea, 2d ed. (Madrid: Ed. Gredos, 1970), vol. 3, p. 124.

3. Ibid.

4. Antonio Iglesias Laguna, Treinta años de novela española (Madrid: Ed. Prensa Española, 1970), vol. 1, p. 271.

5. José Corrales Egea, La novela española actual (Madrid: Ed. Cuadernos para el diálogo, 1971), p. 125.

6. Gonzalo Sobejano, Novela española de nuestro tiempo (Madrid: Ed. Prensa Española, 1970), p. 185.

7. Juan Ignacio Ferreras, Tendencias de la novela española actual (Paris: Ed. Hispanoamericanas, 1970), p. 148.

8. Juan Luis Alborg, Hora actual de la novela española (Madrid: Ed. Taurus, 1958), vol. 1, p. 209.

CHAPTER 6

1. Rafael Bosch, La novela española del siglo XX (New York: Las Américas, 1970), vol. 2, p. 142.

2. Claude Couffon, "Rencontre avec J. F. Santos," Les lettres nouvelles, Paris, no. 62 (July-Aug. 1958), 127-32.

3. Eugenio de Nora, La novela española contemporánea (Madrid: Ed. Gredos, 1962), vol. 3, p. 288.

4. Jesús Fernández Santos, Los bravos (Barcelona: Ed. Destino, 1954), p. 200. All page references given in this chapter are to this edition.

5. Pablo Gil Casado, La novela social española (Barcelona: Ed. Seix Barral, 1968), p. 68.

6. G. Sobejano, Novela española de nuestro tiempo (Madrid: Ed. Prensa Española, 1970), pp. 246-7.

7. Gil Casado, La novela social, p. 72.

8. Ibid., p. 71.

9. Ibid., p. 73.

10. Sobejano, Novela española, p. 245.

11. Ibid.

12. Gil Casado, La novela social, pp. 76-8.

13. Juan Carlos Curutchet, Introducción a la novela española de postguerra (Montevideo: Ed. Alfa, 1966), p. 106.

14. Ibid., pp. 114-5.

15. Ibid., p. 117.

16. Ibid., p. 118.

17. Gil Casado, La novela social, p. 70.

18. See pp. 205-8 of F. Santos' Los bravos for this sustained description into Don Prudencio's life and thoughts.

19. J. Alborg, Hora actual de la novela española (Madrid: Ed. Taurus, 1958), vol. 2, p. 374.

20. Ibid., p. 375.

21. Ibid., p. 377.

22. M. García-Viñó, Novela española actual (Madrid: Ed. Guadarrama, 1967), p. 146.

23. Ibid., p. 147.

24. Ibid., p. 148.

25. J. Corrales Egea, La novela española actual (Madrid: Cuadernos para el diálogo, 1971), p. 66.

26. E. Nora, La novela española, p. 288.

27. J. Ignacio Ferreras, Tendencias de la novela española actual (Paris: Ed. Hispanoamericanas, 1970), p. 160.

CHAPTER 7

1. J. Ignacio Ferreras, Tendencias de la novela española actual (Paris: Ed. Hispanoamericanas, 1970), p. 165.

2. Gonzalo Sobejano, Novela española de nuestro tiempo (Madrid: Ed. Prensa Española, 1970), p. 235.

3. Ibid.

4. Ibid., p. 237.

5. J. Corrales Egea, La novela española actual (Madrid: Cuadernos para el diálogo, 1971), p. 77.

6. E. de Nora, La novela española contemporánea (Madrid: Ed. Gredos, 1962), p. 278.

7. F. Carenas and J. Ferrando, La sociedad española en la novela de postguerra (New York: Eliseo Torres, 1971), p. 37.

8. R. Sánchez Ferlosio, El Jarama (Barcelona: Ed. Destino, 1956), p. 8. The following page reference is to this edition also.

9. S. Sanz Villanueva, Tendencias de la novela española actual (Madrid: Cuadernos para el diálogo, 1972), p. 74.

10. Corrales Egea, La novela española actual, p. 77.

11. Nora, La novela española contemporánea, p. 277.

12. Sobejano, Novela española, p. 236.

13. Rafael Bosch, La novela española contemporánea (New York: Las Américas, 1970), vol. 2, p. 142.

14. Ibid.

15. G. Torrente Ballester, Panorama de la literatura española contemporánea (Madrid: Ed. Guadarrama, 1965), p. 528.

16. Bosch, La novela, p. 270.

17. J. Ortega y Gasset, The Dehumanization of Art and Other Writings on Art and Culture (New York: Doubleday, 1948), p. 1-50.

18. Bosch, La novela, p. 270.

19. Ignacio Ferreras, Tendencias, pp. 165-6.

20. Ibid., pp. 166-7.

21. Ibid.

22. J. L. Alborg, Hora actual de la novela española (Madrid: Ed. Taurus, 1958), vol. 2, p. 339.

23. Ibid., p. 332.

24. Ibid., p. 333.

25. M. García-Viñó, Novela española actual (Madrid: Ed. Guadarrama, 1967), p. 105.

26. Ibid., p. 106.

27. Ibid., p. 107.

28. Ibid.

29. Ibid., p. 108.

30. Ibid.

31. Ibid.

32. Ibid.

33. Ibid., p. 111.

34. Ibid.

35. Ibid., p. 112.

36. Ibid.

37. Sobejano, Novela española, p. 239.

38. Pablo Gil Casado, La novela social española (Barcelona: Ed. Seix Barral, 1968), p. 29.

39. Ibid. , p. 30.

40. Sanz Villanueva, Tendencias de la novela española actual (Madrid: Cuadernos para el Diálogo, 1972), p. 74.

41. J. C. Curutchet, Introducción a la novela española de postgue-rra (Montevideo: Ed. Alfa, 1966), p. 65.

42. Ibid. , p. 40.

43. Susan Sontag, Against Interpretation (New York: Dell, 1961), p. 36.

CHAPTER 8

1. Notes 1 to 7 following were cited from a collection of reviews chosen by Seix Barral for the dust jacket of Las afueras. These particular words of praise come from J. Pasteur in La voz de Asturias, Feb. 19, 1959.

2. P. Corbalan, Informaciones (Madrid), April 17, 1959.

3. J. L. Cano, "Reseña de 'Las afueras'," Insula, no. 151 (June 1959), 12.

4. [Review], Times Literary Supplement (London), Sept. 25, 1959; author not cited.

5. R. V. Zamora, "Review of 'Las afueras'," España (Tangiers), 1959.

6. U. Bandi, "Review of 'Las afueras'," La voce Republicaria (Rome), 1959.

7. "Review of 'Las afueras'," Papeles de Son Armadans, no. 41 (July 1959), 16; author not cited.

8. Blurb from the dust jacket of Las afueras (Barcelona: Ed. Seix Barral, 1958; 200 pages).

9. Rafael Bosch, La novela española del siglo XX (New York: Las Américas, 1970), p. 146.

10. R. Iglesias Ferreras, Tendencias de la novela española actual (Paris: Ed. Hispanoamericanas, 1970), p. 174.

11. E. de Nora, La novela española contemporánea (Madrid: Ed. Gredos, 1962), pp. 317-8.

12. Ibid. , p. 318.

13. Ibid.

14. G. Sobejano, Novela española de nuestro tiempo (Madrid: Ed. Prensa Española, 1970), p. 311.

15. Goytisolo-Gay, Las afueras, pp. 30-1.   Page references in
    this chapter are to this edition; see note 8.

16. Sobejano, Novela española, p. 311.

17. G. Sobejano gives an excellent plot summary of Chapter Six
    of Goytisolo's Las afueras in Novela española, pp. 310-15.

18. Nora, La novela española, pp. 318-9.

19. Sobejano, Novela española, p. 315.

20. Bosch, La novela, pp. 146-7.

21. Ignacio Ferreras, Tendencias, p. 175.

22. F. Olmos García, "La novela y los novelistas españoles de
    hoy," Cuadernos Americanos, vol. 22, no. 4 (July-Aug.
    1963), 234.

23. Sobejano, Novela española, p. 311.

CHAPTER 9

1. I refer to Janet Díaz, Ana María Matute (New York: Twayne,
   1971), and Margaret Jones, The Literary World of Ana
   María Matute (Lexington: University of Kentucky Press,
   1970).

2. Díaz, Ana María Matute, p. 18.

3. In the United States, Primera memoria appeared as School of
   the Sun, transl. by Elaine Kerrigan (New York: Pantheon,
   1963); in England it was called Awakening, transl. by
   James Holman Mason (London: Hutchinson Press, 1963).

4. Interview, Ana María Matute and I, Sitges, July 10, 1968.

5. Ibid.

6. Díaz, A. M. Matute, p. 14.

7. Interview, July 10, 1968.

8. Ana María Matute, Primera memoria (Barcelona: Ed. Destino, 1960), p. 245.

9. Díaz, A. M. Matute, p. 135.

10. Ibid. , p. 134.

11. Matute, School of the Sun, pp. 3-4.

12. Díaz, A. M. Matute, p. 133.

13. Ibid.

14. Rafael Bosch, La novela española del siglo XX (New York:
    Las Américas, 1970), p. 154.

15. Ibid. , pp. 154-5.

16. Díaz, A. M. Matute, p. 134.

17. Page numbers of all quotations from the primary work refer to the American edition, School of the Sun; see note 3.

18. Díaz, A. M. Matute, p. 135.

19. J. Corrales Egea, La novela española actual (Madrid: Cuadernos para el diálogo, 1971), p. 107.

20. Ibid.

21. Ibid.

22. Ibid., p. 108.

23. B. Patt and M. Nozick, Spanish Literature Since the Civil War (New York: Dodd, Mead, 1973), p. 188.

24. J. Ignacio Ferreras, Tendencias de la novela española actual (Paris: Ed. Hispanoamericanas, 1970), p. 146.

25. Quotations in this paragraph are from M. García-Viñó, Novela española actual (Madrid: Ed. Guadarrama, 1967), pp. 151-6.

26. James R. Stamm, A Short History of Spanish Literature (New York: Doubleday, 1967), p. 241.

27. E. de Nora, La novela española contemporánea (Madrid: Ed. Gredos, 1962), vol. 3, p. 265.

28. Ibid., pp. 255-6.

29. Ibid., p. 266, as cited by Nora in a footnote.

30. Interview, July 10, 1968.

31. Ibid.

32. J. L. Ponce de León, La novela española de la guerra civil (1936-1939) (Madrid: Insula, 1971), p. 82.

33. A. M. Matute, Los soldados lloran de noche (Barcelona: Ed. Destino, 1964), pp. 153-4.

34. F. Olmos García, "La novela y los novelistas de hoy," Cuadernos americanos, vol. 22, no. 4 (July-Aug. 1963), 229.

CHAPTER 10

1. D. Sueiro, La criba (Barcelona: Ed. Seix Barral, 1961), p. 7. All page references given in this chapter are to this edition.

2. G. Sobejano, Novela española de nuestro tiempo (Madrid: Ed. Prensa Española, 1970), p. 351.

3. Ibid.

4. Ibid., p. 352.

5. P. Gil Casado, La novela social española (Barcelona: Ed. Seix Barral, 1968), p. 131.

6. Ibid., p. 132.

7. J. Corrales Egea, La novela española actual (Madrid: Cuadernos para el Diálogo, 1971), p. 115.

8. Bosch, La novela española del siglo XX (New York: Las Américas, 1970), vol. 2, p. 159.

9. Ibid.

CHAPTER 11

1. Interview, Juan García Hortelano and I, Madrid, June 27, 1968.

2. See J. Domingo, "Dolores Medio and J. G. Hortelano," Insula, no. 253 (Dec. 1967), 5.

3. See for instance J. Domingo, "Novísimos, nuevos y renovados," Insula, no. 313 (March 1973), 6.

4. R. Bosch, La novela española del siglo XX (New York: Las Américas, 1970), p. 166.

5. G. Sobejano, Novela española de nuestro tiempo (Madrid: Ed. Prensa Española, 1970), p. 339.

6. P. Gil Casado, La novela social española (Barcelona: Ed. Seix Barral, 1968), p. 32.

7. J. G. Hortelano, Summer Storm, transl. by Ilsa Barea (New York: Grove Press, 1962), p. 259.

8. Gil Casado, La novela social española (Barcelona: Ed. Seix Barral, 1968), p. 44.

9. Interview, June 27, 1968.

10. Gil Casado, La novela social, p. 44.

11. Ibid., p. 47.

12. Rafael Bosch, La novela española del siglo XX (New York: Las Américas, 1970), p. 166.

13. Interview, June 27, 1968.

14. Quoted in J. Corrales Egea, La novela española actual (Madrid: Cuadernos para el diálogo, 1970), p. 62.

15. Ibid., p. 89.

16. Ibid., p. 91.

17. Ibid., p. 92.

18. See La novela social española, pp. 41-59, for an extensive
     discussion on García Hortelano's stylistic techniques.

19. On pp. 49-57 Gil Casado pursues G. Hortelano's style re-
     lentlessly, selecting a large number of citations from the
     text of Tormenta.

20. See La novela social española, p. 58.

21. See J. I. Ferreras, Tendencias de la novela española actual
     (Paris: Ed. Hispanoamericanas, 1970), pp. 183-4.

22. Hortelano quoted in F. Olmos García, "La novela y los
     novelistas españoles de hoy," Cuadernos americanos, vol.
     22, no. 4 (July-Aug. 1963), 228.

23. Ibid.

24. Ibid.

25. Interview, June 27, 1968.

26. Sobejano, Novela española, pp. 339-40.

27. George J. Becker, Documents of Modern Literary Realism
     (Princeton, N.J.: Princeton University Press, 1963),
     p. 89.

28. Ramón Buckley linked Tormenta de verano and El Jarama to-
     gether in two chapters of his work, Problemas formales
     en la novela española contemporánea, showing their mutual
     use of cinematic perspectives, image-symbols, "taped"
     dialogues (magnetofonismo dialogal) and subjective-descrip-
     tive techniques and the successful use of these techniques
     by García Hortelano and Sánchez Ferlosio.

CHAPTER 12

1. Gil Casado, Sobejano and Guillermo & Hernández give excel-
    lent summaries (in Spanish) of the plot of Tiempo de si-
    lencio in their respective volumes of criticism cited in the
    Bibliography.

2. From a review by Antonio Vilanova which appeared in the
    magazine Destino, published in Barcelona sometime in
    1962, as cited on the dust-jacket of the novel.

3. J. Corrales Egea, La novela española actual (Madrid: Cua-
    dernos para el diálogo, 1970), pp. 143-4.

4. R. Domenech, "Interview with L. M.-Santos," Insula, no. 208
    (Mar. 1964), 4.

5. E. de Nora, La novela española contemporánea (Madrid: Ed.
    Gredos, 1970), vol. 3, p. 343.

6. F. Carenas and J. Ferrando, La sociedad española en la

novela de postguerra (New York: E. Torres, 1971),
p. 127.

7.   R. Domenech, "Interview," 4.

8.   Gemma Roberts, Temas existenciales en la novela española
de postguerra (Madrid: Ed. Gredos, 1973), p. 131.

9.   Aquilino Duque, "Realismo pueblerino y realismo suburbano:
Un buen entendedor de la realidad," Indice, no. 185 (June
1964), 9.

10. Roberts, Temas existenciales, p. 133.

11. Ibid. , p. 195.

12. Juan Carlos Curutchet, "L. M. -Santos, el fundador," Cuadernos de Ruedo Ibérico (Paris), no. 17 (Feb. -Mar. 1968),
17.

13. R. Buckley, Problemas formales en la novela española contemporánea (Barcelona: Ed. Península, 1968), p. 195.

14. Carenas and Ferrando, La sociedad española, p. 141.

15. Guillermo and Hernández, La novelística española de los 60
(New York: E. Torres, 1971), p. 49.

16. The most interesting articles on Tiempo de silencio I have
read are the following: (1) J. W. Díaz, "L. M. -Santos
and The Contemporary Spanish Novel," Hispania, vol. 51,
no. 2 (Mar. 1968), 234-237; (2) S. Eoff and J. Schraibman,
"Dos novelas del absurdo: 'L'etranger' y 'Tiempo de silencio'," Papeles de Son Armadans, no. 168 (Mar. 1970),
213-241; (3) F. Grande, "L. M. -Santos: 'Tiempo de silencio'," Cuadernos Hispanoamericanos, no. 158 (Feb.
1963), 337-342; and (4) C. Rojas, "Problemas de la nueva
novela española," in La nueva novela europea (Madrid: Ed.
Guadarrama, 1968), pp. 121-137.

17. G. Sobejano, Novela española de nuestro tiempo (Madrid: Ed.
Prensa Española, 1970), p. 362.

18. L. Martín-Santos, Tiempo de silencio (Barcelona: Ed. Seix
Barral, 1962), p. 75. All page references in this chapter
are to this edition.

19. Benito Varela, Renovación de la novela en el siglo XX (Barcelona: Ed. Destino, 1966), p. 30.

20. Guillermo and Hernández, La novelística, p. 63.

21. Gil Casado, La novela social española (Barcelona: Ed. Seix
Barral, 1968), p. 277.

22. M. -Santos, quoted in Ibid. , p. 281.

23. Ibid. , p. 284.

24. Ibid. , p. 286.

25. Ibid. , p. 289.

26. See Mario Bendetti's review of the novel in La Mañana, a newspaper published in Montevideo, as quoted on the dust-jacket of the Seix Barral edition, 1962.

27. Review by Tristan Renaud in Les Lettres Francaises (Paris), 1962, as cited on the dustjacket by the editors of Seix Barral.

28. Felix Grande, "L. M. -Santos: 'Tiempo de silencio'," Cuadernos Hispanoamericanos, no. 158 (Feb. 1963), 341-2.

29. Nora, La novela española contemporánea, p. 343.

30. Ferreras, Tendencias de la novela española actual (Paris: Ed. Hispanoamericanas, 1970); see pp. 187-9.

31. Bosch, La novela española del siglo XX (New York: Las Américas, 1970), vol. 2, p. 160.

32. G. Torrente Ballester, Panorama de la literatura española contemporánea (Madrid: Ed. Guadarrama, 1965), p. 532.

33. Buckley, Problemas formales, p. 205.

34. S. Sanz Villanueva, Tendencias de la novela española actual (Madrid: Cuadernos para el diálogo, 1972), p. 137.

35. Consult Gil Casado, La novela social española, p. 280, and G. Sobejano, La novela española, pp. 353-4.

36. Grande, "L. M. -Santos," Cuadernos Hispanoamericanos, p. 342 [see note 28].

37. This article, part of a collection of essays entitled La nueva novela europea (Madrid: Ed. Guadarrama, 1968), is on pp. 121-36.

38. Ibid. , p. 130.

39. J. Domingo, La novela española del siglo XX, (Barcelona: Ed. Labor, 1973), vol. 2.

40. Ibid. , p. 111.

41. Ibid. , p. 112.

CHAPTER 13

1. J. L. Castillo Puche, Paralelo 40 (Barcelona: Ed. Destino, 1963), pp. 7-9. All page references in this chapter are to this edition.

2. J. Ignacio Ferreras, Tendencias de la novela española actual (Paris: Ed. Hispanoamericanas, 1970), p. 160.

3. José Domingo, La novela española del siglo XX (Barcelona: Ed. Labor, 1973), p. 140.

4. M. García-Viñó, Novela española actual (Madrid: Ed. Guada-
    rrama, 1967), p. 50.

5. Ibid., p. 51.

6. Ibid., p. 52.

7. Ibid., p. 53.

8. Ibid., pp. 54-5.

9. Ibid., p. 57.

10. Sanz Villanueva, Tendencias de la novela española actual (Ma-
    drid: Cuadernos para el diálogo, 1972), p. 102.

11. Brian J. Dendle, The Spanish Novel of Religious Thesis 1876-
    1936 (Madrid: Ed. Castalia, 1968), p. 93.

12. G. Sobejano, Novela española de nuestro tiempo (Madrid: Ed.
    Prensa española, 1970), p. 195.

13. Ibid., p. 188.

14. Iglesias Laguna, Treinta años de novela española 1938-1968
    (Madrid: Ed. Prensa española, 1970), p. 216.

15. G. Roberts, Temas existenciales en la novela española de
    postguerra (Madrid: Ed. Gredos, 1973), pp. 236-61.

16. E. de Nora, La novela española contemporánea (Madrid: Ed.
    Gredos, 1968), vol. 3, pp. 163-4.

CHAPTER 14

1. A large portion of the biographical material in these pages is
    derived from Kessel Schwartz' very excellent book, Juan
    Goytisolo (New York: Twayne, 1970), pp. 9-10 and pp. 19-
    22.

2. J. Corrales Egea, La novela española actual (Madrid: Cuader-
    nos para el diálogo, 1971), p. 62.

3. J. Goytisolo, Señas de identidad (Mexico: Ed. J. Mortiz,
    1966), p. 35. All page references in this chapter are to
    this edition.

4. E. R. Monegal, El arte de narrar (Mexico: Ed. Monte Avila,
    1969), pp. 188-92, passim.

5. K. Schwartz, Juan Goytisolo, pp. 95-7.

6. See Guillermo and Hernández' excellent chapter on Goytisolo
    for a detailed analysis of Señas de identidad, in their book,
    La novelística española de los 60 (New York: E. Torres,
    1971), pp. 111-25, some of which is reproduced in the
    paragraph that follows.

7. Ibid., pp. 118, 121-2.

8. J. Goytisolo, El furgón de cola (Paris: Ed. Ruedo Ibérico, 1967), p. 36.

9. G. Sobejano, Novela española de nuestro tiempo (Madrid: Ed. Prensa Española, 1970), p. 280.

10. P. Gil Casado, La novela social española (Barcelona: Ed. Seix Barral, 1968), p. 296.

11. K. Schwartz, Juan Goytisolo, p. 102.

12. As quoted by K. Schwartz, Ibid., p. 107.

13. S. Sanz Villanueva, Tendencias de la novela española actual (Madrid: Ed. Cuadernos para el diálogo, 1972), p. 161.

14. Bosch, La novela española contemporánea (New York: Las Américas, 1970), pp. 7-8.

15. E. de Nora, La novela española contemporánea (Madrid: Ed. Gredos, 1968), p. 294.

16. R. Buckley, Problemas formales en la novela española contemporánea (Barcelona: Ed. Península, 1968), p. 211.

17. K. Schwartz, Juan Goytisolo, p. 109.

18. Gil Casado, La novela social, p. 216.

19. Carlos Rojas, De Cela a Castillo-Navarro (Englewood Cliffs, N.J.: Prentice-Hall, 1965), p. 133.

20. Kessel Schwartz, "Introduction to Goytisolo's 'Fiestas'," in Goytisolo, Fiestas (New York: Dell, 1964), p. 9.

21. K. Schwartz, Juan Goytisolo, pp. 135, 136, and 134.

22. For an excellent study on alienation and aggression, see José Ortega, Alienación y agresión en Señas de identidad y Reivindicación del conde Don Julián (New York: E. Torres, 1972), pp. 31-76, for his views on Señas.

23. J. Goytisolo, Marks of Identity, transl. by Gregory Rabassa (New York: Grove, 1969), p. 178, 180, 182, 190 and 342.

24. See Juan Goytisolo, "Formalismo y compromiso literario," Casa de Américas, vol. 4, no. 26 (1964), 149.

25. Goytisolo's words, as quoted by K. Schwartz, Juan Goytisolo, p. 21.

26. As quoted in E. R. Monegal, El arte de narrar, p. 197.

CHAPTER 15

1. G. Sobejano, Novela española de nuestro tiempo (Madrid: Ed. Prensa Española, 1970), p. 347.

2. Juan Marsé, Ultimas tardes con Teresa (Barcelona: Ed. Seix

Barral, 1966), p. 334.

3. Guillermo Díaz-Plaja, La creación literaria en España (Madrid: Ed. Aguilar, 1968), p. 82.

4. Ibid. , p. 83, 85.

5. J. Domingo, La novela española del siglo XX (Barcelona: Ed. Labor, 1973), vol. 2, p. 119.

6. Quoted in F. Olmos-García, "La novela y los novelistas españoles de hoy," Cuadernos Americanos, vol. 22, no. 4 (July-Aug 1963), 217-9.

7. Gil Casado, La novela social española (Barcelona: Seix Barral, 1968), p. 305.

8. J. Corrales Egea, La novela española actual (Madrid: Ed. Cuadernos para el diálogo, 1971), p. 146.

9. Ibid. , p. 148.

10. Sobejano, Novela española, p. 344.

11. Ibid. , p. 346.

12. Ibid. , p. 349.

13. Guillermo and Hernández, La novelística española de los años 60 (New York: E. Torres, 1971), pp. 71-3.

14. Mario Vargas Llosa, "Una explosión sarcástica en la novela española moderna," Insula, no. 233 (April 1966), 1.

15. Guillermo and Hernández, La novelística, pp. 88, 89.

16. Vargas Llosa also finds this parallel in the article cited in note 14 above.

17. Vargas Llosa, op. cit. , 1.

CHAPTER 16

1. Interview, Ignacio Aldecoa and I, Madrid, June 26, 1968.

2. Gaspar Gómez de la Serna, Ensayos sobre la literatura social (Madrid: Ed. Guadarrama, 1971), pp. 113-4.

3. G. Sobejano, Novela española de nuestro tiempo (Madrid: Ed. Prensa Española, 1970), p. 304.

4. José Domingo, " 'Parte de una historia': Narrativa española," Insula, no. 252 (Nov. 1967), 4.

5. Ibid.

6. Guillermo Díaz Plaja, La creación literaria en España (1966-1967) (Madrid: Ed. Aguilar, 1968), p. 332.

7. Ibid. , p. 333.

8. Interview, June 26, 1968.

9. Domingo, "Parte," 4.

10. Ricardo Senabre, "La obra narrativa de I. Aldecoa," Papeles de Son Armadans, no. 164 (Jan. 1970), 1.

11. J. Domingo, La novela española del siglo XX (Barcelona: Ed. Labor, 1973), vol. 2, p. 101.

12. J. Corrales Egea, La novela española actual (Madrid: Cuadernos para el diálogo, 1971), p. 127.

13. Interview, June 26, 1968.

14. Eugenio de Nora, La novela española contemporánea (Madrid: Ed. Gredos, 1968), vol. 3, p. 302.

15. Aldecoa, quoted in J. L. Alborg, Hora actual de la novela española (Madrid: Ed. Taurus, 1958), vol. 2, pp. 277-8.

16. Alborg, Hora actual, p. 295.

17. Gómez de la Serna, Ensayos sobre la literatura social, pp. 185-99 passim.

18. In, for example, J. I. Ferreras, Tendencias de la novela española actual (Paris: Ed. Hispanoamericanas, 1970), p. 162.

19. I. Aldecoa, Parte de una historia (Barcelona: Ed. Noguer, 1967), p. 17. All page references in this chapter are to this edition.

20. Interview, June 26, 1968.

21. Gemma Roberts, Temas existenciales en la novela española de postguerra (Madrid: Ed. Gredos, 1973), pp. 100-1.

22. As quoted in Ibid., p. 118.

CHPATER 17

1. Antonio Núñez, "Encuentro con Juan Benet," Insula, no. 269 (April 1969), 4.

2. G. Sobejano, Novela española de nuestro tiempo (Madrid: Ed. Prensa Española, 1970), p. 402.

3. G. Sobejano presents an excellent outline of the plot of Volverás a Región on pp. 401-2 of Novela española, which lends cohesion to the confusions of Benet's story.

4. Ibid., p. 405.

5. Guillermo and Hernández, La novelística española de los años 60 (New York: Eliseo Torres, 1971), p. 129.

6. Ibid., pp. 135-6.

7. Ibid., p. 136.

8. Ibid. , p. 147.

9. Ibid. , p. 149.

10. J. L. Ponce de León, La novela española de la guerra civil
    (Madrid: Ed. Insula, 1971), p. 170.

11. Pedro Gimferrer, "En torno a 'Volverás a Región'," Insula,
    no. 266 (Jan. 1969), 14-5.

12. J. Corrales Egea, La novela española actual (Madrid: Ed.
    Cuadernos para el Diálogo, 1970), p. 211.

13. Gimferrer, "En torno a 'Volverás a Región," 15.

14. Núñez, "Encuentro," 4.

15. S. Sanz Villanueva, Tendencias de la novela española actual
    (Madrid: Ed. Cuadernos para el diálogo, 1972), p. 182.

16. J. Domingo, La novela española del siglo XX (Barcelona: Ed.
    Labor, 1973), vol. 2, p. 157.

17. F. Carenas and J. Ferrando, La sociedad española en la no-
    vela actual (New York: E. Torres, 1971), p. 192.

18. F. Tola de Habich and P. Grieve, Los españoles y el boom
    (Venezuela: Ed. Tiempo Nuevo, 1971), p. 39.

19. Juan Benet, Volverás a Región (Barcelona: Ed. Destino,
    1967), p. 142.

20. Eric Auerbach, Mimesis (New York: Doubleday, 1953), p.
    312.

21. P. Gimferrer, "En torno a 'Volverás a Región'," 4.

22. See Joaquín Marco, Nueva literatura en España y América
    (Barcelona: Ed. Lumen, 1972), pp. 143-5.

23. See J. Domingo, La novela, vol. 2, pp. 157-8 for an analy-
    sis of Benet's latest novels.

24. I refer to an interview reported by Tola de Habich and
    Grieve; see note 18.

CHAPTER 18

1. Luis López Martínez, La novelística de Miguel Delibes (Mur-
    cia: Univ. of Murcia, 1973), p. 11.

2. Díaz, Miguel Delibes (New York: Twayne, 1971), p. 162.

3. J. R. Stamm, A Short History of Spanish Literature (New
    York: Doubleday, 1967), p. 241.

4. See Chapter Two of M. García Viñó's Novela española actual
    (Madrid: Ed. Guadarrama, 1967), pp. 18-46, for Carlos
    Rojas' ideas of the influences on Delibes' fiction.

5. See Carlos Rojas' Introduction to De Cela a C. Navarro
    (Englewood Cliffs, N.J.: Prentice-Hall, 1965), p. 57.

6. See R. Buckley, Problemas formales de la novela contempo-
    ránea (Barcelona: Ed. Península, 1968), pp. 81-138.

7. Ibid., p. 99.

8. Ibid., p. 138.

9. Guillermo Díaz-Plaja, La creación literaria en España (1966-
    1967) (Madrid: Ed. Aguilar, 1968), p. 294.

10. Guillermo and Hernández, La novelística española de los años
    60 (New York: E. Torres, 1970), p. 107; see also
    pp. 91-107 for their penetrating analysis of Cinco horas
    con Mario.

11. F. Olmos García, "La novela y los novelistas españoles de
    hoy," Cuadernos Americanos, vol. 22, no. 4 (July-Aug.
    1963), 222.

12. M. Delibes, "Notas sobre la novela española contemporánea,"
    Cuadernos del Congreso por la libertad, no. 63 (Aug.
    1962), 36-7.

13. Vásquez and Kosoff, "Introduction" to Delibes' El Camino
    (New York: Holt, Rinehart & Winston, 1960), p. xi.

14. Ibid., p. vii.

15. Ibid.

16. F. Tola de Habich and P. Grieve, Los españoles y el boom
    (Caracas: Ed. Tiempo Nuevo, 1971), pp. 133-6.

17. Alonso de los Ríos, Conversaciones con Miguel Delibes (Ma-
    drid: Ed. EMESA, 1971), pp. 158-9.

18. Ibid., p. 135.

19. Díaz, Miguel Delibes, p. 150.

20. Miguel Delibes, Parábola del náufrago (Barcelona: Ed. Des-
    tino, 1969), p. 26. All page references in this chapter
    are to this edition.

21. Díaz, Miguel Delibes, p. 170, footnote 5.

22. S. Sanz Villanueva, Tendencias de la novela española actual
    (Madrid: Cuadernos para el diálogo, 1971), p. 130.

23. G. Sobejano, Novela española de nuestro tiempo (Madrid: Ed.
    Prensa española, 1970), p. 163.

24. Díaz, Miguel Delibes, p. 158.

25. J. Corrales Egea, La novela española actual (Madrid: Cua-
    dernos para el diálogo, 1971), p. 216.

26. Francisco Umbral, Miguel Delibes (Madrid: Ed. ESPESA,
    1970), pp. 49-50.

27. Joaquín Marco, Nueva literatura de España y América (Barcelona: Ed. Lumen, 1972), p. 125.

28. A. Iglesias Laguna, Treinta años de novela española (1938-1968) (Madrid: Ed. Prensa Española, 1970), p. 275.

29. J. M. Martínez-Cachero, La novela española entre 1939 y 1969 (Madrid: Ed. Castalia, 1973), p. 226.

30. Díaz, Miguel Delibes, p. 152.

31. J. Domingo, La novela española del siglo XX (Barcelona: Ed. Labor, 1973), vol. 2, p. 55.

32. Díaz, Miguel Delibes, p. 158.

33. E. Entrambasaguas, "Estudio crítico y biográfico de Miguel Delibes," Las mejores novelas españolas contemporáneas (Barcelona: Ed. Planeta, 1971), p. 41.

34. J. Domingo, "Una Parábola de Miguel Delibes," Insula, vol. 24 (Dec. 1969), 7.

35. Umbral, Miguel Delibes, p. 49.

36. Sobejano, Novela española, p. 163.

37. Sanz Villanueva, Tendencias, p. 130.

38. Marco, Nueva literatura, p. 126.

39. Corrales Egea, La novela española actual, pp. 218-9.

40. "Interview with Miguel Delibes," ABC (Madrid), March 13, 1970, p. 8 (no author was cited).

41. De los Ríos, Conversaciones, pp. 99, 99-101.

42. Díaz, Miguel Delibes, p. 34.

43. "Interview," ABC, p. 8.

44. Entreambasaguas, Las mejores novelas, p. 41.

45. Domingo, "Una Parábola de M. Delibes," Insula, p. 7.

46. Díaz, Miguel Delibes, pp. 154-5.

47. López Martínez, La novelística, pp. 193-4.

48. Díaz, Miguel Delibes, p. 153.

49. Díaz, Miguel Delibes, pp. 153-4.

50. Ibid.

51. Vicente Horia, "El mal mayor: en Ernst Jurger y Miguel Delibes," Estafeta Literaria, no. 451 (Sept. 1, 1970), 45.

52. Isaac Montero, "Un libro insólito y vivo; Parábola," Cuadernos para el Diálogo, no. 77 (Feb. 1970), 46.

53. Leo Hickey, Cinco horas con Miguel Delibes (Madrid: Ed. Prensa Española, 1967), p. 307.

54. Antonio R. de las Heras, "Escritores al habla: M. Delibes," ABC (Madrid), March 13, 1970, supplement, p. 2.

CHAPTER 19

1. See Rafael Bosch, La novela española del siglo XX (New York: Las Americas, 1970), vol. 2, pp. 170-1 for his reviews of Grosso's Germinal, Testa de copo and El capirote.

2. J. Ignacio Ferreras, Tendencias de la novela española actual 1931-1969 (Paris: Ed. Hispanoamericanas, 1970), p. 187.

3. J. Corrales Egea, La novela española actual (Madrid: Cuadernos para el Diálogo, 1971), p. 69.

4. F. Olmos García, "La novela y los novelistas españoles de hoy," Cuadernos Americanos, vol. 22, no. 4 (July-Aug. 1963), 217.

5. Ibid.

6. Ibid., p. 232.

7. Joaquín Marco, Nueva literatura en España y América (Barcelona: Ed. Lumen, 1972), p. 81.

8. F. de Tola de Habich and P. Grieve, Los españoles y el boom (Caracas: Ed. Nuevo Tiempo, 1971), pp. 185-6.

9. J. M. Martínez Cachero, La novela española entre 1939 y 1969 (Madrid: Ed. Castalia, 1973), p. 256.

10. Ibid., p. 256; see footnote.

11. J. Domingo, La novela española del siglo XX (Barcelona: Ed. Labor, 1973), vol. 2, pp. 114-5.

12. J. Domingo, "Del realismo crítico a la nueva novela," Insula (Madrid), no. 290 (Jan. 1971), 5.

13. Ibid.

14. Ibid.

15. Consult Domingo's article, "Del realismo," for a particularly good outline of this novel's somewhat confusing plot.

16. Ibid.

17. A. Grosso, Guarnición de silla (Barcelona: Ed. Seix Barral, 1971), p. 160. Further page references are to this edition.

18. Domingo, "Del realismo," Insula, 5.

19. See Guillermo Díaz-Plaja's review of Inés Just Coming, in Cien libros españoles (Madrid: Ed. Anaya, 1971), pp. 222-4, for his explanation of Grosso's style.

20. S. Sanz Villanueva, Tendencias de la novela española actual (Madrid: Ed. Cuadernos para el diálogo, 1971), p. 171.

21. Ibid., p. 172.

CHAPTER 20

1. J. M. Carrascal, Groovy (Barcelona: Ed. Destino, 1973), p. 161. Further references are to this edition.

2. J. Domingo, "Narrativa española: La rueda de los premios," Insula, no. 318 (May 1973), 7.

3. J. W. Díaz, "Spanish Literary Prizes," Hispania, vol. 56 (Sept. 1973), 723.

4. Ibid.

5. Domingo, "Narrativa española," Insula, 7.

6. George Gissing, quotation from The Private Papers of Henry Ryecroft (1903) vol. 1, p. 16, as found in Bartlett's Quotations (Boston: Little, Brown, 1955), pp. 774-5.

7. The New York Times reported in July 1974, that General Francisco Franco was suffering from phlebitis and internal hemorrhaging. For two weeks he had all political powers transferred to his designated successor, Prince Juan Carlos de Borbón. Though Franco regained his health and with it, his executive powers, many political observers feel that, like Juan Perón (who died in Buenos Aires in June 1974), the end of an era (35 years of "peace") is quite near.

CHAPTER 21

1. Fernando Moran, Novela y semidesarrollo (Madrid: Ed. Taurus, 1971), pp. 319-20.

2. Ibid. , p. 369.

3. Ibid. , pp. 419-20.

4. Ibid. , p. 309.

5. José Domingo, "Narrativa española: Estilo y testimonio," Insula, no. 328 (Mar. 1974), 7.

6. Robert Sheehan, "Review of San Camilo 1936," Hispania, vol. 55, no. 2 (May 1972), 387.

7. See José Domingo, "Narrativa española: Problemática religiosa e histórica," Insula, no. 294 (May 1971), 5.

8. J. Domingo, "Narrativa española: Estilo y testimonio," Insula, no. 328 (Mar. 1974), 7.

9. José Domingo, "Narrativa española: Nóvisimos, nuevos y renovados," Insula, no. 306 (Mar. 1973), 20.

10. José Domingo, "Del hermetismo al barroco: Benet y Grosso,"

Insula, no. 320-321 (July-Aug. 1973), 20.

11. José Domingo, "Narrativa española: Del realismo a la nueva novela," Insula, no. 290 (Jan. 1971), 5.

12. George R. McMurray, "The Hispanic World: Literary Prizes in Mexico," Hispania, vol. 57, no. 2 (May 1974), 358.

13. J. Domingo, "Del hermetismo al barroco," Insula, no. 320-321 (July-Aug. 1973), 20.

14. Pablo Gil Casado, La novela social española (1920-1971), 2d ed. (Barcelona: Ed. Seix Barral, 1973), p. 505.

15. This critique and those that immediately follow were taken from the dust-jacket of the English translation of Juan Goytisolo's Reivindicación del Conde don Julián, i.e., Count Julian, translated by Helen R. Lane (New York: Viking, 1974), 205 pages.

16. Carlos Fuentes, "Review of 'Count Julian'," New York Times Book Review, May 5, 1974, pp. 5-7.

17. Ibid., p. 6.

18. Manuel Durán, "Vindicación de Juan Goytisolo y 'Reivindicación del Conde don Julián'," Insula, no. 290 (Mar. 1971), 1-2.

19. Blurb from the dust-jacket of the English translation, Count Julian (see note 15).

CHAPTER 22

1. Charles L. King, "Review of 'La saga/fuga de JB'," Books Abroad (Oklahoma), vol. 48, no. 1 (Winter 1974), 103.

2. James Abbot, "Review of Francisco Umbral's 'Memorias de un niño de derechos'," Books Abroad (Oklahoma), vol. 47, no. 4 (Autumn 1973), 233.

3. Ana María Novales, in her recent book, Cuatro novelistas españoles: Delibes, Aldecoa, Sueiro, Umbral (Madrid: Ed. Fundamentos, 1974), presents the only serious and extended study of Umbral's writing career to date. She examines, in detail, the following novels: Balada de gamberros, Travesía de Madrid, Las europeas, El Gioconda and Los males sagrados, and discusses others.

4. John Rozier, "Notes and News: Emory Professor Wins Top Award," Hispania, vol. 57, no. 1 (Mar. 1974), 157.

5. See A. Iglesias Laguna, Literatura de España día a día (Madrid: Ed. Nacional, 1972), pp. 307-11 for the complete review of Las hermanas coloradas.

6. José Domingo, La novela española del siglo XX (Barcelona: Ed. Labor, 1973), vol. 2, p. 85.

7. Fuentes, La nueva novela hispanoamericana (Mexico: Ed. Mortiz, 1969), 98 pages.

8. Interview with Ana María Matute in Sitges, Spain, August 6, 1968.

9. Domingo, La novela, vol. 2, p. 59.

10. Ibid., p. 136.

11. Ibid., p. 120.

12. Ibid., p. 38.

13. Ramón Buckley, Problemas formales de la novela española contemporánea (Barcelona: Ed. Península, 1968), pp. 183-6.

14. Domingo, La novela, vol. 2, p. 161.

15. See Laguna, Literatura (note 5), pp. 259-64 for a complete review of Trulock's Inventario base.

16. Domingo, La novela, vol. 2, p. 147.

17. José Domingo, "Narrativa española: Novísimos, nuevos y renovados," Insula, no. 306 (Mar. 1973), 6.

18. See Rafael Conte's Prologue in Manuel Andújar's Vísperas (1970), entitled "El realismo simbólico de M. Andújar."

19. Fuentes, La nueva novela, pp. 17-20.

20. Ibid., p. 80.

21. Rafael Bosch, La novela española del siglo XX (New York: Las Américas, 1970), vol. 2, p. 369.

22. Guillermo Díaz-Plaja, La creación literaria española, 1966-1967 (Madrid: Ed. Aguilar, 1968), p. 438.

23. The following are all from the New York Times except nos. 4 and 7: (1) Richard Eder, Magazine (Sunday), Aug. 27, 1972, pp. 8-10; (2) Henry Giniger, Aug. 3, 1972, p. 3; (3) Giniger, Oct. 10, 1972, p. 38; (4) Time Magazine, Dec. 11, 1972, pp. 55-7; (5) Giniger, Mar. 2, 1974, p. 1; (6) editorial, Mar. 4, 1974, p. 46; (7) Washington Post, Apr. 19, 1974, p. 26; (8) Eder, Mar. 11, 1974, p. 25; (9) editorial, Aug. 22, 1974, p. 22; (10) Tom Wicker, analysis, June 4, 1974, p. 44; and (11) Wicker, news analysis, June 7, 1974, p. 35.

24. Tom Wicker, "Spain on the Brink," New York Times, June 7, 1974, p. 35.

25. Juan Goytisolo, "Writing in an Occupied Language," New York Times Book Review, guest editorial, Mar. 31, 1974, p. 47.

26. Ibid.

27.   Ramón Buckley, "Del realismo social al realismo dialéctico,"
      Insula, no. 326 (Jan. 1974), 1-4.

28.   "Encuesta: Nueva literatura española: Castellet, Gimferrer,
      Ríos," Plural (Mexico) (Oct. 1973), 20-5.

29.   J. Martínez-Cachero, La novela española entre 1939-1969
      (Barcelona: Ed. Castalia, 1973), pp. 245-53.

30.   Marco, Nueva literatura en España y América (Barcelona:
      Ed. Lumen, 1972); see pp. 73-151.

31.   See Montero, "Los premios: 30 años de falsa fecundidad,"
      Cuadernos para el diálogo, vol. 14 (May 1969), 1-15.

32.   Sueiro, "Silencio y crisis de la joven novela española,"
      Revista de la Universidad de México, vol. 23, no. 596,
      30-6.

33.   G. Sobejano, Novela de nuestro tiempo (Madrid: Ed. Prensa
      Española, 1970), p. 460.

34.   Borges on Writing, ed. Giovanni, Halperin and McShane (New
      York: Dutton, 1973), pp. 164-5.

Appendix

STYLISTIC ANALYSIS OF LITERARY PASSAGES

This Appendix intends to provide additional revelations (wherever possible) about the style and thematic considerations of each writer through a detailed analysis of a choice exemplary passage by the novelist in the French manner of <u>explication de texte</u>.

Each of the following passages was chosen because it is typical of the novelist's literary style and production. After a serious reading of the text, I will try to (1) situate the passage in its context, (2) define its general character, (3) describe its structure, (4) analyze it in detail, and (5) sum up my conclusions.

CELA and LA COLMENA

La mañana.

Entre sueños, Martín oye la vida de la ciudad despierta. Se está a gusto escuchando, desde debajo de las sábanas, con una mujer viva al lado, viva y desnuda, los ruidos de la ciudad, su alborotador latido: los carros de los traperos que bajan de Fuencarral y de Chamartín, que suben de las Ventas y de las Injurias, que vienen desde el triste, desolado paisaje del cementerio y que pasaron--caminando desde hace y varias horas bajo el frío-- al lento, entristecido remolque de un flaco caballo, de un burro gris y como preocupado. Y las voces de las vendedoras que madrugan, que van a levantar sus puestecillos de frutas en la calle del General Porlier. Y las lejanas, inciertas primeras bocinas. Y los gritos de los niños que van al colegio, con la cartera al hombro y la tierna, olorosa merienda en el bolsillo ... [p. 221].

This highly descriptive passage begins Chapter Six of Cela's
novel. Its theme is the arrival of morning. The protagonist,
Martín Marco is lying in bed in a brothel with Purita. He has
just awakened to the early morning sounds of the city. The text
generally purports to describe the awakening of a gigantic metropolis in the manner of Dos Passos, Galsworthy, Balzac or Proust.
Its perspective is panoramic. We see and hear how the city
awakens in the morning from near and from far. Structurally, we
proceed from the closest point, Martín's bed, into the street area
near the brothel, and then to the outskirts of the city where Martín
can hear the early sounds of automobile horns and in the distance,
the gentle cries of school children on their way to the colegio. It
is essentially a visual portrait, proceeding from one room and
widening into a panoramic view of Madrid.

This passage is typical of Cela's narrative prose style. It
is essentially descriptive but borders on the lyrical because of its
building of images. It begins first, with shorter sentences, then
longer ones which have a cumulative effect in creating this wide,
panoramic view. The senses are also of vital importance to Cela.
Martín hears the noises of the city, feels the presence of his bed
partner and although he does not see for himself the images he describes in his own thoughts, Cela makes them come alive for us--
los carros de los traperos (the junkman's cart), un flaco caballo (a
sagging horse), un burro gris (a gray donkey), vendedores que
madrugan (early-rising vendors), puestecillos de frutas (small fruit
stands), las calles de Fuencarral, Chamartín, Porlier, (particular
Madrid streets), los colegiales con cartera al hombro, olorosa
merienda en el bolsillo (kids carrying their briefcases with their
lunches tucked inside). In short, Cela chooses the most realistic
details about daily life in Madrid and the city pulsates for us.

Cela's style is visual; he relies heavily on adjectives:
burro gris, olorosa merienda. There is a certain prolongation of
sentences which describe: los carros ... que bajan..., que
suben..., que vienen or Y las voces ... Y las lejanas ... Y los
gritos.... These sentences give his style a certain lingering, run-
on quality and a naturalness in his storytelling. Cela is not given
to any other "stylistic features" here except straightforward narration. His vocabulary is extremely concrete and he prefers to use
words that give a feeling for local color--for example, the diminu-
tive puestecillo instead of puesto. For a Realist description of this
type, Cela's choice of words is very proper. He does not intend
to be very expressive but his choice of words does reveal his attitudes toward the external world. His world is gray, sad, and pessimistic, like Martín's. Note the following images: El triste
desolado paisaje and entristecido remolque de un flaco caballo and
un burro gris. Cela generally favors a kind of gray imagery on
the level of universals in the manner of the novels of Dos Passos.

Most striking is an expressive rhythm that builds cumula-
tively, but not quite to a crescendo, in this particular passage.
This particular text is also quite harmonious. Cela uses the present

tense exclusively to give us a feeling of presentness, a kind of
spontaneity and the idea of multiple actions proceeding with a kind
of simultaneity and flowing.   Ideas are subordinated to images.
The author also stands apart from the text.   His aim is to present
the arrival of morning as Martín Marco sees, hears and feels it,
nothing more.   The pervading tone of the passage is not joyous,
but rather sad and the author's coldness in his description is felt
because of his complete detachment from the scene.   The images
themselves are on the level of abstractions (universals).   Every
citizen of Madrid could conjure images such as the ones Cela has
so aptly caught pictorically, sensitively for us of the sights and
sounds, the arrival of morning in Madrid.

        Summing up, this passage is typical of Cela's descriptive
technique.   It was wholly conceived in the tradition of the Realist
novel (a style from which the author originally intended to depart).
Cela pinpoints the essences of the "awakening" experience on this
particular morning in Madrid or of any large city (which was his
original intent).   His prose is rhythmic, his images keen, his use
of language, sharp, terse, colloquial, colorful (and even colorless)
in this passage.   His detachment from the scene is evident, but
his evocation of this particular morning contains a certain degree
of sadness in its perspective and a kind of majesty or boldness of
vision.   This vision has enhanced Cela's career as a new Realist
writer, still in the tradition of the nineteenth century but aesthetically tempered with a new coldness or "clinical objectivity."
Morning is seen in small snapshots that when placed together form
the entire panorama of a wide-angle shot of Madrid's skyline.   It
is this panorama that Cela unfolds in the best tradition of the
Realist writers but with a vital, rhythmic style.

GIRONELLA and LOS CIPRESES CREEN EN DIOS

        Los hijos no estaban.   Don Santiago Estrada comprendió.
Su esposa estaba en cama; no le dio tiempo a vestirse.   Sintió
unos brazos forzudos, los de Blasco, que la empujaban hacia el
pasillo, escaleras abajo, que la introducían en un coche junto a su
esposo.   Don Santiago Estrada y ella se miraron y cada uno leyó
en el otro el miedo absoluto.   Todo ocurría con sencillez abru-
madora, en el silencio de la noche: el chirriar de los neumáticos,
la sensación de frío, los empujones hacia la pared en la que adi-
vinaban nichos, el vago temblor de unos cipreses, pisadas, ruido
de cerrojos, el abrazo mutuo, una descarga y la muerte [p. 843].

This passage indicates Gironellas' excellent narrative powers. It deals with the death of an aristocrat, Don Santiago, as the Anti-Fascist Revolutionary Committee is in the process of executing, without trial, many of the landed gentry of Gerona near the conclusion of the novel. Typical of the last few chapters, this passage narrates the death of one of the minor but well-known characters with whom the Alvear family is acquainted.

In general, Gironella's prose is dramatic, straight-forward, realistic and in this particular passage, poetically bleak. It is extremely cinematic as well. Structurally, this section has a characteristic rhythm of three to four beats (syllables) at its shortest and nine to twelve beats at its largest phase of the narrative. For example,

$$\begin{array}{ccccccc} 1 & 2 & 3 & 1 & 2 & 3 & 1 \end{array}$$
Los hijos no estaban. / Don Santiago comprendió. /Su

$$\begin{array}{cc} 2 & 3 \end{array}$$
esposa estaba en cama....

The internal rhythm of the passage is so well calibrated that it sets the tone for the final, quick shots that bring death to Don Santiago and his wife. Gironella purposely shows no emotion, leaving himself out of the scene completely. This scene consists mainly of a compilation of a series of images, brought to a crescendo and final resolution while mixing the senses--note how everything occurred with phantom-like simplicity and in the silence of the night --the sound of pneumatic drills, the feeling of cold, the sight of vague trembling of the cypress trees, the sound of clicking hammers of the guns, a mutual embrace (feeling) and death (the final shade).

Gironella avoids most literary devices and utilizes a clear, concise prose, in a journalistic style, reinforced by his use of concrete vocabulary. In fact, Gironella's sense of reporting historical events intrudes heavily into relating the fictional experiences of his characters. The prose is indistinguishable in both cases, creating harmonious effects in the estimation of some critics and a disparaging one to others who are searching for an "artistic style," complete with expressive words, literary devices, revelations about his craft and himself. If one is to judge Gironella's writing style as such, it emanates from the concise prose of a journalist (like Ernest Hemingway) and expresses itself as typically Gironellian with the themes, imagery and rhythm characteristic only of his personal style.

In this passage, Gironella's words are deliberately unexpressive, but the experience of death is portrayed in universal images. He sees the external world as passive and portrays it objectively. His images are bleak and here particularly, there is intentional rhythmic monotony that leads us to the climax (of death). Nevertheless, the passage, with its monotonous tone, engages us with its harmonious effects, since even the blend of imperfect tenses (which describe) and preterite tenses (which present single, conclusive actions) is used with particular skill. Gironella's narration achieves dramatic value because of this interplay of description and action. The single idea of paramount importance is how death is met by this particular family, the Estradas. The tone of the passage and similar scenes throughout the novel is one of pervading, relentless, countless and undisputed tragedy. Gironella is successful in keeping his reader's interest alive despite the repetition of similar scenes.

The analysis of the cited passage conclusively proves Gironella's intentional use of nineteenth-century Realism to explicate his fictional and historical premises in Cypresses. It shows Gironella's individual, simple, journalistic prose superseding the grandiose style of Dickens or a Balzac. One can appreciate Gironella's terseness, honesty and sincerity in creating a harrowing scene and portraying it in a cool, cold manner. Gironella also has his own keenly dramatic, lyrical sense, which can readily be appreciated by the rhythmic and poetic tone he sets in this particular passage. He also shows himself throughout Cypresses to be unaffected by the stylistic innovations of many of his fellow New Wave writers, preferring simplicity of style, an intriguing plot, readily identifiable characters (almost stereotypes) but mostly, a panorama.

Like Balzac, Dickens and Galdós, Gironella can create (and destroy) his own world. Gironella may not be the intellectual equal of these three great writers, but his attempt to do something new with still censorable, fairly intractable material and his intention to write his own Episodios nacionales (National Episodes) in the manner of Pérez Galdós (to chronicle Spain from 1931 to the present day) is admirable as well as commercially profitable for one of the few writers in Spain who makes his career as a continuer of the anachronistic Realist school. Gironella has garnered a popular reputation and his career is an international success story. Although Spanish letters must await Gironella's ultimate evaluation, it is undeniable that he is a writer of paramount importance and one to be observed very closely in the near future.

QUIROGA and ALGO PASA EN LA CALLE

Lo deseó con todas sus fibras, fieramente:

"Que sea un niño. Quiero un niño."

Se abandonaba contra Froilán. Por primera vez desde que estaba casada se dio cuenta que no se trataba de muñecos de carne, nacidos de un momento fugaz, sino de seres humanos que llegaban desde nuestra infancia, desde nuestra vida, cuajados en un momento.

"Será el ser más feliz del mundo. Todo lo que yo no he tenido...."

"Quiero ser madre," pensó porque esta vez iba a ser otra cosa.

La vida. La vida pequeña yendo de ella a aquel incipiente ser humano. Eso era lo que ella daba, no la muerte [p. 178].

This passage demonstrates, in a more conventional manner, Elena Quiroga's highly realistic, yet emotional and lyrical style of writing. It expresses Agatha's realization of her need for a child after the accidental death of her father. It consists of a series of thoughts and descriptions of these thoughts in relationship to her husband Froilán. The passage appears near the end of the novel after Agatha has had several hours to meditate upon the death of her father and the meaning of death and life. Stylistically it is not terribly innovative since it reveals through the use of monologue (not necessarily always interior), her random thoughts expressed directly to the reader about her need for life, love and a child. Quiroga's language is simple, unadorned prose, charged somewhat emotionally but not very colorful or thrilling. In fact, it is rather gray prose lacking imagery. A more innovative passage demonstrating her skill as a Realist writer is the following:

--¿Tú te das cuenta de lo que estás haciendo? Muchacha...

(Hueles a otra mujer. Deseas a otra mujer. Te has negado--amiga de Esperanza, volver a empezar--y vienes a mi desde ella. No importa. Estás humillado porque te has negado.... En lo oscuro estaba yo, sin saber por qué. En lo oscuro, con la fragancia de la noche entrando por la ventana.... Oh no tomas nada que no hayas tomado ya. No dudes. No temas.)

La apartó un poco de sus labios.

--¿Te das cuenta?

Presencia dijo:

--Sí [p. 196].

Presencia is thinking about her romance with Ventura, reliving this dialogue in a half-remembered flashback, half-thought interior monologue. Ventura is dead and Presencia mulls over the past as she awaits the burial of her lover. Quiroga uses poetic prose to describe the sensual nature of their relationship. The underlined (italicized) dialogue represents Ventura's words, remembered by Presencia. "Do you realize what you are doing, girl?" and later, "Do you realize?" In the parentheses, Quiroga describes Presencia's feelings towards Ventura, her former teacher and now lover: "You smell another woman. You desire another woman. You've denied yourself.... It doesn't matter. You're humiliated because you denied yourself. I was in the darkness without knowing why--in the darkness with the fragrance of the night entering through the window--Oh, you're not taking anything that you might not have already taken. Don't doubt it. Don't be afraid!" Presencia gives herself sexually to Ventura and the chapter ends on a vital note suddenly counterpointed by the novel's final chapter which deals strictly with Ventura's burial.

Elena Quiroga writes extremely well. She has a very good ear and a sense of poetic language, especially where her portraits of women and their feelings are concerned. Her language is halting, dramatic. Her short sentences punctuate the atmosphere with truths that demonstrate a particular female sensibility. She states exactly the right words, expressing her protagonist's feeling most artfully if laconically.

Quiroga's main strength as a writer is to develop characters and relationships through their thoughts, monologues and dialogues. She has succeeded in mastering feminine psychology and as this passage indicates, she has lyrically expressed the "feeling" states of her characters. Her unadorned prose is definitely a departure from the journalistic style of Gironella and the colloquial Realism of Cela. Quiroga has succeeded in imparting a level of emotion, feeling and warmth to the contemporary Spanish novel, humanizing it. She is the first New Wave writer to lead the Spanish novel in this direction.

FERNANDEZ SANTOS and LOS BRAVOS

Se detuvo al borde del agua y empezó a beber pausadamente, hasta hartarse. Quedó con la boca abierta, como en espera de un invisible bocado, mirando a la otra orilla. El agua bajaba templada, plagada de insectos y restos de hierba en los remansos. Se adelantó y fue introduciendo el cuerpo en la corriente, hasta mojar el vientre; luego dio una vuelta completa sobre sí, gozándose en aquel placer repentino. De nuevo en la orilla se estremeció con violencia y miró hacia los puertos. Aunque él no las veía, allí estaban las montañas azules, nítidas, con el sol próximo al ocaso proyectando largas sombras sobre cada aguja, cada cresta, sin la más pequeña nube cubriendo sus cumbres....

Se echó a un lado y emprendió un trote corto por la cuesta hasta entrar en el pueblo; le vino el olor de los hombres, olor a

humo y voces. En el portal de la primera casa dos niños juga-
ban.... El mayor le dijo: "toma"....

    Le silbó quedo, y él fue más allá con el vientre pegado al
suelo, rozando la hierba.

    --Toma, toma [pp. 91-2].

    This descriptive, lyrical passage is situated in the middle
of Los bravos and deals essentially, with a dog, not a man, drinking water and playing by a river. It is immediately striking because the scene begins with a series of actions. The protagonist
seems to have a human perspective; "he" looks at the mountains,
enters the water, etc.; then one realizes it is a "dog" that is living the realities of this passage. F. Santos carefully avoids identify-
ing the protagonist here but lets the reader continually search for
his identity, anticipate who the character is as the actions of the
dog are revealed. He utilizes a very important writing technique,
going from the ambiguous to the concrete. The character's identity is fragmented, mysteriously withheld and then is generally revealed.

    F. Santos is careful to present excellent but sober descriptions
of nature intermingled with dialogues that give certain clues until
suddenly, two pages later, the identity of the protagonist is discovered. This is a very long passage. The vocabulary of this
text is replete with images of nature. Sentences are short, full
of images and actions. For the reader, the drama of F. Santos'
prose builds because one is constantly wondering who it is one is
reading about and what his relationship is to the plot. Sentences
contain objective statements, generally in the preterite and imperfect tenses. Their staccato pace gives the passage a dramatic
rhythm with its collection of concrete, objective images.

    Another passage typical of F. Santos' style shows his use of
cinematic elision in the following manner:

    Los truenos se sucedían, prolongando su estrépito sobre las
nubes, y un grato olor a tierra húmeda se esparcía en el aire.
El médico pensó: "Ozono," y dejó vagar la mirada por las juntas
de piedra verdinegra.

         * * *

    La difusa claridad que acompaña a la lluvia invadió suave-
mente el corral, al tiempo que el rumor de la lluvia hacía salir a
Amparo. Miró el cielo y calculó que tendrían lluvia para una
hora ... [pp. 152-3].

At the end of one scene (or chapter), the doctor is caught in a
rainstorm in Alfredo's house. The rain serves as the link between

this scene and the next one (separated by asterisks) in which Amparo is trying to leave her home enroute to the cantina. F. Santos
has created a simple montage of words, using the image of rain
as a film director would provide continuity or a smooth cinematic
transition between scenes. These passages are fairly typical of
F. Santos' style and give an accurate idea of additional perspectives
in the stylistic refurbishing of the Spanish novel because of Santos'
variations of Spanish Realism.

SANCHEZ FERLOSIO and EL JARAMA

Tito miraba el torso asténico de Santos, cuando éste se hubo sa-
cado la camisa:

--¡Qué blanquito!

--Claro, vosotros vais a las piscinas. Yo nunca tengo
tiempo. Va a ser la primera vez que me chapuzo este verano.

--Pues yo tampoco no te creas que habré ido más de un
par de veces o tres. Lo que pasa es que tengo el piel morena de
por mí. Tú te vas a poner como un cangrejo, ya lo verás.

--Ya, si por eso quería yo el albornoz. Mucho sol no me
conviene el primer día [p. 34].

This passage is typical of the conversations between most
of the young group of Madrileños, sunning themselves at the beginning of the novel. Description is held to a minimum and what is
seen by the characters is usually described by the author. When
Santos took off his shirt, Tito could not help but exclaim how pale
Santos was. The young men talk quickly, using generally accepted
colloquialisms like me chapuzo ("It's going to be the first time I
duck into the water this summer"). They discuss only superfici-
alities--"you're skin is darker than mine ... you'll broil like a
crab ... that's why I wanted a cloak ... too much sun the first
day doesn't suit me. " The striking quality about this dialogue and
most others throughout the novel is its banality. Reading El Jarama is like reading a scrupulously transcribed tape recording,
despite the author's claim of objectivism and his supposed portrayal
of "vulgarity. " Apart from some lively descriptions of nature, S.
Ferlosio's dialogues (and their banality) are the chief stylistic feature of the novel with special attention given to Madrileñan slang.

His use of vocabulary is extraordinary. Slang is used
abundantly. One concludes one of the author's special interests is
capturing conventional reality through a rigorous application of linguistic principles. The author is obviously fascinated by slang and
abundantly sprinkles it throughout his characters' conversations.

Imagery appears only in descriptions of nature. His dialogues per-
sist with a rhythmic monotony of everyday chatter and are devoid
of any ideas of much importance, in keeping with his view of with-
holding his own insights and opinions from the novel. S. Ferlosio
makes no attempt to influence the reader, only to report exactly
the conversations as he heard or imagined them. One never feels
S. Ferlosio's presence in the novel during the conversations between his characters. However one does experience the author on
rare occasions, when he describes nature. Note the following passage and the brilliant flash of description:

Desde el suelo veía la otra orilla, los páramos del fondo y

los barrancos ennegrecidos, donde la sombra crecía y avanzaba

invadiendo las tierras, ascendiendo las lomas, matorral a matorral,

hasta adensarse por completo; parda, esquiva y felina oscuridad,

que las sumía en acecho de alimañas. Se recelaba un sigilio de

zarpas, de garras y de dientes escondidos, una noche olfativa,

voraz y sanguinaria, sobre el pavor de indefensos encames mater-

nales; campo negro, donde el ojo de cíclope del tren brillaba

como el ojo de una fiera [p. 227].

Night is falling while Tito and Lucita are alone together
gazing at the banks of the river. Night shadows invade the land,
moving in a "feline" manner. Night itself appears like a wild animal, voracious, sanguine as a lone train moves through the mountains, its headlight of the locomotive compared to a cyclops, shin-
ing like a savage beast. It is only in a passage like this that one
can feel the author's presence in the novel--his mastery of description, his linguistic powers, his enormous sense of rhythm. But
this passage is atypical and rare in the novel. His description of
the onset of night is invested with so much life that even inanimate
objects retain a presence of beings or beasts. The passage is
dramatic, dynamic, striking, because the shadows of night have the
movement and presence of a clawing cat. The locomotive becomes
a giant cyclops. It is inconceivable that Tito and Lucita "see" the
onset of evening in such beautifully descriptive, literary images.
Night itself appears as a clawing, feline creature, illuminated by
the eye of a giant cyclops. These are striking metaphors, dramatically presented.

By employing a concrete vocabulary, S. Ferlosio makes use
of his imagery--his objects--los páramos, los barrancos, lomas,
tierras, matorrales, to conjure a beautiful, imaginative passage
describing nature which is so atypical of the novel. It is obvious
S. Ferlosio can write beautiful, descriptive passages and is a linguist of great capabilities. If only El Jarama had been more subjective in content than objective; if only S. Ferlosio had entered his
characters' minds and hearts more often and made his presence
felt. It is only in these rare, descriptive passages that one can

really appreciate S. Ferlosio's excellent poetic, metaphoric, symbolic prose. It is a pity there are too few of these passages in the novel. I have chosen it deliberately to demonstrate this writer's incredibly immense talent and fertility.

GOYTISOLO-GAY and LAS AFUERAS

--Señor....

--Encantado.

La segunda puerta sonó cortante, como un objeto que cae. Ciriaco se inclinó ante la ventanilla.

--Y perdonen lo de antes, ¿eh, mi alférez? No quise ofender. Pero es eso, creí que molestaba y, en fin, ya me entiende....

--Sí, sí.

--Pues nada, entonces, hasta el jueves...--dijo apartándose. Arrancaron. "Les espero," se oyó con el trepidar del motor. El coche partió calle arriba, adquiriendo en seguida velocidad.

--¡Qué liante!--resopló Nacho--. ¡Qué tío más pesado! Miro por la ventanilla de atrás. El limpiabotas aún seguía parado allá lejos, saludando con la mano.

--Lo que me gustaría es saber qué diablos hubieras hecho si él se guarda tu carnet. Yo no me hubiese arriesgado desde luego...--rió Nacho--. En fin, intentamos salvar lo que nos queda de noche. ¿Dónde vamos?

--Donde quieras.

--Donde quiera no, porque yo iría a un restorán, pero a estas horas ni hay que pensarlo. Podemos cenar a base de bocadillos. Para en el primer sitio que veas un poco decente.

--No. Por aquí, no. En las afueras ... [p. 117].

This passage, taken from Chapter Three, is a dialogue between Victor, the ex-soldier, Nacho, his friend and Ciriaco, Victor's former lieutenant. Victor and Nacho are saying good-bye to Ciriaco after spending many hours chatting with him at several local bars. During the few hours they were together, Ciriaco had insulted a gypsy guitarrist and at the beginning of this passage, he is apologizing to Victor and Nacho as the latter two men are getting into Victor's car to find some peace of mind in the early hours of the morning en las afueras, on the outskirts of the city.

Their conversation, is fast, colloquial, real, as if the author had transcribed a tape recording of them talking together. One feels Victor's and Nacho's desire to flee from Ciriaco and Victor's longing for tranquility and escape. One understands the compassion for the sad figure of Ciriaco waving good-bye to the other two men as Nacho knows intuitively the men will never see each other again despite the planned rendezvous for Thursday next. When Nacho sees Ciriaco's stationary figure through the back window, the reader feels certain of the hypocritical attitudes expressed by all three men when they take leave of each other. Their Thursday meeting will never come to pass.

Unlike Sánchez Ferlosio, Goytisolo adds more descriptive lines that narrate what his characters are doing and looking at, not just what they are saying. Goytisolo is, consequently, less objective and more of a traditional Realist, preferring to use external description when necessary, to present a fuller portrait of the characters and the events that shape their lives. This passage then, somewhat banal but realistic in its delineation of the characters and their problems, is typical of Goytisolo's best use of a realist-objectivist technique. Goytisolo has an excellent ear for dialogue and a unique sensitivity for drama to capture the nuances and the feelings between the lines and in the silences.

MATUTE and PRIMERA MEMORIA

Sobre el arco de la gran puerta dorada, que estaba abierta, había escudos de piedra y las cabezas de los cuatro evangelistas. Por encima de la cúpula de mosaicos verdes, arrancándoles un llamear dañino, estaba el sol, rojo y feroz en medio del cielo pálido. Y me dije: "Casi nunca es azul el cielo." Una cruel sensación de violencia, un irritado fuego ardía allá arriba: todo invadido, empapado, en aquella luz negra. En los batientes de la puerta relucían racimos de hierro. Dentro, la humedad negro-verdosa, como de pozo, se pegaba al cuerpo. En el enorme paladar de Santa María había algo como un solemne batir de alas. Y me dije si acaso en la oscuridad de los rincones andarían murciélagos, si habría ratas huyendo o persiguiéndose entre el oro de los retablos. También la casa de la abuela era sombría y sucia. (Se quejaba Antonio de que era demasiado grande para sólo dos mujeres y únicamente limpiaban las habitaciones habitadas.) Había telarañas y polvo en las porcelanas, la plata y la vajilla que regaló

el rey al bisabuelo, cuando se casó.   Y en la vitrina, en las re-
splandientes estatuillas de jade....   Y las flores.   (En la esca-
lerilla de piedra, donde yo solía sentarme, cuando Borja no me
quería llevar con ellos, tras la pared amarilla de la casa cubierta
de espesas madreselvas, se abrían los gladiolos rojos.)   Dentro
de Santa María, las fascinantes vidrieras de colores, estallaban
entre la negrura y el moho, altas y resplandecientes en la oscuridad, ávidamente lamidas por el sol.   Especialmente aquella, con
su delgado Santo de manos unidas y clavos en los pies.   Un rayo
de luminoso rojo caía al suelo, como una mancha de sangre.   Y
un destello del sol, igual que una mariposa de oro voló de un lado
a otro de la bóveda.   Mosén Mayol cantaba

--De-un Lau-da mus: te Dominum confi-te-mur ... [pp. 78-
80].

This narration is from part one, "The Descent," and is
Matía's description of her first visit to the Church of Santa María.
It is full of images, lyrical and dramatic because it contains words
that chisel the images Matía sees before her eyes--escudos de
piedra (escutcheons of stone), cúpula de mosaicos verdes (cupola of
green mosaics).   Matía feels the ferocity of the sun on the green
mosaics and compares it to a fire blazing above.   And conversely,
everything was steeped in "black light" (todo invadido, empapado
en aquella luz negra) which make one aware of Matía's forebodings
of evil.   She hears the fluttering of wings and believes there are
bats fleeing and chasing one another among the gold altar pieces.
Her mind quickly jumps to Doña Práxedes' home, where Antonia,
the maid, is complaining about its huge size for just two women
to live in.   These remarks, in present time, are in parentheses.
Her inspection of the church causes Matía to think about the cob-
webs and dust in Doña Práxedes' home.

Matute uses concrete language which objectifies her images.
She visualizes, for example, the porcelains, statues of jade and
the flowers.   After her thoughts of red gladiolas pass, she realizes she is still in the Church of Santa María, looking at the highly colored stained glass windows that metaphorically "exploded"
their color among the blackness and the mold, glass that was avid-
ly licked by the sun (lamidas por el sol).   "A ray of luminous light
fell on the ground like a bloodstain"--another example of Matute's
striking use of simile; "... and a flash of sunlight, just like a
gold butterfly, flew from one side of the vault to the other."

Matute is expert at creating brilliant similes and metaphors.
Her choice of images, her predilection for the theme of nature,
and her sympathetic responses to nature are revealed by her

constant use of natural phenomena to explain Matía's feelings.
There is also a special type of rhythm into which her readers are
swept: long, lyrical sentences, punctuated with short, fragmented
statements, half-sentences, images, interjections.   Matute-Matía's
ideas are linked by the visual, although there is a psychological
concomitant triggered visually by certain key colors or images.
In this case, the color black (or Matute's feeling about evil, decadence and corruption which arise contrarily while she is in a
church) leads to stimulation of Matía's memories of Doña Práxedes
and her home.

        Matute's style is best described as expressive, vital, flu-
ent, imprecise at times, but delicate, flowing, and realistic.   Although her use of intense interior monologues with flashbacks that
have all the reality of cinematic dream sequences is strong, yet
they seem fortuitous.   Matute is interested in revealing Matía's
thoughts to us, the mind of a fourteen-year-old adolescent girl, a
fearful child living with relatives on an isolated island.   Through
Matía, Matute gives us, perhaps, her own insights into her personal, adolescent world.   It is because of the alternating vagueness
and clarity of her perceptions or memory states, in the nuances
or shadows of her writing style, that Matute creates her own notion of reality.   Hers is a new world of Realism that is now fragmented and now reconstituted in order to achieve a kind of subjec-
tive-objective reality of the inexorable and yet evanescent feelings
of human consciences, past and present.

        This particular passage also demonstrates the elegiac tone
Matute achieves with her rememberances of time present and experience past.   It is ironic that Matía, unlike Monsignor Mayol,
cannot praise God or confide in him, since Primera memoria proves
to us, if anything, the spiritual emptiness in which Matía dwells.
Matute's writing understates this theme, but readers feel the implicit criticism of the church Matute has suggested here in this
passage.   In fact, it is to the reader's advantage to develop his
own personal notion of the world of Matía and not be explicitly
guided, but simply journey through suggestion, nuance and lyricism,
into the life and mind of Matute's characters.

SUEIRO and LA CRIBA

        Estaba muy cansado.   Agotado.   Volvió la cara hacia la
sombra, hacia el interior de la habitación.   Todos contemplaban al
niño y hablaban, dichosos, alegres.   Su mujer sonreía, hundida en
la almohada, boca arriba.   Le miró.

        Pensó entonces que deseaba respirar en la vida, abarcar en
un solo paso todos los pasos que aún tenía que dar de un lado a

otro, encontrar una mirada, un gesto, una palabra suya que re-
sumiesen y llenasen en aquel instante todas las palabras, todos
los gestos, todas las miradas que eran necesarias y que aún le
quedaban por cumplir a lo largo del tiempo. Lo pensó, mirándola,
mirándola a ella, mirándolos a todos y acercándose para ver a su
hijo, desde el fondo de una infinita tristeza, de una gran soledad,
de un gran silencio; desde el fondo de una inmensa y absoluta
angustia [p. 151].

   This passage is typical of the narrator's thoughts as Sueiro
presents them from his particular view in the third person singular.
The narrator's wife has just given birth (at the very end of Chapter Four) and "he" is visiting his wife just several hours after.
"He" is tired, worn out. Everyone present in his wife's hospital
room is jubilant about the birth; his wife is smiling. However,
rather than turn his thoughts to her, he begins to think only of
himself. If only he could sum up in his mind, in a word, feeling,
or gesture, everything he felt, the enormity of this experience
called birth, of his becoming a father, having a son. But instead,
"he" feels an infinite sadness, a great solitude and silence, an
immense and absolute anxiety to his very depths with which he
cannot reconcile.

   This passage is lyrical and descriptive and like the entire
novel, part of the author's re-creation of the thoughts of "everyman" or "anyman." Sueiro transmits to the reader "his" anxieties
quickly, easily, poetically, graphically. The passage begins somewhat monotonously, building steadily with single images and expands
gradually, dealing with the abstractions of birth (and resultant happiness). But normal or expectant reactions are subverted. Instead
of happiness, one are forced into the narrator's emptiness of spirit.
Sueiro builds expectations rhythmically, using infinitives (respirar,
abarcar) and gerunds (mirando, acercándose) and finally nouns
(soledad, silencio, angustia) to capture accurately the narrator's
pessimistic view of reality.

   The tone of this passage is gray, tragic, frustrating. Although Sueiro uses no special stylistic devices or imagery, his
ideas and rhythmic style are of great importance. They indicate
the narrator's willingness to deal with abstractions, beyond his ken
and Sueiro's turn of mind to make the "unexpressable" feelings
finitely expressable to his reading audience. Sueiro is a poignant
writer; his characters are pathetic. It is precisely the pathos and
delicacy of nature in counterpoint to crude reality that endears his
novel to me, a novel about the vulgarities and profanities of daily
experience from a uniquely artistic, sensitive and at times, lyrically beautiful point of view.

GARCIA HORTELANO and TORMENTA DE VERANO

Un brillo indeciso señalaba el mar. El camino, desde allí, bajaba en pronunciada pendiente hacia la aldea de los pescadores. Las huertas eran más escasas y pobres. Aspiré hondo el olor de la tierra húmeda. No muy lejos, se movió una luz, llevada por alguien que caminaba entre los bancales con un farol de petromax.
Aquella chica tendría familia. Hasta entonces no había reparado en ello. Seguramente contemplarla tan aislada en medio de la arena, bajo una sábana, o en la canasta, con aquel amanecer que daba un espesor de carne muerta a su piel, me había determinado a considerarla como un abjeto, que se sabe tuvo mucho valor. Pero era probable que viviesen sus padres, sus hermanos, incluso que hubiese tenido un hijo. Me recreaba morbosamente en inventarle una vida a la muchacha y decidí seguir andando. Aun así, continué pensando en ella y de una manera diferente hasta como entonces lo había hecho, porque, a partir de aquel momento, la muchacha poesía una especie de vida, una solidez o un valor, en mi memoria [pp. 76-7].

Although the novel is largely composed of dialogue, I have deliberately chosen this prose passage to analyze since it demonstrates G. Hortelano's ideas of sensuality and his protagonist's (Javier's) complex reflections on the nude, dead girl he had just seen hours before on the beach. Javier's anxiety to invent a life for the nude woman, his feeling that people are more than just material objects but have an "added dimension," and his excitement transporting him out of the state of boredom he experienced before the death of this unknown woman are all felt in this selection (from Chapter Eight). Just as each chapter in G. Hortelano's novel generally begins and ends with a prose description by Javier and is interspersed with dialogue in which Javier always participates, this passage is typically descriptive of our narrator's personal thoughts near the end of this chapter. G. Hortelano is good at describing nature in generalities--"un brillo indeciso ... el camino bajaba en pronunciada pendiente..." ("an indecisive (glimmering) light; the path dropped sharply") and its effect on Javier--"aspiré hondo el olor de la tierra húmeda" ("I breathed deeply the smell of the damp earth").

Javier then begins to think about "aquella chica muerta" ("that dead girl"). He begins to question himself (extensively using the conditional and imperfect subjunctives), wondering about her identity and striking the simile "aquel amanecer que daba un espesor

de carne muerta a su piel, me había determinado a considerarla
como un objeto que se sabe tuvo mucho valor" ("the early morning
light that gave her skin the weight of dead flesh, had led me to
think of her as an object, valuable once upon a time"). His imagination leads him to fill in a life for the dead woman--parents, a
possible child of her own--but what is more remarkable is Javier's
own idée fixe, his constant meditation about this dead woman which
seems to fill the void in the already "dead" life he is living in
Velas Blancas.

Although G. Hortelano's vocabulary is not terribly expressive and his ideas not exactly even awe-inspiring, his novel
achieves a certain measure of success because of the "naturalness"
of his writing, with its well-intentioned rhythmic monotony and its
pervading banal tone. Tormenta has a kind of objective realism
beyond El Jarama, since it presents at least one character's interior world (Javier's thoughts)--to the exclusion however of all
other protagonists. Javier is preoccupied with himself and his
own feelings (throughout the entire novel). He is the prism through
which the entire world of Velas Blancas is revealed to the reader.
It is a pity that his (or G. Hortelano's) powers of observation and
intellectual acumen could not transcend the vacuousness of the
world he wrote about in such superficial terms. G. Hortelano's
work is determinedly less "artistic" than his predecessors', but he
applies his simple, concise style to a simple, fairly common subject: the end result is a popular modern novel, a bit flat, like
tepid tea, but drinkable all the same. Tormenta de verano is neither the thrilling revelation of interior worlds nor the daring ex-
posé of Spain's Costa Brava society nor the fascinating social critique nor even the Harold Robbins-like potboiler it could have been.
It may have "... definite affinities with many contemporary works
on the theme of the daily apocalypse of Europes' guilt-ridden, sex
haunted post-war rich," as the blurb of the English translation may
suggest, but it falls far from the mark of great literature and
more into the realm of "detective story" with minor psychological
and stylistic pretensions. The previously cited passages are typical of the level of prose at one of the hero's most excited moments.

MARTIN-SANTOS and TIEMPO DE SILENCIO

Pedro se volvió hacia él interrumpiendo la búsqueda de
otras fuentes de simpatía ya que ésta, al parecer más decisiva,
con tan especial abundancia sobre él se derramaba.

--Así que usted ... (suposición capciosa y sorprendente)

--No. Yo no ... (refutación indignada y sorprendida)

--Pero no querrá usted hacerme creer que ... (hipótesis
inverosímil y hasta absurda)

--No, pero yo ... (reconocimiento consternado)

--Usted sabe perfectamente ... (lógica, lógica, lógica)

--Yo no he ... (Simple negativa a todas las luces insuficiente)

--Tiene que reconocer usted que ... (lógica)

--Pero ... (adversativa apenas si viable)

--Quiero que usted comprenda ... (cálidamente humano)

--No.

--De todos modos es inútil que usted ... (afirmación de superioridad basada en la experiencia personal de muchos casos)

--Pero ... (apenas adversativa con escasa convicción)

--Claro que si usted se empeña ... (posibilidad de recurrencia a otras vías abandonando el camino de la inteligencia y la amistosa comprensión)

--No, nada de eso ... (negativa alarmada)

--Así que estamos de acuerdo ... (superación del apenas aparente obstáculo)

--Bueno ... (primer peligroso de reconocimiento)

--Perfectamente. Entonces usted ... (triunfal)

--¿Yo? ... (horror ante las deducciones imprevistas)

--¡¡Ya me estoy cansando!! [p. 169]

Of the many passages used to describe Martín-Santos' style, I have chosen this particular one as typical because of his use of parenthetical remarks. It is a dialogue between Pedro and the police investigator, Similiano. Its chief strength is that it shows the inability and failure of using language to communicate the truth of the situation. (Pedro is not guilty of performing an abortion which resulted in Florita's death.) The passage is dominated by both Pedro's and the inspector's preconceptions, the latter believing Pedro is guilty before the young medical student can answer the charges. Both men become grotesque marionettes who neither listen to nor reason with each other because of their preconceptions.

The style of this passage may be called exemplary of the Baroque period since the dialogue (which forms the conclusions of the forty-first fragment or section of the book) is overloaded with silences and parenthetical descriptions, characterizing the meaning behind each phrase uttered by the characters. Pedro is not guilty of any crime, but after his talk with Similiano, he has no strength to proceed against authority and the dialogue ends in his agreement, with Similiano, that he is Florita's murderer.

The dialogue begins as the inspector imputes guilt to Pedro, who categorically denies it. Similiano hypothesizes that he really did kill Florita, but Pedro simply disagrees with him while the inspector continues using "logic" (absurdity), his wiles, his humanity, his affirmation of superiority based upon personal experiences with many similar cases, his past knowledge of recurrences of such cases, and his supposed "agreement" with Pedro that the latter perfectly understands the situation. The dialogue ends as Pedro horrifically comprehends Similiano's preconceived deductions while the latter feels he is triumphant, having brilliantly communicated with his prisoner. Pedro falls into despair and bursts forth with, "I'm becoming so tired!"

Readers can appreciate this passage because they are far above the author's prodigious prose exercise. M. Santos' parenthetical remarks help one to characterize intellectually what should be happening in the minds of the participants in the dialogue, but is unfortunately and ironically not occurring. The dialogue itself is elevated by M-Santos' parenthetical commentaries; otherwise, its rendition would be a simple, artless, objectivist reproduction of reality (like a tape recording of their conversation), without any characterization or intellectualized thoughts.

There are roughly four completed thoughts in the entire dialogue--"You understand perfectly," "I want you to understand," "So we are agreed," and "I'm becoming so tired." The rest of the dialogue is characterized by short one- or two-syllable words, short phrases or utterances that punctuate the almost comic tone of the dialogue. There are complete lapses of communication in the silences between the replies. The rhythmic monotony of the dialogue helps to accentuate the emptiness in the minds of both men, Pedro's feeling of despair and the police inspector's vacuity because of his long-time position as a legal fonctionnaire, a mere instrument without mind or will, incapably handling matters of law, life and death, discharging them impersonally without will or conscience. Although this passage is free from most of the commonly used "stylistic devices" that fill the novel, its very terseness provides an authoritative and authentic, expression that markedly reveals (within the conversation's verbal austerity) a routine emptiness found in the path of Spanish justice.

CASTILLO-PUCHE and PARALELO 40

Pasaban los cochazos americanos, cochazos como barcos, cochazos con alas de cometa, cochazos con colas de dinosaurios, cochazos con cuernos de bisonte, brillantes cochazos que venían desde Torrejón a darse un garbeo por el centro de Madrid.

--Te invito--dijo Genaro.

--Pero, no irás a entrar ahí--respondió alarmado Emiliano.

--¿Y por qué no?

--Que ahí no se nos ha perdido nada a nosotros, Genaro.

--¡Quién sabe! Te invito a una copa de coñac--insistió
Genaro.

--Ahí no, hombre. --Y Emiliano puso una cara de súplica
que daba pena.

Era una diminuta pero brillante cafetería que tenía la barra
en forma circular. Por todas partes refulgían los materiales
novísimos: aluminio, plástico, cristal. La barra estaba invadida
por gentes que parecían seres de otro planeta juntados allí por una
extraña carambola. Mezclados había ruidos grandotes y grasientos
con rubios colorados y barbilampiños; negros enormes de cuello
grueso y robusta cabeza con negros de cuello fino y cabeza
minúscula; pelirrojos pecosos con mulatos amoratados, con azules
zambos, con sajones puros; pálidos latinos de tez un poco sucia
como la de los tambores muy usados con puertorriqueños de mirar
receloso y dientes podridos [p. 32].

This passage is typical of Castillo-Puche's graphic, journalistic style. It displays his penchant for trenchant criticism in his
use of the Spanish language. For example, he uses the word
cochazos (huge cars, describing them in detail) in a critical, anti-
American sense. He has an excellent ear for natural but banal
dialogue (note the colorless exchange between Emiliano and Genaro)
and his excellent sense of external description as he narrates, with
graphic intensity, the physical setting and the human elements within a typical American "cafeteria" in "Korea."

The passage is typical of the author's narrative style. His
use of special language (cochazos) his similes, the satirizing of
American values are rife. There is a brittle, satirical edge to
his invective, a kind of hard-edged, impersonal reporting when,
for example, describing the clientele of the cafeteria. When he
describes the various racial and ethnic types intermingling there,
it has the effect of a tarnished but lively melting-pot of personalities. One can appreciate these passages because, like so many
others, they contain the colloquial and strangely honest narrative
perception of a somewhat naïve author.

GOYTISOLO and SEÑAS DE IDENTIDAD

SALIDA

SORTIE

EXIT

AUSGANG

tout le monde est parti

come here my darling

las torres del transbordador aéreo la estación marítima más grúas
       más cobertizos más barcos

con Jaime I el conquistador se inicia una nueva política de expansi-
       ón por la otra orilla del mar Mediterráneo

sexo violento y suntuoso de Changó reconfórtame

materna Yemeya acógeme

dentro de útero escóndeme

no permitas que me arranquen a ti

la Puerta de la Paz la Barceloneta el humo espeso de las fábricas

pero no

su victoria no es tal

y si un destino acerbo para ti como para los otros te lleva

no queriéndolo tú

antes de ver restaurada la vida del país y de sus hombres

deja constancia al menos de este tiempo no olvides cuanto ocurrió
       en él te calles

la geometría caótica de la ciudad las tres chimeneas de la Cefsa
       campanarios y agujas de iglesias jardines

on va rater le car

tu te rends compte

alguno comprenderá quizás mucho más tarde

edificios legañosos buldozers brigadas de obreros barracas en
       ruina nuevas chozas farolas plateadas avenidas

qué orden intentaste forzar y cuál fue tu crimen

INTRODUZCA LA MONEDA

INTRODUISEZ LA MONNAIE

INTRODUCE THE COIN

GELDSTUCK EINWARFEN

These are the very last lines of the novel, the end of Chapter Nine.   It is typical of the poetic-prose-cum-stream-of-con-
sciousness narrative of Alvaro Mendiola as he makes his way from
his French country house to Barcelona.   Alvaro is on the point of
death after surviving a serious heart attack three days ago.   His
thoughts are rambling.   He has just driven to a point on the road
where he can survey for several minutes the city of Barcelona
through a telescope.   He views from afar the tremendous industrial
progress of Spain, the mandate of James I.   But all these phenomena of progress are very much anti-life, anti-sex.

Alvaro wants to hide.   He feels the present regime is vic-
torious in material goals but not in spiritual ones.   Spain will be
restored by those exiles who will not be silent.   He believes within
the realm of material progress, the voices of the émigrés will not
be lost, that "someone will understand what order you tried to resist and what your crime was. "   Alvaro's thoughts form a strong,
urgent but pessimistic plea to the Spanish émigrés not to forget the
past.   Their former ideological and spiritual commitments are
counterpointed with the tourists' inserting coins in the telescope to
"view" the newly industrialized city on the surface (progress); they
do not really see below the surface as Alvaro had done to discover
himself, his nation and his own marks of identity.

This section of Alvaro's thoughts is Goytisolo's most powerful, dramatic and passionate plea of the entire work.   Note the
lack of punctuation, the poetic "look" of the prose, the free form,
the unstructured prose resembling thoughts, the absolute visual appeal of images despite the absurdly heavy abstractions hidden behind the surface prose: Goytisolo's summation is full of internal
resonances--James I, Puerta de la Paz, la Cefsa, Changó, Yemayá.
His sense and nonesense references, however, do not eclipse the
empassioned rhythm of Alvaro's thoughts, his desperate plea to all
Spaniards to remember, his call to past resistence, past hopes,
unfulfilled dreams.   Only by penetrating the surface of Alvaro's
thoughts (through a reading of the entire novel) can these words
provide the proper insights and awareness for Goytisolo's readers.

MARSE and ULTIMAS TARDES CON TERESA

Teresa Simmons en bikini corriendo por las playas de sus

sueños, tendida sobre la arena, desperezándose bajo un cielo pro-

fundamente azul, en el agua en su cintura y los brazos en alto

(un áureo resplandor cobijado en sus axilas, oscilando como los

reflejos del agua bajo un puente) después nadando con formidable

estilo, surgiendo de las olas espumosas su jubiloso cuerpo de finas

caderas ágiles y finalmente viniendo desde la orilla hacia él como

un bronce vivo, sonoro, su pequeño abdomen palpitando anhelante,
cubierta toda ella de rocío y de destellos. Jean Serrat sonriéndole
a él, saludando de lejos con el brazo en alto, a él, al tenebroso
murciano, a ese elástico, gatuno, apostado montón de pretensiones
y deseos y ardores inconfesables, y dolientes temores (la perderé
no puede ser, no es para mí, la perderé antes de que me déis
tiempo a ser un catalán como vosotros, ¡caaaabrones!), que ahora
yacía al sol sobre una gran toalla de colores que no era suya,
como tampoco era suyo el slip que llevaba, ni las gafas de sol,
ni los cigarrillos que fumaba, siempre como si viviera provisi-
onalmente en casa ajena: ¿qué haces tú aquí, chaval, qué espe-
ras de esa amistad fugaz y caprichosa entre dos estaciones, como
de compartimiento de tren, sino veleidades de niña rica y mimada
y luego adiós si te he visto no me acuerdo? Sólo por verla así,
caminando despacio, semidesnuda y confiada, destacándose sobre
un fondo de palmeras y selva inexplorada--¿acaso no era la isla
perdida este verano?--valía la pena, y era suya, suya por el momento más que de sus padres o de aquel marido que la esperaba
en el futuro, más suya que de cualquiera de los muchos amantes
que pudieran adorarla y poseerla mañana [p. 197].

I deliberately chose this narrative passage from the second
part of Marsé's novel because it demonstrates the psychological
apex of Teresa's and Manolo's love idyll. Teresa and Manolo are
frolicking on the beach at Blanes. Teresa imagines herself to be
movie actress Jean Simmons, racing on the beach "of her dreams"
in a bikini against a perfect Hollywood set of blue sky, white sand,
frothy waves and bronzed Manolo. Teresa is caught up in her cinematic fantasy at its height as Manolo thinks he can never possess
this "unattainable" woman, the "movie star" of Teresa's imagination. Manolo is self-conscious of his lack of ownership--of towels,
cigarettes, glasses--his poverty extends itself from physical pos-
sessions to his spirit as he faces his "golden girl. " What can he
expect but a seasonal summer romance? He contents himself with
the sight of her because at least, for the moment, only for the
moment, Teresa is really his. Manolo's thoughts reflect those of
a potential loser, a youngster who knows he will never win or keep
his "golden" girl, Teresa, the girl of his dreams.

In this short, descriptive section, Marsé succeeds deftly
in presenting Teresa's self-image (through a cinematic parody) and
Manolo's personal opinions of himself. It is Marsé's use of language, parody and our intelligence that makes the beach scene,

both physically and mentally, come alive for his readers. Note
the great use of gerunds: corriendo, desperezándose, profunda-
mente, oscilando, nadando, surgiendo, viniendo, the unusually
great length of three sentences which contain several interior
thoughts, some exterior descriptions, gentle sarcasm and some
pathetic sentimentalism. Marsé builds his images beautifully
through his use of gerunds and participles.

This particular passage contains a certain kind of emotional
rhythm generated through Marsé's brilliant repetition of words
meaningful to the protagonist: "era suya, suya por el momento
... más suya que de cualquier de los muchos amantes" ("she was
his for the moment, more his than any of her future lovers").
Marsé's prose is current, colloquial (gatuno, cabrón), ironic,
rhythmical, emotionally expressive, transcient, fleeting, at times
poetic. When this passage is placed in juxtaposition to the quotation from Arthur Rimbaud that immediately precedes it ("O que ma
quille éclate! O que j'aille à la mer! Oh let my body burst! Oh
let me go down to the sea!"), the passage takes on added erotic
and ironic significance. Rimbaud's emotions were pure heartrend-
ings, fulfilled by a kind of savage sexuality. Teresa and Manolo's
"affair" is youthful, juvenile, synthetic, as unreal as the screenplay she is living in her mind, as pathetic as the inferiority complex Manolo reveals to us. Rimbaud was the great sensualist poet-
maudit in tune with the world, jaded but real. Teresa and Manolo
are post-pubescents, adolescents, innocents (at this moment).

Perhaps this passage can be best appreciated now if Marsé's
sardonic wit is taken into consideration, since it is essentially his
wit that raises an otherwise stereotyped situation into a greater
semantic and sarcastic excursion than one originally expected on
first reading. It is within this particular framework that Marsé
has conceived his entire novel. This passage serves us as a
single microcosm, a gem of its kind, heretofore incomparable in
the Spanish fictional prose of this period.

ALDECOA and PARTE DE UNA HISTORIA

Está amaneciendo y el acantilado de la Isla Mayor--viole-
tada, dulzosa--parece perfectamente simétrico con su reflejo en
las aguas calmas del río de mar. Estos minutos crepusculares,
hasta que el urgente sol de Africa ponga sus panes de oro, primero en la cima, luego en la ladera oriental de Montaña Amarilla,
reconcilian los sentidos--a veces hirvientes, a veces desmayados,
en esta latitud--con la naturaleza.

Las falúas, las barcas, el muelle, la población, las dunas,
lo que veo y me rodea, son los testigos de la serenidad que gozo,
sorprendido, hasta que de pronto un gallo estride con su canto,
llega desde la lejanía solemne y rapaz una gaviota, pica el agua de
la caleta un pez perseguido. Vuelvo la cabeza hacia Montaña Amarilla, donde se insinúa, estriando su copete morado, un resplandor.
Comienza la mañana y este milagro--tan doméstico y consabido--
renueva la individualidad de las cosas: el camino a la llanía,
pateado por los camellos; las latas de conservas vacías, brillando
distintamente, en la joyería del muladar, junto a las rocas; tal
cual planta de geranios sobre el perfil de una tapia; los cabezudos
bolardos emergiendo del cemento del muelle.... Un vientecillo
alegre aflora con el sol y arruga la epidermis del mar, que se
descompone en matices, verdeando, azuleando, griseando, negreando hasta los pies del gran acantilado, cuya imagen desaparece
de las aguas. Y al fin el sol, ya brotado de la línea del este,
después de rojear el mar, lo melifica [pp. 116-7].

This passage begins Chapter Thirteen of Aldecoa's novel.
It is his celebration of sunrise and the most salient example of the
author's poetic prose and perfection of beauty through an intense,
highly polished utilization of language. The narrator literally acts
as a pair of eyes, veo (I see), that witness the dawn. The beauty
of nature as reflected in the sensitive artist and narrator is the
theme of the entire passage. Aldecoa visualizes sea gulls, roosters,
"the renovation of the individuality of things" around him. The
camels, the geraniums, the wind that caresses his skin, the dark
greens, blues, grays, blacks, colors that disappear into the sea
when the sun rises are all a part of this early morning celebration of the arrival of dawn. He has captured the reality of the
morning on his artist's pallet.

Aldecoa's choice of language is authentic because he has
experienced the coming of dawn in the very same manner. His
words are fluid and build themselves to a crescendo--e. g. , the
arrival of the bright hues of reds and oranges when the sun approaches its zenith. His use of language is proper, simplified,
refined, accurate, natural, rhythmic. As the images of sunrise
take shape, so does the rhythm of his verses, accentuating the
change of colors, tone and the light of the sea: "se descompone
en matices, verdeando, azuleando, griseando, negreando hasta los
pies del gran acantilado, cuya imagen desaparece de las aguas. "

Every concrete image of Aldecoa's gradually brightening
seascape is mellowed by the reddish-tinted light he casts over the
Isla Mayor. The novelist-poet-narrator is in harmony with the
joy, surprise and splendor he feels within his soul as the spectacle
of nature is revealed to him (and to the reader). Aldecoa's brilliantly stylized prose contains for me the proper lights and darks
of an Impressionist painting by Monet. Just as that painter tried
to express on his canvasses the conscious joy he felt in nature,
so does this sensitive, poetic-prosist.

BENET and VOLVERAS A REGION

--¿Qué dices?   ¿Qué haces ahí?

La conciencia y la realidad se compenetran entre sí; no se
aislan pero tampoco se identifican, incluso cuando una y otra no
son sino costumbres. Raras veces un suceso no habitual logra
impresionar la conciencia del adulto sin duda porque su conocimiento la ha revestido de una película protectora, formada de imágenes
adquiridas, que no sólo lubrifica el roce cotidiano con la realidad
sino que le sirve para referirlo a un muestrario familiar de emo-
ciones. Pero en ocasiones algo atraviesa esa delicada gelatina que
la memoria extiende por doquier--aunque no conoce ni nombre--
para somar con toda su crudeza y herir a una conciencia indefensa,
sensible y medrosa que sólo a través de la herida podrá segregar
el nuevo humor que la proteja; y entonces se convierte en una costumbre refleja, en conocimiento ficticio, en disimulo ya que, en verdad, el miedo, la piedad o el amor no se llegan nunca a conocer.
Hay una palabra para cada uno de esos instantes que, aunque el
entendimiento reconoce, la memoria no recuerda jamás; no se
transmiten en el tiempo ni siquiera se reproducen porque algo--la
costumbre, el instinto quizá--se preocupará de silenciar y relegar
a un tiempo de ficción. Sólo cuando se produce ese instante otra
memoria--no complaciente y en cierto modo involuntaria, que se
alimenta del miedo y extrae sus recursos de un instinto opuesto al
de supervivencia, y de una voluntad contraria al afán de dominio--
despierta y alumbra un tiempo--no lo cuentan los relojes ni los
calendarios, como si su propia densidad conjure el movimiento de

los péndulos y los engranajes en su seno--que carece de horas y
años, no tiene pasado ni futuro, no tiene nombre porque la memoria se ha obligado a no legitimarlo; sólo cuenta con un ayer cica-
trizado en cuya propia insensibilidad se mide la magnitud de la
herida. El coche negro no pertenece al tiempo sino a ese ayer
intemporal, transformado por la futurición en un ingrávido y abor-
tivo presente. El doctor lo comprende y le mira; "vamos, vamos"
porque sabe que el que padeció el abatimiento, el horror, o la
piedad está y inhabilitado para saber lo que son y para buscar su
propia cura; sabe que tampoco es del tiempo aquella mañana en la
fonda del cruce, aquella mañana que degeneró en tarde mientras
esperaba, con sus cabás en el suelo, sentado en la cerca de la
encrucijada, la llegada de María Timoner. Allí está el miedo, el
abatimiento, la pérdida de la justificación de un sí mismo que en
adelante tendrá que desconfiar, rehusar toda esperanza, anhelar un
fin [pp. 92-3].

This passage begins Benet's second chapter. The young boy
whose mother had deserted him is asked by the doctor, "What are
you saying? What are you doing here?" Dr. Sebastián is not interested in his replies. Nine pages of the doctor's thoughts in detail are reconstructed for us in a very, very long monologue (of
which I have chosen about one page, above) before the doctor tells
the boy to sit down and wait. The doctor's thoughts are revealed
to us in the very best literary context of stream of consciousness.
He wonders about the theoretical relationship between conscience
and reality, memory and the wounds memories inflict on us because of our bad experiences, experiences which provoke suffering,
harm, a lack of love and pity. Memories cause scars of the sensibility. Looking at the boy, the doctor reflects upon his own
dreaded pain, the pain of unrequited love for the woman, María
Timoner.

This narrative passage is composed of a logical (and later
on, a somewhat illogical) stream of thoughts, dealing through abstractions with the concrete realities that obsess our daily lives.
There is little imagery. What is extraordinary is the gray, almost cerebral tone and the constant flow of Dr. Sebastián's thoughts.
There is a somewhat "scientific" attitude towards the expression of
his innermost feelings, when the mind is referred to as "esa
delicada gelatina" ("that delicate gelatinous thing"), as he gropes
with the interplay of mind, memory and the events which scar his
life.

Benet's Dr. Sebastián is amazed at the resiliency of his brain, its self-protective devices, its psychological resource of retaining only those events that are largely tied to the emotions, especially fear. His "fear" of seeing María Timoner again is psychologically triggered by the unfortunate boy left at his office by an irresponsible mother. El coche negro (the black car) is the visual symbol or stimulus, the psychological memory trigger reminding him of Timoner's (and the unnamed boy's mother's) disappearance. Dr. Sebastián never resolves his thoughts. Because of Benet's extensive use of the present tense, the reader is very much aware of the immediacy of the doctor's thoughts. Benet achieves flow through the constant use of dashes, setting off a great number of parenthetical remarks which help to explain his abstractions.

Perhaps Benet is expressing here, in this particular passage, the notion of our heavy reliance on our instincts, which at times, superimposes itself over our own ideas of logic or intelligent thought patterns. Time becomes obscured as does the actual memory of events. What remains is the scarred tissue, the abstract feeling, the residue of pain because of María Timoner's failure to arrive as he, Dr. Sebastián waited for his lover, his mistress, just as the young boy will continue to wait for his mother, his loved one.

Except for the principal theme, this passage (a bit clearer than most) is typical of Benet's stylistics. It is entirely possible to lose the thread, as I have done on several occasions, while reading his novel. Only by dividing up Benet's very long monologues into smaller portions can one appreciate their content and evaluate even more carefully the Baroque, behaviorist style in which the entire novel is written.

DELIBES and PARABOLA DEL NAUFRAGO

Le tiemblan las manos y su temblor se comunica a la lámpara que emite un nervioso tintineo, tin-tin-tin. Ya en el servicio (caballeros), mientras orina, se mira al espejo y no se reconoce, el pelo y las barbas blancos ensortijados, de una densidad pilosa desconcertante, como vedijas. Jacinto se acaricia las barbas (al terminar de orinar), se encara consigo mismo y se dice con voz descompuesta, /es inútil dar voces, Jacinto convéncete, / /porque el mundo está sordo y ciego, Jacinto, nadie te escucha, / /¿oyes? nadie desea enterarse de lo que ocurre aquí dentro, / /porque lo que se conoce es como si no sucediera.   Pero yo me/

/pregunto, Jacinto, ¿dónde están los pobres de espíritu, los/
/mansos de corazón, los misericordiosos, los pacíficos, los que/
/lloran, los que padecen hambre y sed de justicia, si es que/
/queda alguno? ¿Dónde están, Jacinto? Anda, dímelo, por favor,/
/te lo pido, tú lo sabes, Jacinto, no seas así, yo necesito en-/
/contrar uno, te lo juro, no es un capricho, tú mismo puedes/
/verlo, que si de aquí a dos dias no aparece un manso de cora-/
/zón, un misericordioso, un pacífico, un hombre con hambre y/
/sed de justicia, Jacinto, despídete, tú me dirás, ¿o es que no/
/te das cuenta? Tú lo estás viendo lo mismo que yo, no es que/
/sea una invención mía, que las cosas, lo mires por donde lo/
/mires, no pueden haberse puesto peor ... / [pp. 210-1; portions
appearing within / marks were entirely in italics in original].

I have deliberately chosen this passage, some twenty pages
before the conclusion of the novel, because it is representative of
several of Delibes' stylistic devices. At this point in the novel,
Jacinto San José is feeling nervous because of the relentless
growth of the hydra that seems to imprison him in his cabin retreat.

The passage begins in the third person singular and Jacinto
is viewed in an erratic, irrational state; his hands are trembling
like the lamp above emitting a nervous tin-tin sound. Having gone
into the bathroom to urinate, he looks at himself in the mirror and
does not recognize his own image, as his beard has turned into
white wool, which is one of the early manifestations of his metamorphosis into a ram. Caressing his beard, he starts to think
about himself, beginning with the words es inútil (it's useless), the
text is now recast into the second person singular as Jacinto, in a
prolonged interior monologue, believes it is hopeless to seek help
since everyone in his society is either blind or deaf to his plight.
In a parody of a religious sermon, he asks, "Where are the poor
of spirit, the kindhearted, the merciful, the pacifists, those who
cry, suffer hunger and thirst for justice? Where are they?" Jacinto reflects on these questions and, as if by talking to a mute or
deaf God (or himself), he is resigned to his fate. Things could
not be worse for him. Apparently, no one will speak out for him
or come to his aid. Could it be that the fierce-of-heart, the
warriors, the torturers, the unjust have dominated the world? Is
there no hope left?

Most of Delibes' novel is as dramatic as the preceding passage indicates. His use of self-interrogation and interior monologue is facile and appropriate to the plot and development of Jacinto's character. This particular section of the novel is characterized by an extended use of the present tense and maintains a

kind of rhythmic harmony in its interrogative pursuit of Jacinto's
predicament. Delibes deliberately uses the present tense to simu-
late actual thoughts in Jacinto's mind. The entire monologue is
framed in a tone of desperation. Jacinto is caught in a cul-de-sac,
not knowing where to turn. His desperation and his provocative
(almost philosophical) analysis of the composition of society can
certainly be appreciated. It is Delibes' own attitudes, I feel, that
form the essence of Jacinto's thoughts. For as Delibes has already admitted, he writes of his own dissatisfaction with the world,
and Jacinto San José is but another mouthpiece for his essentially
pessimistic point of view.

GROSSO and GUARNICION DE SILLA

    Travesía de Madrid que ya termina con las cansinas luces

de Getafe, y de nuevo el silencio, la autopista, para silvar un fox

ya trasnochado y meter la directa. Todo quedó ya atrás, siempre

un mal sueño, este Madrid de Dios, y enfilar hacia el Sur, con

las pupilas un tanto dilatadas de reflejos. Y Aranjuez. Allí pensó

dejarlo, o quizás en Ocaña, pero es mejor hacerlo un poco más

abajo--más oportunidades de ponerse en camino, pasados Madride-

jos y Valdepeñas, desde donde le será más fácil encontrar el

Oeste irremediable. No quiere despertarlo, tendido en la litera,

mientras cruza las luces y hace sonar el claxon, soñando con la

tierra dulce de promisión (bastante menos dulce) de la cada vez

más lejana e inalcanzable Francia.

    Bochorno. Ni frío ni calor. Septiembre ha descolgado su

anuncio de otoñada. La carretera se abre en la llanura mesetaria

de las vides. Huele a lagar y a noche. El acelerador a fondo--

aunque no pese jamás de los sesenta. Un gazapo que no es gazapo

sino rata--cruza el asfalto antes de encontrar la muerte bajo diez

neumáticos. Los grillos cantan lejos, allí donde se levantaron las

eras del verano o en las lindes, o en los ribazos de las alcanta-

rillas [p. 161].

    This selection comprises the second and third paragraphs at
the very beginning of Chapter Five. Ignacio is on the road in his
red sports car. Grosso is narrating Ignacio's way south--from
Madrid to Andalusia along the superhighway leading from Madrid.
It is written in the third person singular. It is a hot day for

September. Ignacio pushes down hard on the accelerator, letting
his throttle out, speeding as he leaves Castille.

This selection is less typical of the kind Grosso writes because it is simpler in style. Nevertheless, it possesses a kind
of rhythm and pace in the prose style he uses to describe actions.
Ignacio is going south to collect the body of his dead brother,
Leonardo, south to "the land of promise," less sweet now because
of what awaits him there. The passage is filled with a sense of
foreboding. Ignacio is very much alone with his thoughts. As he
speeds at sixty kilometers per hour, a rat or a young rabbit crosses
the road. He squashes it under his tires as the crickets chirp in
the distance. There is something lethal, oppressive and cruel in
Grosso's description of nature.

This cited passage is one of the least complicated narrative
sections in the entire novel. One of the striking qualities of
Grosso's prose is his hard-hitting rhythm. He states his theme
immediately--travesía de Madrid, and the rest of his images are
subordinated to this concept, parallelling Ignacio's trajectory south.
There is an excessive use of punctuation (commas) which help
enumerate the adjectivial or ideological pile-up of noun ideas in the
passage. The vocabulary is very concrete. Ignacio's (Grosso's)
world is one of objects--cold, harsh, monotonous, matter-of-fact.
The ideas in themselves as they are conceived in this passage are
of great importance. But one must ferret them out "between the
lines" so to speak.

There is a feeling of profundity in this passage. First the
reader is an observer on the road from Madrid, watching the silent
motorist turning on to the superhighway. Later, the reader pene-
trates "with dilated pupils" the spacious, empty plains, smelling
the essences of wine and nightfall, listening to the crickets in the
ditches of the far-off underground sewers. Grosso forces one to
use his senses, to discover with him (like the sensualist he is) the
sights, smells, sounds, and emotional and physical climate of the
land and its protagonists. Throughout all this activity, Joao Diaz
(probably a Catalan friend of Ignacio's) sleeps, immune to the face
of nature flying by, its odors, the sounds of traffic, the day or
evening light which surrounds him.

The author is detached from this passage; his tone is one
of cold reportage. The use of preterite tenses intermingled with
present and future tenses combined with shortened, incomplete
phrasing, gives one the impression of Grosso as an impersonal
artist. Grosso paints a verbal canvas with short, quick strokes,
suggesting with flashes of paint (words) the entire, cold world of
his itinerant traveler on the road. For this is essentially Grosso's
methodology: instantaneous impressions that provide flashes of insight so the reader may understand, in the aggregate, the meaning
behind his fleeting impressions. Much in the same vein as Impressionist painters like Monet, Seurat or Corot, Grosso's prose follows a similar course, sometimes misleading us, confusing us, but

generally leaving us appreciative of his manipulative (and creative)
use of language.

CARRASCAL and GROOVY

    --Tú también tendrás niños, Pat, así, como te he dicho,
¿entiendes? Estaba anormalmente seria.

--Sí, ma, pero ¿cómo entran ahí dentro?
La soltó casi con miedo. Fuera se adivinaba una maña espléndida
de verano.

--Anda, vete a jugar. Ya te lo explicaré otro día, cuando seas
mayor. No, no está, ya me lo parecía, dijo que iba a trasladar-
se a Broadway, aunque aquello está lleno de cerdos, y esto, ¿para
qué se necesitan tantos cerdos?, ¡mira que si tengo un hijo de
el!, no, no puedo tenerlo, ¿qué día es?, bueno, a lo mejor, pero
no, eso tienes que sentirlo, estoy segura de que cuando pasa, lo
notas, lo sientes, lo, aunque ayer fue tan, no sé, tan ligero, es
lo que te pasa con la hierba, que te vuelves ligera, toda, todo,
voy a mirar por si acaso en el drugstore, pero seguro que tampoco está.

--Pues es mentira que las mamás puedan traer a los niños solas.
Necesitan un hombre, por eso se casan.
Se lo decía en un susurro, inclinada sobre el pupitre para que la
maestra no las oyese hablar. Pat estaba tan indignada que le
costó bajar la voz.

--Eso es mentira, Eve. Se puede tener un niño sin estar casada.
Rosa.... La cortó. Eve era niña de rasgos muy femeninos, muy
bellos, ojos grandes y cabellera castaña [p. 56].

    I have selected these passages from Chapter Two as typical
of the unique writing style of José María Carrascal. The rather
banal dialogue between Pat and her mother deals with pregnancy
and child-bearing. Pat, as a very young girl, cannot understand
the "mechanics" of pregnancy or giving birth. Carrascal reproduces this dialogue in his retrospective-recall approach. Pat was,
perhaps, in elementary school when this conversation took place.
However she remembers it in the middle of a Manhattan thorough-
fare as she stands in the street, wondering (in the third person
singular) why New York needs so many policemen (she calls them

"pigs") as she makes her way towards Broadway thinking about terminating her own pregnancy. She thinks about being "high" on marijuana. Then her thoughts return to her mother talking about the necessity of marriage. We are suddenly in a classroom. Pat remembers saying to her school mate Eve, "You can have a child without marrying. My sister Rose...." And then, Pat's thoughts center on Eve until she is jarred from them and regains her grasp on reality as she walks through the teeming streets of Manhattan's East Village.

Carrascal presents dialogue, description, retrospective-recall and present-time description consecutively with no pauses or breaks in the narrative. His language is colloquial, typical of the New York teenagers making their way in the big city. Dialogue, description and recall follow no logical pattern. Essentially the reader is following Pat's thoughts throughout the entire novel-- disorganized thoughts, speculations, and incomplete ideas, expressed in elliptical phrases. Carrascal makes no attempt to use traditional techniques like simile, metaphor, or symbolism. Pat's vocabulary is quite ordinary. Carrascal's strength is in reproducing language and character as it really is. He relies on a fast succession of images, one piled on the other. Names have connotations. For example, there is Eve, with beautiful large eyes and chestnut hair, the "virginal" girl who we will discover later is Pat's father's lover. And yet, the characters are never really seen completely because of Pat's rapidly jumping thoughts. The reader is given fragments, pieces of a puzzle to work with and must fill in much about the physical description and moral posturing of all the men and women in Pat's life.

Groovy is relentlessly straightforward, direct in its dialogue, accurate and precise in its description of the city, sentimental in its retrospective-recall and blunt in its recapitulation of present action. Like the great Gerald Arpino ballet, Astarte, it assaults one's senses and leaves one coping (usually logically) with one's own lacks of insight, understanding, and factual knowledge until the end of the novel is reached. And even at its conclusion, much like Julio Cortázar's Rayuela (Hopscotch), one is never quite certain if he retained everything he wanted to know about the leading character and her life and the society in which she lives. Groovy is a little like a machinegun sputtering out bullets in rapid succession, bullets that are fast charges of verbal energy, orienting/disorienting one, with few sustained pauses for reflection. The novel's verbal anatomy is skeletal; it is cold and factual, and written almost in the vein of a newspaper story. Carrascal is distinctly absent from the novel. His position is never known--only that he wrote 336 pages of tight, tense prose in a journalistic style that may be characterized as confusing, colloquial and, at times, fascinating.

BIBLIOGRAPHY*

BOOKS

Alborg, Juan Luis. Hora actual de la novela española. 2 vols. Madrid: Ed. Taurus, 1958.

Aldecoa, Ignacio. Parte de una historia. Barcelona: Ed. Noguer, 1967.

Allot, Miriam. Novelists on the Novel. New York: Columbia Univ. Press, 1959.

Amorós, Andrés. Introducción a literatura contemporánea. Salamanca: Ed. Anaya, 1966.

Aranguren, José Luis. La juventud europea y otros ensayos. Barcelona: Ed. Biblioteca Breve, 1968.

Aub, Max. Discurso de la novela española contemporánea. Mexico: Fondo de Cultura Económica, 1944.

Auerbach, Eric. Minesis. New York: Doubleday, 1953.

Ayala, Francisco. La estructura narrativa. Madrid: Ed. Taurus, 1970.

Azuar, Rafael. El diálogo y los personajes en la novela. Publ. by the author, 1970.

Baquero Goyanes, Mariano. Estructuras de la novela actual. Barcelona: Ed. Planeta, 1970.

Baquero Goyanes, Mariano. Proceso de la novela actual. Madrid: Ed. Rialp, 1963.

Becker, George J. Documents of Modern Literary Realism. New Jersey: Princeton University Press, 1963.

Benet, Juan. La inspiración y el estilo. Barcelona: Seix Barral, 1973.

Benet, Juan. Volverás a Región. Barcelona: Ed. Destino, 1967.

Blosch-Michel, Jean. La nueva novela. Madrid: Ed. Guadarrama, 1968.

Bonet, Laureano. De Galdós a Robbe-Grillet. Madrid: Ed. Taurus, 1972.

*See also page 403.

389

Bosch, Rafael. La novela española del siglo XX. 2 vols. New York: Las Américas, 1970.

Bozal, Valeriano. El realismo: entre el desarrollo y el subdesarrollo. Madrid: Ed. Ciencia Nueva, 1966.

Buckley, Ramón. Problemas normales en la novela española contemporánea. Barcelona: Ed. Península, 1968.

Carenas, F. and Ferrando, J. La sociedad española en la novela de la postguerra. New York: Eliseo Torres, 1971.

Carrascal, José María. Groovy. Barcelona: Ed. Destino, 1973.

Casado, Pablo Gil. La novela social española. Barcelona: Ed. Seix Barral, 1968.

Casalduero, Joaquín. Sentido y forma en el Quijote. Madrid: Ed. Insula, 1949.

Castellet, José María. La hora del lector. Barcelona: Ed. Seix Barral, 1957.

Castellet, José María. Nuevo novísimos. Barcelona: Ed. Seix Barral, 1971.

Castellet, José María. Notas sobre la literatura española contemporánea. Barcelona: Ed. Laye, 1955.

Castillo-Puche, José Luis. Paralelo 40. Barcelona: Ed. Destino, 1963.

Cela, Camilo José. La colmena. Barcelona: Ed. Noguer, 1971.

Chandler, R. E. and Schwartz, K. A New History of Spanish Literature. Baton Rouge: Louisiana State University Press, 1961.

Clotas, J. and Gimferrer, P. 30 años de literatura en España. Barcelona: Ed. Kairós, 1971.

Corrales Egea, José. La novela española actual. Madrid: Cuadernos para el diálogo, 1971.

Curutchet, Juan Carlos. Introducción a la novela española de postguerra. Montevideo: Ed. Alfa, 1966.

Delibes, Miguel. Parábola de naúfrago. Barcelona: Ed. Destino, 1969.

Dendle, Brian J. The Spanish Novel of Religious Thesis (1876-1936). Madrid: Ed. Castalia, 1968.

Díaz, Janet. Ana María Matute. New York: Twayne, 1971.

Díaz, Janet W. Miguel Delibes. New York: Twayne, 1971.

Díaz-Plaja, Guillermo. La creación literaria en España. Madrid: Ed. Aguilar, 1968.

Díaz-Plaja, Guillermo. Cien libros españoles: poesía y novela (1968-1970). Salamanca: Ed. Anaya, 1971.

Díez-Echarri, E. and Roca Francesa, J. M. Historia de la lite-

ratura española e hispanoamericana.   Madrid: Ed. Aguilar,
1968.

Domingo, José.   La novela española del siglo XX.   2 vols.   Barcelona: Ed. Labor, 1973.

Ellman, Michael and Ferdelson, Jr. , Charles, Editors.   The
Modern Tradition: Backgrounds of Modern Literature.   New
York: Oxford University Press, 1965.

Fernández Santos, Jesús.   Los bravos.   Barcelona: Ed. Destino,
1954.

Ferreras, Juan Ignacio.   Tendencias de la novela española actual
(1931-1969).   Paris: Ed. Hispanoamericanas, 1970.

Foster, David W.   Forms of the Novel in the Work of Camilo José
Cela.   Columbia: University of Missouri Press, 1967.

Fuentes, Carlos.   La nueva novela hispanoamericana.   Mexico:
Ed. Joaquín Mortiz, 1969.

García Hortelano, Juan.   Summer Storm.   Transl. of Tormenta de
verano by Ilsa Barea.   New York: Grove Press, 1962.

García Hortelano, Juan.   Tormenta de verano.   Barcelona: Seix
Barral, 1962.

García-Viñó, Manuel.   Ignacio Aldecoa.   Madrid: Ed. ESPESA,
1972.

García-Viñó, Manuel.   Novela española actual.   Madrid: Ed.
Guadarrama, 1967.

Gil Casado, Pablo.   La novela social española (1942-1968).   Barcelona: Ed. Seix Barral, 1968.

Gil Casado, Pablo.   La novela social española (1970-1971).   2d ed.
Barcelona: Ed. Seix Barral, 1973.

Giovanni, Halperin and McShane, editors.   Borges on Writing.
New York: Dutton, 1973.

Gironella, José María.   Los cipreses creen en Dios.   Barcelona:
Ed. Planeta, 1953.

Goldman, Lucien.   Pour une sociologie du roman.   Paris: Ed.
Gallimard, 1964.

Gómez de la Serna, Gaspar.   Ensayos sobre literatura social.
Madrid: Ed. Guadarrama, 1971.

Goytisolo, Juan.   Count Julian.   Transl. from Reivindicación del
Conde don Julián by Helen R. Lane.   New York: Viking,
1974.

Goytisolo, Juan.   El furgón de cola.   Paris: Ed. Ruedo Ibérico,
1967.

Goytisolo, Juan.   Problemas de la novela.   Barcelona: Ed. Seix
Barral, 1959.

Goytisolo, Juan. Marks of Identity. Transl. by Gregory Rabassa of Señas de identidad. New York: Grove Press. 1969.

Goytisolo, Juan. Señas de identidad. Mexico: Ed. Joaquín Mortiz, 1966.

Goytisolo-Gay, Luis. Las afueras. Barcelona: Ed. Seix Barral, 1958.

Grosso, Alfonso. Guarnición de silla. Barcelona: Ed. Seix Barral, 1971.

Guillermo, E. and Hernández, J. A. La novelística española de los 60. New York: Eliseo Torres, 1971.

Harss, Luis. Los nuestros. Buenos Aires: Ed. Sudamericana, 1966.

Hickey, Leo. Cinco horas con Miguel Delibes. Madrid: Ed. Prensa española, 1967.

Hoyos, Antonio de. Ocho escritores actuales. Murcia: Ed. Aula de Cultura, 1954.

Iglesias Laguna, Antonio. Literatura de España día a día (1970-1971). Madrid: Ed. Nacional, 1972.

Iglesias Laguna, Antonio. Treinta años de novela española (1938-1968). Madrid: Ed. Prensa Española, 1970.

Ilie, Paul. La novelística de Camilo José Cela. Madrid: Ed. Gredos, 1963.

Jones, Margaret. The Literary World of Ana María Matute. Lexington: University of Kentucky Press, 1970.

López Martínez, Luis. La novelística de Miguel Delibes. Murcia: Univ. of Murcia, 1973.

Lukacs, Georg. The Theory of the Novel. Boston: M. I. T. Press, 1971.

McPheeters, D. W. Camilo José Cela. New York: Twayne, 1969.

Marco, Joaquín. Nueva literatura en España y América. Barcelona: Ed. Lumen, 1972.

Marra-López, José R. Narrativa española fuera de España (1939-1961). Madrid: Ed. Guadarrama, 1963.

Marsé, Juan. Ultimas tardes con Teresa. Barcelona: Ed. Seix Barral, 1966.

Martín-Santos, Luis. Tiempo de silencio. Barcelona: Ed. Seix Barral, 1962.

Martínez-Cachero, J. M. La novela española entre 1939 y 1969. Madrid: Ed. Castalia, 1973.

Matute, Ana María. Los soldados lloran de noche. Barcelona: Ed. Destino, 1964.

Matute, Ana María. Primera memoria. Barcelona: Ed. Destino,
    1960.

Matute, Ana María. School of the Sun. Transl. by Elaine
    Kerrigan of Primera memoria. New York: Pantheon, 1963.

Monegal, Emir R. El arte de narrar. Mexico: Ed. Monte Avila,
    1969.

Moran, Fernando. Novela y semidesarrollo. Madrid: Ed. Taurus,
    1971.

Navales, Ana María. Cuatro novelistas españoles: Delibes, Alde-
    coa, Sueiro, Umbral. Madrid: Ed. Fundamentos, 1974.

Nora, Eugenio de. La novela española contemporánea (1927-1960).
    Vol. III. Madrid: Ed. Gredos, 1962.

Ortega, José. Alienación y agresión en "Señas de identidad" y
    "Reivindicación del Conde don Julián." New York: Eliseo
    Torres, 1972.

Ortega y Gasset, J. The Dehumanization of Art and Other Writings
    on Art and Culture. New York: Doubleday, 1948.

Patt, B. and Nozick, M. Spanish Literature Since the Civil War.
    New York: Dodd, Mead & Co. , 1973.

Pérez Minik, Domingo. La novela extranjera en España. Madrid:
    Taller Ediciones, 1973.

Pérez Minik, Domingo. Novelistas españoles de los siglos XIX y
    XX. Madrid: Ed. Guadarrama, 1957.

Pizarro, Narciso. Análisis estructural de la novela. Madrid: Ed.
    Siglo XXI, 1970.

Pollman, Leo. La "nueva novela" en Francia y en Iberoamérica.
    Madrid: Ed. Gredos, 1971.

Ponce de León, José Luis S. La novela española de la guerra
    civil (1936-1939). Madrid: Insula, 1971.

Quiroga, Elena. Algo pasa en la calle. Barcelona: Ed. Destino,
    1954.

Río, Emilio del. Novela intelectual. Madrid: Ed. Prensa es-
    pañola, 1971.

Ríos, Alonso de los. Conversaciones con Miguel Delibes. Ma-
    drid: Ed. E. M. E. S. A. , 1971.

Robbe-Grillet. Por una novela nueva. Barcelona: Ed. Seix
    Barral, 1965.

Robbe-Grillet, Alain. For a New Novel: Essays on Fiction.
    Transl. by Richard Howard. New York: Books for Libraries
    Press, 1970.

Roberts, Gemma. Temas existenciales en la novela española de
    postguerra. Madrid: Ed. Gredos, 1973.

Rodríguez Monegal, Emir. El Boom de la novela latino-americana.
    Venezuela: Ed. Nuevo Tiempo, 1972.

Rojas, Carlos. De Cela a Castillo-Navarro. New Jersey:
    Prentice-Hall, 1965.

Roman, Rosa. Ana María Matute. Madrid: Ed. ESPESA, 1971.

Sábato, Ernesto. El escritor y sus fantasmas. Buenos Aires:
    Ed. Ensayistas Hispánicos, 1963.

Saínz de Robles, Federico Carlos. La novela española en el siglo
    XX. Madrid: Ed. Pegaso, 1957.

Sanz Villanueva, Santos. Tendencias de la novela española actual.
    Madrid: Cuadernos para el diálogo, 1972.

Sastre, Alfonso. Anatomía del realismo. Barcelona: Ed. Seix
    Barral, 1965.

Schwartz, Kessel. A New History of Spanish American Fiction.
    2 vols. Miami: Univ. of Miami Press, 1972.

Schwartz, Kessel. Juan Goytisolo. New York: Twayne, 1970.

Schwartz, Ronald. José María Gironella. New York: Twayne,
    1972.

Siclier, Jacques. Nouvelle vague. Paris: Ed. du Cerf, 1961.

Sobejano, Gonzalo. Novela española de nuestro tiempo. Madrid:
    Ed. Prensa Española, 1970.

Sontag, Susan. Against Interpretation. New York: Dell, 1961.

Stamm, James R. A Short History of Spanish Literature. New
    York: Doubleday, 1967.

Sueiro, Daniel. La criba. Barcelona: Ed. Seix Barral, 1961.

Sueiro, Daniel. Los verdugos españoles: Historia y actualidad del
    garrote vil. Madrid: Ed. Alfaguara, 1972.

Tacca, Oscar. Las voces de la novela. Madrid: Ed. Gredos,
    1973.

Thrall, Hibbard and Holman. A Handbook to Literature. New
    York: Odyssey Press, 1960.

Tola de Habich, F. and Grieve, P. Los españoles y el boom.
    Caracas: Ed. Tiempo Nuevo, 1971.

Torrente Ballester, Gonzalo. Panorama de la literatura española
    contemporánea. 3d ed. Madrid: Ed. Guadarrama, 1965.

Tovar, Antonio. Novela española e hispanoamericana. Madrid:
    Ed. Alfaguera, 1972.

Tudela, Mariano. Cela. Madrid: Ed. ESPESA, 1970.

Umbral, Francisco. Miguel Delibes. Madrid: Ed. ESPESA,
    1970.

Varela, Benito. Renovación de la novela en el siglo XX. Barcelona: Ed. Destino, 1966.

Vásquez and Kosoff. El camino. New York: Holt, Rinehart & Winston, 1960.

Wellek, René. Concepts of Criticism. New Haven: Yale Univ. Press, 1963.

Several authors. Siete narradores de hoy: Antología. Madrid: Ed. Taurus, 1963.

ARTICLES

Abbot, James. "Review of Francisco Umbral's Memorias de un niño de derechos." Books Abroad, Vol. 47, No. 4 (Autumn, 1973), 233.

Alvarez, Carlos Luis. "Crítica literaria: Paralelo 40." Blanco y negro (June 15, 1953).

Ayala, Francisco. "Nueva divagación sobre la novela." Revista de Occidente, 54 (Sept. 1967), 294-312.

Berraquero, José. "Los objetos en El Jarama." Cuadernos Hispanoamericanos (Madrid), Vol. 263-64 (1972), 561-71.

Bient, A. "The Novels of Elena Quiroga." Hispania, XLII (1959), 210-213.

Bleiberg, Germán and Marías, Julián. "Novelistas españoles actuales." Diccionario de Literatura Española, Madrid: Revista de Occidente, 1972, pp. 643-648.

Bosch, Rafael. "The Style of the New Spanish Novel." Books Abroad (Winter 1965), 10-14.

Botana, José. "J. M. Gironella: Nuevos episodios nacionales." Duquense Hispanic Review (Pittsburg) 6, iii (1967), 13-33.

Buckley, Ramón. "Del realismo social al realismo dialéctico." Insula, No. 326 (Jan. 1974), 1-4.

Cabot, José T. "Dos posibilidades para la "nueva novela" española." Indice, 24 (1 Jan. 1969), 33-34.

Cabot, J. T. "La narración behavorista." Indice de Artes y Letras, No. 147 (Mar. 1961), 8-9.

Cano, José Luis. "El Jarama." Arbor, No. 126 (1956), 313-314.

Cano, José Luis. "Narrativa española: La colmena." Insula, No. 67 (July, 1951), 3.

Cano, José Luis. "Luis Goytisolo: Las afueras." Insula, No. 146 (Jan. 1959), 8-9.

Cano, José Luis. "Narrativa española: Primera memoria." Insula, No. 161 (Apr. 1960), 8-9.

Castellet, José María. "Juan Goytisolo y la novela española actual." La Torre, IX, No. 33 (Jan. -Mar. 1961).

Castellet, José María. "Notas para una iniciación a la lectura de El Jarama." Papeles de Son Armadans, No. 2 (1956), 205-217.

Castellet, José María. "Veinte años de la novela española (1942-1962)." Cuadernos Americanos, XXII, CXXVI (1963), 290-95.

Cela, Camilo José. "Dos tendencias de la nueva literatura española." Papeles de Son Armadans, XXVII, No. 79 (Oct. 1962), 3-20.

Cirre, José Francisco. "El protagonista múltiple y su papel en la novela española." Papeles de Son Armadans, XXXIII (1964), 159-70.

Cirre, José Francisco. "Novela e ideología en Juan Goytisolo." Insula, XXI, No. 230 (Jan. 1966), 1-12.

Coindreau, Maurice E. "Los jóvenes novelistas españoles: R. Sánchez Ferlosio." Cuadernos del Congreso por la Libertad de la Cultura, No. 27 (Nov. -Dec. 1957), 67-71.

Corrales Egea, José. "¿Crisis en la nueva literatura?" Insula (Madrid) No. 223 (June 1965), 3-10.

Corrales Egea, José. "Situación actual de la novela española." Supplement from Insula, No. 282 (May 1970).

Couffon, Claude. "Rencontre avec J. F. Santos." Les lettres nouvelles, Paris, No. 62 (Juillet-Aôut, 1958), 127-132.

Curutchet, Juan Carlos. "L. Martín-Santos, el Fundador." Cuadernos de Mundo Ibérico (Paris) 17 (Feb. -Mar. 1968), 17.

Delibes, Miguel. "Notas sobre la novela española contemporánea." Cuadernos del Congreso por la Libertad de la Cultura, No. 63 (1962), 34-38.

Díaz, J. "J. García Hortelano: Nuevas amistades." Nuestras Ideas, No. 8 (1960), 102-103.

Díaz, Janet W. "L. Martín-Santos and the Contemporary Spanish Novel." Hispania, LI, No. 2 (Mar. 1968), 234.

Díaz, Janet W. "The Novel of Ignacio Aldecoa." Romance Notes, Vol. II (1970), 475-81.

Díaz, Janet W. "Spanish Literary Prizes." Hispania, LVI, (Sept. 1973), 723.

Díaz Lastra, A. "Señas de identidad de J. Goytisolo." Ruedo Ibérico (Jan. -Sept. 1967), 177-180.

Domench, R. "Interview with L. Martín-Santos." Insula, 208 (Mar. 1964), 4.

Domench, Ricardo. "La primera novela de Daniel Sueiro." Insula, Nos. 176-177 (Jul. -Aug. 1961), 8.

Domingo, José. "Análisis de una sociedad conformista: obras de
    Matute y F. Santos. " Insula (Madrid), No. 274 (Sept. 1969),
    7.

Domingo, José. "Anticipación y actualidad en una novela de
    Daniel Sueiro. " Insula, Vol. 24 (May 1968), 7.

Domingo, José. "Del realismo crítico a la nueva novela. " Insula,
    No. 290 (Jan. 1971), 5.

Domingo, José. "Del seminario a la isla: Castillo-Puche, García
    Ramos. " Insula, Vol. 27 (Jan. 1972), 6.

Domingo, José. "Dos novelistas españoles: Elena Quiroga y
    Daniel Sueiro. " Insula, No. 232 (Mar. 1966), 3.

Domingo, José. "La última novela de Goytisolo. " Insula, XXII
    (July-Aug. 1967), 13.

Domingo, José. "Narrativa española: Del hermetismo al barroco:
    Benet y Grosso. " Insula, No. 320-21 (Jul. -Aug 1973), 20.

Domingo, José. "Narrativa española: estilo y testimonio. " Insu-
    la, No. 328 (Mar. 1974), 7.

Domingo, José. "Narrativa española: La rueda de los premios. "
    Insula, 318, XIX (May, 1973), 7.

Domingo, José. "Narrativa española: Problemática religiosa e
    histórica. " Insula, No. 294 (May, 1971), 5.

Domingo, José. "Narrativa española: Tijeras, Torrente, Malvido,
    Benet. " Insula, No. 278 (Jan. 1970), 5.

Domingo, José. "Novísimos, nuevos y renovados. " Insula, No.
    313 (Mar. 1973), 6.

Domingo, José. "Parte de una historia: Reseña. " Insula, No.
    252 (Nov. 1967), 4.

Domingo, José. "Reseña: Dolores Medio y Juan García Horte-
    lano. " Insula, No. 253 (December 1967), 5.

Domingo, José. "Una meditación de Juan Benet. " Insula, No.
    282 (May, 1970), 7.

Domingo, José. "Una parábola de Miguel Delibes. " Insula, XXIV
    (Dec. 1969), 7.

Duque, Aquilino. "Realismo, pueblerismo y realismo suburbano:
    un buen entendedor de la realidad. " Indice, 185 (June, 1964),
    9.

Duque, Aquilino. "Un buen entendedor de la realidad: Luis
    Martín-Santos. " Indice de Artes y Letras, No. 185 (June
    1964), 9.

Durán, Manuel. "La estructura de La colmena. " Hispania, XLIII
    (1960), 19-24.

Durán, Manuel. "Vindicación de J. Goytisolo: Reivindicación del
    Conde don Julián. " Insula, 290 (Mar. 1971), 1-2.

Eder, Richard. "Portuguese Coup...." New York Times, Mar. 11, 1974, p. 25.

Eder, Richard. "Spain's Uneasy Glances at the 'New' Portugal." New York Times, News Analysis, July 7, 1974, Section 4, p. 3.

Eder, Richard. "Spanish Joke...." New York Times Magazine, Aug. 27, 1972, pp. 8-10.

"Encuesta: Nueva literatura española: Castellet, Gimferrer, Ríos." Plural (Mexico) XXV (Oct. 1973), 20-25.

Entrambasaguas, E. "Estudio crítico y biográfico de Miguel Delibes." Las mejores novelas españolas contemporáneas. Barcelona: Ed. Planeta, 1967.

Entrambasaguas, J. de. "Algo pasa en la calle." Revista de Literatura (Madrid), VI (1954), 384-387.

Entrambasaguas, J. de. "La sangre." Revista de Literatura (Madrid) III (1952), 195-200.

Eoff, S. and Schraibman. "Dos novelas del absurdo: L'etranger y Tiempo de silencio." Papeles de Son Armadans, CLXVIII (Mar. 1970), 213-241.

Fernández Almagro, M. "Algo pasa en la calle." ABC, Jan. 9, 1955.

Flasher, John J. "Aspects of Novelistic Technique in Cela's La colmena." West Virginia University Philological Papers, 21 (November 1959), 30-43.

Fuentes, Carlos. "Review of Count Julian." New York Times Book Review, May 5, 1974, pp. 5-7.

Garasa, D. L. "La condición humana en la narrativa española contemporánea." Ateneo, CLXII (1966), 109-139.

García-Viñó, M. "Introducing the Spanish Novel of Today." Topic 15 (1968), 17-29.

García-Viñó, M. "La nueva novela española," La nueva novela europea. Madrid: Ed. Guadarrama, 1968, pp. 47-80.

Georgeseu, Paul A. "Lo real y lo actual en Tiempo de silencio." Nueva Revista de Filología Hispánica (Mexico), Vol. 20 (1971), 114-120.

Gil Novales, Alberto. "El Jarama." Cavileño, No. 39 (May-June 1956), 71-73.

Gil Novales, Alberto. "Narrativa española: Los bravos." Insula, No. 120 (Dec. 1955), 6.

Gil Novales, Alberto. "Nuevas amistades." Cuadernos Hispanoamericanos, No. 126 (June, 1960), 385-86.

Gimferrer, Pedro. "En torno a Volverás a Región." Insula, No. 266 (Jan. 1969), 14-15.

Giniger, Henry. "Franco Delegates Powers as Ruler to Juan Carlos." New York Times, July 20, 1974, p. 1.

Giniger, Henry. "Franco Said to Fight Back After Hemorrhage Alarm." New York Times, July 21, 1974, p. 2.

Giniger, Henry. "Moves to Liberalize Politics in Spain Get Underway." New York Times, July 23, 1974, p. 3.

Giniger, Henry. "Spain Resists Liberalization." New York Times, August 3, 1972, p. 3.

Giniger, Henry. "Spanish Anarchist Executed...." New York Times, Mar. 2, 1974, p. 1.

Giniger, Henry. "University Administration Quits." New York Times, Oct. 10, 1972, p. 38.

Gissing, George. "The Private Papers of Henry Ryecroft." Bartlett's Familiar Quotations. Boston: Little Brown & Co., 1955.

Gómez Gil, Alfredo. "José Luis Castillo-Puche." Cuadernos Americanos, Vol. 177 (1971), 234-247.

Goytisolo, Juan. "The Contemporary Spanish Novel: Crisis, Silence and Change of Direction." Boston University Journal, 19, ii (1971), 24-32.

Goytisolo, Juan. "España 25 años después." L'Express, Apr. 2, 1964.

Goytisolo, Juan. "Formalismo y compromiso literario." Casa de Américas, IV, No. 26 (1964), 149.

Goytisolo, Juan. "Para una literatura popular." Insula, No. 146 (Jan. 1959), 7-11.

Goytisolo, Juan. "Writing in an Occupied Language." New York Times Book Review, Guest Editorial, Mar. 31, 1974, p. 47.

Grande, Félix. "L. Martín-Santos: Tiempo de silencio." Cuadernos hispanoamericanos, No. 158 (Feb. 163), 337-342.

Gullón, Ricardo. "The Modern Spanish Novel." Texas Quarterly, IV, No. 1 (Spring 1961), 79-96.

Henn, David. "La colmena: An Oversight on the Part of Cela." Romance Notes, Vol. 13 (1972), 414-418.

Heras, Antonio R. de las. "Escritores al habla: Miguel Delibes." ABC (Madrid), Mar. 13, 1970, Suplemento, 2.

Horia, Vicente. "El mal mayor: en Ernst Jünger y Miguel Delibes." Estafeta Literaria, No. 451 (Sept. 1970), 45.

Horia, Vicente. "La nueva ola de la novela española." Punta Europa, No. 117 (Jan. 1967), 55-57.

Hutman, Norma C. "Disproportionate Doom: Tragic Irony in the Spanish Post Civil War Novel." Modern Fiction Studies, 18 (1972), 199-206.

Jones, Margaret. "Temporal Patterns in the Works of Ana María
    Matute. " Romance Notes, 12 (1971), 282-88.

King, Charles L. "Review of La saga/fuga de J. B. " Books
    Abroad, Vol. 48, No. 1 (Winter 1974), 103.

Knapp Jones, W. "Recent Novels of Spain: 1936-1956. " Hispania,
    XL (1957), 303-311.

La Rosa, J. M. de. "Juan Goytisolo o La destrucción de las
    raíces. " Cuadernos Hispanoamericanos (Madrid) 237 (1968),
    779-784.

MacMahon, D. "Changing Trends in the Spanish Novel. " Books
    Abroad, XXXIV (Summer 1960), 227-230.

McMurray, George R. "The Hispanic World: Literary Prizes in
    Mexico. " Hispania, Vol. 57, No. 2 (May 1974), 358.

Marías, Julián. "La novela española de nuestro tiempo. " Pro-
    logue to La novelística de Camilo José Cela by Paul Ilie.
    Madrid: Ed. Gredos, 1963.

Marra-López, J. R. "J. L. Castillo-Puche: Paralelo 40. " In-
    sula, 200-201 (Jul. -Aug. 1963), 17.

Marra-López, J. R. "La criba de Daniel Sueiro. " Cuadernos del
    Congreso por la Libertad de la Cultura, No. 58 (Mar. 1962), 91.

Marra-López, J. R. "Tormenta de verano. " Insula, No. 187
    (June, 1962), 4.

Martínez Cachero, J. M. "El novelista Juan Goytisolo. " Papeles
    de Son Armadans, No. 95 (Feb. 1964), 124-160.

Montero, Isaac. "Los premios: 30 años de falsa fecundidad. "
    Cuadernos para el diálogo, XIV (May, 1969), 1-15.

Montero, Isaac. "Un libro insólito y vivo; Parábola. " Cuadernos
    para el diálogo, No. 77 (Feb. 1970), 46.

Núñez, Antonio. "Encuentro con D. Sueiro. " Insula, No. 235
    (June 1966), 4.

Núñez, Antonio. "Encuentro con Juan Benet. " Insula, No. 269,
    (April 1969), 4.

Núñez, Antonio. "Encuentro con J. F. Santos. " Insula, No. 275-
    76 (Oct. -Nov. 1970), 20.

Olmos García, F. "La novela y los novelistas españoles de hoy. "
    Cuadernos americanos, XXII, No. 4 (Jul. -Aug. 1963), 211-
    237.

Ortega, José. "La alienación de la soledad en En el segundo
    hemisferio de Antonio Ferrés. " Cuadernos Hispanoameri-
    canos (Madrid), Vol. 260 (1972), 355-63.

Ortega, José. "Realismo dialéctico de M. -Santos en Tiempo de
    silencio. " Revista de Estudios Hispánicos, Vol. 3 (1968),
    33-42.

Ortega, Julio. "Compromiso formal de M. -Santos en Tiempo de silencio. " Hispania, Vol. 37 (1969), 23-30.

Ortega, Julio. "Juan Goytisolo: Hacia Juan sin tierra. " Plural, XXV (Oct. 13, 1973), 5.

Palley, Julián. "Existentialist Trends in the Spanish Novel. " Hispania, XLIV (Mar. 1961), 21-26.

"Retrogression in Spain. " New York Times. Editorial, Mar. 4, 1974.

Rodríguez Padrón, Jorge. "Alfonso Grosso, a estas alturas. " Cuadernos Hispanoamericanos, Vol. 263-64 (1972), 612-23.

Rojas, Carlos. "Problemas de la nueva novela española. " La nueva novela europea. Madrid: Ed. Guadarrama, 1968, pp. 121-135.

Rozier, John. "Notes and News: Emory Professor Wins Top Award. " Hispania, Vol. 57 (Mar. 1974), 157.

Sánchez Ferlosio, R. "Una primera novela: Los bravos. " Insula, No. 223 (June, 1965), 3-10.

Schraibman, José, with William T. Little. "La estructura simbólica de El Jarama. " Hispanic Studies in Honor of Edward de Chasca-- Philological Quarterly, Vol. 51, No. 1 (1972), 329-42.

Schwartz, Kessel. "Introduction to Fiestas. " New York: Dell, 1964, pp. 7-24.

Schwartz, Kessel. "Juan Goytisolo: Cultural Constraint and the Historical Vindication of Count Julian. " Hispania, Vol. 54 (1971), 960-66.

Seale, Mary L. "Hangman and Victim: An Analysis of Luis M. -Santos' Tiempo de silencio. " Hispania, Vol. 44 (1972), 45-52.

Sénabre, Ricardo. "La obra narrativa de Ignacio Aldecoa. " Papeles de Son Armadans, CLXIV (Jan. 1970), 1.

Sheehan, Robert L. "Gironella and Hemingway: Novelists of the Spanish Civil War. " Golden, Herbert, Ed. Studies in Honor of Samuel Montefiore Waxman. Boston: Boston Univ. Press, 1969, 158-176.

Sheehan, Robert. "Review of San Camilio 1936. " Hispania, LV, No. 2 (May 1972), 387.

Shenker, Israel. "Spain's King-Designate in Power: Prince Juan Carlos. " New York Times, July 20, 1974, p. 3.

Slonin, Mark. "European Notebook. " New York Times Magazine, Dec. 24, 1967, p. 11.

"Spain. " New York Times Encyclopedia Almanac--1972. New York: New York Times, 1971.

"Spain." Reader's Digest Almanac and Yearbook--1967. New York: Reader's Digest Association, 1966.

"Spain." The World Almanac and Book of Facts--1972. New York: Newspaper Enterprise Association, 1971.

"Spain Eyes Portugal." New York Times, Editorial, Aug. 22, 1974, p. 22.

"Spanish Anarchist Executed by Garroting." New York Times, Editorial, Mar. 4, 1974, p. 8.

Spires, Robert C. "Cela's La colmena: The Creative Process as Message." Hispania, Vol. 55 (1972), 873-80.

"Ten Basque Workers Acquitted." Washington Post, Apr. 19, 1974, p. 26.

"Testing Franco's Press Law." New York Times, News Analysis, July 7, 1974, p. 3.

Toledo Silva, Monica R. "El adjetivo de "color" en Rafael Sánchez Ferlosio." Boletín de Filología Española, Vol. 40-41 (1971), 3-8.

Torrente Ballester, G. "La colmena: cuarta novela de Cela." Cuadernos Hispanoamericanos, VIII (1951), 96-102.

Torres Ríoseco, Arturo. "Consideraciones sobre la novela española contemporánea." Homenaje a Federico Onís (1885-1966), 2 vols. Revista Hispánica Moderna, 34 (1968).

Trulock, Jorge C. "La criba de Daniel Sueiro." Cuadernos Hispanoamericanos, No. 139 (July, 1961), 160-62.

"Unsolved Problems of Succession." Time Magazine, Dec. 11, 1972, pp. 55-57.

Valente, José Angel. "Lo demás es silencio," Insula, No. 271 (June 1969), 2.

Vargas Llosa, Mario. "Una explosión sarcástica en la novela española moderna." Insula, XXI, No. 233 (April 1966), 1-12.

Vásquez Dodero, J. L. "Algo pasa en la calle." Nuestro Tiempo (Madrid) IX (1955), 118-121.

Villegas, Juan. "Los motivos estructurantes de La careta de Elena Quiroga." Cuadernos Hispanoamericanos (Madrid) 75 (1968), 638-45.

Werrie, Paul. "La Novelle Vague Espagnole." La Fable Ronde (Paris), No. 225 (Oct. 1966).

Wicker, Tom. "A Miracle...." New York Times, News Analysis, June 7, 1974, p. 35.

ADDITIONAL SOURCES

A listing by chapter of novels, translations, critical
works and articles not elsewhere included in this book
or published after its production began.

CHAPTER 1

Fletcher, Madeleine de Gorgoza. The Spanish Historical Novel
(1870-1970). London: Tamesis Books, 1973.
Sobejano, Gonzalo. Novela española de nuestro tiempo. 2d ed.
Madrid: Ed. Prensa Española, 1975.

CHAPTER 2

Bosch, Andrés and García-Viñó, M. El realismo y la novela actual. Madrid: Ed. Universidad académica, 1975.
Morris, C. B. Surrealism and Spain. Cambridge, England: Cambridge University Press, 1972.

CHAPTER 3

Amoros, Andrés. "Conversaciones con Cela: Sin máscara." Re-
vista de Occidente, Vol. 33 (1971), 267-84.
Henn, David. "Cela's Portrait of Martín Marcos in La colmena."
Neophil, Vol. 55 (1971), 142-49.
Roberts, Gemma. "La culpa y la búsqueda de la autenticidad en
San Camilo, 1936." Journal of Spanish Studies: Twentieth
Century, Vol. 3, No. 1 (1975), 33-64.

CHAPTER 4

Gironella, José María. El mediterraneo es un hombre disfrazado
de mar [travel]. Barcelona: Ed. Plaza y Janes, 1974.
Dougherty, Dru. "Fictive History in Gironella." Journal of Spanish Studies: Twentieth Century, Vol. 2, No. 2 (1974), 77-94.
Suarez-Torres, J. David. "Tratamiento humoristico de la guerra
civil española en las novelas de J. M. Gironella." Disserta-
tion Abstracts International, Vol. 33 (1973), entry no. 5751
A-52A (Boston College).

CHAPTER 6

Freedman, Spencer G. "J. F. Santos: The Trajectory of His
    Fiction. " Dissertation Abstracts International, Vol. 33 (1973),
    entry no. 5173A (University of Massachusetts).
Gainza, Gaston. "Vivencia bélica en la narrativa de J. F. Santos. "
    Estudios Filológicos, Vol. 3 (1967), 91-125.

CHAPTER 7

Sanchez-Ferlosio, Rafael. The One Day of the Week. Transl. by
    J. M. Cohen of El Jarama. New York: Abelard Schuman,
    1962.
Villanueva, Dario. "El Jarama" de S. Ferlosio: su estructura y
    signicado. León: University of Santiago de Compostela,
    1973.

CHAPTER 8

Goytisolo-Gay, Luis. Ojos, círculos, buhos [short stories]. Bar-
    celona: Ed. Anagrama, 1972.
Goytisolo-Gay, Luis. Recuento [novel]. Barcelona: Ed. Seix
    Barral, 1973.

CHAPTER 9

Matute, Ana María. The Lost Children. Transl. by Joan Mac-
    Lean of Los hijos muertos. New York: Macmillan, 1965.
Cannon, Emile T. "Childhood as Theme and Symbol in the Major
    Fiction of A. M. Matute's Novels. " Dissertation Abstracts
    International, Vol. 33 (1973), entry no. 4401 A (Ohio State
    University).

CHAPTER 10

Sueiro, Daniel. Los verdugos españoles: Historia y actualidad
    del garrote vil. Madrid: Ed. Alfaguara, 1971.

CHAPTER 11

Villanueva, Dario. "La última novela de García Hortelano. "
    Camp de l'Arpa: Revista de Literatura, Vol. 6 (1973), 20-
    22.

CHAPTER 12

Martín-Santos, Luis. Time of Silence. Transl. by George Lee-
    son of Tiempo de silencio. New York: Harcourt, Brace and
    World, 1964.
Martín-Santos, Luis. Tiempo de destruccion. Ed. and with a
    Prologue by José Carlos-Mainer. Barcelona: Ed. Seix
    Barral, 1975.
Feal Deibe, Carlos. "Consideraciones sicoanalíticos sobre Tiempo

de silencio de L. Martín-Santos. " Revista Hispánica
Moderna, Vol. 36, No. 1 (1971), 117-27.

CHAPTER 13

Castillo-Puche, José Luis. Hemingway: entre la vida y la muerte
[biography]. Barcelona: Ed. Destino, 1968.
Castillo-Puche, José Luis. De dentro de la piel [short stories].
Madrid: Ed. Nacional, 1972.
Castillo-Puche, José Luis. Revisión de Baroja [criticism]. New
York: Eliseo Torres, 1973.
Gómez Gil, Alfredo. "J. L. Castillo-Puche." Cuadernos Ameri-
canos, Vol. 177 (1971), 234-47.

CHAPTER 14

Goytisolo, Juan. Juan sin tierra [novel]. Barcelona: Ed. Seix
Barral, 1975.
Giles, Mary E. "Juan Goytisolo's Juego de manos: An Archetypal
Interpretation. " Hispania, Vol. 56 (1973), 1021-29.
Gould Levine, Linda. "Don Julián: Una 'Galería de espejos lite-
rarios'. " Cuadernos Americanos, Vol. 188 (1973), 218-30.
Sobejano, Gonzalo, et al. Artículos y ensayos sobre Juan Goyti-
solo por Sobejano, Fuentes, Vargas Llosa, Castellet, Sarduy,
Rodríguez Monegal, Ortega y otros. Madrid: Ed. Funda-
mentos, 1975.

CHAPTER 15

Marsé, Juan. Si te dicen que caí [novel]. Mexico: Ed. Novaro,
1973 [Premio Internacional de Novela Mexico].

CHAPTER 16

García-Viñó, M. "Los cuentos de Ignacio Aldecoa. " Arbor, Vol.
335 (1973), 133-35.

CHAPTER 17

Benet, Juan. Cinco narraciones y dos fábulas [short stories].
Barcelona: Ed. La Gaya Ciencia, 1972.
Benet, Juan. Sub rosa [short stories]. Barcelona: Ed. La Gaya
Ciencia, 1973.
Rodríguez Padrón, Jorge. "Volviendo a región. " Campo de l'Arpa:
Revista de Literatura, Vol. 7 (1975), 27-38.

CHAPTER 18

Delibes, Miguel. Las guerras de nuestros pasados [novel]. Barcelona: Ed. Destino, 1975.
Pauk, Edgar. Miguel Delibes: Desarrollo de un escritor (1947-
74). Madrid: Ed. Gredos, 1975.

406   Spain's New Wave Novelists

CHAPTER 19

Grosso, Alfonso. Florido mayo [novel]. Madrid: Ed. Alfaguara,
     1973.

CHAPTER 20

Carrascal, José María. La muerte no existe [novel]. Madrid:
     Ed. Privado, 1974.
Carrascal, José María. Mientras tenga mis piernas [novel]. Bar-
     celona: Ed. Destino, 1975.

CHAPTER 21

Díaz, Janet W. "Techniques of Alienation in Recent Spanish
     Novels." Journal of Spanish Studies: Twentieth Century,
     Vol. 3, No. 1 (1975), 5-16.
El año literario español 1974 [criticism]. Madrid: Ed. Castalia,
     1974.
Reunión de Málaga 1972 [articles by Angel Asturias, Cela, García
     Pavón, Rojas and Trulock]. Málaga: Instituto de Cultura de
     Málaga, 1973.

CHAPTER 22

Caballero Bonald, J. M. Vivir para cantárlo [poetry]. Barcelona:
     Ed. Seix Barral, 1959.
Caballero Bonald, J. M. Agata ojo de gato [novel]. Barcelona:
     Ed. Seix Barral, 1974.
Gesulla, Luis. Culminación de Montoya [novel]. Barcelona: Ed.
     Destino, 1974 [Premio Nadal].
Irizarry, Estelle. "La cultura como experiencia viva en El jardin
     de las delicias." Papeles de Son Armadans (Mallorca), Vol.
     68 (1973), 249-61.
Leyva, J. La circunsición del señor solo [novel]. Barcelona:
     Ed. Seix Barral, 1972 [Premio Biblioteca Breve].
Martín Gaite, Carmen. Retahílas [novel]. Barcelona: Ed. Des-
     tino, 1974.
Moix, Ana María. No Time for Flowers [novel]. Barcelona: Ed.
     Lumen, 1971.
Moix, Ana María. 24 x 24 [interviews]. Barcelona: Ed. Penínsu-
     la, 1972.
Palls, Byron P. "El tiempo en Ocho, siete, seis de Antonio
     Ferrés." Cuadernos Hispanoamericanos (Madrid), Vol. 277-
     78 (1973), 196-215.
Rojas, Carlos. La guerra civil vista por los exilados [essays].
     Barcelona: Ed. Planeta, 1975.
Umbral, Francisco. Los males sagrados [novel]. Barcelona: Ed.
     Planeta, 1973.
Umbral, Francisco. Los españoles [essays]. Barcelona: Ed.
     Planeta, 1974.

INDEX*

All major novels discussed in this book are listed
under their Spanish title.

*Page numbers underlined indicate location of most extensive infor-
mation. Titles are followed by author's name in parentheses.